Prospects for Social Security Reform

Prospects for Social Security Reform

Edited by Olivia S. Mitchell, Robert J. Myers, and Howard Young

Pension Research Council
The Wharton School of the University of Pennsylvania

University of Pennsylvania Press
Philadelphia

Pension Research Council Publications

A complete list of books in the series appears at the back of this volume.

Copyright © 1999 The Pension Research Council of the Wharton School of the University of Pennsylvania
Printed in the United States of America on acid-free paper

10 9 8 7 6 5 4 3 2 1

Published by
University of Pennsylvania Press
Philadelphia, Pennsylvania 19104-4011

Library of Congress Cataloging-in-Publication Data
   Prospects for social security reform / edited by Olivia S. Mitchell,
Robert J. Myers, and Howard Young.
      p.   cm.
   "Pension Research Council Publications."
   Includes bibliographical references.
   ISBN 0-8122-3479-0 (alk. paper)
   1. Social security — United States.   I. Mitchell, Olivia S.
II. Myers, Robert J. (Robert Julius), 1912–   .   III. Young,
Howard, 1932–   .   IV. Wharton School. Pension Research Council.
HD7125.P733   1998
368.4'3'00973 — dc21   98-41908
                                                                  CIP

Frontispiece: Special Treasury securities, stored in a federal government filing cabinet in West Virginia, represent $700 billion in Social Security Trust Fund assets. Photo: Jeff Baughan.

Dedicated to the Memory of Shannon Schieber

Contents

Preface   ix

I. What Is the Social Security Problem?

1. An Overview of the Issues   3
Olivia S. Mitchell, Robert J. Myers, and Howard Young

2. Measuring Solvency in the Social Security System   16
Stephen C. Goss

3. Criteria for Evaluating Social Security Reform   37
Joseph F. Quinn

4. New Opportunities for the Social Security System   60
Stephen G. Kellison and Marilyn Moon

II. Assessing the Economic Impact of Social Security Reform

5. Social Security Money's Worth   79
John Geanakoplos, Olivia S. Mitchell, and Stephen P. Zeldes

6. Simulating Benefit Levels Under Alternative Social Security
Reforms   152
Gordon P. Goodfellow and Sylvester J. Schieber

7. Stochastic Simulation of Economic Growth Effects of Social
Security Reform   184
Martin R. Holmer

8. Thinking About Social Security's Trust Fund   201
Kent A. Smetters

9. Government Guarantees for Old Age Income   221
George G. Pennacchi

10. Means Testing Social Security   243
David Neumark and Elizabeth Powers

11. Social Security and Employer Induced Retirement   268
Robert M. Hutchens

**III. Political and Practical Considerations Regarding Social
Security Reform**

12. Compliance in Social Security Systems Around the World   295
Joyce Manchester

13. Employer Responses to Social Security Reform   313
Janice M. Gregory

14. An Actuarial Perspective on How Social Security Reform
Could Influence Employer-Sponsored Pensions   333
Christopher Bone

15. An Organized Labor Perspective on Social Security Reform   349
David S. Blitzstein

16. Women as Widows Under a Reformed Social Security System   356
Karen C. Holden

17. Investment and Administrative Constraints on Individual
Social Security Accounts   372
Robert C. Pozen and John M. Kimpel

18. Americans' Views of Social Security and Social Security
Reforms   380
John Rother and William E. Wright

Contributors   395

Index   401

Preface

Olivia S. Mitchell

Social security systems play a central role in old-age income support in most countries on earth. The United States is no exception: many older Americans today rely on the nation's old-age scheme for at least half of their retirement income. Yet the U.S. social security system — like those of many other countries — faces prospective insolvency in the not too distant future. Around the time that the baby boom generation retires, social security benefits payable will exceed payroll tax revenue. If system solvency is to be restored, benefits will have to be cut by one-quarter, or taxes raised commensurately. Alternatively, some experts propose privatization of social security, investing some of the funds in private capital markets.

Why does social security face these problems? What types of reforms should policymakers and interested lay people support, and on what grounds? This book offers a road map for those seeking to understand these questions and to evaluate their answers, in the inevitable reform debates that lie ahead. Our goal is to inform policymakers and practitioners charged with restructuring the social security system, in the context of the transition to an aging — and permanently older — society and a more competitive global economic order.

Because we seek a broad readership, the studies contained in this book include perspectives of a wide range of people including economists, actuaries, fund managers, pension experts, labor market analysts, and policymakers. This interdisciplinary approach, we believe, makes the work particularly interesting to both U.S. residents and those from other countries as well, as they seek to redesign old-age systems in their own context.

In bringing the volume to fruition I owe thanks to the support and guidance of the Institutional Members of the Pension Research Council. Many of our members have actively participated in the research, and continue to play a key role in the ongoing policy debate on social security reform.

Council Board members Robert Myers and Howard Young served as co-editors for this volume, and for their help I am most grateful. The Pension Section of the Society of Actuaries and the Society of Actuaries Foundation provided sponsorship for a conference discussing early results; at the University of Pennsylvania, the Wharton School granted the Council financial assistance in the form of a Wharton Impact grant, and the Penn Aging Research Center also offered financial assistance for the work. Joanne Tang is particularly thanked for her excellent help with logistical and other arrangements for the Pension Research Council.

On behalf of the Pension Research Council at the Wharton School, I thank the many contributors and the several institutions supporting the high-quality research culminating in this volume.

I
What Is the Social Security Problem?

Bk Title

Chapter 1
An Overview of the Issues

Olivia S. Mitchell, Robert J. Myers,
and Howard Young

H55 J26
(U5)

The U.S. social security system has played a central role in improving the well-being of older Americans since the Great Depression. Since the Old-Age, Survivors, and Disability Insurance (OASDI) program was launched during the Great Depression, millions of program participants have relied on the orderly and timely functioning of the system. In 1997, the Social Security Administration paid benefits of about $360 billion to retirees, their dependents, and their survivors, while payroll taxes on workers and their employers amounted to about $400 billion. At the end of 1997, the excess — amounting to about 21 months of benefit payouts — was held in special issue Treasury obligations in the social security trust funds. Currently the OASDI program – which accounts for over a fifth of the federal budget — is hailed by many as a model of efficiency, providing a valuable source of income to approximately 44 million beneficiaries each month for an annual administrative cost of $3.7 billion, which represents $26 per covered worker. Certainly many of today's elderly would live in poverty if not for the social security system, and older people in the United States today have reason to feel more confident about their prospects in old age than do the elderly in the most of the world's other nations.

Despite these accomplishments, Americans have begun to worry about the future of their social security system. This is because, about the time the baby boom retires, the social security system will face serious imbalance. Specifically, payroll taxes along with interest income from the trust funds will fall short of the income flow needed to pay benefits. The fund is insufficient to pay off the estimated large amount needed to prefund all promised obligations, after taking into account future income from taxes and interest. In addition, a growing group of young people believes that it will not "get its money's worth" from the system. These two realities have prompted the most serious rethinking since 1939 of the basic principles on which social

security is based. There is no immediate crisis, since projected system revenues are projected to be adequate to pay promised benefits for about 20
years. But ideally *well* before the crisis does arrive, reforms must be implemented for the social security system to continue to play a key role in Americans' retirement.

The need for reform was powerfully brought to the public's attention
during the mid-1990's by the governmental-appointed Advisory Council on
Social Security (1994–1996). Reflecting a range of political views, age/
ethnic/sex interest groups, employer and employee organizations, and
geographic backgrounds, this 13-member group received testimony from
national experts and held numerous open meetings. But while previous
councils had been able to fashion compromises when required, this Advisory Council issued a final report containing not one but three very different reform plans (Advisory Council 1997). This lack of agreement brought
home to Americans the deep-seated nature of the controversy, and the lack
of easy consensus.

In this volume we put this debate in context by explaining why Americans'
most important old-age support system faces the fundamental challenges
that it does as we enter the twenty-first century. We then offer a range of
perspectives on how to think about reform options going forward, and how
to compare some of the most important reform alternatives available. Toward this goal, we have collected the reasoned thoughts of some two dozen
influential social security experts, people who are united by their concern
for the nation's retirement system but who also frequently disagree about
what should be done about these problems. As will become clear, we do not
impose consensus on these experts, but instead take the opportunity to
present their views so as to stimulate additional thought, discussion, and
more informed policymaking. We believe that it is in hearing the many
different stakeholders' voices about social security that the lessons and pit-
falls become clearer.

Looking across these distinct views, several messages emerge. One is that
alternative reforms offer different ways to spread the risks of old age across
the stakeholders in the economy. Specific old-age risks confronting retirees
include *individual risks*—often attributable to low earnings or job loss producing low retirement saving; *company risk*—arising from corporate financial duress; *national risk*—due to inflation and economic recession; and
international risk—arising in times of global capital market fluctuations such
as the present.[1] Stakeholders in the retirement income system naturally
include individual workers and retirees, their families, and their employers;
moving to the broader view, one might include all members of a given generation, and also those from many different generations—including those
as yet unborn. How these four types of old-age risk impinge on all the different players is a topic we place at center stage in the discussions to follow.

Not only does the identity of stakeholders in the system vary; who they are also affects each group's assessment of costs and benefits and how they judge the menu of reform options. For example, employers, workers, and other groups including women and the poor, will tend to see very differently the appropriateness of keeping the defined benefit approach versus moving to a defined contribution format. Here we not only describe the alternatives, but also offer criteria for judging them and for explaining why reasonable people differ regarding their policy recommendations. We also assess the most important implications of social security system-wide reform, and explore what these changes might do to alter the basic fabric of the economic and social environment as a whole.

In the discussion that follows, we begin with a detailed analysis of what the system does and why social security faces the problems it does. Most people are not aware of the magnitude of the system's unfunded liabilities, and believe that the system is in trouble because of the baby-boomers and the lack of wage growth to generate needed tax revenues. While these do play a role, they are only part of the reason that benefits are projected to exceed the financing, under the intermediate-cost estimate. In fact, much of the burden facing future taxpayers can be explained by the substantial transfers granted to several generations covered under the program during the start-up phase, just as is often done in private pension plans. The burden of this unfunded liability, and the interest required to pay for the debt, implies that virtually all workers today anticipate very much lower net returns from the system than did their parents and grandparents. The question therefore becomes one of how this burden will be borne. Groups asked to carry part of the load will be today's workers, today's retirees, and to some extent, the workers of the future. How to allocate the burden, therefore, is at the crux of the reform debate. While there is no single right answer regarding burden-sharing, we believe that discussions of reform options are better informed when these issues are discussed explicitly rather than obscured.

In the second and third sections of this book, we offer economic and practical assessments of potential reform scenarios. One reason that policymakers may disagree about reform options is that they differ regarding how reforms alter economic actors' behavior. Here several such behavioral responses are explored, including workers' retirement portfolio choices, retirement patterns, employer layoff responses, and government investment and risk-sharing patterns. Another reason that reformers disagree about which reform would work best is that they consciously or implicitly disagree about the criteria that should be used in judging reforms. To this end, we provide a discussion of specific evaluation guidelines that help clarify points of agreement, and make more evident important areas of disagreement in thinking about specific reforms. The book's last section reports special concerns of specific stakeholder groups, as they contemplate alternative plans for social security reform.

Before proceeding with a more detailed overview of the findings, we note that this discussion focuses on the government program providing cash benefits to older retired and disabled workers, as well as to the survivors of deceased and retired workers. We do not examine in detail the Medicare program, which in the United States affords health care to those 65 and older (and to long-term disabled workers). While recognizing the importance of that benefit program and its projected financing difficulties, we believe that repairing the Medicare structure must be dealt with in the very short term. The problems of the nation's OASDI system must be solved with a longer-term perspective.

The Size of the Social Security Problem

In order to judge the urgency of social security reform in the United States, it is essential to have a clear idea of how the system arrived at its current juncture, how the system's predicted insolvency according to the intermediate-cost estimate can be measured, and what the size of the projected funding shortfall might be. Several demographic and economic trends lie behind these projections, as pointed out by Stephen Goss. He emphasizes that low fertility rates after 1965, longer life expectancies, and a large group of baby-boomers projected to attain retirement age will produce a relatively small working age population supporting baby boom retirees. Also, American workers' real pay has failed to rise significantly over the last two decades due to productivity shortfalls, making tax collections grow less quickly than previously forecast. Benefits have also been increased from time to time under the social security program, and in 1975, annual automatic cost of living adjustments were introduced (in 1977 these adjustments were adjusted for what appeared to be over-indexing). Finally, employment and life-style patterns have changed since the program was designed in the 1930s. Higher rates of divorce, job downsizing, and fewer skilled jobs have made the prospects for retirement increasingly uncertain.

What will these trends mean for the future of the social security program? Steven Kellison and Marilyn Moon show how future taxes and benefits under current law are forecast, and estimate that, under current tax and benefit rules, the combined OASDI Trust Funds will be exhausted around 2029, according to agency intermediate-cost assumptions. In addition, they note that these same Trust Funds will become a net collector from, rather than contributor to, overall federal resources around 2020, disappearing by 2029. At that point tax revenues will be sufficient to pay only 75 percent of scheduled benefits, with that ratio decreasing to about 66 percent by 2071. This is in the context of a national shift in private pensions from defined benefit to defined contribution plans, leaving many workers with low overall replacement rates in retirement.

Both Goss and Kellison/Moon understand the limitations of these long-range projections and acknowledge that problems arise in using them as the basis for policy formulation. One concern is that reforms to bring the financing of the system into balance have important economic implications for workers and retirees, potentially including tax increases and benefit cuts. Another concern is that current policymakers may not be able fully to anticipate the needs and priorities of future generations, making periodic revisions in social security probably inevitable. Even with these caveats, however, the message is a gloomy one. The U.S. social security system is not in balance, facing unfunded liabilities estimated at between $5 and $9 trillion in present value terms, as shown by Goss. This debt, and the burden it imposes on the economic system, cannot continue to grow inexorably. The system must be reformed; the status quo cannot be maintained into the indefinite future.

A map for progress in this discussion is offered by Joseph Quinn, who provides several practical criteria that can be used to evaluate alternative social security reform proposals. Drawing on the work of the Technical Panel on Trends in Income and Retirement Saving for the Advisory Council on Social Security (which he co-chaired with Olivia Mitchell), Quinn points out that the social security system has several competing goals. In addition, he notes that the program has diverse and imperfectly understood interactions with overall economic and social activities. Quinn's concern is that behavioral responses to social security taxes and transfers might offset the expected direct impacts of the program, at least in some cases. For example, workers who anticipate high retirement benefit payments from social security would save less on their own, and retire somewhat earlier, than without such a system. It is essential to factor these economic responses into a cost-benefit analysis of any particular change in the system. Quinn also believes that attention must be devoted to the transition mechanisms for implementing program changes, since he foresees that these will dramatically affect public understanding, confidence, and support for the system that emerges from the reform fray.

Options for Social Security Reform

While diverse ways to reform America's social security system can be imagined, it is useful to think of them in terms of three alternative "template" approaches. One such template for reform is to cut benefits so as to live within current tax rates; the second is to raise taxes in order to keep benefit promises more or less untouched; and the third is to convert the present system from a defined benefit to a defined contribution system.[2] The reform options offered by the last (1994–96) Advisory Council on Social Security may be classified according to these templates. Thus the "Maintain Benefits" (MB) plan preserved most current benefit promises while raising taxes to pay for them (see the Appendix to this chapter). The second plan, termed the "Personal Security Account" approach (PSA) by its inventors, cut government-provided benefits and instead provided a flat benefit to all retired workers along with individually managed defined-contribution funded accounts. The third proposal, offered as a compromise plan, was named the "Individual Account" plan (IA), where a small individual account would be married with a government-guaranteed benefit somewhat smaller than current benefits. This does not exhaust the range of options, since, as we shall show below, others have proposed cutting benefits by means-testing them, or limiting social security payouts to those in dire economic need.[3]

Despite the diversity of views over which reform to adopt, most U.S. policymakers do agree that a reform plan must ensure that the old-age system has a solid financial footing for the long term. Further, most experts agree that the "long term" should be thought about in terms of generations rather than simply years or presidential terms; the 75-year perspective currently used for the social security system is generally seen to be about right. Other areas of agreement include the view that social security reforms should be enacted to ensure old-age security sooner rather than later. This is because changes legislated now and implemented gradually into the future will allow workers time to adjust their saving and retirement plans.

More controversy is generated over which of the specific reforms should be implemented and how soon they should go into effect. As we shall show below, part of the dispute stems from differences in evaluation objectives, and part is attributable to the fact that reasonable people disagree about economic and demographic projections 75 or more years into the future. In our view, such disagreement is most productively narrowed by understanding which alternative types of reform are technically feasible, and the importance of likely economic and political behavioral responses to these reforms.

Assessing the Economic Impact of Social Security Reform

The second substantive section of the book offers an economic assessment of specific social security reform proposals, in order to explore how given reforms might affect both household and economy-wide behavior. Olivia Mitchell, John Geanakoplos, and Stephen Zeldes launch the discussion with a critique of several measures frequently offered to compare social security outcomes under different reform scenarios. Specifically, money's worth concepts such as the benefit to tax ratio, the internal rate of return, and net present value are widely used to summarize the relationship between social security participants' lifetime taxes paid and lifetime benefits received. The authors argue that this may be appropriate under some circumstances, but is not useful for comparing alternative social security systems — including systems with privately managed individual accounts investing in equities. The evidence also suggests that money's worth estimates are biased in favor of social security privatization because the measures often do not fully incorporate effects of the transition costs; they often do not appropriately adjust for either aggregate or idiosyncratic risk, both of which would rise under privatization; and they do not account for changes in household behavior as a result of the reform.

The likely pattern of returns potentially available for a PSA or IA accumulation account is studied by Gordon Goodfellow and Sylvester Schieber. In simulation analysis, the authors show that no policy proposal, including the Maintain Benefits plan, will be able to provide benefits consistent with current rules unless *substantially* more new revenues are raised. They then posit that a PSA or IA approach would probably see people investing their retirement funds in diverse ways, and some additional cost would be expended in administrative expenses. In the long term, they believe that returns on contributions experienced in a PSA account can be quite high, if the capital market performs in the future as it has in the past.

Another policy expert, Martin Holmer, also uses stochastic simulation to model the interactions between social security and the broader economy. This study is macroeconomic in spirit, seeking first to replicate the outcomes in the nonstochastic, or deterministic, model that was used by the Social Security Administration in assessing reform options for the Advisory Council. He then goes on to embed his program simulation in a larger model of the economy, in order to explore whether policies appear to have different effects when macroeconomic consequences are taken into account. Holmer estimates the impact of various reforms on national saving, and concludes that GDP would be substantially higher under a system where individual accounts (IA or PSA) were invested in capital markets.

Of course, equity investment need not be restricted to privately held individual accounts, as noted in Kent Smetters's study of investing the social security trust funds in equities. This idea, introduced initially by supporters of the MB plan, has captured the attention of many in the policy arena. A key issue, as Smetters points out, is how risk is transferred intergenerationally, due to variation between expected and actual results of Trust Fund investments. Are retirees at risk for capital market fluctuations, or will future workers have to pay higher taxes in times of depression? The answers to these questions are crucial in determining the nature of risk pooling across and within generations. The author also acknowledges some of the difficult governance and political issues that would arise if the government used politically motivated inclusion or exclusion rules, or if certain stocks were included or excluded from the index fund in which government monies were invested.

This discussion leads naturally to the more general topic that is of special interest to George Pennacchi, who explores the relationship between private retirement saving and government retirement guarantees for pension systems. Drawing on international experience, the author discusses how to model and value government guarantees for retirement income, similar to those provided by other governments in many parts of the world. He uses

contingent claims analysis, or option pricing theory, to value defined benefit as well as defined contribution pension guarantees. This is particular
useful in Chile, for instance, where the government guarantees a minimum
retirement income to participants in the mandatory private pension system.
Even though people hold private assets in their individual accounts, this
government-guaranteed return turns out to be worth many times salary for
a low-paid employee (and less than a year's pay for a highly paid employee).
Clearly guarantees of this sort can dramatically alter the incentives to participate in a defined-contribution individual-account type system and not to
comply fully with the coverage rules, and they also influence the fiscal cost
of individual-account type pension reforms.

Much public opinion tends to favor cutting benefits for the wealthy,
rather than uniform across-the-board reductions for everyone. Hence the
interesting study by David Neumark and Elizabeth Powers explores the potential effects of means-testing social security benefit amounts, by drawing
on evidence from other programs that do implement a means test. Their
specific focus is on the Supplemental Security Income program, from which
the authors conclude that means testing will induce less work prior to old
age. There may be some negative effect on saving rates as well.

Reformers of social security benefits and taxes must also anticipate possible employer responses. In his study, Robert Hutchens asks how social security changes might alter the structure and intent of corporate retirement
policy. Hutchens views social security benefits as a form of early-retirement
program, financed by a non-experience-rated tax. Against this backdrop,
employers structure their employment policy toward older workers, behavior somewhat akin to that seen in unemployment insurance. Hutchens's
stylized model shows how companies hit with adverse demand shocks will
tend to downsize older workers in bad times, with social security benefits
cushioning this transition. The implication of his model is that social security benefit cuts and payroll tax increases could reduce the demand for
older workers. While the results are suggestive rather than empirically con-
clusive, the study does point to some as yet unexpected responses to system-
wide changes in social security.

Political and Practical Considerations

The third section of this book reports on how various stakeholder groups
might react to the proposed social security reforms. One practical issue that
must be confronted by all social security reformers is that of system non-
participation, or more bluntly, payroll tax evasion. Other countries have a
difficult time ensuring that eligible employers and workers actually participate in their national social security systems, particularly in Latin America
and Eastern Europe. While this topic has not warranted much attention in
the United States thus far, it will in the future: researcher Joyce Manchester

points out that one-quarter of American taxpayers admit underpaying their taxes at some point. Her review indicates that social security reforms will be more successful when payroll taxes are lower, benefits are linked more closely to taxes paid, and the number of tax brackets is reduced.

Likely employer responses to social security reform are taken up in the chapters by Janice Gregory and Christopher Bone. Gregory shows how employer pensions have evolved alongside social security over time, a joint evolution process that suggests to her that companies will change their retirement offerings in tandem with changes in social security. One prediction is that if social security benefits were to be reduced, overall retiree benefits would fall since many employers would not be able to make up the difference. If social security taxes were raised to finance existing benefit promises, she predicts that this labor cost increase could curtail employment and would even induce some companies to provoke earlier retirement. If the OASDI program were to move toward an individual-account model, Gregory believes that companies would then be urged by their workers to return to the defined benefit pension model, in contrast to current trends. Some important reactions would be automatic due to formal integration of pension and social security benefits, and in other cases wages might fall if social security taxes were to rise. Bone's chapter is a companion piece outlining additional research needed regarding potential employer responses. Drawing on his actuarial background, Bone emphasizes the tremendous diversity and detail inherent in private pension plan benefit and contribution formulas. While some may be tempted to dismiss the importance of these plan design features, he hypothesizes that they will induce plan sponsors to adapt differently to social security changes. In addition, public and private pension plans are governed by a different regulatory construct, which in turn affects how these costs will be spread among the relevant stakeholders.

Employee groups are also worrying about prospects for social security reform, as is made clear in the chapter by David Blitzstein. Drawing from historical evidence, he posits that organized labor groups would react quite negatively to far-reaching changes in the nation's OASDI system. Many union representatives would tend to oppose a model for social security in which workers are given the responsibility to invest for themselves in individually held accounts. This is because employers and the nation as a whole are perceived to be inherently better able to bear capital market risk and pool longevity risk than are individual workers and their families. For this reason, among others, American organized labor tends to favor reforms that stabilize the system by improving system revenues, rather than by cutting benefits.

Risk of a related sort is the focus of Karen Holden's analysis, in which she argues that individual account programs run the risk of undercutting the insurance aspect of social security for older widows. Her research shows that women, as compared to men, still earn less, have fewer years in the wage labor market, and live longer in retirement. Thus older women run a greater than average risk of falling into old-age poverty, a risk that would potentially be exacerbated by social security reforms that emphasized individual accounts. As a result, Holden points out, the debate over social security benefit cuts or tax increases critically affects how women will be treated by the reformed system as wife and widow beneficiaries. In her analysis, she explores not only what social security changes might help the plight of poor widows, but also evaluates changes in company pensions that might ease their condition.

Years of experience in the pension arena at Fidelity afford Robert Pozen a special vantage point in the analysis of individual social security accounts. His chapter emphasizes the importance of rules that will affect the balance between individual control, risk impact, compliance levels, and administrative costs. Should social security move to a defined contribution format, several alternative formats might be permitted, and Pozen notes some of their strengths and weaknesses. He recommends adopting several regulatory and legal constructs developed for private pension plans under the Employee Retirement Income Security Act (ERISA), including, for example, requiring a provider to offer at least three investment pools.

Economic issues are not the only factors influencing the social security reform environment, a point brought home by John Rother and William Wright. They review data from several recent public opinion polls conducted for the American Association of Retired Persons, asking people about their preferences regarding the current social security system as well as possible changes in the system. Perhaps the most striking conclusion from their data is how confused people seem to be about social security and their own retirement prospects. We know from other sources that Americans are undersaving, yet the AARP polls indicate that many people believe they will not need the national social security system in retirement. This may simply be the flip side of the finding that national confidence in the OASDI system has dropped by a quarter between 1985 and 1996, from 46 percent to 35 percent. The evidence also shows that many of the reforms under active discussion are unpopular. For example, two-thirds of poll respondents opposed raising the normal retirement age to age 70, and about the same fraction opposed raising the payroll tax to meet current benefit promises. By contrast, benefit cuts were favored by many, particularly if the cuts were targeted at the high-income elderly (where the "high income" group was typically defined as people wealthier than the survey respondent!).

Risk Spreading into the Future

To preserve old-age security for current and future retirees, the nation's old-age system must be reformed soon. As we shall demonstrate in what follows, specific proposals differ in terms of how and for whom benefits will be cut, how and for whom taxes will be raised, and whether a private account should be included — and, if so, how large to make this account. Possible responses of economic players are diverse and sometimes undesirable. Those who have a stake in the outcomes are many, including individual workers and retirees, the family, employers, all generations alive today, and additional generations into the future.

But despite these complexities, and irrespective of which reform plan is chosen, any reform plan will ultimately involve allocating risk across different members and groups in society. The form and structure of the restructured social security system that emerges for the future will therefore determine who ends up bearing which types of risk; in the end, the risk of a complex, globally interdependent, and aging society may never be completely avoided or eliminated.

Appendix: An Overview of the Advisory Council Proposals[4]

The 1994–96 Advisory Council on Social Security consisted of persons representing business and labor (3 members each), the self-employed (1 representative) and the public (5 members), and was chaired by University of Michigan economics professor Edward Gramlich. Rather than issuing a single recommendation, the panel proposed three alternative models for social security reform.

The first plan, known as the Maintenance of Benefits (MB) plan, was championed by Robert Ball, a former Commissioner of Social Security, and five other members. This plan intended to keep in place the currently legislated schedule of benefits, including raising the normal retirement age to 67. Revenues needed to pay for the benefits would come from (i) additional federal income taxation of social security benefits and the diversion to the OASDI Trust Fund of the income tax receipts on benefits currently supporting Medicare; (ii) a 1.6 percentage point increase in the combined employer-employee payroll tax rate in the year 2045; and (iii) the allocation of up to 40 percent of Trust Fund reserves to the equity market, which in the past enjoyed a higher rate of return than government bonds. This proposal envisioned no individual accounts and some benefit cuts beyond those already legislated.

The second proposal, known as the Individual Accounts (IA) plan, was authored by Chairman Gramlich and Marc Twinney. This plan would cut benefits for middle and high wage workers through changes in the benefit formula, and index the normal retirement age to changes in longevity. It would also boost payroll taxes by 1.6 percent of covered payroll to finance a small individual defined contribution account. System participants would be permitted limited investment discretion over the funds, which could be invested under the auspices of a government licensed and managed mutual fund. At age 62, retirees could claim an indexed annuity, based on the total accumulation in the account; the funds could not be withdrawn in a lump sum.

The third proposal, named the Personal Security Account (PSA) proposal, was developed by Sylvester Schieber and Carolyn Weaver. This model would replace the current social security defined benefit plan with a two-tiered system, where the first tier would pay all participants a flat benefit independent of earnings histories, thus annulling the defined-benefit nature of the OASDI system. This flat payment would be worth about $410 per month (in $1996), an amount about two-thirds of the poverty level for an elderly individual, and similar to a low-wage worker's social security benefit today. (Pro-rated first-tier benefits would be paid to those with 10–34 years of coverage.) The second tier would consist of a mandatory personal retirement account financed by a tax of 5 percent of payroll which would be a reassignment from the employee 6.2 percent tax rate; the account would be managed by a licensed private investment house under the direction of the plan participant. Accounts could be claimed at age 62.[5] Under this model, a significant unfunded liability from the old system would remain, requiring additional revenues equal to about 1.5 percent of covered payroll over the next 72 years.

Despite their differences, all three proposals contained common elements, including the maintenance of a mandatory, universal, public social insurance program with retirement, survivors, and disability benefits. They all envisioned a progressive benefit structure, with net transfers toward those with low earnings. Each involved additional taxation of social security benefits, with the eventual inclusion of all social security benefits (in excess of contributions already taxed) in taxable income. All recommended mandatory social security coverage of new state and local government employees.

All three plans also favored the provision in present law raising the normal retirement age to 67, and two plans (IA, PSA) would have further indexed it to longevity. None of the plans proposed means-testing benefits or indexing social security benefits at rates lower than the cost of living. All three plans eliminated the forecast 75-year social security imbalance, and all three went beyond this to stabilize the ratio of the Trust Fund reserves to annual expenditures between 2050 and 2070, the last two decades of the current planning horizon. Finally, all three plans relied on private sector investments to generate additional revenues for future retirees or for the OASDI program as a whole.

Notes

1. These concepts are discussed at more length in Mitchell (1988).
2. In this third case, of course, it is likely that benefit cuts and tax increases would still be needed to reach system solvency. See Goodfellow and Schieber, (this volume).

3. Other reform options include one by the Committee on Economic Development (CED 1997), which is perhaps best characterized as a plan halfway between the IA and the PSA plans. See also Carter and Shipman (1996).

4. This section is derived from Quinn and Mitchell (1997).

5. The PSA plan also advocated increasing the normal retirement age.

References

Advisory Council on Social Security. *Final Report of the 1994–96 Advisory Council on Social Security*. 2 vols. Washington, D.C.: Social Security Administration, 1997.

Carter, Marshall N. and William G. Shipman. *Promises to Keep: Saving Social Security's Dream*. Washington, D.C.: Regnery Publishing, Inc., 1996.

Committee on Economic Development (CED). *Fixing Social Security*. New York: Committee on Economic Development, 1997.

Mitchell, Olivia S. "Insulating Old-Age Systems from Political Risk." Presented at the 1997 Conference on "Nine Challenges to Pension Reform" hosted by the Mexican Government, Oaxaca, Mexico, December 1997. Pension Research Council Working Paper #98-4, Wharton School, 1998.

Quinn, Joseph F. and Olivia S. Mitchell. "A New Look at Social Security Reform." *Prospectives on Work*. Industrial Relations Research Association: University of Wisconsin, Madison, 1997: 70–73.

Chapter 2
Measuring Solvency in the Social Security System

Stephen C. Goss

Public confidence in the ability of the U.S. social security program to make expected future benefit payments has been an essential component contributing to the success and popularity of the program since its enactment in 1935. The development and application of measures of solvency have successfully provided advance warning of future financing inadequacy. This warning has provided policymakers and legislators the time needed to develop thoughtful modifications of the program.

Defining solvency depends on one's view of the role and design of the social security program. A range of measures of solvency has evolved to address a variety of concepts of solvency. The current assessment that the social security program, as presently specified, will not be solvent over the long-range future has resulted from the application of these measures. Comprehensive amendments to the Social Security Act will be designed to satisfy these measures of solvency. Therefore, an understanding of these measures is useful for the upcoming discussion and development of legislation.

The Social Security Act requires that the Board of Trustees report annually to the Congress providing the expected operations and status of the Old-Age and Survivors Insurance (OASI) and Disability Insurance (DI) Trust Funds for the next 5 fiscal years and "a statement of the actuarial status of the Trust Funds." The particular measures used in assessing the actuarial status of the social security program are the subject of this chapter. Our measures have been developed to be consistent with the nature of the program and the manner of financing, as set forth in the Social Security Act. The Actuarial Standards Board, in its third draft of the Standard of Practice for Social Insurance, has specifically instructed that valuation measures and tests of financial adequacy for social insurance programs be designed to be consistent with the design and intent of the program financing approach. As a government-administered social insurance program, social security has specifically not been subject to the funding requirements applied for private pensions and insurance. Therefore, the measures described in this paper for assessing the actuarial status and solvency of the social security program differ substantially from the measures used for private pensions and insurance.

Because the social security program is estimated to be inadequately financed over the long run, based on the "best estimate" intermediate assumptions used in the 1997 Trustees Report, future legislative changes are expected to be needed. These changes may retain the basic pay-as-you-go form of the program, as have other amendments over the past 20 years, or they may substantially change the nature of the program and its financing. If substantial changes are made, such as a move toward sustained partial advance funding or a provision for mandatory individual accounts, then new measures may be needed to assess the impact and viability of the new program.

The Nature of Social Insurance and Social Security Financing

Since its enactment in 1935, the social security system has been managed by the federal government with dedicated taxes and, since the 1950's, mandatory participation by nearly the entire population. Unlike private pensions and insurance, this social insurance program is essentially "guaranteed" a stream of new participants indefinitely into the future. For this reason, social insurance can be financed without advance funding for accrued future obligations, contrary to the requirements for private pensions and insurance. While the desirability of such pay-as-you-go financing is debatable, the approach has been implicit in law.

A pay-as-you-go financing approach requires no accumulation of reserves for advance funding, but the lack of authority to borrow makes it prudent for the Social Security Administration to maintain a "contingency reserve fund." Without modest contingency reserves, an unexpected economic downturn could quickly render the program unable to pay full benefits on a timely basis. For example, higher than expected inflation would increase benefits, and lower than expected employment and wages would reduce tax revenues, resulting in an accumulated "loss" equal to 50 to 100 percent of the annual cost of the program within about five years. Thus, a contingency reserve of 100 percent of annual cost (i.e., a 100 percent trust fund ratio) has been accepted as sufficient to "ride out" an unexpected recession or to provide time for the enactment of legislation in the event of a more permanent negative turn in economic trends.

As suggested above, the meaning of solvency, or financial adequacy, for a given period in the context of a social insurance program with pay-as-you-go financing is that all expected benefits will be payable in full when due throughout the period. Reaching and maintaining a projected contingency reserve of 100 percent of annual cost provides a practical working margin that accommodates moderate cycles around expected conditions, and allows time for corrective legislation in the event of a negative shift in underlying conditions.

The specified level of payroll taxes has been modified throughout the history of the social security program, from initial levels of 1 percent for employers and employees each, to the current level of 6.2 percent each. Most of this increase is the result of the maturation of a program that started by taxing essentially all workers while paying benefits only to recent retirees, but has since reached the state where over 95 percent of the nation's elderly population is eligible for benefits. Benefit levels have risen and benefits have been extended to cover additional contingencies such as disability. Since 1935, however, financing has been maintained on a roughly pay-as-you-go basis with projected reserves rising substantially above 100 percent of annual program cost only for temporary periods.

Measuring Social Security Solvency

The Social Security Act requires an annual report on both the status of the trust funds for the next five years and a statement of the "actuarial status" of the funds for the long-range future. Different measures of solvency, or financial adequacy, have been developed for the (10-year) short range period and the (75-year) long range period.

Short-Range Measures

Solvency is defined as the expectation that benefits will be payable in full when due, so it is sufficient to examine projected trust fund levels over the next decade. If trust funds are not exhausted during this period, then the program is projected to be solvent in the short range period.

Based on the recommendation of the Technical Panel on Assumptions and Methods appointed by the 1991 Advisory Council, a short range test of financial adequacy has been adopted that requires that (1) the trust fund ratio remain at or above 100 percent through the next 10 years, if it is at least 100 percent initially; or (2) the trust fund ratio rise to at least 100 percent by the end of 5 years and remain at or above 100 percent for an additional 5 years, and that benefits are payable in full when due throughout the next 10 years, if the trust fund ratio is below 100 percent initially. This test adds the practical requirement that a contingency reserve be developed and maintained. For the 1997 Trustees Report, the combined OASI and DI Trust Funds were projected to remain above 100 percent of annual cost for the next 10 years under the intermediate alternative II assumptions. The social security program was thus found to meet the test of short range financial adequacy.

Long-Range Measures

The actuarial status over the long term has been analyzed using a number of measures. An examination of annual values for a 75-year period (or longer) being cumbersome, a number of single-value summarized measures and indicators have been developed over the years.

Actuarial Balance. This most basic and useful summarized measure has been designed to provide a value of zero when the program is projected to be financed precisely on a pay-as-you-go basis, on average, over a specified valuation period. The actuarial balance is defined as the difference between the long-range summarized income rate (tax revenue) and the long-range summarized cost rate (benefit payout). However, the method of summarization, the length of the long-range period, and the components included in cost and income have all changed over the years.

Prior to 1965, projections were made into perpetuity. The long-range summarized cost rate was defined as the present value of projected future cost into perpetuity divided by the present value of projected future taxable payroll into perpetuity. Summarized income rates were defined as the present value of projected future payroll taxes divided by the present value of projected future taxable payroll.

In the 1965 Trustees Report, the long-range valuation period was changed to 75 years, reflecting the recommendation of the latest Advisory Council. Estimates had been assumed to level off after 85 or 90 years and the Council felt that it served "no useful purpose to present estimates as if they had validity into perpetuity" (Board of Trustees, 1965: 68). The 75-year period encompasses essentially the entire future life span of all current workers and beneficiaries, even the youngest current workers, at the beginning of the 75-year period. It also provides a projection period long enough to illustrate the complete and mature effects of past amendments and potential future changes to the Social Security Act. Restricting the long-range period to 75 years lowered the estimated long range cost by only about three percent in 1965, largely because estimates were made on a level cost basis, discounted by the full expected trust fund interest rate.

Under the level-cost approach, no increase in either the average wage level or the level of prices was assumed for the future. This approach was developed because the law at that time provided for no automatic increase in either the maximum taxable wage or the benefit formula. While "present law" estimates for the Trustees Report could not explicitly presume the enactment of likely changes in future legislation, the use of constant future price and wage levels made implicit the assumption of such changes.

But when projections were made assuming no increase in either price or average-wage levels, discounting by the full assumed nominal interest rate meant that the summarized long-range cost and income rates put very little weight on benefits, payroll, and taxes for distant future years. Thus, inclusion of estimated values for years beyond the 75th projection year in the summarized rates made little difference.

With the adoption of automatic benefit indexing and automatic indexing of the maximum taxable earnings level in the 1972 Social Security Amendments, dynamic assumptions were used beginning with the 1973 Trustees Report. Under dynamic assumptions, explicit increases in average wage and price levels were specified for the future projections. The 1973 Trustees Report also changed the method of summarizing cost and income rates. As a matter of simplification, an approximation of the present-value approach was adopted. Under this approach, the summarized cost rate was computed as the arithmetic average of the annual cost rates for the 75 years in the long-range period. The summarized income rate was defined similarly. This approach, called the "average cost method," was retained through the 1987 Trustees Report. The average cost method is equivalent to the present value method where the growth rate in the aggregate taxable payroll is used as the annual discount rate. This approach was deemed appropriate at the time because it yielded values that were very close to present-value calculations (the growth in aggregate taxable payroll was very close to the current interest rate on the trust funds), and the summarized rates were more easily replicated without access to main-frame computers.

In 1988, calculation of the summarized cost and income rates returned to the present value method. Trust fund interest rates had become substantially different (larger) than the growth rate in aggregate taxable payroll, and computers and programmable calculators had become widely available. These last two changes in the actuarial balance were to include the starting trust fund balance in the summarized income rate (beginning with the 1988 report) and to include the present value of a target trust fund balance equal to 100 percent of annual cost in the summarized cost rate (beginning with the 1991 report). With these changes, exact actuarial balance (i.e., an actuarial balance of zero) indicates that the present value of projected income over the next 75 years, along with the starting trust fund balance, is enough to cover the present value of all costs over the next 75 years, leaving a trust fund balance equal to 100 percent of annual outgo at the end of the period.

Table 1 indicates the projected actuarial balances for the social security (OASDI) program based on the Trustees' intermediate assumptions of Trustees Reports for years 1973 through 1997. Evident in these estimates of OASDI actuarial balance are the large improvements made at the enactment of the 1977 and 1983 Social Security Amendments, and the deterioration of the actuarial balance before and after these amendments. The size of the actuarial deficit immediately prior to enactment of the 1983

TABLE 1. Summarized Long-Range (75-Year) OASDI Rates Based on Intermediate Assumptions

Year of Report	Summarized Cost Rate	Summarized Income Rate (%)	Actuarial Balance (%)
1973	10.95%	10.63	−0.32
1974	13.89	10.91	−2.98
1975	16.26	10.94	−5.32
1976	18.93	10.97	−7.96
1977	19.19	10.99	−8.20
1978	13.55	12.16	−1.40
1979	13.38	12.19	−1.20
1980	13.74	12.22	−1.52
1981	14.08	12.25	−1.82
1982	14.09	12.27	−1.82
1983	12.84	12.87	0.02
1984	12.95	12.90	−0.06
1985	13.35	12.94	−0.41
1986	13.40	12.96	−0.44
1987	13.51	12.89	−0.62
1988	13.52	12.94	−0.58
1989	13.72	13.02	−0.70
1990	13.95	13.04	−0.91
1991	14.19	13.11	−1.08
1992	14.63	13.16	−1.46
1993	14.67	13.21	−1.46
1994	15.37	13.24	−2.13
1995	15.44	13.27	−2.17
1996	15.52	13.33	−2.19
1997	15.60	13.37	−2.23

Source: Annual OASDI Trustees Reports.
Note: Alternative II-B for years 1981–90, alternative II for all other years.

Amendments, based on preliminary intermediate assumptions for the 1983 Trustees Report, was 2.09 percent of taxable payroll. Estimated actuarial deficits have once again exceeded this level since the 1994 Trustees' Report.

The deterioration of the OASDI actuarial balance since enactment of the 1983 Amendments is the result of changes in five areas. Changes in (1) economic assumptions, (2) disability experience and assumptions, (3) actuarial projection methods, and (4) the starting and ending year of the 75-year valuation period have each worsened the actuarial balance by an amount equal to about one-third of the current actuarial deficit. Changes in (5) demographic experience and assumptions have improved the actuarial balance by an amount equal to about one-third of the current actuarial deficit.

The size of an estimated actuarial deficit may be usefully characterized as the magnitude of the increase in the combined payroll tax rate that would be needed to eliminate the actuarial deficit, effective at the beginning of the valuation period, thus restoring solvency for the program over the long-range period. It must be noted, however, that this is merely a convenient characterization, and that an infinite number of solutions involving benefit reductions and/or revenue increases would similarly eliminate the actuarial deficit.

Advancing the starting and ending year of the valuation period for each annual Trustees' Report currently increases the size of the actuarial deficit by 0.08 percent of taxable payroll. This worsening is the result of the inclusion of an additional year (the 76th year of the prior Trustees Report projection) which has a substantially larger deficit than the other years in the period, on average. The first year of the prior Trustees Report valuation period is not excluded from the new valuation, because the net operations for that year, and for all prior years, are reflected in the starting trust fund balance, which has been included in the summarized income rate since the 1988 Trustees Report.

As mentioned earlier, the long-range valuation period was limited to 75 years, starting in the 1965 report, to avoid dominating the actuarial balance with the level of annual balances at and beyond the 75th projection year. If the actuarial balance had been computed into perpetuity for the 1996 report, an OASDI actuarial deficit of about 4.7 percent of taxable payroll would have been calculated. This value is much closer to the annual deficit of 5.51 percent of payroll estimated for 2070 than it is to the actuarial balance for the 75-year valuation period 1996–2070 of 2.19 percent of payroll.

Annual Cost Rates, Income Rates, and Balances. Annual cost and income rates are computed as the dollar annual cost and annual tax income, respectively, divided by the annual taxable payroll. Cost includes both benefits and administrative expense. Tax income includes both payroll tax receipts and revenue transferred to the trust funds from the general fund of the United States Treasury equal to the amount collected for federal income taxation of OASDI benefits beginning in 1984 (a portion of this amount is also allocated to the Hospital Insurance Trust Fund).

The annual balance is the difference between the annual income rate and the annual cost rate. Because interest income is excluded from the annual income rate, the annual balance indicates how close the program is to operating on a pay-as-you-go basis for the year. Excluding interest from the income rate also makes sense because the interest is needed primarily to maintain the level of the contingency reserve. The interest rate on trust fund assets is close enough to the rate of increase in aggregate program cost so that interest on the assets is just about the amount needed to maintain a constant trust fund ratio (assets to annual cost) from the beginning to the end of the year, particularly for a relatively small contingency reserve fund.

TABLE 2. Projected OASDI Annual Cost Rates, Income Rates and Balances, and Cost as a Percentage of GDP, Based on the Intermediate Assumptions of the 1997 Trustees Report

| Year | OASDI Annual Rate as % of Payroll | | | OASDI Cost as % of GDP |
	Income	Cost	Balance	
1996	12.63	11.49	1.14	4.66
2010	12.73	12.48	0.26	4.87
2030	13.09	17.47	−4.38	6.57
2070	13.32	19.18	−5.86	6.68

Source: 1997 OASDI Trustees Report

In addition, annual cost rates are useful as an indication of the cost to society of providing benefits, regardless of how the cost is financed. Similarly, annual cost as a percentage of GDP is a useful indicator of the cost of the program to the society.

Table 2 provides selected annual rates based on the intermediate assumptions of the 1997 Trustees Report. These rates indicate the dramatic rise in the cost rate, both as a percentage of payroll and as a percentage of GDP, as the baby-boom generation retires between 2010 and 2030. Increases both before and after this period are relatively modest. Cost rates do not drop back down to earlier levels as the baby-boom generation dies off. The continuing increase in cost rates after 2030 reflects the assumed continued increase in life expectancy, primarily after reaching retirement age, and the ultimate total fertility rate at a level of 1.9 children per woman. Figure 1 (from the 1997 Trustees Report) illustrates projected annual cost and income rates for the OASDI program under the intermediate alternative II as well as under the low-cost alternative I and the high-cost alternative III assumptions.

The size of the annual balance at the end of the period is of particular interest. If the annual balance at the end of the period differs significantly from the actuarial balance for the period, then the actuarial balance for the next Trustees Report will move in the direction of the ending annual balance. The relationship between the ending (75th year) income rate and cost rate is also indicative of the proportion of projected program cost that is covered by the specified tax revenues in the law. For example, based on the values in Table 2 for the intermediate assumptions of the 1997 Trustees Report, the projected tax revenues alone would cover about 74 percent of program cost in 2029, the year of combined trust fund exhaustion, and about 68 percent of program cost by 2071. The percentage of cost covered by specified tax rates indicates the relative extent that benefits would need to be reduced, or revenue increased, in order to achieve balance between the annual income and cost rates.

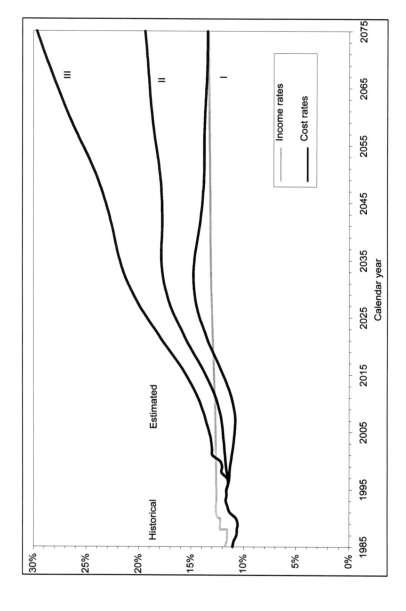

Figure 1. Estimated OASDI income and cost rates by alternative, calendar years 1985–2075 (% of taxable payroll). Source: 1997 OASDI Trustees Report.

Trust Fund Ratios, Year of Trust Fund Exhaustion, and Stability at the End. The trust fund ratio is, of course the ultimate measure of solvency, defined as the ability to pay all benefits in full when due. The date of trust fund exhaustion, which would occur during the year 2029 for the combined OASDI program based on the intermediate assumptions of 1997 Trustees Report, is of particular significance. Figure 2 (from the 1997 Trustees Report) illustrates the projected trust fund ratios under each of the three alternatives.

It is worth noting that the combined trust funds are not exhausted during the 75-year long-range projection period under the low-cost alternative I assumptions (the alternative I and III assumptions will be discussed further below). The trust fund ratios for alternative I serve to illustrate two additional considerations. First, the actuarial balance for a valuation period is directly related to the trust fund ratio at the end of the period. A trust fund ratio of 100 percent is, of course, associated with an actuarial balance of zero, with a positive actuarial balance indicating an ending balance greater than 100 percent and a negative actuarial balance indicating an ending trust fund ratio of less than 100 percent. In practice, under present law, a negative trust fund ratio is not possible because there is no authority to borrow.

The second consideration regarding the ending trust fund ratio is the stability of the ratio around the end of the valuation period. If the trust fund ratio is stable at the end of the long-range period, we can be assured that in the absence of major changes in assumptions, the actuarial balance for the current Trustees Report will change little for subsequent reports for the foreseeable future. This results from the fact that there is a one-to-one correspondence between the trust fund ratio and the actuarial balance. A stable trust fund ratio implies a stable actuarial balance. For this reason, most recent proposals to eliminate the long-range OASDI actuarial deficit have also been designed to achieve a stable trust fund ratio at the end of the long-range period (like that illustrated under alternative I assumptions). This is true for the each of the proposals of the 1994–96 Advisory Council and S. 825, proposed earlier by Senators Kerrey and Simpson.

Test of Long-Range Close Actuarial Balance. This test is not a test of solvency or financial adequacy. It represents an attempt to characterize, with a single-value summarized measure, whether the program is at least close to being solvent throughout the long-range 75-year period. The requirement for being only close to solvent is intended to reflect the inherent uncertainty in making projections very far into the future.

For many years the test of close actuarial balance required that the summarized long-range income rate be between 95 and 105 percent of the summarized long-range cost rate. When the income rate was near the lower end of the range, the trust fund would be exhausted prior to the end of the long-range period, but the financing of the program would arguably be within "striking distance" of the level needed to achieve solvency. The range

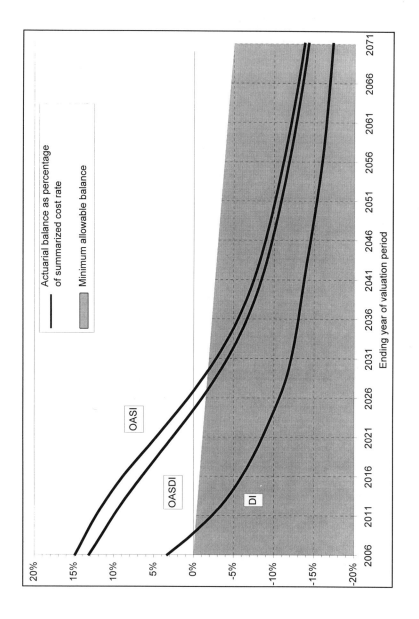

Figure 2. Comparison of estimated long-range actuarial balance with the minimum allowable for close actuarial balance (Alternative II) by trust fund. Source: 1997 OASDI Trustees Report.

of "tolerance" allowed that there would be no call for corrective legislation as long as the size of the actuarial balance or deficit was small. When the size of the actuarial balance or deficit grew larger, more than 5 percent of the cost rate, then a need to begin serious study toward enactment of corrective legislation would be indicated. Significantly, this earlier version of the test called for action not only when the program was significantly under-financed relative to pay-as-you-go financing, but also when the program was significantly over-financed relative to pay-as-you-go financing.

Based on the recommendation of the Technical Panel on Assumptions and Methods appointed by the 1991 Advisory Council, the test for close actuarial balance was modified in two ways. First, the "upper limit" for actuarial balance was removed. This was done in recognition of the fact that the 1977 and 1983 amendments both provided for temporary advance funding substantially in excess of the contingency reserve level. The temporary advance funding was described as a way to alleviate some of the burden on workers during the retirement years of the baby-boom generation by having the baby-boom generation contribute more than necessary for pay-as-you-go financing during their working years to establish reserves that could be utilized when they retired.

Second, the test was subdivided into 66 separate sub-tests, each of which must be passed in order to meet the test of close actuarial balance. These sub-tests are based on the 66 valuation periods, each beginning with the initial projection year, the first ending with the 10th projection year, and each successive period extending one year so that the 66th sub-period encompasses the entire 75-year period. The maximum permissible size for an actuarial deficit is zero percent of the summarized cost rate for the first period and 5 percent of the summarized cost rate for the 66th period; the permissible percentage is linearly interpolated for intervening periods. This expansion of the test assures that a program will not be found to be in close actuarial balance if it meets the test condition for the full long-range period (the 66th sub-period) but has a substantially larger deficit for a shorter period. Figure 3 illustrates how nearly the OASI, DI, and combined OASDI programs meet the test based on the intermediate assumptions of the 1997 Trustees Report.

The OASI program meets the test for valuation periods of length 10 through 33 years. The DI program meets the test only for valuation periods of length 10 through 12 years. The combined OASDI program meets the test for valuation periods of length 10 through 30 years. In each case, the test is not met for longer periods. Therefore, under the intermediate assumptions of the 1997 Trustees Report, each of the programs fails the test for long-range close actuarial balance.

It is not apparent that failure of the test for close actuarial balance alone has been particularly successful in motivating serious movement toward corrective legislation in the social security program. The 1977 Amendments

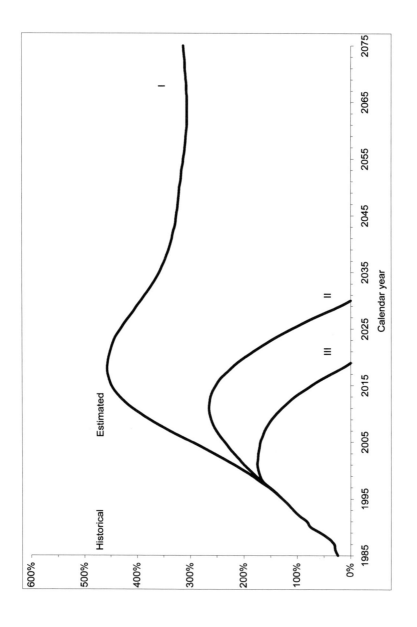

Figure 3. Estimated trust fund ratios, OASDI and DI trust funds combined, by alternative, calendar years 1985–2075 (assets as % of annual expenditures). Source: 1997 OASDI Trustees Report.

failed to bring the OASDI program within the limits of close actuarial balance; the test was not passed until 6 years later when the 1983 Amendments, motivated in part by a near-term solvency crisis, eliminated the long-range deficit altogether. Only six years later, in the 1989 report, the program was again out of close actuarial balance, and continues to be so today without immediate prospect for correction. The lack of a near-term OASDI financing crisis and the greater immediacy of the financial shortfall of the Medicare Hospital Insurance program are largely responsible.

Variation, Stochastic Simulation, and Sensitivity Testing

Due to the inherent uncertainty in projections of future experience, it is desirable to convey some sense of the plausible range of possible future conditions. This can be accomplished either with specified sets of assumptions that are intended to illustrate this variation or with stochastically varying scenarios that provide a sense of how likely it is that the true actuarial status of the program will turn out to be within a given distance range around the actuarial status based on intermediate projections.

Variation in Alternatives

For many years, Trustees Reports have provided projections for at least three full scenarios intended to describe a plausible range of possible long-term outcomes. For this purpose the intermediate alternative II assumptions, which represent the best guess of what future economic and demographic conditions will hold, are modified in each element to create the low-cost alternative I and the high-cost alternative III sets of assumptions. For these variations, the individual elements of the assumption set are varied by selecting levels around the intermediate assumption that are thought to be quite unlikely to be achieved on the average in the long run, but are, nonetheless, plausible. In this manner, each element is modified, generally in the direction that tends to result in lower program cost for alternative I and higher cost for alternative III.

The selection of assumptions on this basis results in variation of many elements from the intermediate assumptions in ways that are inconsistent with interrelationships among elements observed in past data. Thus, the low-cost and high-cost alternatives incorporate, by the method of their construction, an additional reinforcing element that moves toward low or high cost, that of structural change in the historical relationship among elements. In this way it is intended that alternatives will describe a fairly wide range of variation that is likely to encompass future experience.

Figures earlier in this chapter illustrate the range of variation in several measures of solvency based on these assumptions. Alternative I assumptions result in projected cost rates that are very close to projected income rates, and trust fund ratios that are stable or rising. Alternative III assumptions, on the other hand, result in projected trust fund exhaustion substantially sooner than under the intermediate assumptions.

Stochastic Simulation

Stochastic simulation of future long-range economic and demographic trends and their interrelationships would provide a quantitatively, rather than qualitatively, derived basis for illustrating possible future variation in the measures of solvency of the social security program. On the plus side, it would provide a clearly defined probability distribution of measures like year of trust fund exhaustion and actuarial balance. On the minus side, it would not provide unambiguous sets of assumptions that are consistent with the various points in the distribution.

The initial challenge in developing a meaningful stochastic simulation of long-range ultimate trends is to determine what are reasonable distributions for the various elements in the assumption set. It is quite a different matter to establish a probability distribution for long-range 75-year trends in a variable than it is to establish year-to-year stochastic variation around a specified central trend. The latter distribution is readily specified using data for the past 2 or 3 decades or so. But to specify the distribution of possible 75-year trends requires either data for a *very* long period encompassing a number of independent 75-year periods where underlying conditions are reasonably similar to expected future conditions, or a presumption about the nature of the distribution. Because appropriate long-term data are not available, the distribution for each element must be based on presumption. The validity of the distribution of the measures of solvency can only be as good as the presumed distributions for the elements and their interrelationships.

The more fundamental question, however, is for what specific purpose is the stochastic variation in measures of solvency might be useful. It is clear that for private insurance, where the solvency of the insurer is essential, and the insurer cannot rewrite the terms of the contract after the insurance is issued, a probability distribution of outcomes is needed. The insurer must charge premiums that are large enough to ensure that the risk of having expenses (losses) in excess of premium income is acceptably small. And even a small risk of excessive expense may be covered with reinsurance.

Social insurance is different from private insurance in several ways. First, social insurance is not a contractual obligation, or liability. The insurer, the Federal Government, can unilaterally modify the terms of the plan if expenses turn out to be either higher or lower than expected. The 1977 and 1983 Social Security Amendments are examples of such action by the government where substantial reductions in future benefits were enacted, including benefits for current beneficiaries and fully insured workers. For this reason, social insurance can be financed based on the expected cost, and not on the basis of something higher in order to avoid unsustainable losses. The government retains the right to lower benefits or raise taxes unilaterally; if either gains or losses occur, the plan can be modified. Moreover, it can be argued that the government should not charge more than the expected cost for social insurance. It is the ultimate reinsurer and does not set premiums with the expectation of profit. If we conclude that the government can, or even should, charge for social insurance on the basis of expected cost, then the prime function of stochastic simulation for private insurance would appear not to apply to social insurance.

Sensitivity Testing

The Trustees Reports provide summarized cost and income rates and actuarial balances projected on the basis of the intermediate assumptions in all respects except that each of the elements of the set of economic and demographic assumptions is, in turn, replaced with the high-cost and the low-cost values. This provides an additional measure of the sensitivity of the program to variation beyond that provided by projections based on the three alternative sets of assumptions.

Specifically, this sensitivity testing allows readers of the Trustees Reports who disagree with one or more of the elements of the assumptions to estimate roughly how much the solvency of the program, as measured by the actuarial balance, would be affected by modifying the assumption(s) in question.

Other Measures of Solvency

Several important measures of solvency for pension and insurance plans are based on and expressed in dollar amounts, generally present-value dollar amounts. These include the open-group surplus or deficit for a social insurance program, the closed group (to new entrants) surplus or deficiency of a plan, and the plan-termination unfunded accrued liability of a private pension or insurance plan. Each of these has a possible application to the social security program.

The open group concept is consistent with the pay-as-you-go financing approach and is thus directly applicable for the social security program. This can be referred to as the open-group unfunded obligation for social security. The term obligation is used in lieu of the term liability, because liability indicates a contractual obligation (as in the case of private insurance) that cannot be altered by the plan sponsor without the agreement of the plan participants.

The closed group (to new entrants, i.e., persons just reaching working age) surplus or deficiency may have specific application in cases like that of the Federal Government closing the Civil Service Retirement System (CSRS) plan to persons newly hired after 1983. This is a concept that is only appropriate to a plan that has been intended to be fully advance funded, such as plans covered under ERISA. For a social insurance plan that was designed to be financed on a pay-as-you-go basis with the expectation of a continuing pool of new entrants, like social security, this concept cannot apply as a measure of solvency because it is inconsistent with the design and intent of the program. However, the concept can apply in the context of a continuing program that is converting to another form, where there is a desire to keep the financing of the old and new forms of the program separate. In this case the closed group surplus or deficit may be referred to as the closed group (to new entrants) transition gain or cost.

Similarly, the plan-termination unfunded accrued obligation concept may be applied when a continuing plan that has been financed on a pay-as-you-go basis is being converted to a new form that will apply not only for new entrants but also with respect to all future taxes or premiums of still-active workers. In this case, the unfunded obligation of the old form may be referred to as the maximum transition cost.

Open Group Surplus or Deficiency

The open group surplus or deficiency is essentially equivalent to the actuarial balance as it was produced for the 1988 through 1990 Trustees Reports. That is, it is the difference between (a) the present value of the projected tax income over the next 75 years plus trust fund assets at the beginning of the period and (b) the present value of projected cost of the program over the next 75 years. This measure differs from the actuarial balance concept used in 1988–90 only in that the open group surplus or deficiency is not divided by the present value of taxable payroll over the 75-year projection period. It further differs from the concept of actuarial balance used since 1991 in that it excludes the cost of building and maintaining a contingency reserve by the end of the period. Table 3 lists estimates of open group surplus and deficiency provided over the years to the Department of the Treasury for their annual reports "Statement of Liabilities and Other Financial Commitments of United States Government . . ." These values are consistent with estimates based on the intermediate assumptions of the Trustees Report of the year of the valuation date; in some cases estimates of the starting fund balance are updated and the effects of legislation enacted after the Trustees Report are included.

Closed Group (to New Entrants) Transition Gain or Cost

This value was provided to the Department of the Treasury for inclusion in the report cited above through 1994. Since 1995 this value has been judged

TABLE 3. OASDI Open Group Surplus or Deficiency and Closed Group (to New Entrants) for the OASDI Program, for Valuation Years 1973 Through 1997 (billions of $)

Valuation Year	75-Year Open Group Surplus or Deficiency (−)	100 Year Closed Group (to New Entrants) Transition Gain or Cost (−)	Lowest Age in Closed Group	Ultimate Valuation Interest Rate (%)
7/1/1973	−176	−2,118	23	6.00
7/1/1974	−1,312	−2,460	19	6.00
7/1/1975	−2,027	−2,710	20	7.38
10/1/1976	−4,176	−4,148	21	6.60
10/1/1977	−4,787	−5,362	17	6.60
10/1/1978	−930	−3,971	18	6.60
10/1/1979	−848	−4,225	19	6.60
10/1/1980	−1,464	−5,601	15	6.08
10/1/1981	−1,555	−5,858	16	6.08
10/1/1982	−1,641	−5,808	17	6.08
10/1/1983	+148	−5,059	18	6.08
10/1/1984	+37	−4,208	15	6.08
10/1/1985	−269	−4,647	15	6.08
10/1/1986	−343	−5,394	15	6.08
10/1/1987	−378	−5,580	15	6.08
10/1/1988	−664	−5,740	15	6.08
10/1/1989	−850	−6,098	15	6.08
10/1/1990	−1,244	−7,121	15	6.08
10/1/1991	−1,185	−6,595	15	6.39
10/1/1992	−1,773	−7,376	15	6.39
10/1/1993	−1,864	−7,201	15	6.39
10/1/1994	−2,838	−8,390	15	6.39
10/1/1995	−2,833	−8,129	15	6.39
10/1/1996	−3,094	−8,856	15	6.39
10/1/1997	−2,922	−7,913	15	6.29

Source: Annual Issues of "Statement of Liabilities and Other Financial Commitments of the United States Government . . ." from the Department of the Treasury and unpublished estimates from the Office of the Chief Actuary, Social Security Administration

to be inappropriate for inclusion in the report of liabilities and other commitments. These values are included in Table 3 representing the closed-group transition gain or cost for continuing the social security program in another form for new entrants on the valuation date and later and for evaluating the old and new benefit forms separately.

The values in Table 3 are present values discounted to the valuation date and thus represent current dollars on the valuation date. Therefore, they tend to increase by the annual valuation interest rate from one valuation to the next, in the absence of any change in assumptions, methods, or the benefit and financing provisions of the program.

Maximum Transition Cost

This value represents the transition cost for continuing the social security program in a different form, with all payroll taxes for work after the valuation date credited to the new benefit form. The maximum transition cost is computed as the difference between (a) the value of the assets on the valuation date plus the present value of revenue from taxation of future benefits payable on the old form and (b) the present value of all future benefits payable after the valuation date based on earnings credited under the old form, that is, based on earnings prior to the valuation date. Based on the intermediate assumptions of the 1997 Trustees Report, the maximum transition cost computed on this basis is $8,927 billion for a valuation date of 10/1/97 and a 100-year valuation period.

This value is only 13 percent greater than the closed-group-to-new-entrant transition cost for the same period and valuation date. The difference between these two measures is equal to the difference between (a) the present value of future payroll taxes payable by the closed group after the valuation date plus the present value of revenue from taxation of benefits earned based on these payroll taxes, and (b) the present value of additional benefits earned under the old form (beyond the past service credits described below) based on these payroll taxes. This means that the incremental revenue (a) is only slightly larger than the incremental benefits (b) described above.

Future benefits under the old form for workers who have not yet reached benefit eligibility age (62) are calculated on a proportional past service credit basis. The approach is similar to the approach developed for past service credits under the Personal Security Account (PSA) plan for the 1994–96 Advisory Council. The balance of this section describes the detailed method for computing the past service credits for the interested reader.

For each such worker, a monthly benefit amount based on the old form would be computed on the valuation date as if the worker had become disabled. For workers who survive without disability to retirement eligibility age (62), this amount would be indexed by the average wage in the national economy and multiplied by the proportioning factor derived as $P = $ (age on valuation date $- 22)/40$.

For individuals who are disabled continuously from the valuation date until the earlier of death or reaching retirement conversion age (their normal retirement age under the old form), all future benefits payable on the account will be as under the old form. For individuals disabled on the valuation date who recover from disability before reaching retirement eligibility age (62) and survive, disability benefits before retirement age continue under the old form and benefits after reaching retirement eligibility age are the combination of (a) the final disability monthly benefit payment wage indexed to retirement age and multiplied by the factor D = (years disabled between 22 and 62)/40, and (b) the monthly disability benefit payable on the valuation date, wage indexed to retirement age and multiplied by the factor P' = (non-disabled years between 22 and the valuation date)/40. Finally, for individuals who are not disabled on the valuation date but who become disabled thereafter, but before retirement eligibility age, disability benefits are equal to the old form disability benefit computed as if disabled on the valuation date, wage indexed to the date of disability, and multiplied by the factor D' = (age on valuation date − 22)/(age at disability − 22). Benefits at retirement conversion are computed in the same manner as for the individual who is disabled on the valuation date but recovers.

Conclusion

As with any pension or insurance plan, measuring the solvency of the social security system requires careful attention to the nature of the program and its intended financing method. The U.S. social security program is a social insurance plan, meaning that it expects a steady stream of mandatory participants in the future. For this reason, the program has been financed essentially on a pay-as-you-go basis since its early years, with only temporary periods of partial advance funding like the one we are entering as a result of the provisions of the 1977 and 1983 Amendments.

Because the social security program is financed on an essentially pay-as-you-go basis and has a guaranteed stream of new participants in the future, appropriate measures of solvency have been developed and are presented annually by the Trustees in their report to the Congress. These measures include the actuarial balance, annual cost and income rates and balances, annual trust fund ratios and the projected year of trust fund exhaustion, the short range test of financial adequacy and the long-range test of close actuarial balance, and of more recent interest, the size of the annual balance (deficit) at the end of the long-range 75-year projection period and the stability of the trust fund ratio at the end of the period. The combination of these measures provides an array of analytical information intended to assist policymakers, including the President and the Congress, in assessing the actuarial status of the program under current law and the financial implications of the numerous changes to the program that are considered each year.

Absent from the list of measures generally used to assess the solvency of the social security program are such measures as unfunded accrued liability. This measure is entirely appropriate in assessing the solvency of a private pension or insurance program that must by law be fully advance funded at all times, because a cessation of new entrants is always a possibility.

Among the proposals being studied for the correction of the current projected actuarial deficit for social security are a variety of plans that would fundamentally modify the social security program. These proposals would not terminate social security but would modify its form, retaining a substantial mandatory plan providing retirement, survivors, and disability benefits as does the current system. Interestingly, these proposals do present a use for a measure like the unfunded accrued liability that is necessary for fully advance funded plans. The usefulness of the deficit measure in the context of social security is that it represents the maximum potential transition cost that may be incurred in modifying the current social security program into a fully advance-funded defined contribution individual savings plan. This fact was pointed out by Carolyn Weaver and others during the proceedings of the 1994–96 Advisory Council.

Any measure of solvency, especially in the long run (75 years), can only be as accurate as the assumptions used in its application, but the measures described above appear to be accomplishing their purpose. Interest in the long-range financing of the program has seldom been greater. And with the tools now available to make more exhaustive calculations more rapidly than ever before, there is every prospect that the next comprehensive amendments to the Social Security Act will produce a financing structure more robust than any previous one.

Of course, this does not mean that the social security program will be either fixed or "set" forever by the next amendments. Members of every generation have had and will have their own ideas about the type of social insurance system they desire. After all, it is the system's ability to be retailored to some extent for each generation that has helped maintain its broad appeal for over 60 years.

The author wishes to acknowledge members of the Office of the Chief Actuary at the Social Security Administration, past and present, for their dedication and effort in developing the measures discussed in this chapter. Seung An, Orlo Nichols, and William Ritchie have been instrumental in developing the measures and estimates of solvency presented here and in the annual reports of the Social Security Board of Trustees. Opinions are solely those of the author.

References

Board of Trustees of the Social Security Administration. *Annual Report of the Board of Trustees of the Federal Old-Age and Survivors Insurance and Disability Insurance Trust Funds.* Washington, D.C.: USGPO, 1972–1996.

U.S. Department of the Treasury. *Statement of Financial Liabilities and Other Financial Commitments of the United States Government.* Valuation Dates June 30, 1973 through September 30, 1995. Washington, D.C.: Department of Treasury, various dates.

U.S. House of Representatives, Committee on Ways and Means. *Compilation of the Social Security Laws Including the Social Security Act, as Amended, and Related Enactments Through January 1, 1995.* U.S. Congress, Washington, D.C.: USGPO, 1995.

Chapter 3
Criteria for Evaluating Social Security Reform

Joseph F. Quinn

Because of its long-range funding deficit, reform of social security is inevitable. This is one of the themes of this volume. Some combination of increased revenues and decreased or delayed benefits is necessary. It is not a matter of "if" reform will occur, but rather of when and how it will occur.

There is much debate on the appropriate timing of reform legislation and implementation. Some argue that there is no need to legislate reform now, both because the long-range liability prediction is based on a 75-year forecast (and therefore is subject to considerable uncertainty) and because, even if this forecast turns out to be accurate, the OASDI trust funds will not be depleted for over three decades. Seventy-five years ago was 1923. Even economists, usually willing to predict anything, anytime, anywhere, would have been hard pressed to forecast the last 75 years with much accuracy! Why institute reform, especially radical reform, say some, to solve a problem that may turn out to be considerably less serious than it appears to be today?[1] And even if the problem remains, will not future generations, with more and better information than we have today, be in a better position to decide on the best alternative? Others point out, however, that there should be a significant lag between legislation and implementation, to allow citizens to adjust to the new environment, and that whatever reform changes are introduced can be smaller the sooner they are implemented. Both points argue for prompt legislative action.

Whatever the timing, there are many ways that revenues can be raised or future benefits curtailed. The Technical Panel (1997) described, discussed and evaluated a number of them for the Advisory Council on Social Security. Future benefits could be lowered by raising the normal retirement age (which is nearly equivalent to an across-the-board benefit cut), adjusting benefits at less than the cost-of-living, means-testing benefits or by changing the initial benefit calculation formula. Additional revenues could be generated by raising the payroll tax rate, raising the earnings limit on which these taxes apply, expanding the definition of taxable income (for example, to include the value of some employee benefits), subjecting more social security benefits to federal income taxation, adding general tax revenues to the system, including all new state and local government employees in the program, or investing some of the trust fund reserves in equities.

The last Advisory Council on Social Security (1997) has provided a framework for debate on these issues by presenting three very different visions of social security's future, each of which addresses the long-range deficit.[2] The three plans are described in the introductory chapter of this volume. The Maintain Benefits (MB) plan would preserve the current structure of the social security system, and rely primarily on revenue increases (as has usually been done in the past) to finance the benefits that have been promised. The Individual Accounts (IA) proposal would also maintain the basic structure of the social security program, but would rely more on benefit decreases to balance future finances. The IA plan would also add a new and very controversial component — mandatory, defined-contribution, individual retirement accounts over which individuals would have some management discretion. The third option, the Personal Security Accounts (PSA) plan, would also mandate individual savings accounts (but much larger ones than in the IA proposal, with funds diverted from the current payroll tax stream), and proposes fundamental changes in the basic structure of the social security system. The PSA plan would replace traditional earnings-related social security benefits with a two-tiered system — a lower tier, flat-rate benefit, independent of earnings, and an upper tier, defined-contribution, mandatory savings account, over which individuals would have considerable management discretion, both during the accumulation and the distribution of the assets.

How does one choose among these or any other social security reform proposals? Rational discussion of alternatives requires a framework for analysis — a set of criteria against which the proposals can be compared. The purpose of this chapter is to present and discuss a range of such criteria.

The Roles and Goals of the Social Security Program

The criteria used to evaluate a social security program or proposed changes in it depend on its goals. In the U.S., the over-arching goal is a straightforward one — to improve the economic security of current and future recipients, primarily retirees, but also survivors and the disabled. The debate concerns how best to achieve this goal.

The Importance of Social Security Income

Social security benefits are the most important of four principal income sources upon which older Americans rely, and are more than twice as impor-

TABLE 1. Income Shares for Aged Units Aged 65 or Older by Age and Income
Quintile, 1994 (%)

| Source of Income | Age | | | | | |
	Total	65–69	70–74	75–79	80–84	85+
Social Security	42	31	43	48	56	57
Earnings	18	33	16	8	5	2
Employer Pensions	19	18	21	20	17	13
Income from Assets	18	15	17	20	19	22
Other	4	4	3	4	3	5

| Source of Income | Income Quintile | | | | | |
	Total	First	Second	Third	Fourth	Fifth
Social Security	42	81	81	66	48	23
Earnings	18	0	2	6	11	29
Employer Pensions	19	3	7	14	24	21
Income from Assets	18	3	5	10	14	24
Other	4	13	4	4	3	3

Source: Grad (1996), tables VII.1 and VII.5.

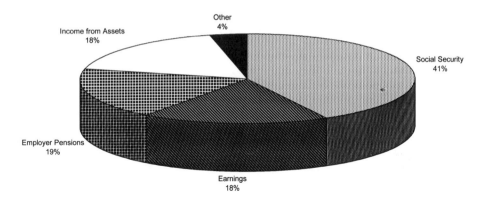

Figure 1. Income shares for aged units age 65 or older, 1994. Source: Grad (1996),
Table VII.1.

tant as the next source. Almost all—91 percent—of all household units
aged 65 or older received social security benefits, and this single source
provided 42 percent of their total cash income in 1994 (see Table 1 and
Figure 1). Three other sources each provided about one-fifth of the aggregate income: employer pensions (19 percent), earnings (18 percent) and
asset income, primarily interest and dividends (18 percent).[3] Two-thirds of
all older household units received some asset income, but many had only

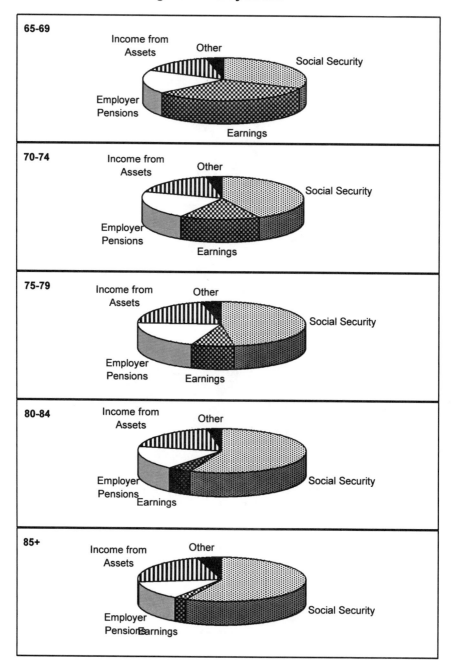

Figure 2. Income shares for aged units by age, 1994. Source: Grad (1996), Table VIII.1.

small amounts. About 40 percent of these households received pension income, and about one-fifth reported earnings (Grad 1996).

The aggregate importance of social security benefits differs dramatically by the age and income status of the recipient. The social security share of total income increases monotonically from 31 percent for those aged 65 to 69 to 56 percent for those aged 80 or older (see Table 1 or Figure 2). Earnings drop dramatically over the same age range, from about a third of total income (for those aged 65 to 69) to less than 5 percent (at ages 80 or older). The shares from asset income and from employer pension benefits are more stable over this age range.

Among the poorest two quintiles of Americans aged 65 or over, social security benefits provided 81 percent of all cash income in 1994 (see Table 1 and Figure 3). For the lowest quintile, public assistance provided another 11 percent, leaving only 8 percent from all other sources.

Those with earnings or pension benefits are rarely found in the lowest quintile. Among those in the highest quintile, in contrast, social security benefits provided less than a quarter of aggregate income in 1994. Earnings (29 percent) was the most important source in this quintile, followed by asset income (24 percent), social security benefits (23 percent) and employer pension benefits (21 percent).

The importance of social security benefits has been increasing, although not steadily, over time. In 1962, social security benefits provided only 31 percent of aggregate income for older Americans (Grad 1997). After the large increases in real social security benefits in the late 1960s and early 1970s, the share increased and then remained stable — in the 36 to 39 percent range between 1976 and 1990. Since 1990, the share has increased again, from 36 percent to 42 percent (1994).

The message here is that social security benefits are a very important component of the financial well-being of most older Americans, especially the poor and the very old. At the same time, however, other sources do provide nearly 60 percent of the aggregate income of those 65 and older, and over three-quarters for those in the top quintile. Thorough analysis must include not only the direct effects of reform on social security benefits, but also any indirect impacts that reform proposals might have on these other important sources of income — earnings, pensions and income from accumulated savings.

The Goals of Social Security

The U.S. social security system is a complex institution that plays many roles simultaneously. In some ways, it behaves like a mandatory *savings* program, a savings account, or a pension. Like these other instruments, it reallocates income over time, taking contributions during one's working years and then paying benefits during retirement. It is also an *insurance* program, like

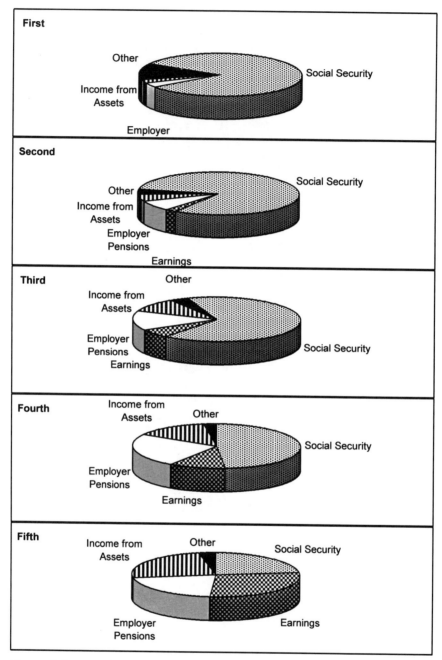

Figure 3. Income shares for aged units by income quintile, 1994. Source: Grad (1996), Table VIII.5.

fire or automobile insurance, since it replaces some of the income lost following the disability or death of a covered worker, and thereby cushions the household's economic decline. Finally, the social security system is a very important *income redistribution* program, like the federal income tax and transfer system. Its progressive benefit structure transfers income from high-earning to low-earning participants, both within and between generations. Of all the federal transfer programs, it is the only one that explicitly bases the transfer on a *life-time* measure of economic status — average monthly earnings over most of an individual's working life.

These multiple roles create multiple goals, and changes therefore require multiple evaluation criteria. The insurance and income redistribution roles suggest that *income adequacy* should be a concern. Are benefits sufficient for recipients to maintain some minimum standard of living? The savings aspect, on the other hand, suggests *individual equity* as an appropriate criterion. What is the relationship between what an individual contributes to the system and what that individual can expect to receive in return? What is the rate of return? Is it a good investment?

The size of the social security system suggests that it might also have important macroeconomic effects. It can affect the economic decisions of individuals, firms, and the government, and therefore can influence the rate of *economic growth* of the economy. Since future retirees will not be directly consuming social security checks or trust fund reserves, but rather the goods and services actually being produced during their retirement, the productive capacity of the economy in the future will be a key determinant of the economic well-being of workers and retirees alike.

Other important considerations discussed below include the administrative costs of proposed reforms, the impact of reform on public confidence in the social security program, and the complexity and ease of transition of reform. One must also consider the general equilibrium effects of reform on other sources of retirement income — employer pension benefits, asset income, and earnings. Finally, it is important to assess the impact of changing a program as important as social security on social cohesiveness.

We take up these issues next, taking as a starting point the criteria proposed by the Advisory Council's Technical Panel on Trends and Issues in Retirement Savings (1997).

Evaluation Criteria

Income Adequacy

The United States social security system grew out of the experiences of the Great Depression in which unemployment and old-age poverty were widespread. Legislative leaders became convinced that the nation was best served by the introduction of a national old-age retirement program based on the principles of social insurance.[4] A primary goal was to assist in the provision of income security in retirement, without the stigma of a public assistance or welfare system.

Social insurance usually has a number of characteristics (Thompson and Upp 1997). It is mandatory for certain categories of individuals (e.g., workers), sponsored, regulated and in some cases managed by the government, and is financed by contributions from the eventual beneficiaries (or their family members). The contributions determine eligibility and sometimes the benefits levels, which are set by law. These characteristics allow the system to avoid the adverse selection problems of private insurance (i.e., the poorer risks are more likely to want the insurance coverage), and permit explicit income redistribution between or within cohorts of participants, something which is difficult to do in a voluntary or privatized system.

Without social security benefits, many older Americans would enter their retirement years without adequate income. Some have lived in or near poverty all their lives, have had irregular work histories without pension coverage, and have been unable to save on their own. Others have been myopic, and have either refused to consider the savings needed to support consumption in retirement or miscalculated what would be required. Others may have had bad luck, hampered by limited personal endowments or by being in a profession whose skills became obsolete, or in an industry or a geographic location doomed to economic decline. Social insurance is designed to dampen the economic implications of any of these unfortunate circumstances.

Through 1950, social security in the U.S. was less important than means-tested old-age assistance, measured by either the number of recipients or the total benefits distributed (Berkowitz 1997). Amendments in 1950, however, increased the social security program's coverage and benefit levels, as well as the tax rates and the taxable earnings base. Since then, it has been much more important than public assistance in supporting the elderly. Disability benefits were added in 1956. The program continued to expand during the 1960s and 1970s and is now the first line of defense against economic distress among older Americans.

Although social security benefits were never designed to be a sole source of support, income adequacy remains the primary and most important criterion by which to judge the success of the program. Income adequacy should be considered with respect to old age, survivors and disability recipients.

Income adequacy can be measured in at least two ways: relative to one's prior income (for example, a replacement rate) or relative to some absolute measure of need, like the U.S. poverty threshold. One of the program's greatest accomplishments has been the dramatic reduction in elderly poverty, from about 30 percent (and twice the national average) in 1967, to half that rate only seven years later, following large increases in real social security benefits beginning in 1968. This decline occurred during a time when Americans were retiring earlier and earlier, making the progress all the more remarkable. Since 1982, the elderly poverty rate has been slightly below that of the entire population.

Neither replacement rates nor poverty indices are perfect measures of income adequacy. A replacement rate is static in nature. It compares retirement income in the first year of retirement to earnings the year before, and ignores changes in income flows thereafter. Depending on whether or not income flows (such as employer pension benefits) are indexed to inflation, a given initial replacement rate could be associated with very different levels of economic well-being later on.

The American poverty concept is an absolute measure, based on the cost of a particular basket of consumption goods. Although the cost of the basket is adjusted for price changes, the market basket itself is not adjusted for the changes in the overall standard of living that occur over time as real incomes rise. Nonetheless, both the replacement rate and the poverty rate are useful summary statistics.

The analysis of any reform proposal should address the likely impacts on the replacement rates of future recipients—retirees, survivors and the disabled—by income level. Who is likely to gain and who is likely to lose from the changes proposed? The analysis should pay particular attention to those at the lower end of the income distribution, those most dependent on the income redistribution built into the social security benefit structure.

A closely related issue is that of risk—who will bear the risk if the forecasts of the future turn out to be inaccurate, as they undoubtedly will? In a defined benefit plan, the risk falls primarily on whoever defined the benefit—the government (and therefore the taxpayers) in the case of social security, or the firm sponsoring an employer pension plan. In a defined contribution plan, the financial risk of disappointing performance falls on the individual. Analysis of reform proposals should consider not only the most likely forecast, but also the income adequacy implications of a range of future economic scenarios.

These forecasts are difficult, particularly when projected many years into the future and especially if they include anticipated stock market returns.[5] The difficulty is compounded by the fact that changes in the social security system may well result in changes in the other sources of future income (earnings, employer pension benefits, and asset income), as employers and individuals respond to the new social security environment.

Individual Equity

Whereas income adequacy is the oldest (and, I would argue, the most important) criterion for evaluating the social security program, individual equity may be the newest. This criterion takes an individual rather than a social insurance perspective, and analyzes the relationship between an individual's total contributions to the system (the payroll tax paid by the employee and employer) and the total benefits that he or she is likely to receive in return.

Historically, individual equity has not been an important part of the social security debate. One reason is that before the system matured, all cohorts of retirees received several times what their (and their employers') contributions would have produced had the funds been invested in similarly safe investments, such as government bonds. Favorable demographics — the high ratio of social security contributors to beneficiaries in the early years of the program — coupled with significant real wage growth permitted generous benefits to retirees without undue burden on workers and employers.[6] Because of the progressive nature and the gender neutrality of the benefit structure, the "rate of return" varied with income level (it is higher the lower one's average lifetime earnings) and gender (since women live longer than men).[7] But social security proved to be a good "investment" for all types of current and prior retirees, and therefore individual equity was not a bone of contention.

But this will not be the case for future cohorts of retirees. Because of the changing demographics, the aging of the population, and the decline in the ratio of social security contributors to recipients, rates of return from social security are falling. Steuerle and Bakija (1994) estimate that the net transfer for average- and high-wage single males has already turned negative, and will do so for high-wage single females and high-wage two-earner couples turning 65 in the years 2000 and 2005 respectively.[8]

In 2030, when the youngest of the baby-boomers will have reached 65, high-wage single men can expect to receive from OASI less than half of what their and their employers' contributions could have provided had they been invested at a 2 percent real rate of return (Steuerle and Bakija 1994). For high-wage females and high-wage two-earner couples, analogous figures in 2030 are about 60 and 75 percent.[9] The absolute size of the expected net transfers from these individuals to social security (the difference between the value of the expected OASI benefits and the proceeds from investment) at a 2 percent real rate of return, are large — approximately $250,000 (in 1993 dollars), $190,000 and $180,000 for high-wage single males, single females and two-earner couples, respectively, who turn 65 in 2030 (Steuerle and Bakija 1994). The negative transfers are slightly larger for subsequent cohorts.

To many young workers, therefore, participation in the social security system no longer looks like a good investment. It is not surprising that "money's worth" calculations are now part of the reform debate and that they have engendered some adverse reactions to the traditionally very popular social security system.

The comparison here is between expected lifetime social security contributions and benefits, and the goal is a closer relation between the two.

According to this individual equity criterion, the social security system should look more like a savings account or an Individual Retirement Account, and less like the income redistributional system that is designed to be. In evaluating reform options, analysts should compare the expected internal rates of return (or the net transfers) of proposed changes with those under the current system, both across generations (that is, by age cohort) and by income class and demographic type within generations.[10]

Economic Growth

Social security expenditures are the largest single item in the federal budget. In 1996, social security outlays, excluding Medicare, totaled $354 billion, nearly a quarter of all federal government expenditures, and nearly 5 percent of gross domestic product. Old-age, survivors and disability benefits were paid to 44 million recipients, and payroll taxes were collected from 144 million workers (Board of Trustees 1997). Changes in a program of this magnitude can have significant macroeconomic effects and can influence the growth rate of the economy.

As mentioned above, economic growth is of paramount importance, because the consumption of future retirees will come from the goods and services being produced at that time. Social security benefits and other sources of retiree income will provide a claim on those future goods and services. Much of the discussion about social security reform focuses on the distribution of future output — the share that retirees will or should have. As important as the share of the pie, however, is the size of the pie being shared.[11]

There are two primary ways in which the social security program can affect economic growth: through its influence on individual labor-leisure choices, and through its impact on aggregate national saving.

Individual labor-leisure choice. The social security system can affect labor supply decisions through the typical income and substitution effects, both during the work life and, more importantly, at retirement. To the extent that participation in the system increases the lifetime wealth of participants, as it has for the vast majority of current and previous retirees, it should increase the consumption of all normal goods, including leisure. Much of this increased leisure has been taken late in life, in the form of earlier retirement. Research suggests that increases in social security wealth may be responsible for about one-third of the post-war decline in elderly labor force participation rates.[12]

But social security taxes and benefits also affect the net wage rate earned by current workers. To the extent that employees view their mandatory OASDI contribution as a tax, it lowers the marginal wage rate for those earning below the maximum taxable earnings.[13] This could have a distortionary effect on labor supply, although evidence suggests that it is a small one, at least for primary workers (Council of Economic Advisors 1997). Once one is eligible for social security benefits, however, the incentives get more complicated. After age 62, additional earnings over the exempt amount have two offsetting effects.[14] They decrease current benefits (to zero, if earnings are high enough), but they also increase the future benefit stream, both because of the recalculation of average earnings and because of the delayed retirement credit. Depending on one's discount rate, life expectancy, and average lifetime earnings, the net result could be an increase or a decrease in expected total benefits — an increase or decrease in lifetime social security wealth. One's true compensation during the year of work includes both the paycheck and the change (the increase or decrease) in social security wealth. If the total amount of expected lifetime social security benefits declines with additional work, then social security acts as a tax, or a pay cut. To the extent that additional work provides both a paycheck and an increase in lifetime benefits, social security acts as a subsidy, and increases true compensation. Considerable research has shown that workers do respond to these incentives, and that they are more likely to leave a job and often the labor force as well, the stronger the retirement incentives (the implicit pay cuts) they face.[15]

Reform proposals that either tighten the relationship between contributions and benefits or make the benefit calculation rules at retirement more age-neutral (i.e., the total expected value of future benefits does not depend on when benefits are first claimed) reduce the labor market distortions of the system, and would be viewed favorably according to this criterion.

Individual consumption-saving choice. Social security rules can influence not only the allocation of time between work and leisure, as discussed above, but also the allocation of income between consumption and saving. Many analysts believe that Americans save too little, both from a macroeconomic perspective and with respect to maintaining consumption levels after retirement. Americans save less than they used to, and less than the citizens of many other industrialized countries.[16]

Economic theory and common sense (synonyms, according to some!) suggest that the public provision of retirement income should affect the amount of discretionary private saving that individuals will do on their own for retirement. The higher the social security benefits promised or the level of private saving mandated (as proposed in two of the Advisory Council plans), other things equal, the less one has to save through other means to maintain a given standard of living. But other things may not be equal. Retirement decisions are affected by the generosity of social security benefits (the net transfer from the system to the individual), which creates an offsetting effect. An increase in benefits and therefore an earlier planned labor market exit could induce an increase in private saving to finance the additional years of retirement (Council of Economic Advisors 1997).

The theoretical effect of the social security system on private saving is ambiguous, as is the empirical literature.[17] Some authors have found substantial negative impacts on private saving (Feldstein 1974), while others have found small or no impacts (Munnell 1974; Danziger, Haveman, and Plotnick 1981). This same ambiguity is found in the related literature on the impact of government savings incentives, such as favorable IRA and 401(k) tax provisions, on net private savings. Some authors find considerable net new saving, while others, sometimes analyzing the same data, find that the saving in these vehicles is just a reallocation of saving that would have occurred in other forms.[18]

Regardless of the difficulty of measuring it, the impact of proposed social security reforms on private saving decisions is an important evaluation criterion, because the sign and magnitude of the effect will influence the amount of asset income that individuals can rely on in retirement, the amount of capital accumulation, and therefore the future productive capacity of the economy at large.

Aggregate national saving. Private saving by individuals is only one part of aggregate saving. Another key component is federal government saving, through the social security program directly and through the rest of the federal budget.

The social security system is currently running large surpluses. In 1996, an OASDI surplus of $71 billion was added to trust fund reserves. This lowered the official federal government deficit by the same amount. The annual OASDI surpluses are scheduled to increase to about $130 billion per year early next century, and then fall, turning negative by about 2019, according to the intermediate forecasts in the Trustees Report (1997). Anticipated revenues and withdrawals from OASDI reserves would then be sufficient to pay benefits until the year 2029.

Social security reform could change government saving in two ways: by directly affecting the revenue or expenditure stream of social security, and by indirectly affecting other government decisions. For example, reform proposals that reduce social security surpluses (e.g., by diverting some of the revenue stream into mandatory individual savings accounts) would increase the measured government deficit. How would the federal government respond to the increased deficit? Would Congress attempt to maintain the current budget deficit path by reducing spending or raising other taxes to replace the diverted revenue stream? If so, this would represent an increase in aggregate savings. Or would Congress slow the time path to budget balance, by maintaining current expenditure and taxation plans and borrowing the diverted funds from the market (from the individuals themselves) rather than from the social security trust funds? In the latter case, the measured increase in private saving (the new savings accounts) would be offset by the increase in government dissaving, and national saving would remain unchanged.[19]

Forecasts of this type are extremely difficult, because they require predictions of future Congressional behavior. Nonetheless, they should be included in the discussion, because the behavioral decisions made could have significant effects on aggregate national saving and therefore on future economic growth.

Administrative Costs

Because of the large scale and the mandatory nature of the social security system, administrative costs are very low, less than 1 percent of benefits paid in 1996 (Board of Trustees 1997). Two of the three reform options proposed by the Advisory Council (1997) include the creation of mandatory individual retirement accounts over which participants would have some management discretion.

Mitchell (1996) has estimated the administrative costs that might accompany alternatives to the current social security system by analyzing the administrative costs of mutual funds and defined-contribution employer pensions, such as 401(k) plans. She argues that the additional costs of investing some of the social security Trust Fund reserves in the equities market (as proposed by the Maintain Benefits plan) would be very small, as long as the investment strategy remained passive and political pressures to favor or avoid particular industries or stocks were resisted.[20] On the other hand, proposals that involve the investment of mandated saving by individuals, like the Personal Security Accounts plan, could result in considerably higher administrative and management costs, depending on the details of the plan; for example, the breadth of investment options allowed, the frequency of asset reallocations permitted, the extent to which the new saving accounts were added to existing mutual funds or 401(k) plans, and whether the accumulated assets could eventually be withdrawn in a lump sum or had to be converted into an annuity.[21] Mitchell (1998) points out that these additional costs would not just be new fees for the same service (i.e., a pure cost increase), but rather would be associated with new investment and portfolio options for participants.

In analyzing the three reform proposals, the Advisory Council (1997) assumed administrative costs of 0.5 basis points per year for the Maintain Benefits plan, 10.5 basis points for the passively-managed Individual Accounts plan, and 100 basis points or 1 percent per year for the Personal Security Accounts plan. Flexible investment options offer advantages but they come at a cost, and both should be considered when evaluating these or any other social security reform proposals.

Confidence in the Social Security System

Public opinion polls suggest a widespread lack of confidence in social security. A 1994 EBRI/Gallup poll, for instance, showed that 43 percent of those surveyed stated that they were "not confident" that social security income would be available throughout their retirement years (Reno and Friedland 1997). Analogous numbers for employer pensions (24 percent) and personal savings (19 percent) were much lower, indicating more confidence in those retirement income components. There were also large differences by age. For respondents under the age of 55, over half were "not confident" in the social security program, compared to only 16 percent of those aged 55 or older.

Further investigation clouds the interpretation of these responses, however, since in an earlier (1991) EBRI/Gallup survey, 93 percent of the respondents said that they expected to receive social security benefits, and nearly half (45 percent) expected they would be "a major source" of their retirement income (Reno and Friedland 1997: 188). (Only 27 percent expected social security benefits to be their "most important" source of income.) In addition, many people support the social security program, even if they harbor some doubts about its future viability. For instance a 1994 poll found that 80 percent of people not receiving social security benefits said that they favored or strongly favored the fact that "part of every working person's income goes to support the social security program," and nearly three-quarters opposed a decrease in spending on social security benefits (Reno and Friedland 1997: 186).

Irrespective of whether these survey results reflect snap reactions or thoughtful judgments, they are a matter of concern, since the future of the social security system depends on the political support of the electorate. Hence any reform must be assessed in terms of the likely impact it would have on public confidence, both through the financial details of the proposal and through the effects of any educational components that it might include.

Complexity and Ease of Transition

Although some of the details of the social security program are complicated, Americans have a good general understanding of its goals and features. Most know that social security benefits are based on earnings and are financed by payroll taxes, that current taxes largely pay for current benefits, and that benefits are not directly means-tested (Reno and Friedland 1997: 183). As noted above, the vast majority claim that they expect social security benefits to be part of their incomes in retirement.

Reform will revise the current rules, as it must. An important consideration is the nature of the transition from the current system to whatever replaces it. Those nearing retirement age should be protected from sudden and dramatic changes in what they have been led to expect.[22] And for all participants, young and old, one should consider the complexity of any proposal, and ask whether citizens can be expected to understand the important parameters of the new system. It may be more difficult to maintain political support for a system whose features are only vaguely understood by the population.

Changes in Employer Pension Plans

Because of the magnitude of the social security system and the number of participants and beneficiaries, changes in the system can be expected to have impacts in other parts of the retirement environment and in the economy as a whole. The private savings responses of individuals and the behavioral responses of Congress to possible changes in the federal budget deficit were mentioned above. Equally important are the responses of employers through their pension plans.[23] Since pension benefits are a key component of retirement income (about half as important as social security benefits, in the aggregate) and because pension receipt is rarely associated with poverty, changes in pensions in response to social security reform could have important implications for the economic well-being of the elderly.[24]

Some response to changes in social security benefits would be automatic under current rules, because nearly two-thirds of full-time pension participants are in plans that are formally integrated with social security (Mitchell 1992).[25] This means either that pension benefits are directly reduced by some proportion of social security benefits received, or that the pension formula applies a lower rate to earnings that are subject to social security tax than to earnings that are not. Unless these rules were changed, part of any social security benefit decrease would be automatically offset for some pension recipients.

Of more interest, however, are the discretionary changes that might follow social security reform. Would a decline in the size of social security's defined benefit (e.g., as in the Personal Security Account plan) increase the demand by employees for defined benefit employer pensions? Would a universally mandated defined contribution plan result in a decrease in the number of these plans at work, or a decrease in the matching rate offered by employers? Would employees contribute less to these plans, even if they were still available? In general, anyone already saving can offset at least part of any new saving mandate, by simply saving less elsewhere.[26] One "elsewhere" is in the discretionary component of employer-based pension saving.

Since private and institutional savings (through the social security system or through employer pension plans) are all means to the same end, it is plausible that there would be offsetting effects to major social security reform. It is difficult to predict what would happen to the structure of employer pensions or to the total contributions of employers and employees, but the impact of any such changes could be very important.

Social Cohesiveness

Social security is one of the few programs in which nearly all Americans participate, either directly as workers or indirectly as spouses or dependents enjoying survivors insurance. Many analysts have lamented the decline of common purpose in the United States.[27] An important criterion for consideration is what effect particular reforms would have on the viability of the social security program in the future.

Opponents and proponents of radical reform acknowledge the importance of this issue, but to opposite purpose. Those opposed to the partial privatization component that exists in two of the three Advisory Council plans fear the long-run political implications of formally separating the social security program into two parts. They foresee the development of one component of primary interest to the poor — the defined benefit part, the means of redistribution — and another part of primary interest to the middle and upper classes — the defined contribution, mandatory saving part.[28] They wonder if the defined benefit part would take on a welfare aura, like Supplemental Security Income, especially in the PSA plan, where the income redistribution occurs through a flat-rate benefit, independent of earnings. If the public perception of this component does change, privatization opponents worry that the social insurance aspect of the program, its original reason for existence, will atrophy over time, and higher and higher proportions of the payroll tax would be moved into the upper tier.

Proponents of privatization, on the other hand, claim that political support for the current social security system will inevitably decline over time, as it becomes a poor investment for more and more involuntary participants. They argue that continued political support for the system requires radical change — the replacement of the old engines of population and real wage growth with the new engine of the equities market.

Whomever is right, I suspect that these long-range political issues will turn out to be as important to the well-being of future retirees as are the economic forecasts of benefit levels under the various reform proposals.

The Financial Health of the Social Security System

This was the last of the six criteria adopted by the Advisory Council's Technical Panel (1997). It is obviously important, since the unfunded liability facing the system is largely what prompted this round of interest in social security reform. Any proposal for change should be analyzed for its long-range fiscal implications. Since all of the Advisory Council's proposals would eliminate the 75-year unfunded liability, given the assumptions, this criterion will not help us differentiate among these three, but it may distinguish them from other reform plans that do not achieve this goal, or even move us further away from it.

Conclusion

Because of the favorable age distribution of the population during the maturing of the American social security system — the high ratio of contributors to beneficiaries — the program was able to make a major contribution toward the economic security of low-earning workers while simultaneously providing an outstanding financial return on the contributions of all cohorts of Americans, rich and poor alike. In the future, however, this will not be possible, and the inherent tension between the goals of income adequacy and individual equity will become clear. Income redistribution explicitly treats different people differently — that is the point of it. The primary goal of the social security system, income adequacy for its recipients, must now be balanced against the political implications of a mandatory program in which certain citizens can expect to be significant net contributors over their lifetimes.

The social security system should not be viewed solely as a savings vehicle. Social insurance provides more than an individual return on investment. It provides to individuals insurance against certain risks, and to society some protection against the inequalities and inequities that are inevitable in an advanced capitalistic state. These considerable benefits must be weighed against their costs, and under the current rules, these costs differ significantly by income class.

In this chapter, I have discussed various criteria by which to evaluate proposals for social security reform, including income adequacy, individual equity, economic growth, the complexity and administrative costs of any new system, its effects on public confidence and social cohesiveness, and how other components of income security in old age, particularly employer-sponsored pensions, would be likely to change. Most analysts would agree that most or all of the criteria discussed in this paper should be part of the social security reform debate, although many would disagree about their relative importance. I agree with the Council of Economic Advisors (1997), who ended its discussion of the economic challenges of an aging population by concluding that "a variety of approaches [to social security reform] should be considered, but any possible changes must . . . ensure that the benefits of reduced poverty and increased economic security for the aged and disabled are not put at risk."

The author would like to thank his Boston College colleagues Eric Kingson and John Williamson, as well as Olivia Mitchell and Robert Myers, for insightful comments on an earlier draft of this chapter.

Notes

1. As an example, a 1996 Advisory Commission to the Senate Finance Committee estimated that the official consumer price index overstates changes in the actual cost-of-living by about 1.1 points per year. Were this estimate adopted by the social security actuaries and future benefit decreased by this amount, about two-thirds of today's 75-year deficit would disappear.

2. See Chapter 1 (this volume), Quinn and Mitchell (1996), and Advisory Council (1997) for the details of these proposals.

3. All other sources of income provided less than 4 percent of aggregate income for the elderly in 1994. Public assistance, including Supplemental Security Income, provided less than 1 percent (Grad 1996). Employer pensions include private pensions and annuities, government employee pensions, and railroad retirement pensions. Some income from pension accumulations may be mislabeled as asset income, if lump sum pension distributions is invested in financial instruments and their income then listed under interest or dividends. For a detailed analysis of this issue, see Woods (1996).

4. The Committee on Economic Security, whose recommendations established the basic framework for the U.S. social security system, rejected two other approaches to old-age income security—a noncontributory, universal pension system funded by general revenues, and a means-tested program (Thompson and Upp 1997). For a discussion of means-testing in the current reform debate, see the chapter in this volume by David Neumark and Elizabeth Powers. For a concise history of the early decades of the social security program, see Berkowitz (1997) or Bryce and Friedland (1997).

5. Goodfellow and Schieber (this volume) simulate benefit levels in the future under various social security reform alternatives.

6. In 1960, the maximum annual OASDI contribution of the employee and employer combined was only $288, or about $1,500 in 1996 dollars. In 1970, the maximum was $655, about $2,650 in 1996 dollars (Social Security Administration 1996). In 1998, the maximum combined OASDI contribution was $8,482, more than a five-fold increase in real terms since 1960.

7. Estimates of real rates of return in the Old-Age and Survivors components of social security, net transfers (OASI benefits–OASI taxes paid), and the ratio of benefits to taxes for various types of participants can be found in Steuerle and Bakija (1994). The Committee on Ways and Means (1993: 1301–5) has also calculated net transfers and the ratio of benefits to taxes for men and women retiring in 1980, 1992 and 2000. Finally, Burtless and Bosworth (1997) have estimated internal rates of return on OASDI contributions, by birth cohort. All of these estimates tell the same story—low-wage workers do better than high-wage workers, and early cohorts (those born in the 1920s and 1930s) have done better than subsequent cohorts will.

8. Steuerle and Bakija (1994) use a 2 percent real rate of return on alternative investments. An internal rate of return from the social security system in excess of this implies a net transfer to the individual; a rate of return less than 2 percent real implies a negative transfer—a transfer from the individual to others in the social security system. The estimates I am using adjust for the chances of death before receiving old age benefits. Steuerle and Bakija also calculate net transfers assuming survival to age 65, and in these calculations the bad news is delayed a bit, but the trends are the same. See also Mitchell, Geanakoplos, and Zeldes (this volume).

9. Because of the progressive benefit structure, low-wage workers of all types continue to receive more than a 2 percent real rate of return from the social security

system, even in 2050. Because of the subsidy in the spousal benefit, single-earner couples also continue to do well.

10. Leimer (1995) also provides an excellent nontechnical discussion of frequently used money's worth measures, the assumptions behind them, and their uses and limitations.

11. See the chapter by Martin Holmer (this volume) for simulations of the potential impacts of social security reform on economic growth.

12. See Hausman and Wise (1985) and Ippolito (1990). Hurd and Boskin (1984) attributed nearly all of the decline in the labor force participation rates of older Americans to the generosity of social security. Moffit (1984) is skeptical of the claims, and points out that aggregate social security wealth rose significantly in the 1950s (because of increases in coverage; more categories of workers were included in the system, and they enjoyed large windfall increases in wealth) without any dramatic declines in labor force participation rates.

13. In fact, the payroll tax is not a pure tax for most workers, since the earnings associated with the payroll tax increase future social security benefits. As discussed above, for most current and past retirees, social security has in fact been a substantial wage *subsidy*, not a tax, since each dollar of contribution has generated several dollars of eventual benefit. For many workers today and in the future, however, this will not be the case.

14. In 1998, beneficiaries aged 62 to 64 could earn up to $9,120 without losing any social security benefits. Beyond that, benefits were reduced by $1 for each $2 earned. For those aged 65 to 69, the exempt amount was $14,500, and the benefit loss was $1 for each $3 additional earned. The 1998 exempt amount for those 62 to 64 was indexed to average earnings in the country. For those 65 to 69, legislation will increase the exempt amount dramatically, to $30,000 by the year 2002. At age 70, there is no earnings test, and one can receive full benefits regardless of earnings.

15. For more discussion of these issues, see Quinn, Burkhauser, and Myers (1990), Quadagno and Quinn (1997) or the Technical Panel (1997).

16. Gramlich (1997) estimates that private saving, calculated from the National Income and Product Accounts, has dropped by about one-third since the 1960s, as a percentage of Gross National Product. Aggregate national saving has dropped more dramatically, from 8.6 percent (during 1962–65) to only 2.0 percent (during 1991–1994) of GNP, primarily because of the large increases in federal government deficits. At the individual level, Poterba, Venti, and Wise (1996) estimate that the median level of personal financial assets (excluding housing and estimated social security and pension rights) of households with heads aged 55 to 64 was only $8,300 in 1991. Trends and issues in national saving are discussed by the Technical Panel (1997).

17. The Council of Economic Advisors report (1997) contains a concise discussion of the effects of social security on saving, distinguishing among three different time periods: the start-up phase, the current mature system, and the future.

18. See Poterba, Venti, and Wise (1996) and Engen, Gale, and Scholz (1996) for these opposing views.

19. This assumes that individuals do not offset some of the mandated savings themselves. Bosworth (1996) and Burtless and Bosworth (1997) argue that it is difficult to use social security accumulations to augment national savings, because, in practice, the surpluses are integrated into the federal budget and treated like any other revenue source. This same argument suggests, however, that reducing social security surpluses, as the Personal Security Account plan proposes, might lead to Congressional actions to offset this loss in revenues, and therefore would result in an increase in national saving.

20. Mitchell (1998) estimated that these administrative costs would be at the lower end of the one to 20 basis point range.

21. The Individual Accounts proposals would permit participants to select from a small number of investment vehicles managed by the government (a TIAA-CREF model) and would require conversion of the assets to an annuity when they are claimed. The Personal Security Accounts plan would have individuals invest their mandated savings on their own (a 401(k) model), within some regulatory framework to be determined, and would permit lump-sum dispersal at or after age 62.

22. The most controversial of the three Advisory Council proposals, the Personal Security Account plan, would exempt current participants aged 55 or older in 1998 from the basic structural change to a two-tiered system. They would continue in the current system and would receive the benefits promised under current law, subject only to changes in retirement ages and benefit taxation that apply to all. Those under 25 in 1998 would lose any rights under the old system, and receive benefits only under the new system. Those aged 25 to 54 would receive a combination of their benefits as determined by the current system and the Tier I (flat rate) benefits under the new proposal, each prorated by the number of years spent working in each of the two systems (Advisory Council 1997).

23. This is the topic of the chapter by Janice Gregory, in this volume.

24. Grad (1996) reports that only seven percent of aged units in the bottom income quintile received any employer pension income, and that it amounts for only three percent of their total cash income.

25. This estimate is based on 1989 data. Mitchell (1992) notes that there was little change in the percentage of participants in integrated plans between 1985 and 1989.

26. Theoretically, even someone not saving at all could offset the mandate, by borrowing today to finance the required saving (leaving consumption unchanged), and then repaying the debt when the assets are made available in the future. For most of those without savings, however, this avenue is unlikely.

27. Putnam (1995) documents numerous examples of declining civic engagement, in government affairs (declining voter turnout), religious affiliation (declining church attendance), labor unions (declining membership), civic and fraternal organizations (he cites numerous examples of decline) and even participation in bowling leagues (down 40 percent between 1980 and 1993, while the total number of bowlers increased by 10 percent!) Although he does acknowledge some countertrends, Putnam concludes that social capital in the United States is eroding.

28. In the Personal Security Account plan, for example, maximum-wage workers, in the steady-state, are predicted to receive about 80 percent of their total benefits from the upper tier, compared to only 40 percent for low-wage workers. In the Individual Accounts plan, with a smaller defined-contribution part, the analogous numbers are 40 and 20 percent (Advisory Council 1997).

References

Advisory Commission to Study the Consumer Price Index. *Toward a More Accurate Measure of the Cost of Living.* Washington, D.C.: U.S. Senate Finance Committee, December 1996.

Advisory Council on Social Security. *Final Report of the 1994–1996 Advisory Council on Social Security.* Vol. 1, *Findings and Recommendations.* Washington, D.C.: USGPO, 1997.

Social Security Administration. *Annual Statistical Supplement to the Social Security Bulletin.* Washington, D.C.: Social Security Administration, August 1996.

Berkowitz, Edward D. "The Historical Development of Social Security in the United States." In Eric R. Kingson and James H. Schulz, eds., *Social Security in the 21st Century.* New York: Oxford University Press, 1997: 22–38.

Board of Trustees of the Social Security Administration. *Annual Report of the Board of Trustees of the Federal Old-Age and Survivors Insurance and Disability Insurance Trust Funds*. Washington, D.C.: USGPO, 1997.

Bosworth, Barry P. "Fund Accumulation: How Much? How Managed?" In Peter A. Diamond, David C. Lindeman, and Howard Young, eds., *Social Security: What Role for the Future?* Washington, D.C.: National Academy of Social Insurance, 1996: 89–115.

Bryce, David V. and R. B. Friedland. "Economic Security: An Overview of Social Security." In *Assessing Social Security Reform Alternatives*. Washington, D.C.: Employee Benefit Research Institute, 1997: 29–41.

Burtless, Gary and R. A. Moffitt. "The Effect of Social Security Benefits on the Labor Supply of the Aged." In Henry J. Aaron and Gary Burtless, eds., *Retirement and Economic Behavior*. Washington, D.C.: Brookings Institution, 1984: 135–71.

Burtless, Gary and Barry Bosworth. "Privatizing Social Security: The Troubling Trade-Offs." *Brookings Policy Brief* 14. Washington, D.C.: Brookings Institution, March 1997.

Committee on Ways and Means, *Green Book*. U.S. House of Representatives, Washington, D.C.: USGPO, 1993.

Council of Economic Advisors. *Economic Report of the President*. Washington, D.C.: USGPO, 1997.

Danziger, Sheldon, Robert Haveman, and Robert Plotnick. "How Income Transfer Programs Affect Work, Savings and the Income Distribution: A Critical Review." *Journal of Economic Literature* 19, 3 (1981): 975–1028.

Engen, Eric M., William G. Gale, and John Karl Scholz. "The Illusory Effects of Saving Incentives on Saving." *Journal of Economic Perspectives* 10 (1996): 113–38.

Feldstein, Martin S. "Social Security, Induced Retirement and Aggregate Capital Accumulation." *Journal of Political Economy* 82, 5 (1974): 905–26.

Grad, Susan. *Income of the Aged: 1994*. Washington, D.C.: Social Security Administration, 1996.

———. *Presentation Before the Social Security Advisory Board*. Washington, D.C., March 21, 1997.

Gramlich, Edward M. "How Does Social Security Affect the Economy?" In Eric R. Kingson and James H. Schulz, eds., *Social Security in the 21st Century*. New York: Oxford University Press, 1997: 147–55.

Hausman, Jerry A. and David A. Wise. "Social Security, Health Status, and Retirement." In David Wise, ed., *Pensions, Labor, and Individual Choice*. Chicago: University of Chicago Press, 1985: 159–91.

Hurd, Michael D. and Michael J. Boskin. "The Effect of Social Security on Retirement in the Early 1970s." *Quarterly Journal of Economics* 99, 4 (1984): 767–90.

Ippolito, Richard A. "Toward Explaining Early Retirement After 1970." *Industrial and Labor Relations Review* 43, 5 (1990): 556–69.

Leimer, Dean R. "A Guide to Social Security Money's Worth Issues." *Social Security Bulletin* 58, 2 (1995): 3–20.

Mitchell, Olivia S. "Trends in Pension Benefit Formulas and Retirement Provisions." In John A. Turner and Daniel J. Beller, eds., *Trends in Pensions 1992*. Washington, D.C.: USGPO, 1992: 177–216.

———. "Administrative Costs in Public and Private Retirement System." In Martin Feldstein, ed., *Privatizing Social Security*. Chicago: University of Chicago Press, 1998: 403–56.

Moffitt, Robert A. "Trends in Social Security Wealth by Cohort." In Marilyn Moon, ed., *Economic Transfers in the United States*. Chicago: University of Chicago Press, 1984: 327–347.

Munnell, Alicia H. "The Impact of Social Security on Personal Savings." *National Tax Journal* 27, 4 (1974): 553–67.

National Academy of Social Insurance. *Social Insurance Update*, Vol. 1, No. 3, December 1996.

Olsen, Kelly. "Keeping Track of Social Security Reform Proposals: A Summary." In *Assessing Social Security Reform Alternatives*. Washington, D.C.: Employee Benefit Research Institute, 1997: 113–22.

Poterba, James M., Steven F. Venti, and David A. Wise. "How Retirement Saving Programs Increase Saving." *Journal of Economic Perspectives* 10, 4 (1996): 91–112.

Putnam, Robert D. "Bowling Alone: America's Declining Social Capital." *Journal of Democracy* 6, 1 (1995): 65–78.

Quadagno, Jill and Joseph F. Quinn. "Does Social Security Discourage Work?" In Eric R. Kingson and James H. Schulz, eds., *Social Security in the 21st Century*. New York: Oxford University Press, 1997: 127–46.

Quinn, Joseph F., Richard V. Burkhauser, and Daniel A. Myers. *Passing the Torch: The Influence of Economic Incentives on Work and Retirement*. Kalamazoo, Mich.: W. E. Upjohn Institute for Employment Research, 1990.

Quinn, Joseph F. and Olivia S. Mitchell. "Social Security on the Table." *American Prospect* (May/June 1996): 76–81.

Reno, Virginia and Robert B. Friedland. "Strong Support but Low Confidence: What Explains the Contradiction?" In Eric R. Kingson and James H. Schulz, eds., *Social Security in the 21st Century*. New York: Oxford University Press, 1997: 178–94.

Steuerle, C. Eugene and Jon M. Bakija. *Retooling Social Security for the 21st Century*. Washington, D.C.: Urban Institute Press, 1994.

Technical Panel on Trends and Issues in Retirement Savings. *Final Report of the 1994–1996 Advisory Council on Social Security*, Vol. 2. Washington, D.C.: Social Security Administration, 1997.

Thompson, Lawrence H. and Melinda Upp. "The Social Insurance Approach to Social Security." In Eric R. Kingson and James H. Schulz, eds., *Social Security in the 21st Century*. New York: Oxford University Press, 1997: 3–21.

U.S. Department of Commerce, Bureau of the Census. "Population Projections of the United States by Age, Sex, Race, and Hispanic Origin: 1995 to 2050." *Current Population Reports*. Washington, D.C.: USGPO, 1996: 25–1130.

Woods, John R. "Pension Benefits Among the Aged: Conflicting Measures, Unequal Distributions." *Social Security Bulletin* 59, 3 (1996): 3–30.

Chapter 4
New Opportunities for the Social Security System

Stephen G. Kellison and Marilyn Moon

The U.S. social security system is in need of reform to close the anticipated gap between income and costs after the baby boom generation begins to retire in 2010. Our goals in this chapter are to discuss the financing problem facing the social security system, and then to raise issues we believe need further analysis in the reform. These issues pertain to approaches for at least partially solving the system's financing problem — investment of a portion of the reserve now accumulating in equities rather than in government bonds, or the creation of funded individual investment accounts. These topics are ones in which we have particular interest as the two public members of the Board of Trustees of the Social Security and Medicare Trust Funds. But as Trustees, our highest interest is in increasing public understanding of the alternatives for reform, so that support for a specific reform plan can build. This process is urgent, because even though there is not an immediate crisis in social security program financing, reforms enacted sooner will spread more broadly the burden of those changes across different age groups.

For an informed public debate about the extent and type of reform that is necessary, many questions need to be addressed. These questions run the gamut from philosophical issues — such as whether in post-industrial economies individual self-reliance is preferable to social insurance — to highly technical issues such as measurement of the cost-of-living index for adjustment of benefit amounts. We will not attempt to list, much less answer, all of these questions, but as the debate about change intensifies it is important, to keep in perspective the breadth of possible reforms of the social security program. The legislative process tends to narrow discussion quickly and focus on specific proposals, but it is axiomatic that changes cannot be made in the social security program unless and until the public accepts those changes.

The Social Security Financing Problem

The Social Security Board of Trustees is required by the Social Security Act to report to the Congress each year on the current and projected future financial status of the social security program. Information is provided separately in the report for the Old-Age and Survivors Insurance (OASI) and the Disability Insurance (DI) programs, since each has its own tax rate, benefit provisions, and trust fund. However, the two trust funds are frequently considered together as OASDI for discussion purposes.

Workers entering the labor force today may be receiving benefits as much as 75 years from now; the 1997 Trustees Report provided social security financing projections that far into the future — until 2071. But it is crucial to recognize the enormity of the task of making such projections. A review of social security financing projections across recent Trustees Reports shows that the future cannot be predicted with certainty, even if the social security law remains unchanged. This is because future income from payroll taxes, interest, and other sources, and future expenditures for benefits, will depend upon a large number of unknowns including the size and characteristics of the work force subject to payroll taxes, the level of workers' earnings, and the size and composition of the population receiving benefits as well as the level of those benefits. These unknowns depend in turn on future rates of birth, marriage, divorce, death, disability, migration, labor force participation, unemployment, productivity gains, wage increases, changes in the cost-of-living (and in its measurement), and many other economic and demographic variables.

The complexity of the social and economic factors involved and the long time horizon used mean that alternative sets of assumptions are required to give a range of possible future outcomes. Currently the Trustees Report provides projections under three sets of economic and demographic assumptions, to show a range of possible future program experience. The intermediate (Alternative II) set of assumptions in the Trustees Report reflects the Trustees' best estimate of future experience. The low-cost, Alternative I, assumptions are more optimistic; while the high-cost, Alternative III, assumptions are more pessimistic. Current discussions about changes in OASDI financing, like the discussions preceding the social security legislative changes in 1977 and particularly in 1983, generally rely on point estimates using the intermediate assumptions and, at least implicitly, treat them as exact. In the future, when considering social security financing changes, we should try to help policymakers and the public keep in mind the purpose of the more optimistic Alternative I and the more pessimistic Alternative III sets of assumptions in the Trustees Report. They help stress the fact that the Trustees' long-range projections provide a range of future possibilities rather than a single point estimate.

When experience deviates from the best estimates, or when estimates of future experience are revised and the long-range financial result worsens (as has happened since the 1983 financing changes), some might conclude that there is a flaw in the social security program. In fact, what has happened since 1983 is that experience generally has provided additional evidence of economic and demographic trends that had to be taken into account by the Trustees when selecting alternative assumptions for financing projections. Primarily as a result of these real-world changes, the system is now projected to have an actuarial deficit over the next 75 years under the intermediate assumptions (Goss, this volume). Table 1 tracks changes in the key intermediate assumptions used since 1983.

One alternative to basing financing changes on a *specific* point estimate 75 years into the future would be to legislate self-correction mechanisms. Thus as key variables affecting social security financing changed (such as life expectancy for retirees), program provisions associated with those variables (such as the normal retirement age) could automatically change in tandem to keep projected income and expenditures in balance. Sweden, for example, recently indexed its retirement age to changes in life expectancy. In the United States, the 1972 enactment of annual cost-of-living benefit adjustments for increases in prices and indexing of the amount of earnings subject to OASDI taxes (called the "earnings base") to growth in average wages placed those particular determinants of social security financing on automatic pilot. Thus far, while the theoretical possibility of automatically adjusting other determinants has been mentioned from time to time, it has not been widely considered in practice.

We do not mean to endorse such changes at this point. It is useful, nevertheless, to raise the issue of automatically adjusting the major factors that determine social security financing. The absence of such automatic indexation, combined with the almost certain likelihood that future experience will *not* be exactly as projected under the Trustees' intermediate assumptions, means that the system inevitably will move out of balance in a positive or negative direction every few years. This, in turn, could necessitate periodic reconsideration of various policy options to bring the system back into balance. Although in many areas the genius of American politics has been in adjusting programs as needed, the prospect of addressing social security financing every 10 or 20 years is not generally viewed as desirable. Given the inherent uncertainty of 75-year projections, however, aiming for exact financial balance and expecting that balance to be maintained will certainly disappoint and will also push us toward arbitrary changes to achieve periodic exact balances.

Looking backward, a good example of a financing change that appears to have been chosen primarily to satisfy a 75-year point estimate of funding status (rather than being made on policy grounds) is the schedule adopted in 1983 for increasing the retirement age for full social security benefits.

TABLE 1. History of Long-Range Assumptions for the OASDI Program, Intermediate Assumptions[a]

Publication	Fertility Rate in 2050	Average Life Expectancy in 2050	Annual Change in CPI	Average Annual Real Wage Differential	Average Unemployment Rate	Disability Prevalence Rate[b]	Real Interest Rate[c]
1997 TR, II	1.9	80.3	3.5%	0.9	6.0%	41.0	2.7%
1996 TR, II	1.9	80.0	4	1.0	6.0	41.0	2.3
1995 TR, II	1.9	79.8	4	1.0	6.0	40.3	2.3
1994 TR, II	1.9	79.8	4	1.0	6.0	37.4	2.3
1993 TR, II	1.9	79.6	4	1.1	6.0	34.0	2.3
1992 TR, II	1.9	79.7	4	1.1	6.0	34.0	2.3
1991 TR, II	1.9	79.8	4	1.1	6.0	30.8	2.3
1990 TR, II-A	1.9	79.7	3	1.7	5.5	30.8	2.5
1990 TR, II-B	1.9	79.7	4	1.3	6.0	30.8	2.0
1989 TR, II-A	1.9	79.7	3	1.7	5.5	30.8	2.5
1989 TR, II-B	1.9	79.7	4	1.3	6.0	30.8	2.0
1988 TR, II-A	1.9	80.0	3	1.9	5.5	30.8	2.5
1988 TR, II-B	1.9	80.0	4	1.4	6.0	30.8	2.0
1987 TR, II-A	2.0	80.1	3	2.0	5.5	30.8	2.5
1987 TR, II-B	2.0	80.1	4	1.5	6.0	30.8	2.0
1986 TR, II-A	2.0	80.2	3	2.0	5.5	29.1	2.5
1986 TR, II-B	2.0	80.2	4	1.5	6.0	29.1	2.0
1985 TR, II-A	2.0	80.1	3	2.0	5.5	28.3	2.5
1985 TR, II-B	2.0	80.1	4	1.5	6.0	28.3	2.0
1984 TR, II-A	2.0	80.0	3	2.0	5.5	25.9	2.5
1984 TR, II-B	2.0	80.0	4	1.5	6.0	25.9	2.0

Notes:
[a] Principal assumptions include those which have the greatest effect on the actuarial estimates (fertility, mortality, CPI, and disability prevalence rates) and one which draws attention (unemployment rate) but which does not have a major effect on the actuarial balance. In 1984–90 there were two sets of intermediate assumptions which shared the same demographic assumptions but used different economic assumptions; alternative II-B was cited in most policy discussions.
[b] Average age-adjusted prevalence rate per 1,000 disability insured workers in 2050, based on 1980 population aged 20–64.
[c] Average annual rate for special public-debt obligations issuable to the trust funds.
Source: Data kindly supplied by the SSA Office of the Actuary.

This provision increases the retirement age for people reaching age 62 in 2000–2005 by two months per year for each birth-cohort for six years; makes no further change for 12 years; and then again increases the retirement age by two months per year for another six years. The end result, of course, is to raise the age for full retirement benefits from 65 to 67 by 2027. Two of the financing plans put forth by the last Advisory Council (1997) would eliminate the apparently arbitrary 12-year hiatus in this schedule and index the retirement age after it attains 67 to increases in longevity. Again, we stress that our use of this example does not mean we endorse a specific change; rather, the example shows how premising consideration of financing changes on meeting a 75-year point estimate as of the simple point in time can lead policymakers to enact changes that are not examined on their merits to the extent we might wish.

Is there some other way to keep the system automatically in balance, while recognizing the uncertainty inherent in 75-year estimates, short of indexing everything we can? (Of course, indexing raises other questions, as the debate over the cost of living index illustrates. Here, the question has been, what index should be used and how it should be measured.) We know of no mathematical answer to this question. But we do think the formulation of social security financing policy would produce better results if policymakers and the public came to understand that seeking "exact" actuarial balance at the end of any given 75-year period may dictate policies that otherwise seem questionable. Second, policymakers and the public need to recognize that, because there is no way to predict the future perfectly, even our best efforts at policy changes in any given year can only be approximations that will need periodically to be updated, just as we update the Trustees Report assumptions each year based on recent experience and new information about future trends.

The difficulty and inexactness of making projections over a 75-year period have led some observers to question whether such a forecast should be undertaken at all. Some observers suggest that the 75-year period be shortened, for example. We strongly disagree with this view. Most of the current financing problems facing social security are attributable to major demographic changes, ones that are well established and that will take several decades to unfold. A long projection period, such as 75 years, is essential to assess the full impact such demographic forces will exert on the social security system.

A great difficulty with regularly updating benefit programs like social security is that it is much more difficult to reach political agreement when benefit programs must be adjusted downward or their growth slowed, than it is to create new benefit categories and increase benefits. Nevertheless, it is critical for policymakers and the public to come to accept that social security financing is directly affected by changes in our population and in our economy. It follows that social security financing provisions will have to change if the factors that affect income and expenditures evolve in ways that are not precisely projected under the Trustees' best estimates — as we know will almost certainly happen over a period as long as 75 years.

OASDI Projections

The long-term financial status of OASDI can be measured in several ways. One of the simplest is current cash flow. Under the intermediate (Alternative II) assumptions, income to OASDI from payroll taxes alone is projected to exceed benefits paid in each of the next 15 years. In 2012 and thereafter, payroll tax income plus a portion of annual interest income will be needed to equal annual expenditures. However, beginning in 2019 and continuing through 2029, current tax income plus annual interest plus a portion of the trust fund reserves will be needed to pay benefits. In 2029, the accumulated assets of OASDI will be exhausted. With assets exhausted, tax income in that year is projected to equal about three-quarters of social security benefit costs, and this ratio is projected to decline to about two-thirds at the end of the 75-year projection period in 2071.

A different measure of OASDI's long-term financial status is the percent of total earnings subject to OASDI taxes (called "taxable payroll"). This relative measure is useful because it avoids the difficulty of comparing dollar amounts for different periods. The 1997 Trustees Report indicates that the shortfall in OASDI financing using this measure is 2.23 percent. This number can be interpreted as the required increase in the current payroll tax rate of 12.4 percent — for a total of 14.63 percent — in each of the next 75 years, or the amount that would have to be subtracted from the benefit rate, to bring the system into financial balance.

One significant result of using a 75-year projection period is that in each new Trustees Report, a new, relatively higher, cost year is added at the end of the period. Social security costs are higher in those far distant years because future beneficiaries are anticipated to live significantly longer in retirement than do beneficiaries today. Currently, adding a new distant year to the projection period increases the deficit by .08 percent of taxable payroll. Approximately one-third of the 1997 deficit of 2.23 percent of payroll that has developed since the 1983 Amendments is due to the rolling forward of the projection period into years that have significantly higher costs on average than those between 1983 and 1996. But the value of making 75-year projections — even when we know they cannot be exact — is that these projections alert us to possible changes in economic and demographic conditions long before they occur, giving us time to plan for such changes.

Changes in key demographic and economic assumptions on the OASDI financing projections are also significant. For example, the 1997 Trustees Report assumed that, in the future, women in the United States will have during their lifetime an average of 1.9 children each. A 0.1 change in the fertility rate assumption changes the long-range actuarial balance by 0.12 percent of taxable payroll. Similarly, a 0.1 percentage point change in the assumption regarding the rate at which wages will rise per year after inflation, changes the balance by 0.11 percent of taxable payroll. Although a change of 0.1 percent is small in any single year, the "magic of compounding" over a 75-year projection makes small changes important. Thus, selecting the assumptions used in projecting OASDI financing is among the most important duties of the Board of Trustees and is based on the best technical advice and analysis available both inside and outside the government. The importance of the process of selecting the assumptions and preparing the projections is recognized in the Social Security Act by requiring that the Chief Actuary of the Social Security Administration provide a written opinion in each report regarding the methods and assumptions used in preparing the report.

Changing the individual components in any set of assumptions can have a significant effect on the financing balance, but often individual changes have offsetting effects. The purpose of having alternative sets of assumptions is to show what would happen if future experience regarding *all* the assumptions in a set were either more positive or more negative for the financing of the social security program. As would be expected, the effect on the balance of such variation across the whole set of assumptions is large. Thus, while the actuarial balance in 1997 under the intermediate assumptions is −2.23 percent of taxable payroll, the balance under the low-cost (Alternative I) assumptions is +0.21 and under the high-cost (Alternative III) assumptions is −5.54. The range of possible future experience projected under the three sets of assumptions underscores, we believe, the need for policymakers and the public to accept the likelihood that periodic adjustments will be needed, as demographic and economic conditions fluctuate, to keep the social security program financed on a sound basis.

On the positive side, the range established by the three sets of assumptions is intended to cover a wide variety of plausible economic and demographic conditions. This range is not mathematically determined, and no traditional statistical measures can be attached to it. But a critical point to keep in mind regarding the high- and low-cost projections is that if the economic and demographic experience in this country in the next 75 years were to approach the path described by either of those sets of assumptions, every aspect of our society, not just the social security program, would be affected significantly.

When Is Social Security Financing Change Needed?

If the system were to be balanced annually, legislation would be needed virtually every year due to the variation in the 75-year projections of OASDI financing that occurs as a result of even small changes in key assumptions.

The Trustees have for many years used a target of "close actuarial balance," where the 75-year summarized cost rate is not allowed to exceed the summarized income rate by more than 5 percent. This concept indicates that some variation in the 75-year actuarial projection is to be expected and does not necessarily require action. Conversely, the "close actuarial balance" concept implies that action to reduce the projected deficit is needed when the deficit exceeds 5 percent. By this test, action has been needed for over a decade, since 1989. The summarized 75-year income rate in 1997 of 13.37 percent of taxable payroll is only 86 percent of the summarized cost rate of 15.60 percent. Furthermore, OASDI costs are projected to rise steadily, even after the baby boom generation's retirement, due to continuing increases in life expectancy. Thus, the need for attention to social security financing is clear, not only because the program is out of "close actuarial balance" but also because the financing shortfall can be expected to increase in each new Trustees Report even if we make no changes in our assumptions about the future.

Another important consideration regarding the timing of action on social security financing is that the sooner changes are enacted, the more broadly can the burden of closing the financing deficit be distributed across different age groups. One way to illustrate this point is that if it were decided to raise payroll taxes in 1998 to eliminate the OASI projected deficit, employers and employees each would have to pay about 18 percent more in all future years (i.e., an OASI tax rate of 6.3 percent rather than 5.35). If such a change were not effective until 2010, the tax rate would have to be increased by almost a quarter (to 6.57 percent), and if delayed until 2025, that tax rate would have to be increased by more than a third (to 7.22 percent). Reductions in benefits or other types of changes would have similar increases in size if their effective dates were delayed. Thus, while we have time to consider carefully what changes should be made in the social security program, we should act as soon as support for a plan can be developed.

What Are the Options to Improve Social Security Financing?

Prior to 1977, social security financing was kept in relative balance by increasing the payroll tax rate and earnings base, and by expanding the fraction of jobs subject to the payroll tax. In 1977 and thereafter, financing provisions were enacted to reduce the growth of future program costs. Examples of such changes include elimination of "faulty indexing" in the computation of benefits in 1977, cutbacks in benefits in the early 1980s, and increases in the normal retirement age in 1983. There are obviously a wide variety of options today for increasing income or reducing the cost of OASDI. To bring social security financing into balance in these ways, however, would require increasing the tax rate, as noted earlier, by about 18 percent throughout the 75-year period, or by reducing benefit costs by about 15 percent — or some combination of the two. That such choices are less than attractive perhaps explains why no legislative action has occurred, even though the system has been out of "close actuarial balance" throughout the decade of the 1990s.

This problem is complicated by the fact that the rising cost of health care has attracted more attention to Medicare than has been given to the social security deficit in recent years. Although the social security program and Medicare are usually considered separately, their financing is closely related. Both depend on the payroll tax for most of their income, and for many retirees the amount of their social security benefit largely determines how much they are able to pay in premiums, deductibles, and co-insurance for health care. Also, both the social security program and Medicare are vying for the same limited resources, and in the long run the shape of both programs will be driven by the same demographic forces that are leading us to an aging society. Given, then, that the options of raising the payroll tax rate or reducing benefit costs each raise hard issues, it is perhaps not surprising that some have tried to find other possible solutions to the social security financing problem.

A different option for social security reform is argued cogently by Bosworth (1996), who proposes increasing the size of the future economic pie, so that the higher costs of retirement can be met with a lower tax rate than would otherwise be necessary. In other words, a richer society can afford a richer social insurance program. One way to accomplish this, Bosworth suggests, is actually to save and invest in equities the billions of dollars by which annual social security payroll taxes currently exceed benefit payments — the trust funds. Bosworth notes that, via the 1977 and 1983 Social Security Amendments, Congress began to move away from a pay-as-you-go system of financing the social security program toward a partial reserve system. An implication of this policy appears to be that assets can be built up in the social security trust fund while the baby boomers are still working, to be used, along with interest earned on those assets, to help pay the cost of the baby boom generation's retirement.

The problem with Bosworth's plan, however, is that unless the buildup in social security assets actually increases net national savings and investment, economic growth will not be increased, and the share of the economic pie that will have to be used to pay retirement costs will be unchanged. And experience shows that, immediately following the 1983 amendments, assets of the trust fund rose, but so too did dissaving by the federal government via larger budget deficits. The key to the Bosworth option, then, is to use the buildup in the trust fund reserve to increase national saving and thus economic growth, but not to let the trust fund be offset by larger federal deficits. The recent deficit reduction agreement represents progress, but this agreement includes both social security income and expenditures in measuring the budget deficit. And since social security income exceeded outgo by $66 billion in fiscal year 1996, this helped offset deficits in the rest of the budget. Increasing national saving requires that the current annual buildup in social security trust fund assets not be used for current consumption.

One way Bosworth seeks to protect the social security trust fund buildup from being offset by the federal budget deficit is to invest the reserves in private securities, rather than in government bonds. Another would be to let individual workers invest a portion of their payroll tax in individual saving accounts, similar to IRAs, or in a limited number of carefully regulated investment funds. These ideas have become, of course, key elements of the financing plans put forth, or suggested for study, by the last Social Security Advisory Council.

The concept of investment of the trust fund reserves in private securities is of particular interest to us, since it is the responsibility of the Board of Trustees under Section 201 (c) of the Social Security Act to "Hold the Trust Funds. . . . Review the general policies followed in managing the Trust Funds, and recommend changes in such policies." The last major review of trust fund investment policy (in 1960) expressed concern about government investment in private securities, and led the 1960 Advisory Council to recommend that social security trust fund investments be limited to securities backed by the federal government. Since that time, the development of efficient, passively managed, and broadly indexed investment funds may have mitigated some of the earlier concerns. But, thus far, there has been relatively little analysis of the questions that would have to be answered before any change in trust fund investment policy could be accepted. We would like to enumerate a few of those questions in the hope of stimulating additional analysis.

Questions Regarding Investment of Trust Fund Reserves in Private Securities

1. *How much would investment risk increase?* One of the key arguments for holding trust fund reserves in *federal* securities (as is presently the case) is that it is the safest investment possible — there is little to no risk of loss of principal. Investment safety is more important for the social security program than for most investors, because it is the basic source of retirement income on which workers rely and to which they are expected to add, if possible, additional retirement income from work-related pensions and personal savings. Thus, safety of investment would seem to be more critical for the social security program than for other investors. Indeed, the safety of social security allows individuals to take more risk in other parts of their retirement savings. If this is so, one must ask whether it makes sense to

expose the social security program to the same risk as pensions and personal saving in private securities.

The principal method of assessing the difference in risk of investing in government bonds versus private securities has been to look at long-term past experience. Such analysis shows both higher rates of return and higher volatility of returns for private securities. This greater volatility would have to be taken into account when designing a plan to invest social security program reserves in private securities. In addition to the financial risk, there also would be considerable political risk. For example, how would Congress and the American public react to a stock market crash, if a significant portion of the social security reserves were invested in equities? As another example, during the period of 1968 to 1982, nominal asset values zig-zagged around a flat trend, but real values after inflation declined substantially.

2. *How much additional return could the social security trust fund expect for investment in private securities versus government bonds?* The last Advisory Council (1997) relied in its discussions on an analysis of historical experience showing that stocks outperformed government bonds by an average of 4.7 percent per year over the period 1900–95. But, as every financial prospectus tells us, future performance may not resemble that of the past. For example, would historical yield differentials between the equity and debt markets continue with such a reallocation between markets? After all, someone would still have to hold the federal debt that the social security trust funds would no longer be buying.

As Trustees we are well aware of the difficulty of using past experience to forecast the future. In fact, there is no perfect methodology for doing so, and we must be careful to avoid extrapolating from past experience just because it is the easiest thing to do. Nevertheless, it will be critical to reach some broad consensus on the additional return that the trust fund could expect from investing in private securities, if such an investment policy is to be seriously considered by policymakers.

3. *Would private investment of the trust fund reserves actually increase net national saving and, if so, by how much?* Investment of trust fund reserves in private securities may or may not affect private saving, and the net effect on public saving, or dissaving, is unclear. As difficult as reaching the recent deficit reduction agreement has been, the deficit calculation still includes the social security trust fund reserve annual buildup projected over the next 15 years. Whether a trust fund buildup could be saved over this period would depend not only on continued strong economic performance, but also on convincing policymakers that the federal budget should be balanced *exclusive* of increases in social security reserves, to raise the national saving rate. This would obviously be a daunting political challenge. Hence, investing the social security trust fund reserves in private securities would not necessarily increase total national saving unless the budget deficit were reduced by a like amount.

4. *How much additional economic growth could an increase in net national saving produce?* This is, of course, a fundamental macroeconomic question, and one that is currently very much under debate in regard to the economic benefits of implementing a deficit reduction plan. There seems to be some level of agreement that additional national saving produced by reducing the deficit would have a measurable, but small, effect on economic growth in the short term, with the possibility of larger positive effects in the longer run. The problem with measuring the effect of additional saving is that the rest of the economy cannot be held constant while savings increases. Nevertheless, it will be necessary to argue that additional growth would occur if the budget is balanced exclusive of the buildup in social security reserves, so that the buildup can actually have a positive effect on national savings.

5. *Could procedures be established for investment of social security reserves in private securities so as to avoid political involvement in investment decisions?* A positive aspect of the current trust fund investment policy is that it avoids the need to make choices of sectors, industries, or companies in which to invest. Today, such issues might be avoided even in private sector investment of the trust fund, by investing only in passively managed funds indexed to the broad market. The public is familiar with mutual funds, and they have become the preferred method of investing for many. This undoubtedly makes it easier for people to consider investing the trust fund reserves in private securities, but convincing the public that such investments could be insulated from political interference would be a major hurdle. Moreover, many raise a question of whether governmental ownership of a significant portion of private industry should be considered at all.

6. *How would the currently projected need for the social security trust fund to draw down reserves on a predictable schedule as the baby boom retires affect investment in private securities?* A fundamental rule of investing is not to put at risk money needed to pay next month's bills, or retirement money that will be needed next year. Yet, under current projections, the social security trust fund will need to draw down its reserves when the baby boom retires. This would appear to limit the possibilities for investment of the reserves long enough to obtain significant additional return, and would also put the trust fund at risk of facing a down market at the time it needs to disinvest. One way to meet this problem would be to invest only trust fund monies not needed to pay current benefits. This solution, however, requires that to make a substantial enough investment to provide significant additional return to the fund, additional amounts would be needed now for the fund to invest. Bosworth proposed raising the payroll tax rate now, arguing that it would reduce the need in the future for greater tax rate increases or benefit reductions. The last Advisory Council also recognized the timing problem and agreed that only trust fund reserve amounts never projected to be needed to pay current benefits should be invested privately. The bottom line seems

to be that wide agreement exists that trust fund assets needed to pay current benefits should not be invested in private markets.

These questions are not intended to be an exhaustive list of the issues that must be resolved before changing the law to allow investment of trust fund reserves in private securities. They do show, however, that both good analysis and good will among policymakers would be required in any effort to allow such a major change in trust fund investment policy.

Arguments over these questions led some members of Congress and supporters of one of the Advisory Council plans to avoid these issues completely, by allowing or requiring workers to invest on their own a portion of their annual payroll tax in personal accounts similar to IRA's. Such individual accounts would transfer to the individual worker all of the issues of risk, return, and administrative cost that would be faced by the social security trust fund if its reserves were invested in private markets. An individual-account approach also is attractive to some because it ensures that the federal budget balance will not include the contributions to those accounts. The Board of Trustees may not have any responsibility for such individual savings account plans, but, since we have listed difficult issues regarding trust fund investment in private securities, we acknowledge that there are also similar issues under individual account plans. There are also difficult issues regarding private saving plans, and we list several major ones next:

Questions Regarding Individual Investment Plans for Retirement Income

1. *Is it good social policy to reduce the redistributional elements of social security and to increase links between benefits received and taxes paid into the program?* The social security program has historically provided a balance between (a) relating benefits to taxes paid, and (b) redistribution from higher earners to lower earners and from individual workers to workers with families. The purpose of the redistributional, or "social adequacy," element of the social security program is to ensure that lower-income workers and their families receive an adequate benefit. Individual saving accounts, particularly if funded by a reduction in the payroll tax, would affect this balance by decreasing the redistributive feature of the program.

2. *To what extent should options for investment of workers' saving be limited to a set of passively managed, broadly indexed funds?* Such a limitation would reduce the time and information that workers would need to devote to their investments and reduce the possibility of poor return as a result of bad luck or poor individual investment decisions. However, such a limitation would be resisted by some as an unacceptable reduction in individual freedom in investing personal assets.

3. *What, if any, would be the government's responsibility for investment return?* In

Chile, for example, the government guarantees a relative annual rate of return on workers' investment in mandatory private saving funds and a minimum pension benefit (Turner and Watanabe 1995; Pennacchi, this volume). If the U.S. markets experienced another period like that between 1968 and 1982 when the equities market was virtually flat, people retiring in those years might view the result as unfair and expect government action on their behalf.

4. *How much of a worker's investment for retirement should be subject to market risk?* Private pensions in the U.S. have been moving from defined-benefit to defined-contribution plans for a number of years, thereby making pension benefit depend on market performance. If social security were to become partly a defined contribution plan, this would subject more of workers' retirement income to market risk or the risk that some workers would invest too conservatively to achieve the average rate of return available over past periods.

5. *How much enforcement and regulation would be needed if all workers were required to invest in private plans on their own?* Since the government would have residual responsibility for retirement income through needs-based plans, it would be important to ensure a high degree of compliance with individual investment account requirements.

6. *What would be the administrative cost for individual investors?* There is virtually no administrative cost for social security trust fund investment in government bonds, whereas the cost of administering individual investment accounts for 145 million workers would be larger. Could ways be found to reduce those administrative charges? What would be fair compensation to private money managers for "social security" accounts? Do the advantages of such a program outweigh the considerable extra administrative expenses that would be incurred? Answers to these queries are not yet known.

7. *Would people be required to annuitize their saving at retirement to ensure a stream of payment however long they lived beyond that point?* If so, could a broad market for such annuities be developed and administrative charges held down? If not, what would be the additional cost to government needs-based programs for those who exhausted their individual savings? Experience in the private sector teaches us that assets in defined-contribution plans are rarely used to provide periodic lifetime income.

8. *Will mandating private savings for retirement translate into an increase in national savings?* As people see funds build up in their individual accounts for retirement, they may reduce savings elsewhere. Also, people may demand and receive the right to use these individual account funds for purposes other than retirement income. How such factors evolve could reduce the positive economic effects that private savings accounts are often promised to produce.

As these questions illustrate, requiring individual workers to have private accounts raises a different set of thorny issues, ones no simpler than those compared to the ones that arise if the social security Trust Fund were to buy equities.

Conclusion

We join with other members of the Board of Trustees in calling for timely action to resolve the projected long-term social security financing problem. Although the OASDI system is projected to be able to pay benefits for many years, we need to develop policy options soon. Early action should be taken for several reasons. First, the earlier changes are implemented, the more incremental they can be. Second, implementing changes soon would permit time for phasing them in and for workers to adjust their retirement plans. Third, there has been an alarming erosion of public confidence in the social security system over the past few years, particularly among younger generations (see Quinn, and Rother and Wright, this volume). Early attention to the social security program's longer range financing problems is vital to restore public confidence in the program.

As Public Trustees we are quite disturbed about the public's loss of confidence that the social security program will be there for future generations. And, if the public is convinced (rightly or wrongly) that the social security program will not be there when it reaches retirement age, it may feel that it has no option but to replace the program.

New approaches regarding social security financing fall outside the traditional "box" of tax increases and benefit reductions to meet rising retirement costs. They center on increasing national saving to increase economic growth, so that the cost of retirement when the baby boom generation retires and beyond will require a smaller portion of national income than it otherwise would. With a larger economic pie and higher wages, a given payroll tax rate will provide more income to the trust fund to pay benefits. To achieve this result, the income that the trust fund receives in excess of current needs would have to be added to national savings, and this can occur only if that excess is not offset by increases in federal budget deficits. Fortunately, the prospects for this change appear better now than at any time in recent years, but there is still a long way to go to reach that objective. Faster economic growth would also increase the attractiveness of investing the Trust Fund reserves in private securities. An alternative would be to allow workers to invest a portion of their payroll taxes in private savings accounts. Either alternative could channel part of the additional growth into retirement income, but both approaches raise very tough questions that would need to be resolved before agreement on such changes could be reached.

It would be foolhardy to rush to judgment on these new approaches for meeting the rising costs of retirement, but it is vital that informed debate help resolve long-range social security balance. We cannot reliably predict the future. But reaching agreement on changes will be easier, if we recognize that searching for a set of changes that meet a specific point-estimate 75 years into the future is less important than moving ahead soon with those changes that seem to make the most sense, with full realization that the social security program cannot be insulated from all future social and economic change. The strength of the social security program is that it can adapt as our national circumstances change; our acceptance of the necessity for change is more difficult, eased only by having the information needed to believe that we understand why change is necessary and in which direction it should take us.

References

Advisory Council on Social Security. *Final Report of the 1994–1996 Advisory Council on Social Security.* Vol. 1, *Findings and Recommendations.* Washington, D.C.: Social Security Administration, 1997.

Board of Trustees of the Social Security Administration. *Annual Report of the Board of Trustees of the Federal Old-Age and Survivors Insurance and Disability Income Trust Funds.* Washington, D.C.: Social Security Administration, 1997.

Bosworth, Barry P. "Fund Accumulation: How Much? How Managed?" In Peter A. Diamond, David E. Lindeman, and Howard Young, eds., *Social Security: What Role for the Future.* Washington, D.C.: Distributed by the Brookings Institution for the National Academy of Social Insurance, 1996.

Pennacchi, George G. "Government Guarantees for Old-Age Income." This volume.

Rother, John and William E. Wright. "Americans' Views of Social Security and Social Security Reforms." This volume.

Turner, John A. and Noriyasu Watanabe. *Private Pension Policies in Industrialized Countries.* Kalamazoo, Mich.: W. E. Upjohn Institute for Employment Research, 1995.

II
Assessing the Economic Impact of Social Security Reform

Chapter 5
Social Security Money's Worth

John Geanakoplos, Olivia S. Mitchell, and
Stephen P. Zeldes

HSS
J26   [US]

"Money's worth" measures play a prominent role in the U.S. social security reform debate. For example, the Social Security Advisory Council (1997) recently scored three reform plans according to the internal rate of return, the discounted benefit-to-tax ratio, and the net present value, and it concluded that all three plans would substantially improve social security's performance on money's worth criteria. In the popular press, pundits and politicians compare rates of return anticipated under the current social security system with historical average returns on U.S. capital markets. After realizing how much higher market returns have been than those projected on social security, some observers conclude that shifting from our current underfunded social security system to an individual-account, defined contribution program would lead to higher returns for all. Thus presidential candidate Stephen Forbes (1996) declared that "the average worker retiring today receives a lifetime return of only about 2.2 percent on the taxes he has paid into the system. Contrast this with the historic 9–10 percent annual returns from stock market investments. . . . The advantages of an IRA-type approach are overpowering."[1]

This chapter offers a critical assessment of money's worth measures as they are used in the context of social security reform. These measures have been used for two distinct purposes by policy analysts: to compare how different groups fare relative to each other under a *given* social security system,[2] and to compare how a given group fares under *alternative* systems. In this chapter we concentrate on money's worth measures as used in the second context — for instance, in comparing cohorts' returns under the current, pay-as-you-go, mostly unfunded system with returns under other systems that require more or less funding, different benefit structures, or some other format altogether. In so doing, we are interested in assessing how alternative social security systems would affect different cohorts over time.

The study begins with a stylized model of multiple generations. We assume a constant annual real interest rate of 2.3 percent and a constant growth rate of 1.2 percent, and simulate the actual economy to a surprising degree of accuracy. We show that declining social security returns are the inevitable result of having instituted an unfunded (pay-as-you-go) retirement system that delivered benefits to people already old at the time the system started. We prove that in an ongoing social security system, with or without a trust fund, the net present value of transfers to all generations must sum to zero. If early participants received substantial positive transfers from the system, then later generations must receive negative transfers. Later generations must earn low rates of return on their social security contributions because early cohorts received high returns. Part of social security taxes should thus be seen as payments on past debt incurred to transfer money to retirees soon after system startup, not as investments in assets producing future income.

An important element of system reform concerns the fate of the accrued benefits for past contributions. There are several ways of computing this liability. Goss (forthcoming) describes a method similar to what we will call the straight-line method that at shut-down would entitle someone who worked three-quarters of his or her worklife to three-quarters of the retirement benefit. We propose instead a constant-benefit calculation, one that allocates to each dollar of contributions the same present value in benefits (discounted to the contribution date). The former method gives accrued benefits in our stylized economy of $9.1 trillion discounted to 1997; the latter gives $9.9 trillion. If the social security system were ever shut down, this $800 billion difference might be an important source of controversy.

A popular argument suggests that if social security were privatized, everyone could earn higher returns. We show that this is false. That is, suppose the old unfunded system were shut down and workers' new payroll taxes were invested in capital markets. Suppose that explicit debt were issued to replace accrued benefits, and the path of this explicit debt were kept identical to what the path of the present value of accrued benefits would have been in an ongoing system. Then after-tax returns on privatized accounts would be identical to the low returns received under the old system. For example, in our stylized economy, workers receive only 71 cents in benefits in present value terms for each dollar of contributions to the current system. In a privatized system, each dollar of contribution would have to be taxed 29 cents to make payments on the bonds replacing accrued benefit obligations, yielding the same 71 cents of benefits.

Next we turn to an analysis of how money's worth measures are derived in practice, drawing on and comparing the pioneering research of Leimer (1994), Goss (forthcoming), and Advisory Council (1997). Their results reveal that the U.S. social security system heavily subsidized more than 50 birth cohorts alive when the system was implemented. When these groups pass on, they will have received a net subsidy of around $9.7 trillion (in $1997 present value terms). The current unfunded liability, or the present value of accrued benefits minus the current trust fund, is $8.9 trillion calculated according to a method close to the straight-line method. This is close to the $9.1 trillion obtained in our stylized economy, and it suggests that the constant-benefit method would have produced something like $9.7 trillion for the actual U.S. economy. According to both Leimer and Advisory Council estimates, actual rates of return have fallen steadily through time. Under current law, they will not fall as low as we projected in our stylized economy, but that is because current law cannot be sustained. Our social security system is in actuarial imbalance; that is, based on a 75-year horizon, the present value of projected future tax revenues under current law is projected to be less than the present value of future projected benefits by about $3 trillion (Goss, forthcoming). Raising future taxes, or cutting benefits, to bring the system into actuarial balance will reduce returns to levels very close to those presented in our stylized model.

We also examine the Advisory Council money's worth estimates for three reform plans involving investment in the stock market through a central trust fund or individual accounts. Money's worth estimates for these plans are higher than those for other reforms that restore actuarial balance by raising taxes or cutting benefits. In fact, the more money a plan puts into the stock market, the better it "looks" according to the money's worth measures. But this approach is incorrect, in that it replaces uncertain outcomes with their expected values and then discounts them at the risk free rate. This might have the effect of assigning a higher money's worth to one plan even though everyone would be better off under some other plan. Money's worth numbers must be adjusted to reflect risk. In general, how they should be adjusted depends on a detailed knowledge of household preferences. Nevertheless, we show that one does not need to know preference parameters under four conditions pertaining to optimization, intergenerational trade-offs, price stability, and spanning. Then market value defines a money's worth measure with the property that any reform producing a higher money's worth will also give higher welfare, independent of household preferences. Under these conditions, one should not assign a money's worth of $3.85 to $1 of stocks and a money's worth of $1 to $1 of bonds, yet in effect this is what the Advisory Council does. In the real world, of course, one or more of these conditions is likely to fail, so a utility-independent money's worth measure does not exist. We discuss how to modify market value money's worth when some of the conditions are violated. This moves the results toward the non-risk adjusted numbers, but by no means all the way.

Next, we apply the theoretical analysis to concrete reform proposals and provide estimates of how money's worth measures should be modified. Recognizing that some households are constrained from holding stocks themselves, we find that there is likely to be a gain from social security diversi-

TABLE 1. Cash Flows in a Stylized PAYGO Social Security Model: Ongoing System

IRR (%)	PVB/PVT (%)	NPV ($1997)	Cum NPV ($1997)	Birth Year	Calendar Year														
					1938	1948	1958	1968	1978	1988	1997	1998	2008	2018	2028	2038	2048	2058	2068
97.0	2263	63	94	1860	8.3														
11.1	336	379	2453	1870	9.3	9.3													
4.7	162	596	7856	1880	-3.6	10.5	10.5												
2.2	98	393	12698	1890	-4.1	-4.1	11.8	11.8											
1.2	71	193	15525	1900	-4.6	-4.6	-4.6	13.3	13.3										
1.2	71	-8	16352	1910	-5.2	-5.2	-5.2	-5.2	15.0	15.0									
1.2	71	-166	15233	1920		-5.9	-5.9	-5.9	-5.9	16.9	16.9	16.9							
1.2	71	-149	13672	1930			-6.6	-6.6	-6.6	-6.6	19.1	19.1	19.1						
1.2	71	-133	12271	1940				-7.5	-7.5	-7.5	-7.5	-7.5	21.5	21.5					
1.2	71	-120	11013	1950					-8.4	-8.4	-8.4	-8.4	-8.4	24.2	24.2				
1.2	71	-107	9885	1960						-9.5	-9.5	-9.5	-9.5	-9.5	27.3	27.3			
1.2	71	-96	8872	1970							-10.7	-10.7	-10.7	-10.7	-10.7	30.7	30.7		
1.2	71	-87	7963	1980									-12.0	-12.0	-12.0	-12.0	34.6	34.6	
1.2	71	-78	7147	1990										-13.5	-13.5	-13.5	-13.5	39.0	39.0
1.2	71	-70	6415	2000											-15.3	-15.3	-15.3	-15.3	43.9
1.2	71	-63	5757	2010												-17.2	-17.2	-17.2	-17.2
1.2	71	-56	5167	2020													-19.4	-19.4	-19.4
1.2	71	-50	4638	2030														-21.8	-21.8
1.2	71	-45	4163	2040															-24.6
				Total annual contributions	-184	-207	-233	-263	-296	-333	-371	-375	-423	-477	-537	-605	-682	-768	-865
				Total annual benefits	184	207	233	263	296	333	371	375	423	477	537	605	682	768	865
				Annual deficit	0	0	0	0	0	0	0	0	0	0	0	0	0	0	0
				PV (1997$) of trust fund*	0	0	0	0	0	0	0	0	0	0	0	0	0	0	0

Source: Authors' calculations. See text for explanation. Entries are in billions of 1997$ unless indicated otherwise.

Notes: "Ongoing" refers to computations performed for an unfunded open ended Social Security program assumed to continue into the infinite future.

* Also equal to cumulative NPV (1997$) of annual surplus.

fication into stocks. But this gain is only about 20 percent as large as the Advisory Council analysis has suggested.

We are sympathetic to policymakers' efforts to assess whether workers and retirees get their money's worth from the social security system. Yet our analysis shows that popular money's worth measures are often biased when used to compare workers' and retirees' positions under different reform scenarios. In particular, a correct money's worth calculation would show that the net advantage of privatization and diversification are substantially less than popularly perceived.[3]

Money's Worth Measures in a Stylized Economy

To illustrate key issues, we begin with a stylized version of an unfunded social security system in an overlapping generations economy model with no uncertainty. We show how to calculate money's worth measures in this economy; they are unambiguous and easy to compute. We then explain why these money's worth measures are low under our current system, and use this model to analyze the transition costs of moving to a privatized system.

Consider a matrix of numbers with each row (i) representing a birth year and each column (j) representing a calendar year (see Table 1). For simplicity we shall assume all individuals born in the same year are identical. Entry (i,j) represents the total net cash flows in year j to or from all individuals born in year i. Contributions (or taxes) are represented as negative entries and benefits as positive entries.

Assume that all households enter the workforce at 20, retire at 60, and live until age 80. People pay social security taxes each year they work and receive social security benefits during each year of retirement. We let real earnings for each cohort be constant over the worklife, but productivity growth and population growth cause the aggregate earnings, social security taxes, and social security benefits of households born in year t to be $(1+g)$ times as great as those of households born in year i. For this discussion, we also assume that there is no uncertainty. The model is normalized so that total social security benefit payments in the table are equivalent to actual aggregate U.S. system benefits in 1997 (= $371 billion).

In keeping with the Advisory Council's predictions of future long run productivity growth, we suppose that the rate of growth g is 1.2 percent.[4] We further assume that our stylized social security system began in 1938 and will continue to operate forever, as a pay-as-you-go (PAGYO) program with no accumulated trust fund. That is, the model posits that every retired individual over the age of 60 began to receive benefits in 1938, funded fully by taxes raised on workers during that same year. These benefits are equal to what the worker would have received, had he paid social security taxes (at the same rate as current workers) all of his life. Likewise in each calendar year thereafter we suppose the total of all taxes raised from workers is equal to the total of all benefits paid to retirees. Thus the sum of each column in Table 1 is equal to zero. We display only part of Table 1, extending 75 years into the future, but in principle these cash flows would continue infinitely into the future. To make the table easier to read, every tenth row and column of the underlying matrix are shown.

In this stylized framework, one can easily evaluate the different money's worth statistics. All widely used measures of social security money's worth are single numbers that are used to compare the stream of social security taxes paid by an individual with the stream of social security benefits received. We focus on the three most popular measures. The real "internal rate of return" (IRR) is the inflation-corrected discount rate that equates, for each individual, the present value of the stream of social security benefits to the present value of the stream of the taxes paid. The "benefit/tax ratio" (PVB/PVT) represents, for each individual, the present value of lifetime social security benefits received divided by the present value of lifetime social security taxes paid. Finally, the "net present value" (NPV) is equal to the present value of social security benefits minus the present value of taxes paid.[5]

The internal rate of return (IRR) for each cohort appears as the first column; computing it does not require a market interest rate (discount rate). Column two lists the ratio of the present value of benefits to the present value of taxes for each cohort (PVB/PVT). The net present value of benefits minus taxes (NPV) for each cohort i appears in the third column of Table 1.[6] Each present value is taken as of 1997, and uses the annual real rate of interest (r) for discounting. We assume a value for r of 2.3 percent. This is approximately the arithmetic average of the annual real rate of interest earned on intermediate maturity government bonds over the last 70 years, as is shown below. It is also consistent with the Advisory Council's (1997) estimate of the average future real rate of interest.

The fact that r is greater than g is very important to the qualitative features of a pay-as-you-go social security system such as the one sketched here, although the exact magnitudes of the numbers are not. If instead r were less than g forever, then any expansion of a pay-as-you-go social security system would make everybody better off, at least up until the point that the market interest rate r rose back to g. Indeed, if $r < g$, it is not even possible to assign a finite number to total social security benefits.[7] Most economists, we believe, would subscribe to the idea that the real market rate of interest is greater than the rate of growth of the economy.[8]

The supposition that $r > g$ allows us to discount the future to a finite number. But it also makes the past loom large. As we shall see, one extremely important reason that our social security system imposes such a burden on today's young is that the system transferred a great deal of wealth to the generations retiring just after the Great Depression. Since $r > g$, the present value in 1997 of a transfer in 1940 is a larger fraction of 1997 GDP than the actual transfer was of its contemporaneous GDP.[9]

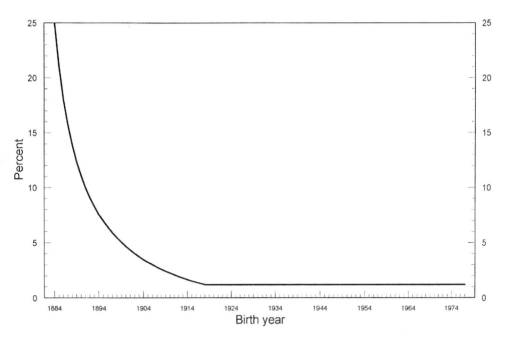

Figure 1. Real internal rate of return on social security, stylized PAYGO model.
Source: Authors' calculations based on stylized PAYGO model.

Internal Rates of Return Must Fall in a Pay-as-You-Go Social Security System

This framework generates a time series of IRR's by birth year, plotted in Figure 1. It will be noted that IRRs start out very high: in fact they are infinite for the very first set of cohorts, fall to about 15–20 percent for early cohorts, and then decline toward 1.2 percent.[10] Early participants earned returns much higher than the market rate of interest (2.3 percent, in our stylized model), while later participants earned rates that were below the market rate of interest. While not shown in the figure, Table 1 indicates that the PVB/PVT ratio started out much above one and ended up below one. Similarly, the NPV for each cohort is positive for early generations and negative for later generations.

It is easy to see that the falling IRR is not a result peculiar to our example, but instead is an outcome produced in any steadily growing economy with a pay-as-you-go system. Generations born before 1918 received all their benefits but did not pay taxes in some or all of their working years. Clearly, then, their rate of return will be very high. By contrast, generations born after

1918 pay taxes from the first year they work, so their internal rate of return must be equal to the rate of growth g of the economy.[11] It must be emphasized that these deteriorating money's worth patterns appear even though we hold constant life expectancy and the age structure of the population. That is, falling money's worth in this model is *not* due to the aging of baby boomers, increased life expectancy, or massive administrative inefficiency, but rather to the simple arithmetic of the pay-as-you-go system.

The Redistributive Implications of a Pay-as-You-Go Social Security System

We next exploit the connection between IRR and NPV to explain why IRRs must fall, and also to make clear the inherently redistributive nature of a pay-as-you-go social security system. Recall that IRR is greater than the rate of interest if and only if NPV is greater than zero. The analytical advantage of NPV over IRR is that NPVs can be aggregated. In a pay-as-you-go social security system, the sum of the NPVs across all cohorts must be zero. If one cohort gets net benefits from the system, the other cohorts must pay. If one cohort has an IRR bigger than r, some other cohort must have an IRR less than r. We now explain why.

The entry for the ith row of the fourth column of Table 1 is the cumulative NPV: that is, the sum of the third column across all rows up to and including row i. We can see that after 1910 or so, the number steadily drops toward 0 as we go down the column (i.e., as i increases). We claim that, in a steady state economy in which $r > g$, this cumulative NPV must always tend to zero as i grows indefinitely large.

Since the entries in the matrix in Table 1 grow at rate g but are discounted back at rate $r > g$, we can safely sum present values over all the infinite entries after the system began in 1938. We need not worry about diverging series or the order in which we take the sums and present values. Each column in Table 1 sums to zero because the system is pay-as-you-go. It follows that the present value of each column sum must equal zero, and therefore that the sum across *all* columns of these present values must be zero as well. Changing the orders of summation and present value, it follows that the sum of the present value of all the rows must also be zero, as claimed.[12]

Since the early generations under the system receive large net present value surpluses from social security, it follows that, on average, current and future generations must lose money to social security (in present value terms). In an unfunded PAYGO system every generation after the initial few *must* lose money in present value terms under social security. Because rates of return were high for the first generations, rates of return must be low for later generations.

In this stylized example we supposed that the social security system never built up a trust fund. The same logic applies, however, if the system borrows money or accumulates a trust fund: in either case, the sum of the NPVs across all generations must be zero. It is only necessary that the trust fund borrows and invests at the rate of interest r, and that the contemporaneous value of the trust fund grows at a rate smaller than r. Under these circumstances, the present value as of a fixed year (say 1997) of the trust fund will increase from some year T to $T+1$ only to the extent that taxes exceed benefits in that year (in present value). In other words, the cumulative NPV of the column sums up to any year T plus the present value of the trust fund in year T must sum to zero for all T. If the contemporaneous value of the trust fund grows at a rate less than r, then the present value of the trust fund must eventually converge to zero. Hence the cumulative column NPV must also converge to zero. As above, this implies that as we go to the limit the cumulative cohort (row) NPVs also converge to zero.

Consider, for example, a variation on Table 1 in which income grows faster than g for some years, say from 1938 to 1973, and then reverts to a growth rate of g forever after. Suppose the tax *rates* are the same as in Table 1 and held constant forever, and the benefit rates are held constant at least until 1973 and increased sometime thereafter. Then the social security system would build up a trust fund in the years up to 1973, from which it could ultimately increase benefits. This, however, would not change the previous conclusions. To the extent that early generations receive benefits in excess of their contributions, later generations must make up the deficit. The presence of the trust fund is a sign that previous NPVs and IRRs were not as high as they could have been. In and of itself, the presence of the trust fund is not sufficient for future IRRs to be above r.

Investment Illusion

Many people look at their low money's worth numbers from social security and assume that these must be the result of systemic administrative inefficiency. Because social security taxes are paid early in life and benefits are received later in life, they tend to think of the taxes as investments paying inadequate dividends. These people believe that, if their contributions could instead be invested in capital markets, they would achieve a higher benefit. However, this perception suffers from investment illusion, since social security taxes should instead be thought of as payments on an old debt. This can be illustrated by imagining a sickly patriarch with no money facing huge medical bills. His children might be called upon to pay the bills. If the expenses were sufficiently high and the number of children sufficiently low, one might imagine that the third generation, the grandchildren, would also be asked to pay. They could do so by waiting until they grew up and their parents got old to give them some money, thus partly repaying and also reenacting their parents' gift to the patriarch. If the bills were astronomically high, and the children and grandchildren together could not afford them in their entirety, the debt might be rolled over to the fourth generation, the great-grandchildren. By renewing the gift each generation, all the descendants of the patriarch can share in the paying of his medical bills. Each generation would pay money when young, and receive less back when old. This fourth generation might never have known or even heard of the patriarch, yet as a result of his legacy they would be born into an obligation to their parents. Not knowing or caring about the health of the patriarch, they might be tempted to renege on the debt and let him face the consequences of less medical care. But by the time they would make this decision his life and illness and medical care would have already come and gone. Defaulting on the debt would hurt not the patriarch but rather the third generation, their parents. This would likely prove difficult to do.

Our social security system functions something like this parable of the family and the sick patriarch. As illustrated earlier, initial cohorts attaining old age after the Great Depression received a net transfer, in turn imposing costs on succeeding generations — perhaps long after they and the reasons they needed so much care have been forgotten. Furthermore, by the iron logic of compound interest, payment deferred is payment increased; thus $100 borrowed once at 2.3 percent real interest requires payment of $2.30 plus an inflation correction every year in perpetuity, long after the purpose of the original loan is forgotten.[13] It is tempting to think that the small number of early generations receiving the transfer and the robust economic growth of the last five decades must surely dwarf the tiny transfers made when the social security system was established. Indeed, if this parable were only about one family, its subsequent success might eventually enable succeeding children to pay off the original loan in its entirety. But this is not the case for an entire economy, since the technological breakthroughs that enriched the economy also helped to maintain high real interest rates, rates that increased the burden of the repayment.[14] In addition, many generations subsequent to the first did not help pay the interest or repay the principal of the initial implicit debt but instead received transfers themselves that caused the implicit debt to grow faster than the rate of interest.

The Unfunded Liability of Social Security

An important question relevant to the current social security reform debate is what would happen if the current system were shut down and replaced by a different system. In such an eventuality, we believe it inconceivable that previously promised benefits would be completely eliminated. The cohort of 1938, for example, which worked and paid into the old system for 40 years, could not be abandoned without benefits at the age of 60 if the system were shut down in 1998.

To give an idea of policy alternatives using our stylized model, we evaluate a "1997 shut-down" scenario which includes only contributions made and benefits received through 1997, plus future benefits accrued based on contributions through 1997 but to be paid after 1997. The present value as of 1997 of all accrued future benefits ($PVAB_{1997}$) represents benefits already "earned" by workers in the system. These are the liabilities that people in our stylized example might be worried about losing if circumstances suddenly changed. If, for example, the population did not continue to grow at the same rate, or if future taxes were reduced, or if the system shut down, these accrued benefits might be in jeopardy. In general, the unfunded liability as of the end of 1997 (UL_{1997}) is defined as the present value of these accrued benefits (in 1997 dollars) minus any accumulated trust fund (TF_{1997}); i.e., $UL_{1997} = PVAB_{1997} - TF_{1997}$. There are no assets in the system to guarantee these unfunded liabilities, except the implicit promise of the government to tax future generations.[15] In our pure pay-as-you-go example there is no accumulated trust fund, so the unfunded liability of the system is simply equal to the present value of all accrued benefits.

It is not necessarily obvious how accrued benefits would be assigned in the event of an actual shutdown of the current social security system; one can think of several potential formulas. The first approach we will call the "straight line" method. Suppose that a system shutdown occurred in 1997, at which point a given worker has labored for s years out of the normal 40. That worker would then be entitled, after age 60, to a benefit worth $s/40$ of the value that he would have received had the system continued in operation and had he continued to work until age 60, at the same average real wage. The straight line accrued benefits as of 1997 in our stylized example are presented in the penultimate line of Table 2a. In the last line we compute their present value (that is, the unfunded liability) to be $9.1 trillion ($1997).

One might say that the straight line method provides a lower bound on social security's unfunded liability, because a dollar of contributions in the last year of a worker's career yields the same benefits as a dollar contributed 40 years earlier. By contrast, if the worker could have deposited his or her contributions in the bank, a dollar contributed at age 20 would yield much more at age 61 than a dollar contributed at age 60. By ignoring the time value of money, the straight line method gives smaller rates of return, and smaller benefit/tax ratios to younger workers at the time of shutdown. In columns 1 and 2 of Table 2a, we see that IRR and PVB/PVT decline as the cohorts get younger at shutdown. PVB/PVT, for example, drops all the way to 51 percent.

An alternative formula for accrued benefits, which we call the constant IRR method, assigns accrued benefits so that a worker gets the same internal rate of return on actual taxes and benefits as he or she would have earned

TABLE 2a. Cash Flows in a Stylized PAYGO Social Security Model: Shutdown Case (Straight Line Method)

IRR (%)	PVB/PVT (%)	NPV ($1997)	Cum NPV ($1997)	Birth Year	Calendar Year														
					1938	1948	1958	1968	1978	1988	1997	1998	2008	2018	2028	2038	2048	2058	2068
		63	94	1860	8.3														
		379	2453	1870	9.3	9.3													
97.0	2263	596	7856	1880	-3.6	10.5	10.5												
11.1	336	393	12698	1890	-4.1	-4.1	11.8	11.8											
4.7	162	193	15525	1900	-4.6	-4.6	-4.6	13.3	13.3										
2.2	98	-8	16352	1910	-5.2	-5.2	-5.2	-5.2	15.0	15.0									
1.2	71	-166	15233	1920		-5.9	-5.9	-5.9	-5.9	16.9	16.9	16.9							
1.2	71	-149	13672	1930			-6.6	-6.6	-6.6	-6.6	19.1	19.1	19.1						
1.2	70	-135	12268	1940				-7.5	-7.5	-7.5	-7.5	20.4	20.4	20.4					
1.0	63	-120	10984	1950					-8.4	-8.4	-8.4		16.9	16.9	16.9				
0.9	57	-90	9936	1960						-9.5	-9.5			12.3	12.3	12.3			
0.8	51	-45	9271	1970							-10.7				6.1	6.1	6.1		
				1980															
				1990															
				2000															
				2010															
				2020															
				2030															
				2040															
				Total annual contributions (past)	-184	-207	-233	-263	-296	-333	-371								
				Total annual contributions (after shutdown)								0	0	0	0	0	0		
				Total annual benefits (past)	184	207	233	263	296	333	371								
				Total annual benefits (accrued as of shutdown)								375	392	347	256	138	35		
				PV ($1997) benefits accrued as of shutdown							9106								

Source: Authors' calculations. See text for details. Entries are in billions of 1997$ unless otherwise indicated.
Notes: "Shutdown" refers to computations performed for an unfunded Social Security program terminated in 1998. Benefits accrued prior to 1998 are assumed to be paid, but no future benefits are accrued. Method for accrual: straight line.

having worked until 60 at the same average wage. Since the constant IRR method gives some time value to money, the accrued benefits are somewhat larger with this method than with the straight line method. Table 2b presents the accrued benefits with the constant IRR method for our stylized example. Note that the IRR in column 1 remains constant at 1.2 percent. The unfunded liability now works out to $9.5 trillion.

Goss (forthcoming) proposed a method of calculating accrued benefits that closely resembles the straight line method, and that agrees with it when there is no productivity growth in the economy. When there is positive growth, the Goss method lies somewhere between the straight line method and the constant IRR method.

The simplest approach to figuring accrued benefits, which we term the "constant benefit/tax ratio method," or "constant benefit" method for short, provides that each dollar of social security contributions generates the same $b in benefits in present value terms (discounted back to the year the contribution was made). For our stylized case, b equals 0.71, which is the ratio of the present value of benefits to the present value of contributions for any generation that contributed to the program over a 40-year worklife. Table 2c summarizes the result of implementing the constant benefit/tax ratio method. Since the constant benefit/tax ratio method fully recognizes the time value of money, we would expect to see the highest accrued benefits under this method. Indeed, we find that the unfunded liability works out to be $9.9 trillion. The divergence between methods for calculating accrued benefits may become an important source of controversy if social security is ever shut down and workers stake their claims to accrued benefits.

The annual social security transfer. Table 1 reports the present value of the transfer that each birth cohort makes or receives over the course of its life after the economy reaches the steady state (where generations pay taxes for the full 40 years). Another way of looking at the transfer is in annual terms for all cohorts together. The transfer a cohort makes in year t is the difference between the contributions it makes in that year and the present value of the benefits those contributions bring, which in turn depends on the formula for accrued benefits. In the simplest case, where there is a constant benefit/tax ratio, 29 cents on every dollar of contributions is transferred to pay off the implicit debt. In 1998 for example, Table 1 tells us that total contributions are $375 billion. We know that those households will only get back 71 cents on each dollar in present value of benefits. Hence the transfer made that year, in 1998 dollars, is $(.29) \times (\$375 \text{ billion}) = \$108.8$ billion. Had we used the straight line method or the constant rate of return method for generating accrued benefits, the transfer would have been slightly lower (because under these methods households would have already given up greater transfers in prior years).

No matter how accrued benefits are calculated in a steady state economy the transfers made by all cohorts in year $t+1$ must equal $(r-g) \times$ (un-

TABLE 2b. Cash Flows in a Stylized PAYGO Social Security Model: Shutdown Case (Constant IRR Method)

IRR (%)	PVB/PVT (%)	NPV ($1997)	Cum NPV ($1997)	Birth Year	Calendar Year														
					1938	1948	1958	1968	1978	1988	1997	1998	2008	2018	2028	2038	2048	2058	2068
		63	94	1860	8.3														
97.0	2263	379	2453	1870	9.3	9.3													
11.1	336	596	7856	1880	-3.6	10.5	10.5												
4.7	162	393	12698	1890	-4.1	-4.1	11.8	11.8											
2.2	98	193	15525	1900	-4.6	-4.6	-4.6	13.3	13.3										
1.2	71	-8	16352	1910	-5.2	-5.2	-5.2	-5.2	15.0	15.0									
1.2	71	-166	15233	1920		-5.9	-5.9	-5.9	-5.9	16.9	16.9	16.9							
1.2	70	-149	13672	1930			-6.6	-6.6	-6.6	-6.6	19.1	19.1							
1.2	67	-132	12273	1940				-7.5	-7.5	-7.5	-7.5	19.1	19.1						
1.2	64	-106	11091	1950					-8.4	-8.4	-8.4		20.6	20.6					
1.2	61	-74	10199	1960						-9.5	-9.5			18.1	18.1				
		-36	9661	1970							-10.7				13.9	13.9			
				1980												7.4	7.4		
				1990															
				2000															
				2010															
				2020															
				2030															
				2040															
Total annual contributions (past)					-184	-207	-233	-263	-296	-333	-371								
Total annual contributions (after shutdown)												0	0	0	0	0	0		
Total annual benefits (past)					184	207	233	263	296	333	371								
Total annual benefits (accrued as of shutdown)											375	375	397	366	286	161	43		
PV ($1997) benefits accrued as of shutdown											9532								

Source: Authors' calculations. See text for details. Entries are in billions of 1997$ unless indicated otherwise.
Notes: "Shutdown" refers to computations performed for an unfunded Social Security program terminated in 1998. Benefits accrued prior to 1998 are assumed to be paid, but no future benefits are accrued. Method for accrual: IRR = 1.2%

TABLE 2c. Cash Flows in a Stylized PAYGO Social Security Model: Shutdown Case (Constant PVB/PVT Method)

PVB/PVT (%)	IRR (%)	NPV ($1997)	Cum NPV ($1997)	Birth Year	1938	1948	1958	1968	1978	1988	1997	1998	2008	2018	2028	2038	2048	2058	2068
		63	94	1860	8.3														
		379	2453	1870	9.3	9.3													
2263	97.0	596	7856	1880	−3.6	10.5	10.5												
336	11.1	393	12698	1890	−4.1	−4.1	11.8	11.8											
162	4.7	193	15525	1900	−4.6	−4.6	−4.6	13.3	13.3										
98	2.2	−8	16352	1910	−5.2	−5.2	−5.2	−5.2	15.0	15.0									
71	1.2	−166	15233	1920		−5.9	−5.9	−5.9	−5.9	16.9	16.9	16.9							
71	1.2	−149	13672	1930			−6.6	−6.6	−6.6	−6.6	19.1	19.1	19.1						
71	1.2	−129	12277	1940				−7.5	−7.5	−7.5	−7.5		20.8	20.8					
71	1.3	−94	11177	1950					−8.4	−8.4	−8.4			19.1	19.1				
71	1.4	−60	10421	1960						−9.5	−9.5				15.3	15.3			
71	1.5	−27	10001	1970							−10.7					8.6	8.6		
				1980															
				1990															
				2000															
				2010															
				2020															
				2030															
				2040															
			Total annual contributions (past)		−184	−207	−233	−263	−296	−333	−371								
			Total annual contributions (after shutdown)									0	0	0	0	0	0		
			Total annual benefits (past)		184	207	233	263	296	333	371								
			Total annual benefits (accrued as of shutdown)									375	402	383	312	182	50		
			PV ($1997) benefits accrued as of shutdown								9907								

Source: Authors' calculations. See text for details. Entries are in billions of 1997$ unless indicated otherwise.
Notes: "Shutdown" refers to computations performed for an unfunded Social Security program terminated in 1998. Benefits accrued prior to 1998 are assumed to be paid, but no future benefits are accrued. Method for accrual: PVB/PVT = 71%

funded liability at the end of year t). For instance, under the constant benefits/tax ratio plan, we calculated above that transfers in 1998 = \$108.8 billion. Define UL_t as the unfunded liability at the end of year t. If we instead calculate the transfers as $(r - g) \times UL_{1997}$, this equals $(.023 - .012) \times (\$9.9$ trillion) = \$108.8 billion. The same would hold true under the other plans, though the transfer is harder to compute. Let us see why.

Consider what would happen if the system did not shut down until 1998 rather than in 1997. Recall that $UL_t = PVAB_t - TF_t$. This implies that:

$$\Delta UL_{1997,1998} = \Delta PVAB_{1997,1998} - \Delta TF_{1997,1998}.$$

The change in the present value of accrued benefits from 1997 to 1998 can be derived as the sum of three terms. It includes first a term $r \times PVAB_{1997}$ because the old accrued benefits are now one year closer, and so their present value must go up by the rate of interest between 1997 and 1998. Second, accrued benefits are increased according to the benefit formula $f(C_{1998})$, as a result of the additional contributions made in 1998 (C_{1998}). Third, unfunded liabilities are diminished by the benefits B_{1998} paid out in 1998. Thus:

$$\Delta PVAB_{1997,1998} = r \times PVAB_{1997} + f(C_{1998}) - B_{1998}.$$

The transfer (TRANS) in 1998 is the difference between contributions in 1998 and the corresponding change in accrued benefits. Defining the annual social security surplus (SUR) as the difference between annual contributions and annual benefits,[16] we have:

$$TRANS_{1998} = C_{1998} - f(C_{1998}),$$
$$SUR_{1998} = C_{1998} - B_{1998},$$
$$\Delta PVAB_{1997,1998} = r \times PVAB_{1997} - TRANS_{1998} + SUR_{1998}.$$

Similarly, we can decompose the change in the trust fund from 1997 to 1998 into three components. First, it increases by $r \times TF_{1997}$ because it earns interest. Second, it rises due to additional contributions made in 1998, and third, it falls due to benefits paid during 1998. This gives:

$$\Delta TF_{1997,1998} = r \times TF_{1997} + SUR_{1998}.$$

Putting these together yields:

$$\Delta UL_{1997,1998} = \Delta PVAB_{1997,1998} - \Delta TF_{1997,1998}$$
$$= r \times (PVAB_{1997} - TF_{1997}) - TRANS_{1998} + SUR_{1998} - SUR_{1998}$$
$$= (r \times UL_{1997}) - TRANS_{1998}.$$

TABLE 3. Social Security Present Values by Birth Year: Stylized PAYGO Model

Birth Year	Age in 1997	PV of Past Benefits Received Less PV of Past Contributions Made	PV of Future Benefits Already Accrued Based on Past Contributions	PV of Future Benefits to be Accrued Less Future Contributions to be Made	Row Total (NPV from Table 1)	Cumulative Row Total
1859–1917	80+ (dead)	15.7[a]	0[a]	0[b]	15.7[c]	15.7
1918–1937	60–79 (living and retired)	−6.2[a]	3.1[a]	0[b]	−3.1[c]	12.6
1938–1977	20–59 (living and working)	−9.5[a]	6.0[a]	−.9[b]	−4.4[c]	8.2
1978+	≤19 (not yet working or not yet born)	0[a]	0[a]	−8.2	−8.2	0
	Total	0[d]	9.1	−9.1	0	

Source: Authors' calculations.
[a] Derived from Table 2a.
[b] Derived from Tables 1 and 2a.
[c] Derived from Table 1.
[d] Equal to accumulated trust fund (=0 since system is PAYGO).

Rewriting this gives $\text{TRANS}_{98} = r \times \text{UL}_{1997} - \Delta\text{UL}_{1997,1998}$.

Next, realize that in a steady state system all the accrued benefits in matrices 2a,b,c must grow at the rate g as the shutdown year rises. In particular, comparing the 1998 and 1997 shutdown scenarios shows $\text{UL}_{1998} = (1+g) \times \text{UL}_{1997}$ or $\Delta\text{UL}_{1997,1998} = g \times \text{UL}_{1997}$, no matter how accrued benefits and hence unfunded liabilities were measured (provided they are linear functions of all the contributions). Putting these together, we get $\text{TRANS}_{1998} = (r-g) \times \text{UL}_{1997}$, as was to be shown. We deduce that the transfer made in 1998 under the straight line method of figuring accrued benefits is $100.1 billion = (0.023 − 0.012) × ($9.1 trillion). Under the constant ratio method it is $104.5 billion = (0.023 − 0.012) × ($9.5 trillion).

Table 3 summarizes the transfers for different cohorts and distinguishes between the transfers paid in the past and those to be paid in the future, in this stylized model. (Later we offer a similar table based on actual U.S. data.) For illustrative purposes, the cohorts are collected into four groups: past participants no longer alive (birth years 1859–1917), those currently alive and retired (birth years 1918–1937), those currently alive and working (birth years 1938–1977), and those currently too young to be working or not yet born (birth years 1978+). The column labeled row total gives the NPV (or net subsidy) aggregated from Table 1.

The early birth cohorts (those no longer living in 1997) received net subsidies of $15.7 trillion (in 1997 present value dollars). Subsequent cohorts will receive negative net subsidies; that is, they will pay transfers. If the system continues, those currently living and retired will pay $3.1 trillion in net transfers, those currently working will pay another $4.4 trillion in net transfers, and those yet to be born will pay $8.2 trillion in net transfers.

The next step is to determine how much of that total transfer has already been made and how much is yet to be collected. For those already dead or not yet working, the answers are obvious. But for those who are currently working or retired, we need to use a combination of Tables 1 and 2a. The third column of Table 3 gives the present value of past cash flows and the fourth column gives the present value of future benefits already accrued (both from Table 2a).[17] The sum of these two is the net subsidy (positive entries) or net transfer (negative entries) based on contributions already made. The fifth column is calculated based on the difference between Tables 1 and 2a, and is equal to the net subsidy to be received based on future cash flows. In this stylized model, current workers have already paid $3.5 trillion more than they have accrued (= −9.5 + 6.0), leaving only a $0.9 trillion net transfer to be paid based on future contributions.

Reform Options in the Stylized Economy

We turn next to a brief evaluation of reform options in this stylized economy. To do so it is useful to clarify three often-confused terms: privatization, prefunding, and diversification of social security.[18] By privatization, we mean replacing the current social security system with a defined contribution system of individual accounts held in workers' names. By prefunding, we mean reducing the system's unfunded liability, whether explicit or implicit. And by diversification, we mean investing social security funds in a variety of private capital market assets, via either individual accounts or the social security trust fund. These concepts are distinct. It is possible for a reform plan to implement any one or two without the other(s). In what follows we focus on reforms with prefunding and privatization; in subsequent sections we take up the diversification issue in detail.

Privatizing social security without prefunding does not improve welfare in the stylized economy. Consider what would happen in this stylized economy if the social security system were privatized so that all new contributions were channeled into individual accounts.[19] Suppose that all past contributions were ignored and no benefits accrued under the current system were paid. In this case, all future social security taxes would earn the market return of 2.3 percent, almost double the 1.2 percent under the current system. But then the entire $15.7 trillion cost of subsidizing cohorts born prior to 1917 would, in effect, be carried by the current middle-aged and old who would then have paid into the system for years without being entitled to any benefits. Column 3 of Table 3 shows that current retirees would lose $6.2 trillion and current workers would lose $9.5 trillion.

Alternatively, one could shut down the old system and privatize but continue to pay all benefits accrued to date, based on past contributions. Recognition bonds could be issued to workers and retirees for the full amount of their accrued benefits. The $15.7 trillion burden carried by current workers and retirees would then be reduced to $6.6 trillion ($= 15.7 - (3.1 + 6.0)$); the recognition bonds would equal the system's current unfunded liability of $9.1 trillion. If the government did not default on these bonds, new taxes would have to be raised to pay interest on the recognition bonds. One way to do so would be to set the new taxes to keep the path over time of recognition bond debt the same as the path of implicit debt under the current system.[20] In this event, these new taxes would correspond exactly to the transfers described in the last section. In other words, it can be shown that the new taxes raised would eliminate *all* the higher returns on individual accounts. Current workers and retirees would themselves face extra taxes, which would raise their net loss back to the $7.5 trillion ($= 3.1 + 4.4$) it was scheduled to be under the current system. Let us see why.

As pointed out earlier, the implicit tax paid in each year through the continuing social security system is $(r - g) \times$ (the unfunded liability at the end of the previous year). If suddenly, at the end of 1997, social security were privatized and recognition bonds were issued, their market value would have to equal the unfunded liability of $9.1 trillion (or to $9.9 trillion if accrued benefits are calculated according to the constant PVB/PVT method). The government would then have a choice whether to pay off the recognition bond coupon payments in their entirety as they came due or to roll over some of the debt. Suppose the government decided to keep the recognition bond debt growing at the same rate g as the economy. Then taxes in 1998 would have to be raised in the amount $(r - g) \times$ (unfunded liability of 1997). The extra taxes needed to finance the payments on the recognition bonds would thus be identical to the transfers made in the old social security system. This is true, not just for 1998 but, by the same logic for every year thereafter. By choosing the tax rates appropriately, the tax burden could be made to fall exactly on the same people who were contributing more to social security than they were receiving in benefits.[21] Aside from the transfers, participants in the current pay-as-you-go social security system are in effect earning the bond rate of return on their money. In a privatized system in which households invested their forced saving in bonds, they would have to pay in new taxes exactly what they paid before in transfers.

To emphasize this point, Table 4 presents a simplified two-period version of the stylized economy. For each cohort, all the work years are summarized into one period (period 1) and all the retirement years into another (period 2). Under the pay-as-you-go system, all period 1 contributions by the young (T_1) are used to fund benefits to the old (also $= T_1$). From the vantage point of period 0, the present value of these benefits, equal here to the unfunded liabilities, is $T_1/(1+r)$. Since aggregate wages grow at rate g,

TABLE 4. Rates of Return with Privatization but no Prefunding in a Two-Period Model

time →	0	1	2	3
Current style PAYGO system				
payments by young	$T_1/(1+g)$	T_1	$T_1(1+g)$	$T_1(1+g)^2$
receipts by old	$T_1/(1+g)$	T_1	$T_1(1+g)$	$T_1(1+g)^2$
rate of return		g	g	g
unfunded liability[a]	$T_1/(1+r)$	$T_1(1+g)/(1+r)$	$T_1(1+g)^2/(1+r)$	$T_1(1+g)^3/(1+r)$
Privatized system with no prefunding (that begins in period 1)				
outstanding "recognition bond" debt	$T_1/(1+r)$	$T_1(1+g)/(1+r)$	$T_1(1+g)^2/(1+r)$	$T_1(1+g)^3/(1+r)$
payments by young (= deposits to accts ignoring tax)		T_1	$T_1(1+g)$	$T_1(1+g)^2$
receipts by old (ignoring tax)		T_1	$T_1(1+r)$	$T_1(1+g)(1+r)$
rate of return (ignoring transition tax)		r	r	r
payments by young		T_1	$T_1(1+g)$	$T_1(1+g)^2$
new taxes on young to finance debt payments		$(r-g)T_1/(1+r)$	$(r-g)T_1(1+g)/(1+r)$	$(r-g)T_1(1+g)^2/(1+r)$
net deposits to individual accounts (after new taxes)		$T_1(1+g)/(1+r)$	$T_1(1+g)^2/(1+r)$	$T_1(1+g)^3/(1+r)$
receipts by old		T_1	$T_1(1+g)$	$T_1(1+g)^2$
rate of return (including transition tax)		g	g	g

Notes:

[a] Unfunded liability after taxes received and benefits paid for the period.

g = growth rate of wage base = rate of return on social security under current PAYGO system.

r = real riskless rate of return = rate of return on privatized system ignoring transition costs $> g$

Privatization occurs by issuing recognition bonds to pay for accrued benefits (rolling over enough interest and principal to keep the debt/GDP ratio constant), and channeling all new contributions into individual accounts.

the young in period 2 will contribute $T_1(1+g)$, the same amount that will be paid out to the old. The rate of return that young households will receive on their period 1 social security payments is $[T_1(1+g)/T_1] - 1 = g$.

What would be the effect of privatizing the social security system just after time 0? This could be accomplished by leaving social security tax rates undisturbed but, from time $t = 1$ onward, putting all future social security contributions into individual accounts invested in bonds instead of transferring them to the old. The generation that is young in period 1, and every succeeding generation, would then receive when old the returns from the riskless asset. To make payments to the period 1 old, "recognition bonds" would need to be issued to fully cover the present value of the social security benefits they would have received under PAYGO. If these bonds were issued in period 0, they would have to be of size $T_1/(1+r)$, namely the outstanding unfunded liabilities.[22]

If we ignore any additional taxes to pay interest on these recognition bonds, then all the contributions of the period 1 young are paid directly into individual accounts. In period 2, these households will receive a payout from their accounts of $T_1(1+r)$; that is, they will receive rate of return $r > g$ on their contributions. However this does not reflect their net proceeds, since the government must also collect *new transition taxes* to pay at least some of the interest on the new recognition bonds.

Each period $t > 0$, the government must either pay off the recognition bond debt by raising new transition taxes, or roll it over by borrowing again from the generation t young. Suppose the government were to collect only enough new transition taxes to keep the outstanding debt from the recognition bonds growing at the same rate as the economy (g), that is, keeping the debt/GDP ratio constant. Then at each date t the value of the outstanding recognition bonds would be exactly equal to the unfunded liability under the old pay-as-you-go system. New transition taxes (assumed for simplicity to be raised on the young) would initially (in period 1) have to equal $(r-g)$ $T_1/(1+r)$.[23] Therefore, *net* deposits into individual accounts (these taxes are paid) would equal $T_1 - (r-g) T_1/(1+r) = T_1(1+g)/(1+r)$. When they are old, they will get back this amount multiplied by $(1+r)$, which equals $T_1(1+g)$. Since they pay T_1 and receive back $T_1(1+g)$, the net rate of return to the old people, after taking account of the tax to finance the relevant interest payments on the recognition bonds, is exactly g! In other words, participants under the privatized system receive the identical rate of return as under the unfunded pay-as-you-go system. This is true not just in period 2 but in all subsequent periods as well. It is also true regardless how large the difference is between r and g.[24]

Notice also that the pattern of payments in a privatized system with the above debt path is identical to the pattern of payments in a pay-as-you-go system. Generation 1's investment in the riskless asset when young is tantamount to buying the recognition bonds when it is young via its privatized social security account. Generation 1 then cashes out (i.e., it sells the bonds) to generation 2 when it is old. As before, generation 1 gives up money when it is young and receives money when it is old (previously called social security benefits, and here called interest and principal on bonds). Thus in a dynamically efficient economy in which the market return is r, the return to the social security participant is $g < r$, because the transfer each generation makes to the start-up generation is on the order of $r - g$.

This point is a general one. When money's worth measures exclude the extra transition taxes needed to finance interest payments on the recognition bonds, they yield a misleading indicator of the value of switching to a privatized system. In this example, there is no change in any net cash flows to any households, yet the naive money's worth comparison would indicate a large gain moving from a pay-as-you-go system to a privatized system.[25]

Privatizing and prefunding social security. Suppose, alternatively, that taxes were raised disproportionately on current cohorts so that the outstanding value of recognition bond debt started out lower, and/or grew over time at a rate slower than g (possibly even decreasing over time). In this case, privatization would be accompanied by prefunding. This outcome is favored by many economists, who believe that social security prefunding would increase national saving.[26] Prefunding could also occur under the current system if taxes were raised or benefits cut and the proceeds deposited into a central trust fund. Many also believe that prefunding is more likely to occur if accompanied by some privatization, on the political argument that Congress is less likely to increase government spending or cut taxes outside social security if the accumulation of any increased social security surplus is done in private accounts rather than through a central trust fund (see, e.g., Feldstein 1998a).

How prefunding would change cohort-specific money's worth measures is of some interest. The higher prefunding diminishes the recognition bond debt facing later cohorts, and consequently prefunding reduces taxes needed to repay the interest on this smaller debt. For these later cohorts, then, returns earned on social security contributions net of recognition bond taxes are higher than anticipated under the current system. But for current workers, returns on a prefunded system net of the higher taxes are inevitably lower than under the current system. For this reason, it should be clear that the current debate should focus on whether this tradeoff is worth making, rather than whether there is a free lunch.[27]

Money's Worth Measures in Practice

We now turn to money's worth measures calculated for the actual economy, as opposed to the stylized system described above.[28] Money's worth measures figured prominently in the Social Security Advisory Council's recent report (1997), where the Council compared outcomes under benchmarks based on the current system with outcomes under three specific reform plans.[29]

Practical Issues in Measuring Money's Worth

In calculating money's worth estimates, a number of practical questions arise. In this section, we discuss the most important of these.

Should estimates be based on actual cohort data or hypothetical worker data? Two approaches to computing cohort measures of social security money's worth are prevalent in the literature. One technique is to use actual administrative data on all individuals (or on a sample of individuals) in a cohort, following them over their worklives and into retirement. This micro-based approach relies on longitudinal data, usually the Social Security Administration's Continuous Work History Sample (CWHS); among those taking this tack are Leimer (1994) and Duggan, Gillingham, and Greenlees (1993).

A second technique calculates tax and benefit profiles for hypothetical workers or households. This approach is much simpler since actual people do not have to be tracked over time, and for this reason it is the more prevalent approach in policy settings.[30] For example, the Office of the Actuary at the Social Security Administration (SSA) used the simulated worker approach in its money's worth analysis for the Advisory Council (1997).[31] It must be noted that the SSA hypothetical earnings profiles are not derived from *actual* cohort specific age-earnings profiles. Rather, the SSA "average" worker experiences earnings growth at the same rate as the growth in economy-wide average covered earnings. Of course, there is no theoretical reason for these to be the same. For example, economy-wide earnings growth could be zero, even though each individual cohort might enjoy 5 percent per annum (or for that matter any arbitrarily high) real wage growth over its lifetime due to experience-related productivity growth. Alternatively, economy-wide earnings growth could be 1.2 percent even if no individual experienced any real wage growth over his or her lifetime; this was assumed in the stylized example of the last section. Hence social security taxes paid and benefits received for the SSA "average" simulated earner will almost certainly misrepresent taxes and benefits of an actual cohort. Whether the bias is consistently positive or negative is a subject for future research.

Which taxes and benefits should be included? In computing money's worth measures, experts disagree about which social security payroll taxes should be included. For instance, some actuaries offer these computations using only taxes paid by employees (e.g., Myers and Schoebel 1992). By contrast, most economists contend that taxes paid by employers should also be included in the money's worth computation, because workers pay for employer-side social security taxes out of reduced wages (Gruber 1995). The estimates we present below include both the employee and the employer-side contributions, that is, the full 12.4 percent payroll tax currently dedicated to the program.

A related issue pertains to which social security benefits should be considered and to whom they should be attributed. Some previous studies examine only retirement benefits, which overlooks the important role of disability payments available through the social insurance system. Other studies have focused only on single worker benefits, which ignores the important spouse and survivor benefits payable if an insured worker with dependents dies. The Office of the Actuary appropriately, in our view, counts the entire relevant set of benefits including retiree, spouse, survivor, and disability insurance payments in its money's worth calculations.[32] If spouse and survivor benefits are included, there is the added question of *which* birth cohort these should be attributed to — the male or female member of the married couple, or the children. The Office of the Actuary makes the simplifying assumption that the husband and wife are of the same age, and attributes children's benefits to the workers' cohort.[33] By contrast, Leimer (1994) assumes that benefits paid to a surviving spouse or dependent child, for example, accrue to that spouse's or child's birth cohort, rather than the cohort of the working member(s) of the household.

Should historical social security taxes and benefits be computed ex-ante or ex-post? When comparing social security benefit and tax streams, the question arises as to whether money's worth computations should be undertaken on an ex-ante or ex-post basis. In other words, should *actual* histories be used for taxes, benefits, and opportunity costs of funds, or should *expected values* be employed? If expected values are used, as of what date or on what information set should the measures be conditioned?

In practice, most estimates use realized (or ex-post) macroeconomic data on earnings, real interest rates, and tax and benefit rules.[34] They also use realized values of cohort earnings (for actual cohort estimates) or economy-wide earnings (for hypothetical worker estimates). Actual mortality patterns are also used to determine the size of the taxpaying population through time, by cohort.[35]

How should future taxes and benefits be forecasted? To analyze the money's worth of social security for generations that are still living, future taxes and benefits by cohort need to be forecasted. These forecasts, and therefore the resulting money's worth estimates, are highly dependent on underlying estimates of future economic and demographic factors, along with forecasted paths for future social security benefit and tax rules. In each case, of course, there is ample room for professional disagreement. Demographers disagree about what is the best forecast of future fertility, immigration patterns, and mortality. Economists disagree about the best forecast of real wage growth, labor force participation, retirement patterns, disability rates, and unemployment, as well as the magnitude of behavioral effects. Yet others argue about future evasion rates. There is also controversy about whether the economic and demographic forecasts are internally consistent; a discussion of the assumptions used to make social security forecasts is provided by the Technical Panel on Assumptions and Methods (1997).[36]

Money's worth calculations are inevitably a mix of historical and fore-casted data. Measures for cohorts retiring when the system was new, in the 1940s and 1950s, reflect mainly ex-post data for taxes, benefits, discount rates, and mortality. More recent system entrants are not yet fully retired, and few have died as yet. As a result, the more recent is the birth cohort, the less important are historical data and the more important are ex-ante fore-casts for money's worth estimates.

What discount rate should be used? Two of the three money's worth mea-sures, NPV and PVB/PVT, require the selection of a rate to discount cash flows. In practice, the SSA discounts past real benefit and tax flows using a rate equal to the realized historical real yield on trust fund assets. To dis-count future flows, the agency uses the intermediate assumptions for the real rate on U.S. Treasury Special Public Debt Obligations.[37] No adjustment is made to the discount rate to take into account the riskiness of the cash flows, an important issue that we return to below.[38]

Finally, to compare net present values across cohorts, the dollar tax and benefit amounts must be expressed in common units.[39] Leimer (1994) uses interest rates to convert into a common year's dollars. By contrast, the Office of the Actuary expresses all dollar figures in constant wage units, by calculat-ing present values as of age 22 and converting these to a common year's dollars using the actual past and the expected future nominal wage index.

Policy Analysts' Money's Worth Estimates

In this section, we present money's worth estimates based on "real world" data on the U.S. system, and compare these with estimates from the stylized model contained in Table 1. We present estimates of money's worth mea-sures under current law and various reform proposals.

Present law and reforms that leave intact the basic structure of social security. We begin with estimates based on historical data and current U.S. law; this benchmark is commonly termed the "Present Law" (PL) case. We hasten to add, however, that the system is in actuarial imbalance: that is, the present value of expected future benefits exceeds the trust funds plus the present value of expected future contributions.[40] For this reason, present law is not a particularly useful benchmark. We therefore also examine two reforms that keep the basic structure of social security the same, but either raise taxes or cut benefits to eliminate the 75-year actuarial imbalance. The "Holdtax" reform maintains current tax rates constant and cuts benefits sufficiently to make the payouts consistent with the revenue raised. The "Holdben" re-form keeps benefit formulas constant, but assumes taxes are increased as needed to finance these benefits.[41]

An excellent study of cohort money's worth using administrative data is that of Leimer (1994), which uses administrative data through 1988 and the 1991 Trustees Report assumptions.[42] Figure 2 presents estimates of IRRs by

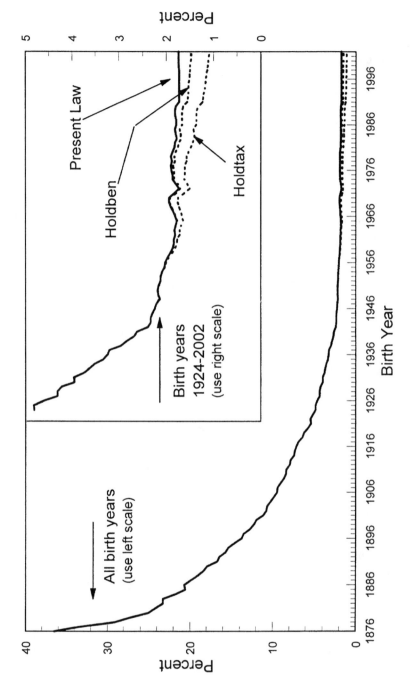

Figure 2. Estimated real internal rates of return on social security contributions. Source: Derived from Leimer (1994).

cohort from this study. Consistent with popular discussion of social security, Leimer's results indicate that early cohorts received very high IRRs—real returns per annum of almost 40 percent. Later birth cohorts fare worse, with IRR figures predicted to remain below 2 percent in real terms into the foreseeable future.

Comparable estimates produced by the Office of the Actuary are shown in Figure 3, based on the hypothetical worker approach described above. We present a "composite worker" estimate equal to a weighted average of a range of worker types (e.g., varying by sex, marital status, age-earnings profile).[43] Under the present law simulation, the internal rate of return will fall from 5 percent for the 1920 cohort to 2.5 percent for workers born in the 1960s; thereafter it remains around 2.5 percent. Under the Holdben approach, returns are roughly similar for cohorts until 1970; thereafter tax increases required to maintain benefit promises drive down the IRR to below 2 percent. Under the Holdtax profile, returns fall below 2 percent sooner, for the group born in the late 1950s. In other words, under either solvency scenario, members of the baby boom generation will be the first generation in the history of social security to receive rates of return on their taxes significantly below the market rate of return. This result is what gives rise to comments such as those quoted as the outset of this chapter.

In Table 5 we compare the IRR paths derived using Leimer's "actual" data with those using the SSA "composite worker" data. It is interesting to note that the IRR estimates tell substantially the same story regarding trend over time: IRRs are projected to be much lower for future cohorts than for past workers.[44] Nevertheless, there are important differences between the two projections, in that the returns projected by the Office of the Actuary exceed Leimer's for the baby boom generations forward; and the magnitude of the difference is substantial, on the order of 20 to 30 percent. The differences are probably due to the fact that Leimer's estimates are based on 1991 rather than on 1997 figures and use actual rather than hypothetical worker data.

We next present NPV estimates for the benchmark case. Figure 4 illustrates the results using (our modification of) Leimer's estimates, where we focus only on the Holdben scenario. The first series in the figure (left scale) presents the NPV of social security for each birth cohort converted from 1989 to 1997 dollars using the appropriate interest factors. (Comparable numbers based on our stylized model appear in the third column of Table 1.) The figure clearly demonstrates that the social security system has redistributed wealth substantially toward earlier birth cohorts. This is consistent with the stylized model, which showed that in the start-up phase of an unfunded defined benefit pension plan the initial elderly receive retirement benefits above what they paid into the system. More surprising to many will be the size and persistence of the wealth transfers under social security over time. That is, based on these computations, it appears that the

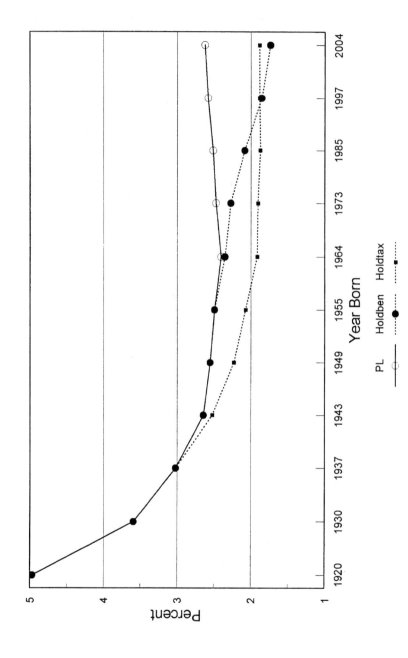

Figure 3. Social security IRR, Benchmarks: Present Law, Holdben, Holdtax for composite worker. Source: Unpublished data supplied by the SSA Office of the Actuary.

TABLE 5. Internal Rates of Return (IRR) Estimates Using Alternative Methods

Birth Year	IRR Leimer (1994) Holdben Type Plan	IRR Advisory Council (1997) Holdben Type Plan	Percentage Difference
1920	5.68	4.97	−13
1930	3.95	3.59	−9
1937	3.20	3.02	−6
1943	2.33	2.64	13
1949	2.17	2.55	18
1955	2.04	2.49	22
1964	1.80	2.35	31
1973	1.76	2.27	29
1985	1.72	2.08	21
1997	1.51	1.85	23
2004	1.45	1.73	19

Sources: Col. 2 from Leimer (1994); Col. 3 = Composite worker estimate derived by authors from data provided by the SSA Office of the Actuary; Col. 4 = (Col 3 − Col 2)/Col 2.

U.S. social security system continued to deliver positive and substantial net benefits well after the first generation of retirees aged out of the program. Indeed, the evidence shows that the social security subsidy was granted to more than 50 birth cohorts, with NPVs turning negative only for cohorts born after 1937.

The second series (right scale) in Figure 4 represents the cumulative sum of the first series, that is, the sum across all birth cohorts prior to the indicated year of the NPVs. This corresponds to column 4 in our stylized example. This cumulative net transfer reaches its maximum in 1937 at approximately $9.7 trillion in present value ($1997). It is of interest to note that this $9.7 trillion figure is in the same ballpark as the cumulative net present value of $12 trillion for 1937 generated in our stylized example in Table 1. By 1977 Leimer's accumulated NPV fell to $7.2 trillion, while our stylized number fell to $8.2 trillion. In general, we should expect Leimer's numbers to be a bit smaller than ours, because the economy actually grew faster than 1.2 percent between 1938 and 1997. This is partly offset by the fact that generations born between 1908 and 1937 in fact continued to receive subsidies from social security, whereas in our stylized example, they did not.

These results are combined with other estimates of social security unfunded liabilities from Goss (this volume) in Table 6 to approximate the net transfers already paid and to be paid by different sets of cohorts, in a way directly comparable to Table 3. Here we see that the system's cumulative net subsidy to date, counting all those living and working today, stands at about $7.2 trillion (last column, third row). This figure is in the same range as our stylized model's $8.2 trillion valuation. Future benefits already accrued

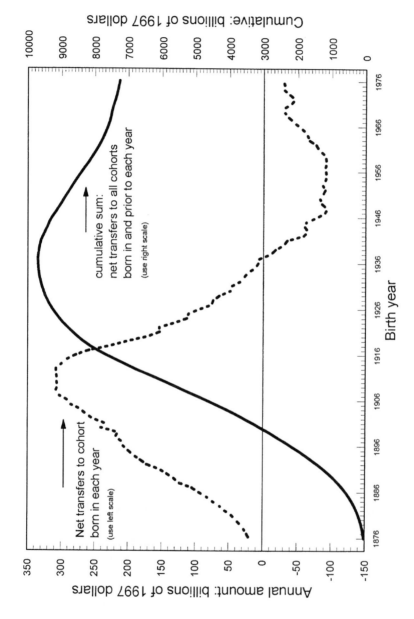

Figure 4. Social security net intercohort transfers. Source: Leimer (1994) tax increase balanced budget scenario and authors' calculations. All figures are present values as of 1997.

TABLE 6. Social Security Present Values by Birth Year: U.S. System

Birth Year	Age in 1997	PV of Past Benefits Received Less PV of Past Contributions Made	PV of Future Benefits Already Accrued Based on Past Contributions	PV of Future Benefits to be Accrued less Future Contributions to be Made	Row Total	Cumulative Total
1859–1917	80+ (dead)	7.9[e]	[0][d]	0	7.9[a]	7.9
1918–1937	60–79 (living and retired)	−8.5[e]	9.5	[0][d]	1.8[a]	9.7
1938–1977	20–59 (living and working)			−1.7[e]	−2.5[a]	7.2
1978+	≤19 (not yet working or not yet born)	0	0	−7.2	−7.2[e]	0
	Total	−0.6[c]	9.5[b,c]	−8.9[e]	0	

Notes: [a] Derived from Leimer (1994)
[b] Derived from Goss (1998)
[c] Derived from Trustees Report (1998) (accumulated trust fund)
[d] Derived from authors' assumptions
[e] Derived from the above and economic theory

based on past contributions are \$9.5 trillion. If we subtract the current value of the trust fund of about \$0.6 trillion, we arrive at the estimate of the unfunded liability of \$8.9 trillion, close to what we found in our stylized model. This can be divided into two pieces. The transfer still to be paid by current workers (based on future contributions and the corresponding benefit to be accrued) is about \$1.7 trillion, while the burden "owed" by future cohorts not yet working or not yet born is on the order of \$7.2 trillion.

Next we illustrate the other money's worth estimates, under the alternative benchmark scenarios. Advisory Council estimates of the path of the net subsidy are given in Figure 5, and the PVB/PVT ratio in Figure 6. The patterns depicted indicate that both the net subsidy and the benefit to tax ratio would be projected to rise given present law (PL) but these paths are not feasible since the current system is unsustainable. More realistic projections under the Holdben and Holdtax scenarios indicate that the net subsidy would remain substantially negative, and the benefit-to-tax ratio would remain well below 100 percent, into the foreseeable future. There are also interesting distributional differences across the benchmark scenarios: thus the negative net subsidy is more similar across cohorts under the Holdtax plan, while as-yet-unborn cohorts pay more over their lifetimes in the Holdben approach.

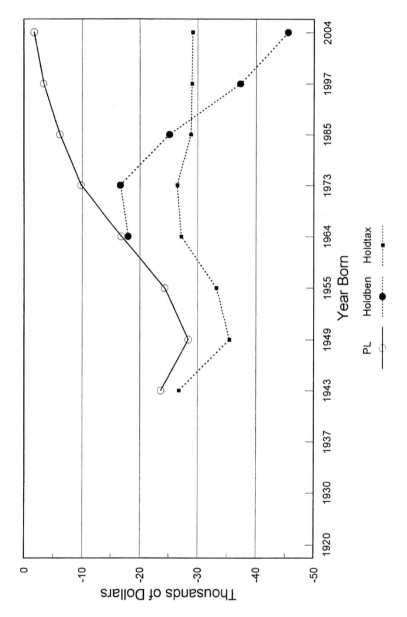

Figure 5. Social net subsidy, Benchmarks: Present Law, Holdben, Holdtax for composite worker. Source: Unpublished data supplied by the SSA Office of the Actuary.

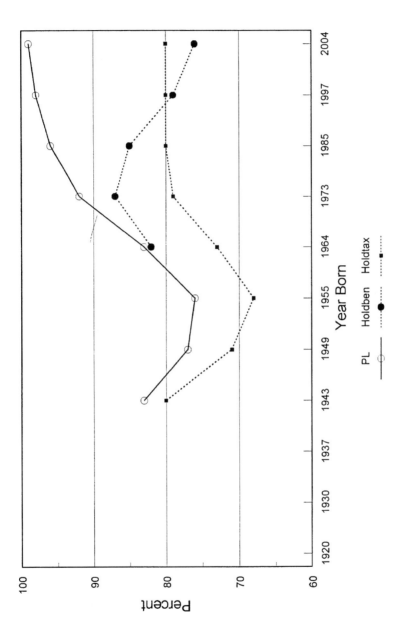

Figure 6. Social security PVB/PVT, Benchmarks: Present Law, Holdben, Holdtax for composite worker. Source: Unpublished data supplied by the SSA Office of the Actuary.

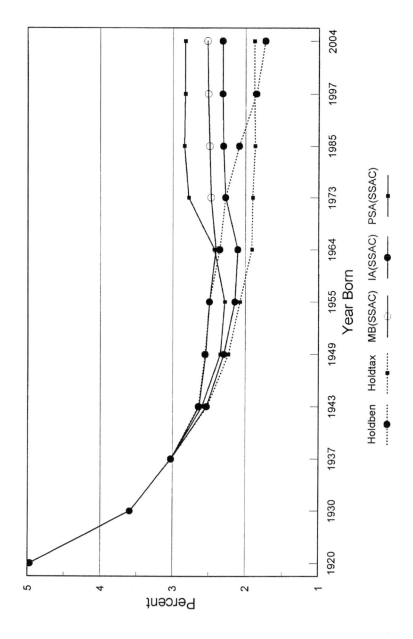

Figure 7. Social security IRR: SSAC proposals, composite worker. Source: Unpublished data supplied by the SSA Office of the Actuary.

Money's worth estimates for more fundamental reform options. Next, we compare the money's worth statistics for the three Advisory Council plans described in Chapter 1 of this volume, along with the Holdben and Holdtax benchmarks. In this case, we present the Advisory Council estimates for the "Maintain Benefits" (MB) approach, which attempts to keep benefit promises more or less fixed by raising tax revenue to finance them; the "Individual Account" (IA) approach, which pares down government-paid benefits somewhat and creates a small individually-owned government-managed defined contribution account; and the "Personal Security Account" (PSA) plan, which would cut benefits to a relatively low uniform per-worker payment, supplementing this with a privately-managed defined contribution plan like that of a 401(k) pension.[45]

The IRR profiles associated with these options appear in Figure 7, where both Holdben and Holdtax profiles end up with IRRs under 2 percent in the long run. The Advisory Council reform plans all have projected IRRs greater than Holdtax IRRs for all cohorts depicted, and they exceed Holdben IRRs for birth cohorts after 1973. Comparing the three reform proposals, the PSA plan's return is projected to be highest, followed by MB plan returns, and then IA plan returns for birth groups after about 1960.[46]

Net social security subsidy patterns appear in Figure 8, where once again the PSA plan dominates the others for cohorts born after the mid-1960s. Figure 9 provides the money's worth ratio (PVB/PVT) patterns by reform plan. The benefit-to-tax ratio for the PSA plan dominates those of the other two reform plans for virtually all birth cohorts, and rises above 100 percent for cohorts after about 1970. Thus it is understandable how one could conclude that each of these three plans—and probably the PSA plan in particular—would be preferable for most cohorts relative to Holdben or Holdtax. Below we show that this conclusion is not generally warranted.

Conceptual Framework for Evaluating Money's Worth Measures: When Is a Single Statistic Sufficient?

Having seen how social security money's worth is computed in practice, we turn next to describing the conditions under which a single statistic accurately reflects the costs and benefits of different social security programs. Not surprisingly, the main difficulty is that the future cannot be perfectly predicted. One approach, favored by the Advisory Council (1997), is to replace the vast multiplicity of possible future worlds with a single average scenario in which all cash flows are discounted at the riskless rate of interest. The trouble with this approach is that households might strongly prefer the average outcome for sure rather than the distribution of possible outcomes; that is, people might be willing to pay much more for the certain plan than for the uncertain plan, yet the Advisory Council approach would assign both plans the same money's worth. Money's worth measures that ignore the

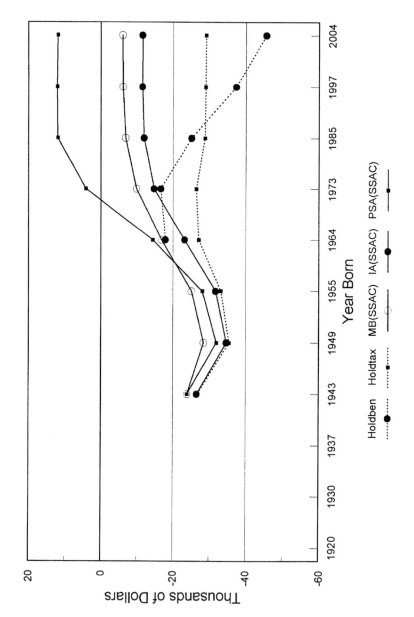

Figure 8. Social security net subsidy, SSAC proposals, composite worker. Source: Unpublished data supplied by the SSA Office of the Actuary.

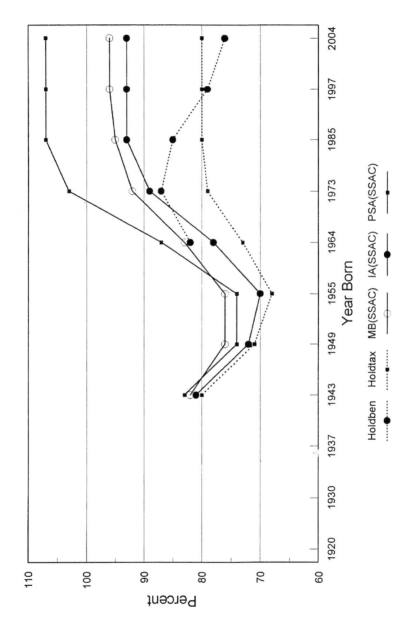

Figure 9. Social security PVB/PVT, SSAC proposals, composite worker. Source: Unpublished data supplied by the SSA Office of the Actuary.

disutility of risk are then biased in favor of uncertain plans that offer high average outcomes.

The underlying point is that money's worth measures should reflect choice and welfare. That is, it would be undesirable to assign a higher money's worth to one plan over a second, when we knew the first plan would reduce the welfare of all participants as compared to the second. In the most general situation, then, accurate money's worth numbers require a detailed knowledge of all households' preferences, including their attitudes toward risk. Since these preferences are not generally known, it might seem hopeless to derive a useful set of summary statistics that can be used for comparing different social security systems.

There is, however, a set of special conditions under which precise money's worth numbers *can* be obtained without knowledge of individual preferences. This scenario serves as our benchmark case in the analysis below. We show that under such conditions, the type of money's worth measures offered by groups such as the Advisory Council are biased whenever there is any genuine uncertainty about outcomes, and the bias is usually in favor of privatization. In actuality, of course, none of these special conditions is satisfied precisely, so we then consider how one might adjust money's worth estimates to account for deviations from the theoretical case. This adjustment moves some components of the theoretically sound money's worth calculations in the direction of the Advisory Council numbers, but other components move in the opposite direction. In any case, a substantial bias in the non-risk adjusted approach remains.

Simple Money's Worth Measures Require Four Conditions

Four conditions must hold for the risk-adjusted net present value money's worth measure to correctly compare the welfare effects of different social security regimes. These four conditions pertain to optimization, intergenerational tradeoffs, price stability, and spanning. If all are satisfied, and all relevant cash flows are included, then the net present value measure extended to the uncertainty case (via the risk-adjusted probabilities or risk-adjusted discount rates) accurately summarizes the costs and benefits of different social security regimes. The four conditions together are sufficient (as well as necessary) to insure that a higher NPV guarantees higher welfare, no matter what the form of the household utility functions.[47] When one or more of these conditions fails, an accurate money's worth calculation requires specific knowledge of individual preference orderings. In this case, we say that a utility-independent money's worth does not exist, or for short, that simple money's worth measures are not valid.

Inconsistent optimization and forced savings. The first condition that must hold for money's worth measures to be valid is that households must be

consistent optimizers. In other words, people must understand the investment opportunities available to them, which in turn should be defined by
market prices and taxes, and they must be "foresightful". For example, if
consumers immediately spent every dollar of income they received, then
the timing of taxes and benefits would be crucial to welfare, and no single
number could possibly summarize a lifetime stream of taxes and benefits
(without explicit knowledge of peoples' utility functions).

Experts long have argued that a primary rationale for social security (and
the reason the current system has survived so long) is that many households
left to their own devices would undersave and then, when old, either live in
poverty or throw themselves on the mercy of the rest of society.[48] Thus the
raison d'être of social security contradicts the first necessary condition for
the validity of money's worth. By taxing individuals when they are young and
employed, and paying them when they are old and retired, social security in
effect is a forced savings plan (assuming that workers cannot undo everything by borrowing when young against their future social security income).
But standard money's worth measures miss completely the benefits of this
forced saving aspect of social security. Indeed, if the rate of return on the
social security taxes were equal to the riskless real interest rate, then none of
the money's worth measures would discern any difference between social
security plans of different sizes; no social security at all would rank on a par
with the social security system currently in place.[49]

As it happens, most reform plans, including all those proposed by the
Advisory Council, maintain approximately the same amount of forced saving — that is, they differ more over what is to be done with the taxes than in
how high they should be. The next three conditions, therefore, are likely to
have a larger impact on the accuracy of money's worth measures in the
present context.

Intergenerational and intragenerational tradeoffs. The second necessary condition for money's worth to be accurate when comparing different social
security regimes is that the relative ranking of the plans should not differ
across households. For example, one social security program might be less
generous to the current old, but more generous to future generations. In
this event, money's worth numbers would be informative because they
would reveal the intergenerational tradeoffs, but they would not in themselves suggest which was the better plan across all households.

Similarly, a key motive for the current social security program is intragenerational redistribution — transferring consumption from wealthier
members of a cohort to less well-off ones. Comparing the current program
to say a privatized system that has less redistribution would give money's
worth rankings that differ across types of individuals. In general, there are
likely to be benefits and costs to society from redistributive policies that are
not captured by money's worth measures (Myers 1996).[50]

Stable prices (and stable shadow prices). A third necessary condition that must be satisfied in order for money's worth numbers to reflect welfare unambiguously is that prices should not change across regimes. Below we discuss the importance of modeling the general equilibrium impact of a massive social security structural change. Here we simply point out that, if a new social security regime were to change real interest rates, then discounting the cash flows at the old interest rates would give a biased assessment of household opportunities. If changes in social security taxes change the shadow price on leisure, then measuring money's worth with the old after-tax wages would also give a distorted picture. We also note that changes in the social security tax rates or benefit rules may change relative incomes, and since households are heterogeneous, this in turn may change demand for various goods and assets, which in turn might change many prices. Once prices change across regimes, it is impossible to rigorously rank alternative regimes by a one-dimensional statistic like money's worth.

Spanning. The fourth necessary condition for the validity of money's worth calculations is that households must be able to duplicate all social security income streams (including benefits and taxes) using cash flows of securities that can be marketed and traded by all households. This condition is usually called "spanning." When spanning obtains, it is appropriate to represent each income stream with its market value, that is, by the price of the marketed security (or combination of securities) giving the identical cash flow. The reason, of course, is that a household decision-maker who had the money instead of the income stream could purchase the same cash flow; conversely, with the income stream, he or she could sell the cash flow and get the money. A gift of either the income stream or its market price would, in the end, yield the person the same utility assuming that he or she optimized the rest of the portfolio after receiving the gift. When such an income stream is small, its market price is the correct measure of its money's worth, even if the person does not reoptimize after receiving the stream. The reason is that by optimizing his portfolio before being given the income stream, the consumer will have chosen to hold enough similar income streams so that the marginal utility of the new income stream is equal to the marginal utility of its market price.

In a world with no uncertainty, with households that are foward-looking and that can borrow and lend at some common riskless rate of interest, all income streams are in effect marketed. But in a world with uncertain payoffs and incomplete markets, there may be no market price to attach to a future stream of contingent cash flows. Also many households may not have access to all capital markets, even if they exist. In this event, and in the absence of detailed knowledge of individual utility preferences, no money's worth statistic can accurately summarize the welfare benefit of the social security income streams. Below we offer ways to guess what the money's worth of social security might be when spanning fails, provided that households have special kinds of preferences.

Let us next consider the situation where a payment stream is marketed but we cannot directly observe its market price. This frequently occurs when an income stream is a complicated linear combination of marketed streams, but is not directly marketed itself. (This situation also arises when we try to forecast the future. We know, for example, that in five years stocks and bonds will both be marketed, but we do not now know what those market prices will be.) One can ascertain what the market price would have to be by applying the principle of "no arbitrage": that is, if one stream of payments is a linear combination of other streams, then its price must be the same linear combination of the other market prices. To implement this scheme we would have to find the right linear combination of marketed securities to reproduce the cash flow of the stream in question, an exercise that is often quite time-consuming. The so-called arbitrage pricing theorem assures us that there is always a direct way, which we now describe, of computing the market price without explicitly finding the spanning securities.

When a marketed income stream is perfectly predictable (it can fluctuate over time, but in a way that leaves no room for surprises), then its market price can be obtained by discounting each of its cash flows by the riskless rate of interest for the corresponding maturity. When the cash flow is stochastic but still marketed, the market price can still be recovered, but only through a much more complicated calculation that takes into account the extra risk. This is a multi-step process: one must forecast first the collection of possible cash flow paths, and the probability of each; one must also forecast the collection of possible short interest rate paths, and the probability of each. Additionally one must estimate the joint probabilities of interest rate paths and cash flow paths. (The security will be worth less if its high cash flows only occur on paths that also exhibit high interest rates.) Finally, one must also forecast the joint probabilities of the interest rate cash flow paths and economy-wide aggregate consumption. (Cash flows that are high only along paths in which the economy as a whole is rich, effectively pay only when people do not need the money, and they should therefore be worth less.) In the end, money's worth values will depend on the expected cash flows discounted at the riskless rate, and (negatively) on some measure of the covariance of the cash flows with a benchmark measure of aggregate consumption.[51]

This complicated series of estimates and calculations is sometimes referred to as "discounting the expected cash flows at the *risk-adjusted* interest rate," or the "risk-adjusted net present value." The final result is likely to be quite different from discounting expected cash flows at the *riskless* rate of interest. In practice, the full-bodied calculation is very difficult to do correctly, although Wall Street research has applied this methodology to specific security cash flows. The non-risk-adjusted approach, namely discounting expected cash flows using the riskless interest rate, is only appropriate if the cash flows are independent of both interest rates and aggregate consumption. This point is frequently overlooked when policymakers value social security cash flows.

Money's Worth with Optimization, Generational Homogeneity, Stable Prices, and Spanning

Under the maintained hypotheses of optimization, generational homogeneity, stable prices, and spanning, the correct money's worth measure of any social security plan for any individual is the risk-adjusted net present value, calculated as the market value of his or her stream of benefits minus the market value of the stream of contributions. More precisely, suppose the market value of benefits less taxes is higher for every generation under one social security system than it is under a different social security system. Then (assuming optimization, stable prices, and spanning), the welfare of every generation must be higher in the first system than in the second, no matter what the preferences of the households regarding consumption, impatience, or attitudes toward risk. The proof of this assertion is immediate. Since prices are the same across the two plans (stable prices), and since individuals properly exploit their opportunities (optimization), and since the first plan offers each individual more opportunities than the second plan (spanning plus higher market values), the comparison does not depend on preferences.

Though the assertion is straightforward, its implications are often missed. We shall apply our analysis to the current reform debate below, but here we list three implications. Subsequently we explore the meaning of money's worth if the spanning and stable prices hypotheses fail.

Stock market money's worth. The stock market is a marketed collection of assets, just as are bond markets. One approach to social security reform involves replacing the trust fund's bond holdings with stock holdings; other reforms involve privatization, where individuals are permitted to invest directly in the capital market. It is tempting to presume that the substitution of stocks for bonds would dramatically improve the money's worth of social security, since the stock market has historically earned a much higher rate of return than government bonds. We have just seen, however, that, under the assumptions stated above, marketed income streams such as stock market returns should be assigned a money's worth equal to their market prices. A dollar's worth of stocks can be worth no more than a dollar's worth of bonds, and so a switch between bonds and stocks should not alter money's worth, correctly calculated.

This conclusion might seem odd, given that the arithmetic average annual real total return from 1926 to 1996 was 9.4 percent on the S&P 500 stock index, while it was only 2.3 percent on intermediate term government bonds (Ibbotson and Associates 1997). But to understand the conclusion it is necessary to ask what drove the historical pattern of returns and whether it is reasonable to expect the past to characterize the distribution of future returns.[52] Three possible explanations of the past returns immediately come to mind, two of which suggest the future might well be like the past. None of these explanations contradicts the view that a dollar of stocks should have the same money's worth as a dollar of bonds.

One explanation is that stocks are riskier than bonds; that is, stocks historically have a much higher standard deviation of return than bonds. And more important, stock market returns are correlated with aggregate consumption — the stock market pays off most just when people are the wealthiest and need the money the least. The higher expected returns are necessary to compensate investors for the higher risk, as we have seen in the past and may continue to see in the future.

Some have argued, however, that the higher risk is not sufficient to explain the high historical returns — this is the so-called "equity premium puzzle" (Mehra and Prescott 1985). Others have argued that over a sufficiently long time horizon stocks are actually less risky than Treasury bonds or bills. For example, there are no 22-year periods since 1926 in the U.S. in which stocks did not outperform bonds.[53] This suggests another explanation for the high return on equities: many people may be irrationally afraid of holding stocks. Yet another possibility is that the performance of the U.S. stock market has been uniquely favorable; that is, the U.S. received a particularly good realization of history that we should not expect to be repeated. Using data gathered from all stock markets in existence around the world since 1900, Brown, Goetzmann, and Ross (1995) show that stocks on average just barely outperformed bonds.

Our conclusion that a dollar of stock and a dollar of bonds should have the same money's worth holds regardless of the explanation, provided our four assumptions are maintained. For example, if households are irrationally afraid of holding stocks, it might seem to follow that the social security system should not fall prey to these irrational fears, and therefore it ought to encourage or force additional investment in the stock market. But under the assumptions of optimization and spanning this will not help. That is, households who are irrationally afraid of stocks will probably avoid equities if offered choice in individual accounts, for the same reason they hold too few stocks in the remainder of their portfolios. If they were in turn mandated to hold some nonzero amount of equities, they will be aware that their social security money is now subject to stock market risk, and they will compensate by holding fewer stocks in their own portfolios (or even by selling stocks short).[54] In other words, the same anxiety that causes an investor to value a dollar of stocks equal to a dollar of bonds ought also to be recognized by the social security participant if part of social security is invested in equity.

What about a future move into stocks? In order to calculate the money's worth for future generations of holding stock in social security, we require — but of course do not know — future stock prices. Therefore it is understandable that analysts seek to forecast stock payoffs and then back out the money's worth of holding stock in the future. But a rigorous application of money's worth would still have to assign a future dollar's worth of stocks the same value as a future dollar of bonds.

Risky benefits and contributions. Since current benefits under our pay-as-you-go system actually depend on the gross domestic product (GDP), that in turn is correlated with the stock market, similar reasoning suggests that we should regard current social security benefits as risky and discount them at a higher risk-adjusted rate. Tax revenues, too, depend on GDP and are probably correlated positively with stock returns, so we should regard these cash flows as risky under the current social security program and discount them using a risk-adjusted rate as well. It is likely that the appropriate rates for discounting taxes and benefits will differ.

Privatizing may not matter. Suppose the current social security program were replaced by a system of individual accounts. Suppose also that taxes were raised in order to pay off the current unfunded liabilities. As argued in the first section of this chapter, in a world of certainty, these taxes can be raised so that the market value of the taxes on each household is exactly equal to the market value of the old social security plan. The same logic can be extended to the case of uncertainty. It follows that that if there is optimization, stable prices, and spanning, then no household money's worth will change, and welfare will be unaffected.

Choosing Between the Money's Worth Measures

In keeping with the Advisory Council's usage, we have presented three different money's worth measures — the internal real rate of return, the benefit-to-tax ratio, and the net present value metric. There remains the question of which of these money's worth measures is most useful, and for what purpose.

The IRR and PVB/PVT have the advantages that they are unit-free and easy to understand. They facilitate comparisons between different birth cohorts inside the same social security plan.[55] However, these measures can lead to incorrect conclusions when comparing systems of different scale.

The shortcomings of the IRR and PVB/PVT measures can be illustrated as follows. Consider a social security system in which taxes are the sum of one component (T_A) representing the portion of the social security tax invested at the riskless market interest rate and returned to the worker as benefits later in life, and a second component (T_t) representing the interest that must be paid on government bonds given to the old at the system's inception and rolled over into the indefinite future, interest that never reverts back to the worker. As we have seen, our current social security system resembles this hypothetical situation. All three measures of money's worth will reflect the fact that every cohort after the start-up ones gets a "bad deal" compared to no social security system at all.

Now let us compare our hypothetical system to another one in which T_A is increased. If all households are rational and able to participate fully in capital market transactions, the size of the social security taxes that earn the riskless return would be completely irrelevant. That is, households will simply undo in their own private portfolios whatever the social security system forces them to invest. This truth is revealed by the NPV measure of money's worth, but is confused by both IRR and PVB/PVT. Consider first the NPV:

$$\text{NPV} = \text{PVB} - (T_A + T_t) = [T_A(1+r)]/(1+r) - (T_A + T_t) = -T_t.$$

Increasing the portion T_A of social security that reflects a riskless return on taxes collected has no effect on NPV. On the other hand, if we measured money's worth by the PVB/PVT method we would get:

$$\text{PVB}/\text{PVT} = \text{PVB}/(T_A + T_t) = T_A/(T_A + T_t)$$

and this number increases (converging to 1) as the program is expanded and T_A is increased (to infinity). Similarly, it can be shown that increasing T_A will raise the IRR, because the IRR is a weighted average of the return on T_A and the return on T_t.

The general point is that any reform plan that increases the size of social security through an increase in the funded part will show an improvement in the PVB/PVT and IRR, even though the correct measure, NPV, will show no change. In other words, part of the apparent superiority of these reform plans over the pay-as-you-go benchmark is based on the misleading advantage that comes with greater scale when the wrong measure of money's worth is used to compare plans.

Overall, our view is that the risk-adjusted NPV measure is most helpful for ranking alternative social security plans. In a world with spanning and optimization, this measure corresponds precisely to market price and is therefore the correct money's worth statistic. The same cannot be said for IRR or PVB/PVT.

Money's Worth When Spanning Fails

Though money's worth measures are informative given the four theoretical conditions just described, we recognize that none of these conditions is likely to be perfectly satisfied in the real world. As described above, in a world with uncertain payoffs and incomplete markets, there may be no market price to attach to a future stream of contingent cash flows. For example, even under the current pay-as-you-go system, benefits are contingent on a variety of economic factors and not easily reproduced via a portfolio of marketed securities. In practice, benefits vary with aggregate shocks like demographic changes; as we have seen in the past, the larger the pool of young workers, the higher tend to be the benefits to old workers. Benefits also tend to depend on productivity changes (i.e., the higher the average wage of young workers, the higher the benefits to old workers), and, most important, they depend on policy changes. It is difficult to find a marketed security that pays off precisely when Congress decides to change social security benefit rules. Additionally, retiree benefits also depend on idiosyncratic shocks to earnings, length of life, and disability. Once again, it is hard to find a marketed security that pays off precisely when a particular household has a few bad earnings years.

The stock market and limited participation. More than half of all U.S. households invest no money in the stock market, either directly or indirectly. This strongly suggests that the spanning hypothesis — that every household can freely trade every asset — is violated. If so, "constrained" households might be helped by a policy that increased their stockownership levels. The question is, how does this change the way that money's worth calculations should be done?

Consider a "constrained" household that holds no stock because it faces a fixed cost of learning about the stock market or because it has no wealth outside of social security. Suppose the household's income is independent of stock market returns. Then the correct money's worth from a small incremental holding of stock can be obtained by discounting the expected payoff of the stock at the risk-free rate.[56] That is, the appropriate money's worth for constrained households from small equity investments is the non-risk-adjusted money's worth. The reason is that the first few dollars of stock bring negligible risk, and therefore increase utility proportional to their expected payoff, with no risk adjustment.

In our view, the fundamental rationale for social security investment in the stock market rests on the existence of people who are currently constrained from holding equities. It is interesting to note that those who would benefit the most from social security investments in equity are probably the poor, since this group is least likely to hold stocks now.

Quantifying the money's worth to a constrained household of a large movement into the stock market is more difficult. It is clear, however, that a discount rate higher than the risk-free rate should be used in computing the money's worth of the stock payoffs.[57] The reason is that, as households gain more exposure to stocks, they would perceive their old age income as more and more at risk.

Suppose the trust fund invests in the stock market, and pays out benefits that depend correspondingly on the return from its stock market investments. Quantifying money's worth as a whole of these trust fund investments in the stock market depends on a host of questions. For example, how many of the households that do not currently hold stock are constrained, and how many of them chose not to hold stocks? For those that are constrained, how much stock would they have held, were they not constrained? In other words, how risk averse are they, and how independent is their income of stock returns? Finally, how big is the stock market investment?

Below, we offer quantitative answers to these questions. For now, we summarize by saying that in the presence of constrained households, a shift of one dollar of social security trust fund investments from bonds into stocks should raise social security money's worth, correctly calculated (even though it does not change market value), but by much less than the non-risk-adjusted money's worth would suggest.

Accounting for idiosyncratic risk. There are several reasons that the non-risk adjusted approach to money's worth estimates for the current social security system are too low, arising from the failure of the spanning assumption described above. Such failures arise because many of the risks that households face — uncertainty about earnings, length of life, disability, and health expenses — may not be fully insurable or hedgeable in private markets. These events are not perfectly insurable due to moral hazard and adverse selection. While the government cannot overcome moral hazard, it can overcome adverse selection by making participation mandatory; indeed, this is one of the rationales for mandatory national social security systems.[58]

To the extent that social security provides insurance with no private substitute or an imperfect private substitute, it is inappropriate to discount the expected benefits at a risk-free rate.[59] That is, the benefit flows of the current social security system are negatively correlated with individual income, and hence the discount rate should be *smaller* than the riskless rate. The non-risk-adjusted approach to money's worth calculations therefore tends to understate the benefits of social security because it calculates benefits at actuarial probabilities, neglecting the insurance premium that participants would be willing to pay beyond those expected benefits to receive the social security stream of benefits.

As an example of this problem, consider longevity risk. Under a mandatory national social security system, longevity risk is pooled since social security benefits are annuitized, paying benefits irrespective of how long the retiree lives. If the private markets could not provide annuities at all, households would be exposed to the risk of living too long (and outliving their resources). They would likely hedge against this by saving more; that is, they would be forced to give up resources when they are younger. They would be made worse off by this loss of government-mandated insurance.[60] If the private markets did provide annuitization, but less efficiently due to adverse selection, households would again be worse off in an ex-ante sense.[61]

Accounting for intergenerational aggregate risk. Social security's contingent benefit and tax streams share risk across generations. The most important way the current system does so is by making retiree benefits for one generation depend explicitly on the wage bill of the next generation; this creates a type of earnings insurance for the young of one generation paid for by the old of the previous generation. It is hard to imagine even a fledgling private market arising to displace this type of intergenerational risk-sharing since the young and the old are never young at the same time, when they might perceive the advantage of entering into a generational contract. Reforms that rely heavily on individual stock market accounts would no doubt reduce the level of intergenerational insurance, a fact overlooked by standard money's worth calculations.[62]

To pursue this idea further, one might imagine restructuring social security benefit and tax formulas in order to provide better old-age consumption insurance by making both depend inversely on the past few decades of stock market performance. This recognizes that a generation blessed with remarkable stock market returns (such as the current baby boomer cohort) might not require as much compensation when it is old, because it would be able to accumulate more than the average generation. Such a generation would then receive lower government-supplied benefits, in turn reducing the taxes paid by the next generation's young. Conversely, a generation experiencing abnormally low stock returns (e.g., the Great Depression) would receive higher benefits, financed by raising taxes on the next generation. Depending on how sharp are the tax changes, the burden of poor stock market performance could be shared by several succeeding generations.

This type of intergenerational risk pooling could be implemented more directly by leaving the benefit formula unchanged but instead investing part of the social security trust fund in the stock market. Taxes on the next generation to pay the benefits would be raised or lowered depending on the performance of the equity market. If the trust fund held stock, then unconstrained households would, in equilibrium, hold correspondingly less, and so their risk exposure would be reduced as in the above insurance scheme.[63] In effect, the stock is transferred to the next generation because its taxes would rise precisely when the market performed poorly (Smetters, this volume; Bohn 1998; Diamond 1997). This scenario implies that the money's worth of a social security defined-benefit system coupled with trust fund investment in the stock market should be higher than a mechanical computation obtained by discounting trust fund stock returns at a risky rate.

A more general point can be made as follows. The stocks of any generation are assets to which neither constrained households living at that time, nor future generations (constrained or not), have access. Social security reforms that effectively take stock out of the hands of today's unconstrained households, and transfer their returns to today's constrained households and to tomorrow's households, do not change the market value of the system. But they can very well improve risk-bearing in a world in which spanning fails, and therefore improve welfare. Both non-risk-adjusted money's worth and market based, risk-adjusted NPV miss this beneficial result.[64]

General Equilibrium Effects and Money's Worth

Almost any social security reform is likely to alter relative prices in the economy. For example, if a significant amount of money were transferred from bonds to stocks by the social security system, and if not all individuals could fully offset these changes in their own portfolios, then stock prices could be expected to rise and bond prices to fall. Consequently the return on bonds would be expected to rise and the return on stocks would fall. This implies that the historical spread between stocks and bonds, so key to the alleged advantage of social security investment in stocks, would diminish.

The beneficiaries of privatization would then be old stockholders who would gain from the rise in stock prices but would not live long enough to be hurt by the fall in subsequent returns. The losers would be future workers with access to the stock market who would then earn lower returns on their stock investments. The menu of investments undertaken by the economy would also probably change, moving to more adventurous risky projects, since the old stocks would now be effectively spread out over more people (including some of the previously constrained households). These subtleties are missed by market-driven money's worth, and by non-risk-adjusted money's worth measures.

Changes in social security may also produce changes in lifetime wealth and effective tax rates on labor. Workers may respond by changing their labor supply, which in turn might alter equilibrium wages. All these direct and indirect effects of social security reform are missed by standard money's worth measures. Under the current social security system, taxes paid while young do not directly translate into benefits received while old. As we have seen, for the typical workers, each payroll tax dollar raises the present value of expected future benefits by less than a dollar (e.g., only 71 cents), and therefore alters hours and retirement age decisions.[65]

Suppose social security taxes were increased to improve funding of the system, and the revenues were not reflected in higher retirement benefits for current workers but rather were used to reduce the transfers paid by future generations. This would likely increase the distortion in the labor supply decision of current workers, and, assuming substitution effects dominate income effects, reduce labor supply. It would, however, reduce distortions faced by future workers, since they would receive a better return on each dollar of social security contributions. In general, the effects of various reform options on labor supply depend on how the transition burdens are shared. Similarly, if the system's progressivity were altered by moving to individual accounts, this would raise the net benefit per dollar of contributions for some groups and lower it for others, thus altering labor supply and retirement incentives.[66] None of these effects are captured by standard money's worth estimates.

Money's Worth and the Current Reform Debate

In this section we examine two of the more prominent types of social security reform proposals, in light of our critique of money's worth. The first sort of plan we assess is usually referred to as (partial or full) privatization, where the objective is to replace (part or all) of the current social security system with a system of individual defined-contribution accounts. The second type of proposal we evaluate is one which would maintain the defined-benefit nature of the current social security system, but would change the program's investment policy: part or all of the social security trust fund would be held in equities. Our goal is to evaluate money's worth measures in each case.

Money's Worth of Individual Accounts

Perhaps the most prominent argument offered in favor of privatization is that individual accounts would pay a higher rate of return than would the current system. The recent Advisory Council report (1997) suggested that moving toward a system of individual accounts would raise the rate of return that participants receive under the social security program. Echoing Forbes (1996) cited above, Michael Tanner of the Cato Institute argued for privatization because "the system remains a bad deal for most Americans, a situation that is growing worse for today's young workers. Payroll taxes are already so high that even if today's young workers receive the promised benefits, such benefits will amount to a low, below-market return for those taxes. Studies show that for most young workers such benefits would amount to a real return of one percent or less on the required taxes. For many, the real return would be zero or even negative. These workers can now get far higher returns and benefits through private savings, investment, and insurance."[67]

This justification of individual accounts flows from two premises. First, proponents note that projected rates of return promised under the current social security system are low, between 1 and 1.5 percent in real terms (Board of Trustees 1997). Second, if the past is a reliable guide to the future, real returns anticipated on private investments are likely to be much higher even than riskless rates of return, which themselves are higher than 2 percent. For example, real stock returns averaged 9.4 percent and real government bond returns averaged 2.3 percent per year, over the 1926–1996 period in the U.S. (Ibbotson and Associates 1997). Proponents then conclude that if social security were privatized and people were allowed to invest their contributions directly in U.S. capital markets, everyone would achieve higher rates of return and be better off. The problem is that the two premises on which the argument rests are accurate, but as we shall show next, it is not correct to make the subsequent leap to the policy prescription.

To understand why, we proceed in three steps. Our starting point considers a simple case where social security is privatized with no additional prefunding. In this first case, we assume that the future is known with certainty and the only available assets are riskless bonds. This sheds light on the effect of moving to mandated individual accounts where these accounts can be held only in riskless bonds. Next, we examine the changes arising from prefunding, achieved by raising taxes on current workers, so as to decrease the social security system's unfunded liability. Finally, we study the results when we add uncertainty and allow individuals to shift assets in their individual accounts from riskless bonds into stocks.

Privatization without prefunding: the certainty case. A fundamental error of the simple privatization argument is that it ignores the accrued benefits earned for past contributions by current workers and retirees. If these are paid in full without changing the degree of prefunding in the system, and if the money is raised via taxes on private accounts invested only in bonds, then the excess of market return above the current social security return will be completely dissipated in the new taxes.

Suppose the old social security system were shut down and all new social security taxes deposited into individual accounts earning the riskless market rate of return. It is important to acknowledge that privatization *could* be implemented with no additional prefunding. For example, if the old social security system were shut down, the government could issue each former participant "recognition" bonds equivalent to the present value of accrued benefits under the old system (which they would then be required to hold in an individual account until retirement). Since the government selects the mix of new taxes and borrowing from which to pay the principal and interest on these recognition bonds, it could choose to keep the explicit recognition bond debt growing along exactly the same trajectory that the old unfunded liability would have followed had the old system continued. Prefunding would then be the same, because the new recognition bond debt would have precisely replaced the old unfunded liability.

For concreteness, let us assume an economy that is in a steady state of growth g equal to 1.2 percent with a riskless rate of interest r equal to 2.3 percent. Then each individual (after the start-up generations) would look forward to a 1.2 percent return under the old pay-as-you-go social security system, versus a 2.3 percent return if the same money were invested directly in (riskless) bonds. While 2.3 percent may not seem much higher than 1.2 percent, the accumulated difference grows large over a long worklife. For example, given constant real contributions for 40 years, and constant real benefits paid out over 20 years so as to yield a rate of return of 1.2 percent, the benefits would need to be raised by about 40.8 percent in order to increase the rate of return to 2.3 percent. Put another way, individuals who had individual accounts earning the riskless market return could pay 29 percent (40.8/1.408) less each year into their individual accounts and still receive the same retirement benefit as they would get from their social security contributions.

But as we showed above, this apparent gain is illusory. If the government were to shut down the old underfunded social security system and move to individual accounts, funds would still need to be raised to cover accrued social security liabilities. Suppose we use $9.9 trillion as our estimate of the unfunded liability.[68] One method for covering these liabilities would be to issue $9.9 trillion in recognition bond debt, and then to roll over just enough interest and principal to keep this debt growing at the rate the unfunded liability would have grown under the old system.

Computing the exact path of payments required to achieve this target precisely is beyond the scope of this chapter, but we can derive a reasonable approximation based on the steady state scenario discussed above. The required extra taxes to keep the debt-to-GDP ratio constant would clearly need to be $(r-g) \times$ (value of the bonds). With a real interest rate of 2.3 percent, a growth rate of 1.2 percent, and an unfunded liability of about $9.9 trillion fully transformed into recognition bond debt, this would involve taxes equal to $109 billion in the first year $(=(2.3 \text{ percent} - 1.2 \text{ percent}) \times \$9.9 \text{ trillion})$.[69] Using the current OASDI benefits of about $375 billion, and ignoring the current operating surplus by assuming these are equal to contributions,[70] the required new taxes represent 29 percent of annual payroll tax collections, or about 3.6 percent of payroll. Put another way, the new tax required to cover payments on the new recognition bond debt would equal 29 percent of all contributions to the new individual accounts.[71] This is equivalent to every generation (forever) paying a 29 percent commission or load on all funds invested in the individual accounts. But this is the entire surplus from market returns. It is worth emphasizing that, as long as r is greater than g, the conclusion still holds: all the extra returns from investing in capital markets will be dissipated by these transition costs. It does not matter whether the difference between the return on capital markets and the return on the existing social security system $(r-g)$ equals 1.1 percent, 3 percent, or even 10 percent!

Many popular discussions of social security privatization ignore these transition costs entirely. For example Beach and Davis (1998) of the Heritage Foundation state:

If Americans were allowed to direct their payroll taxes into safe investment accounts similar to 401(k) plans, or even super-safe U.S. Treasury bills, they would accumulate far more money in savings for their retirement years than they are ever likely to receive from Social Security. Had they placed that same amount of lifetime employee and employer tax contributions into conservative tax-deferred IRA-type investments — such as a mutual fund composed of 50 percent U.S. government Treasury bills and 50 percent equities — they could expect a real rate of return of over 5 percent per year prior to the payment of taxes after retirement.

Some analysts are more circumspect. For example, the Advisory Council made a concerted effort to include additional transition taxes in their money's worth calculations. The PSA plan puts 5 percent of pay into workers' individual accounts and imposes a 1.52 percent transition tax that lasts until 2070.[72] This added tax is incorporated into the Advisory Council's money's worth calculations (1977: 177).

Senator Moynihan has proposed to reform social security through partial privatization. In his plan, workers from now on would be allowed to deposit up to 2 percent of their payroll tax into an individually-managed account.[73] The rest of the system would apparently function like a scaled down version of the current social security system, except that all the current accrued benefits would continue as liabilities of the new system. Because the current social security system is running a surplus, for the next 10 or 15 years the Moynihan plan has the effect of redirecting into individual accounts the surplus that would have otherwise flowed into the social security trust fund. Though workers will earn high market returns on the 2 percent that goes into their individual accounts, the system will eventually be unable to maintain the same benefit formula appearing in the current social security system because the trust fund will be smaller. Though the rate of return on the privatized piece will be above the current social security return, the rate of return on the non-privatized piece will fall, leaving the total return unaffected.

Privatization with increased prefunding. Issuing recognition bonds that grow in value at the same rate as the unfunded liability would have grown under the current system is only one of several ways to finance the transition toward a privatized social security system. (Recall that in a steady state, the current system's unfunded liability will grow at the same rate as GDP.) A dramatic (and probably unpopular) alternative would be to finance the transition cost with a one-time lump sum tax, levied on each current worker. This would generate a tax bill of about $68,000 per worker ($9.9 trillion / 147 million workers). Another equally dramatic solution would be to default completely on all the accrued benefits, forcing current workers and retirees to shoulder the entire $9.9 trillion loss. Both these alternatives reduce the debt of the social security system relative to what the unfunded liability would have been, and thus in our terminology they constitute a shift toward greater funding.

Many economists believe that reducing social security's unfunded liability would enhance national saving and output, and hence they support prefunding on its own merits.[74] But increasing the system's funding level would not immediately raise the rate of return on social security. Indeed, the $68,000 tax would reduce the return of today's workers, and defaulting on the unfunded liabilities would reduce the return of today's retirees and older workers. In general, cohorts that are required to pay higher transition taxes would receive a lower rate of return (less than g), while later cohorts would expect a higher return (eventually r, if the debt were paid off entirely). Feldstein and Samwick (1996, 1997) would require members of the baby boom generation to pay higher taxes, so that their children and future generations would benefit relatively more. Alternatively, the trust fund could be increased by cutting benefits, helping future generations as in the Feldstein-Samwick approach, but at the expense of current retirees instead of current workers. Under a partially funded social security system (i.e., one with a trust fund), the rate of return on social security would be a weighted average of g and r, where the weight on r depends directly on the size of the trust fund.[75]

Privatization without prefunding: incorporating uncertainty. Consider now a privatized system with individual accounts and with recognition bonds replacing all the accrued benefits. Suppose there is also uncertainty in the world, and that workers have the option of moving the money in their individual accounts from riskless assets to risky securities, such as stocks, which have higher expected returns.

It is clear from our analysis in the previous section that, if all households have access to stock investments on their own (i.e., if spanning and optimization hold), then permitting equities in the individual accounts will have no effect on anyone's wellbeing. In effect, the stocks that workers buy for their individual social security accounts will be purchased from their own private portfolios. Their overall portfolios will end up absolutely unchanged.[76] The next question is what would be the effect of this switch from bonds into stocks on money's worth measures. As described earlier, conventional money's worth estimates are based on expected values of contributions and payouts and do not incorporate any adjustment for risk. Inasmuch as mean equity returns are higher than mean bond returns, this change in investment pattern would then raise the individual accounts' internal rate of return as typically computed, as well as the NPV and the PVB/PVT ratio.

As an example, consider switching $100 from bond into stocks for 30 years. Figuring out the "money's worth" of this change depends on how one values the stock. Of course, transferring $100 from bonds into $100 of stocks does not change the market value of the position, nor does it change the welfare of anybody in the system, assuming spanning and optimization. But the conventional money's worth approach yields a very different answer. The Advisory Council's methodology assumed that stocks would return an annual 7 percent real rate and bonds would pay 2.3 percent. Someone who invested $100 in stocks would see the money grow in expected value by 7 percent per year over 30 years, to $761. Discounting this amount to the present using a 2.3 percent rate produces a net present value of $385 = $100 × $(1.07)^{30}/(1.023)^{30}$. According to this calculation, $285 of value has supposedly been created, that is, the estimated net present value of this change is $285. But we would contend that a *risk-adjusted* discount rate should be used to measure the true money's worth of stocks and, under spanning, the appropriate risk-adjusted rate is the expected return on stocks, 7 percent. Naturally, using a 7 percent rate to discount future risky cash flows earning 7 percent produces a present value equal to $100 = $100 × $(1.07)^{30}/(1.07)^{30}$ and a net present value of zero.

In other words, money's worth calculations using an appropriate risky discount rate deviate considerably from those found in the literature, since all benefit payouts that depend on stock market returns must be discounted by a higher rate than the Treasury risk-free rate.[77] In general, a money's worth measure that assumes high returns on stock but discounts by a risk-free rate will overstate the benefit of social security diversification, and the overstatement will be greater the more stock assumed held in the social security accounts.

Policy analysts have not computed money's worth measures for individual account plans correcting for risk in the manner we suggest. However a useful set of equivalent calculations is available from the Office of the Actuary for variants of the IA and the PSA plans. Specifically, these alternative money's worth statistics assume that the rate of return earned on stocks is equal to that on bonds (approximately 2.3 percent). All three of the money's worth statistics (IRR, NPV, PVB/PVT) based on this approach are well below those reported earlier, and, indeed, most of the money's worth advantage for the IA and PSA plans relative to the Holdtax benchmark disappears (Figures 10, 11, and 12).[78]

A somewhat different analysis applies if spanning does not hold. As we have argued elsewhere (Geanakoplos, Mitchell, and Zeldes 1998), some households are probably unable to access the capital markets on their own. Economic theory suggests that allowing some portion of the individual accounts to be held in equities could well make these households better off. This is because people whose income is uncorrelated with stock returns should hold some stock in their portfolios, so as to benefit from the higher expected returns stocks provide compared to safe assets. Such constrained individuals would find that changing the first dollar from bonds to stocks would raise returns with negligible added risk. Additional stock investments

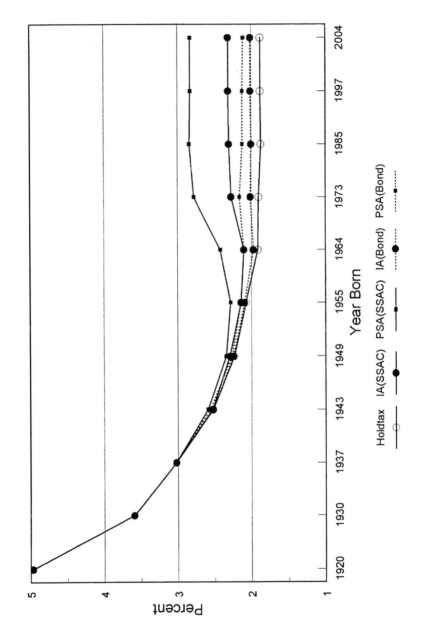

Figure 10. Social security IRR: IA and PSA plans. Mixed stock/bond returns versus bond return for composite worker. Source: Unpublished data supplied by the SSA Office of the Actuary.

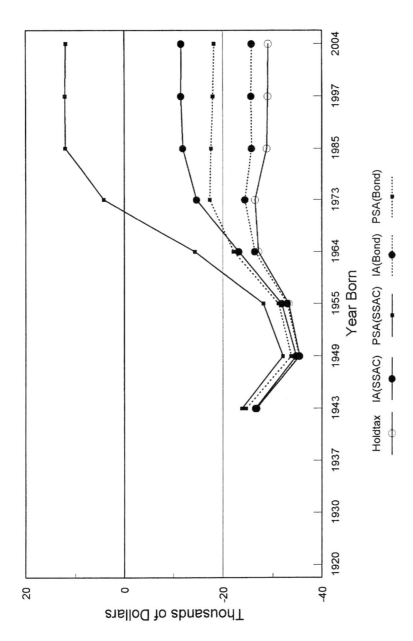

Figure 11. Social security net subsidy, IA and PSA plans. Mixed stock/bond returns versus bond return for composite worker. Source: Unpublished data supplied by the SSA Office of the Actuary.

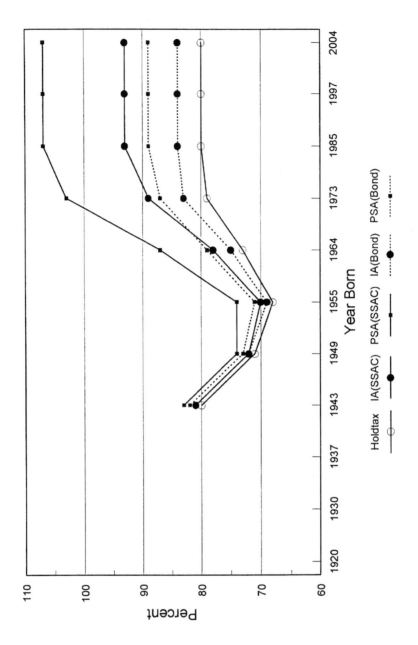

Figure 12. Social security PVB/PVT, IA and PSA plans. Mixed stock/bond returns versus bond return for composite worker. Source: Unpublished data supplied by the SSA Office of the Actuary.

would raise returns further, but at the cost of additional risk, so that risk-adjusted returns would rise, but by less than non-adjusted returns. (Sooner or later risk-adjusted returns would actually fall. Determining the optimal level of stock investment in the accounts depends on household wealth levels and their risk tolerances.)

Additional research must evaluate how many people are constrained in their private portfolios from holding stock, what types of people they are, and how much they would benefit from investing part of their individual accounts in equities under a privatized system. Some two-fifths of the U.S. population held stock in 1995, either on their own account or in defined contribution pensions or mutual funds (Kennickell, Starr-McCluer, and Sunden 1997; Ameriks and Zeldes, in progress). Of the remaining three-fifths, some are young and will perhaps accumulate stock later in life; half of the middle-aged population (44–54) held some stock in 1995. This is probably a lower bound estimate of future stockownership over individuals' work-lives for two reasons. First, these estimates are based on a cross-section of households at only one point in time. Second, there has been a secular upward trend in stockholding by households, one likely to continue. Not all those currently lacking stocks would necessarily benefit greatly from additional equity exposure. For example, very risk-averse workers who face a small fixed cost of market entry might benefit a bit but not very much from putting some equities in their individual social security accounts. Furthermore, some people would not benefit at all from holding stocks — for example, those whose pay or business income is sufficiently highly correlated with the equity market.

A back-of-the-envelope guess about the magnitude of these effect might go as follows. Consider a fully constrained household with no wealth outside social security. This household should regard the first \$100 of stock in its individual social security account as almost riskless, and therefore attach a present value to it of \$385 as calculated earlier. The substitution of \$100 of stock for \$100 of bonds thus increases net present value by \$285. Additional increments of stock, however, lead to more substantial risk for this household. Suppose, for example, that 2 percent of payroll, or one-sixth of all social security contributions, were allowed to be put into stock through individual accounts. If we presumed that the optimal (unconstrained) portfolio consisted of half stocks and half bonds, this would move the constrained household one-third of the way toward this optimum. Using a linear interpolation,[79] this lowers the average gain to investing in stock, from \$285 to $(5/6)(285) = \$237$ for this constrained investor.[80] Assuming that about half of the population is constrained, and that only half of these are substantially constrained, an investment of 2 percent of payroll from social security contributions into equities in private accounts would therefore bring a present value gain in the aggregate of approximately \$59 $(= (1/2) \times (1/2)(\$237))$ for each \$100 in stock.[81] This figure is far smaller than the gain of $285 attributed by a non-risk-adjusted calculation, but sufficiently larger than zero to justify further investigation.

A related consideration is that allowing additional equities to be held in household portfolios would likely increase the demand for, and hence lower the return on, stocks.[82] This would moderate the benefits to constrained households, who in the main are likely to be younger workers, and would actually hurt young unconstrained workers who have not yet accumulated stocks. (Conversely, older and wealthier people who held stock prior to the change would tend to benefit by the increased demand for stock.)[83] It is interesting to note that the potential for this cross-generational wealth transfer — away from today's young — has been overlooked by those who would argue that the young would be most likely to experience higher returns from individual accounts.

When evaluating individual accounts, it is essential to recognize still other types of risk in addition to the stock market risk that has been our focus thus far. Recall that participants' exposure to risk in earnings, health, length of life, and inflation would rise under an individual account plan as compared to the current defined benefit plan. If private financial markets cannot provide all the benefits that the national old-age program offers, or provides them less efficiently, this raises the risk-adjusted return on the government run plan relative to an individual account plan, but is not reflected in standard non-risk-adjusted money's worth estimates. On the other hand, publicly-run, underfunded programs are subject to political risk, which many believe is greater than in an individual account model. Current workers in a pay-as-you-go system are unsure that future (born and unborn) generations will support them when they are old; they well know that benefit and tax payments vary according to political pressures. Since there is no market that can be used to protect against such risk, those potentially more able to bear the risk cannot trade with those less willing to bear it. Correcting for political risk would very likely increase the money's worth of a funded, individual account plan.

In summary, money's worth measures should not be compared across plans containing different levels of funding and portfolio compositions unless transition costs are incorporated and appropriate risk adjustments are carried out. Once these adjustments are undertaken, some people would benefit from individual accounts, others would see no change in their money's worth, and yet others would see declines. On balance, risk-adjusted money's worth would be significantly less favorable toward individual accounts than the typical analysis implies.

Money's Worth of Investing the Trust Fund in Equities

Some analysts find it attractive for social security to move toward equity investments, but believe that diversification into stocks is better achieved through central trust fund investment rather than individual accounts. Thus Munnell and Balduzzi (1998: 5) contend that "investing in equities could provide a lot of additional money to the trust fund," a logic that explains why architects of the Maintain Benefits plan for the Advisory Council proposed to devote 40 percent of the trust fund to equities. Since the Advisory Council did not risk-adjust its money's worth measures, this change in trust fund investments substantially boosts the money's worth value of the MB plan, as compared to a reform that was otherwise similar but invested only in bonds.[84]

For the population at large, it should be obvious that shifting the trust fund into equities will have some of the same effects that we saw when discussing the shifting of individual accounts into equities.[85] The exact effects depend on who bears the risk of the trust fund investments. If the risks are passed on directly to the beneficiaries, and households understand this, then unconstrained investors would offset changes in the social security account by altering their private portfolios, as we saw above. For these households, there would be no net change in the correctly calculated money's worth of an MB-type plan from investing the trust fund in equities, once the additional risk of holding equities is taken into account. Constrained households as well as financially unsophisticated or irrational households (Advisory Council 1997: 114) might be better off if the social security program undertook stock investments on their behalf. But some would be worse off, including those who optimally chose to hold only a small amount of stocks before the change, perhaps because they are risk averse. These people might be forced to hold too much equity in their social security account after the trust fund bought stocks. In general, the more heterogeneous are constrained households in their risk tolerance, and the wiser we think constrained households would be in their investment choices, the more attractive is privatization relative to trust fund investment as a means of achieving diversification. The more homogeneous are constrained households in their tolerance of risk, and the more myopic we think constrained households would be in their investment choices, the more attractive is trust fund investment as a means of achieving diversification.

An alternative approach to risk bearing would be to have all stock market risk borne by future taxpayers through tax rate changes.[86] As described earlier, this could improve intergenerational risk sharing as compared to the status quo. Estimating the value of this potential intergenerational risk pooling is a research question of substantial theoretical and practical interest, one left to future research.

Conclusion

The most popular argument in favor of social security privatization is that it would increase rates of return for all retirees. We have shown that this argument is false. The U.S. social security system's unfunded liability stands at around $10 trillion, based on the constant benefit/tax ratio method for calculating accrued benefits. Privatizing the system would allow households to earn market returns on their social security contributions. But if those contributions were taxed just enough to keep the unfunded liability a constant fraction of GDP, then in the absence of uncertainty, extra market returns would be entirely dissipated. Future workers would not perceive any higher *net* investment returns than they would under the current social security system, because, for every dollar of social security contributions, they would have to pay about 29 cents in tax to meet payments on the unfunded liability inherited from transfers to previous generations. If part of the unfunded social security liability were paid down faster via new taxes, or if the system's unfunded liability were reduced (for example by cutting accrued benefits), then it would be possible for future generations to earn more after privatization than they would from the current system. But these gains will come at the expense of either today's workers or today's retirees.

Some policy analysts use money's worth calculations to endorse privatization for the purposes of increasing workers' investments in equities. They support their contention by reminding us that equity returns have historically been higher than bond returns. But we show that extending money's worth to a world of uncertainty is a difficult business. If four assumptions pertaining to optimization, time homogeneity, stable prices, and spanning hold, then market value gives the correct measure of an asset's money's worth. Under these circumstances, the alleged superiority of equity returns over bond returns is irrelevant, since one dollar of stocks is worth no more than one dollar of bonds. This contrasts with computations offered by the Advisory Council attributing a money's worth of about $3.85 per dollar of stock, obtained by discounting expected stock returns of 7 percent using a riskless rate of 2.3 percent.

In the real world the four assumptions required for money's worth measures may not hold, with the spanning assumption especially likely to fail. In its absence, market value will not provide an accurate measure of money's worth. We estimate that if social security equity holdings reached 2 percent of payroll, then each dollar of stock would yield about $1.59 of money's worth rather than $3.85. Our analysis depends on the educated guess that perhaps one-quarter of households are substantially constrained from holding stock. The failure of spanning also changes our assessment of current social security benefit streams. That is, the market probably can duplicate some but not all of the socially provided benefits (such as real annuities, income insurance, and disability insurance). Once the value of the social insurance benefits is taken into account, the money's worth advantage of privatization becomes smaller than generally recognized by advocates.

There are other costs and benefits of social security reform that are difficult to incorporate into money's worth measures but which may nevertheless exert an important influence in the growing debate. Under the current system, no markets exist to protect against future benefit and tax changes when people are most vulnerable during retirement. Under an individual account format, by contrast, these political risks may be diminished, and people may also have a greater sense of ownership and control over their individual accounts. It is also possible that privatization may make prefunding more politically feasible. On the other hand along with these accounts may come the danger of inexperienced investors making imprudent decisions.

In sum, money's worth measures are well suited to comparing benefits and costs for different income groups, and even different cohorts, under the same social security system. But the typical approaches do not fare well at making comparisons across different reform plans, primarily because they do not properly account for differences in risk and/or transition costs. Developing money's worth measures that are capable of this task is more difficult. Further efforts to adapt money's worth measures to incorporate these elements will play a compelling role in the continuing debate over social security restructuring.

Support for this research was provided by the Cowles Foundation at Yale University (Geanakoplos), the Pension Research Council at the Wharton School (Mitchell), and Columbia Business School (Zeldes). This research is part of the NBER programs on Aging and Public Economics. The authors are grateful to Stephen Goss for supplying data used in the analysis, but absolve him and the Office of the Actuary from responsibility for opinions and any errors. We thank Julie Kozack for research assistance, and Stephen Goss, Dean Leimer, Robert Myers, and fellow members of the National Academy of Social Insurance Panel on Social Security Privatization for helpful comments. Opinions remain those of the authors and not of the institutions with whom the authors are affiliated.

Notes

1. In a similar vein, Stephen Moore (1997) of the Cato Institute appeared before Congress to "enumerate the economic advantages of converting out of our pay-as-you-go government-run Social Security system to a program of PSAs. . . . Privatization offers a much higher financial rate of return to young workers than the current system . . . if Congress were to allow a 25 year old working woman today to invest her payroll tax contributions in private capital markets, her retirement benefit would be two to five times higher than what Social Security is offering."

2. So this first approach might compare returns under the current system for a minimum-wage worker to that of a high-wage worker in the same cohort, or for a single worker to those paid to a married couple. Or one might analyze how an earlier cohort fared vis à vis a cohort born at some later date using a money's worth measure.

3. As we discuss below, there are other reasonable rationales for supporting social security privatization; see Mitchell and Zeldes (1996). For example, a privatized individual account system may better protect benefits against political risk than the

current (projected to be insolvent) system. In addition, an individual-account system may induce fewer labor supply distortions than the current system if the individual-account plan is less redistributive than the current program, and it is likely to provide households with expanded options for portfolio choice. And compared to a federally-run plan that invests the social security trust fund directly in the capital market, an individual-account plan may be better insulated against politicians' efforts to influence investment decisions.

4. This is somewhat lower than for the historical period between 1938 and 1973, but not so different from actual growth rates since then.

5. Leimer (1996) also mentions the payback period and the net transfer as a percentage of the present value of lifetime earnings in an excellent summary of these and other money's worth measures.

6. The fourth column is the cumulative NPV (i.e., the running sum of column 3). We will return to this later.

7. It would not make sense to calculate present values of infinite streams in a social security program with r less than g. In such a case the calculations would be completely dominated by events in the distant future.

8. The conditions under which discounting is feasible $(r>g)$ are the same as those for the dynamic efficiency of an economy. In a world with time-varying but non-stochastic r and g, the required condition is that a type of average of r is greater than average g. If r and g are stochastic, the analysis becomes significantly more complicated. Abel et al. (1989) argue that the empirical evidence supports dynamic efficiency, even in a stochastic world.

9. To the extent that the actual historical rate of growth was closer to the real market rate of interest, our stylized numbers will exaggerate the importance of the past. But we shall see when we look at actual numbers that our stylized numbers still convey appropriate magnitudes.

10. For very early cohorts, the IRR is infinite in this model because these people received benefits but paid no taxes. In the actual U.S. system, only those who had made some contributions received any benefits.

11. To see this, note that each column of taxes and benefits must sum to zero by definition in a pay-as-you-go system. The column under 1997, for example, sums to zero because taxes raised in that year are exactly equal to benefits paid in our hypothetical pay-as-you-go system. But these same 1997 numbers turn out also to equal the present value, in 1997 dollars but figured at a rate of return g, of the benefits and taxes of the generation born in 1918. Hence the rate of return on the taxes paid by the 1918 cohort is g, as claimed. By the homogeneity property of rates of return, the rate of return of every other cohort born after 1918 must also be g.

12. This follows from the commutative law of addition for absolutely convergent series. Note that for any finite set of entries, such as those shown in Table 1, we do not expect the cumulative sum of the row NPVs to be zero just because the corresponding cumulative NPV of the column sums is zero. The first t rows cover a very different set of entries from the first t columns. It is only when we consider the infinite sum that all the columns cover exactly the same set of entries as all the rows.

13. Thus extra consumption by the Depression-era generations must be paid for by an infinity of reduced consumption when added over all future generations. One might well ask whether a social planner ought to weight the importance of the Depression-era generation so heavily that this would be seen as a fair exchange: that is, when should one discount the welfare of future generations at the market rate of (real) interest? The answer to this question is moot, of course, since the decision was made by the social security system's architects in the 1930s. But a similar question may be formulated going forward, namely, how much do future generations owe the gen-

eration that kept the nation together during the Depression, fought and won World War II, and built the markets that enabled future generations to be so productive?

14. Indeed we show below that one natural way of spreading the debt burden is to tax each generation in the same proportion $k(r-g)$ of its income. As long as $r-g$ is the same, higher g does not reduce the proportional burden of the debt overhang from the Depression-era generations.

15. The concept of unfunded liability is different from that of actuarial imbalance. Actuarial imbalance is defined as the present value of expected benefits over some period (often 75 years) minus the present value of expected tax receipts over the same period, minus the current value of the trust fund. The U.S. currently has a 75-year actuarial imbalance of about 2.2 percent of payroll per year, or about $2.9 trillion dollars in present value (Goss, this volume).

16. This surplus is equal to zero in our stylized pure PAYGO system.

17. Since the accumulated trust fund in our setup is zero, the sum of the entries in the fourth column equals the unfunded liability, $9.1 trillion.

18. For a longer discussion of these distinctions see Geanakoplos, Mitchell, and Zeldes (forthcoming).

19. See also Leimer's (1991) analysis of this topic.

20. In a steady state, this would correspond to keeping constant the ratio of outstanding recognition bond debt to GDP.

21. There are different ways of measuring accrued benefits, and each method would require a different tax scheme to make taxes in a privatized system just equal to transfers in the current social security system. We give one example. Suppose accrued benefits are defined according to the present benefit/cost ratio method. Then a proportional tax of $(1 - .71) \times 12.4$ percent $= 3.6$ percent would leave everyone exactly as well off in a privatized system as he would have been in the current pay-as-you-go social security system. For the straight line method, taxes would need to be cohort-specific. In particular, taxes could be reduced for current workers and kept at 29 percent for future workers.

22. This simple example is not too dissimilar in spirit from what Chile did in 1981 as it privatized a major portion of its old-age retirement program (Mitchell and Barreto 1997).

23. Observe that the ratio of new transition taxes $T_1 (1+g)^{t-1}(r-g)/(1+r)$ to income $Y_1 (1+g)^{t-1}$ for each generation depends on the difference $r-g$, not on the magnitude of g, for small values of r and g.

24. A higher r makes privatized returns higher but, as we have just seen, it also increases the interest burden of the unfunded liability.

25. By the same argument, if transition costs are ignored, the other money's worth measure comparisons are also biased in favor of privatizing social security.

26. This presumes that improved funding of social security has a sufficiently small effect on the government budget deficit. For a discussion of this point see the discussion in Technical Panel on Trends and Issues in Retirement Income (1997). There is no reason to believe that privatization without prefunding would necessarily increase national saving (see for instance Mitchell and Zeldes 1996).

27. This point is acknowledged by some analysts (e.g., Feldstein 1997, 1998b) though most popular accounts of privatization overlook the point, as we have noted above.

28. Examples of previous studies focusing on the tax and benefit flows under social security include Boskin and Puffert (1987), Boskin et al. (1987), Caldwell et al. (1998), Duggan et al. (1993), Hurd and Shoven (1985), Leimer (1994), Moffitt (1984), Myers (1996), Myers and Schoebel (1992), Panis and Lillard (1985), and Steurle and Bakija (1994).

29. As explained below, the fact that the current social security system faces insolvency implies that is it not a viable benchmark. In other words, alternative reforms must be compared to benchmarks that have incorporated changes sufficient to make the overall system solvent.

30. One reason the representative worker (or set of workers) is used for Social Security Administration money's worth computations is that year-by-year payroll tax data on individuals are not available for years prior to 1951. The Social Security Administration is able to compute benefits because it keeps data on the sum of the wages on which taxes were paid, which is all that is required to construct benefit amounts (Myers 1993: App. 2-5). While exact data are not available for these very early birth cohorts, approximations could be made based on the data that are available.

31. Hypothetical workers' money's worth calculations have also been undertaken by many researchers, most recently Caldwell et al. (1998).

32. If these benefits are not included, the full tax rate should not be included either.

33. Personal communication, Office of the Actuary, SSA, August 1997.

34. See Miron and Weil (1998) for a historical comparison of ex-ante and ex-post tax and benefit rules.

35. Because these calculations follow all those alive at around the time of labor market entry and take into account mortality probabilities, they naturally differ from a computation that compares benefits received versus taxes paid by those surviving to age 65 (e.g., Thompson 1983).

36. Forecasts of future mortality are developed by age and sex, and show a continuing gradual improvement in life expectancy over time. For a full discussion of social security program benefit formulas and eligibility requirements see Myers (1993) and Board of Trustees (1998) or see www.ssa.gov on the internet.

37. For the future, the forecasted real rate is equal to 4.3 percent in 1997, falling to 3.4 percent by 2000, and to 2.3 percent by 2010 where it is assumed to hold (Board of Trustees 1996: 56–57).

38. As we note below, there is no particular reason to use the historical rate of return on trust fund assets to discount benefit and taxes since the social security system is essentially unfunded (trust fund assets at the end of 1997 equaled approximately 175 percent of one year's benefit outlays). The riskiness of tax and benefit flows are, in principle, not related to the riskiness of trust fund assets.

39. For IRR and PVT/PVB, the choice of units is irrelevant.

40. This is based on the intermediate cost assumptions in the Trustees Report (Board of Trustees, various years). These present values are typically calculated using a 75-year horizon as described in Goss (this volume).

41. For the Advisory Council (1997) estimates, the Holdben plan raises payroll taxes to keep the OASDI trust fund ratio from falling below 100 percent. The Holdtax plan cuts benefits as needed so payroll taxes need not be raised.

42. Leimer's estimates were derived based on data as of 1991. We are hopeful that in the future additional microeconomic data will become available from the Social Security Administration to update the Leimer computations, but these are not available as of this writing.

43. The underlying IRR, NPV, and PVB/PVT estimates were kindly supplied to us in 1997 by the SSA Office of the Chief Actuary for a range of birth cohorts and workers of several stylized types. To create the weights for the composite worker we used Table W, p. 205 (Advisory Council 1997). The IRR composite worker figures represent weighted averages of the underlying worker types, rather than being the IRR for a composite worker.

44. The graph only includes data going back to the 1920 birth cohort, because data for earlier cohorts were not available to us.

45. See Chapter 1 for a more complete description of the Advisory Council plans.

46. These IRR "crossovers" illustrate the key point that one birth cohort will perceive its money's worth differently from another cohort's, depending on how it is likely to fare under the plan.

47. The conditions that must be met in order to compare *different* social security regimes can be significantly weakened when comparing welfare of different people or sets of people (say, different income classes) under the *same* regime. For example, it may be reasonable to support that, though all people are myopic, they are all similarly myopic; it may be acceptable to suppose that all individuals in the economy face the same prices (though across different social security regimes, prices can change), and so on.

48. See, e.g., Kotlikoff (1989) and Tobin (1996). One reason the young might undersave is myopia: they fail to foresee their eventual discomfort when old. Ex-post, each cohort will realize that it should have saved more and consumed less when it was young. Another reason the young (or some subset of the young) might undersave is that they might act strategically, in that they count on the sympathy of their children or the government to support them in old age (the "Samaritan's dilemma"; cf O'Connell and Zeldes 1993).

49. In the presence of borrowing constraints and no myopia, money's worth is biased in the opposite way: workers would be made worse off by a larger plan than a smaller plan (or no plan), even if the plans all paid market rates of return and had identical money's worth measures.

50. There is a fine line between redistribution and insurance (discussed below); what differentiates the two is the information set that we condition on. From the perspective of someone with no information about lifetime wages and mortality prospects other than population averages, transfers from high-earners to low-earners can be seen as insurance. Ex-post, however, households have more information about lifetime earnings profiles as well as life expectancy. In the light of this additional information, social security transfers are seen as redistribution.

51. Precisely which measure of aggregate consumption, and how big the penalty should be per unit of covariance, does depend on the particular prices of the marketed securities. So the arbitrage pricing theorem does not really free us from checking all the marketed securities. But it clarifies precisely how the non-risk-adjusted approach might go wrong.

52. The Advisory Council (1997) assumed a future mean real return on stocks of 7 percent, lower than the historical arithmetic average.

53. For related evidence see Siegel (1997).

54. We can capture the phenomenon of "irrational risk aversion" while maintaining our hypothesis of optimization by supposing that, in addition to the utility they get from the financial payoffs of the stock, households also get disutility from holding these securities (for concreteness, say they lose $\epsilon \times S^2$, where S is equal to the dollar value of shares held). In equilibrium, stocks will necessarily have a higher return in order to get people to hold them and be compensated for the disutility.

55. It is not clear how best to compare NPVs across cohorts. The Advisory Council report (1997) selected an aggregate earnings index to convert NPV estimates into a common year's dollars; this is only one of many alternative choices.

56. "Small" means that the payoffs to the individual from the portion of his social security benefits that depend on stock returns are small relative to his consumption in those periods when he is receiving benefits.

57. A rate higher than the risk-free rate, but lower than the return on equity,

should also be used for households who already have 100 percent of their financial assets in the stock market and would like more.

58. We recognize that even in a mandatory national social security program, people can and do evade taxes for at least part of their work lives (Manchester, this volume). To the extent that such evasion is possible, it may produce adverse selection — for example, by people expecting not to live very long. This will undermine a national program's ability to pool retirement system risk across the population.

59. Consider the analogy to homeowners' fire insurance. Suppose no private market for fire insurance existed, and the government introduced this insurance at actuarially fair rates. If there were no administrative costs, the NPV of this insurance, based on discounting expected cash flows at a risk-free rate, would equal zero. Yet ex-ante households would clearly be better off with the insurance, as it reduces the risks faced by households.

60. Households would be worse off in an ex-ante sense, prior to any private information being revealed.

61. If individuals waited until retirement age to purchase annuities (as is currently generally the case), the private markets are likely to be plagued by substantially more adverse selection than if indiviudals annuitize at earlier ages. For an empirical assessment of the adverse selection and administrative costs on private annuities, see Mitchell et al. (1999). Even if no adverse selection were present, if the government could provide annuities with lower administrative cost, current money's worth estimates would underestimate the value of the current system relative to a privatized one. The reserve would be true if the private sector costs were greater than that of the government. A similar argument holds for disability insurance coverage.

62. Some intergenerational insurance would remain in both the IA and PSA proposals developed by the Advisory Council (1997) since both include a mandatory minimum defined-benefit guarantee financed by pay-as-you-go taxes.

63. Constrained households would be better off under this approach because under the previous plan they would effectively be forced into a short position in the stock market.

64. There is no particular reason that the government should undertake this risk-sharing through social security. In fact, the argument above assumes that no other tax and transfer scheme is accomplishing the same risk sharing.

65. For recent surveys of the literature on how social security has influenced retirement in the United States over time, see Diamond and Gruber (1997) and Lumsdaine and Mitchell (forthcoming).

66. We also recall that these distortions go hand in hand with increased insurance (Diamond 1977).

67. Tanner's testimony to the Social Security Advisory Council (March 5, 1995) is reported on the internet at www.socialsecurity.org/testimony/. A number of World Wide Web sites now provide taxpayers with the opportunity to compare their own rates of return under a system of privatized accounts to those under the current social security system; see for example www.socialsecurity.org. Some of these sites provide money's worth results using the rate of return, while others provide anticipated levels of retirement income under alternate scenarios.

68. As described earlier, Goss (this volume) uses a method close to the straight-line method to estimate the U.S. unfunded liability to be $8.9 trillion, close to the $9.1 trillion in our stylized model using the straight-line method. We have no estimates of the U.S. unfunded liability computed according to the constant PVB/PVT method described in the first section, but it seems reasonable to assume that it would be close to the $9.9 trillion estimate from our stylized model using the PVB/PVT method.

69. Subsequent payments would rise at 1.2 percent per year.

70. OASDI taxes inflows in 1997 were actually closer to $415 billion, or about $45

billion more than benefits, because the current baby boom demographics have given rise to a temporary surplus.

71. Had we used the straight line method for computing accrued benefits, giving an unfunded liability of $9 trillion, and had we used actual OASDI contributions of $400 billion, then we would have obtained a ratio of new taxes to payroll contributions of about ($99 billion)/($400 billion) = 25 percent, as given in our earlier paper (Geanakoplos, Mitchell, and Zeldes 1998).

72. See the Advisory Council report (1997) and Chapter 1 (this volume) for more discussion of the specifics of the PSA plan.

73. For a description of the Social Security Solvency Act of 1998 (S. 1792) see the internet site at www.senate.gov/~moynihan.

74. This perspective is summarized in Technical Panel on Trends in Income and Retirement Saving (1997).

75. A different approach might be to establish individual accounts from some other source, for example by using funds from a federal budget surplus. Thus President Bill Clinton recently suggested that Congress preserve the anticipated budget surplus for social security; see *Wall Street Journal* (1998). This would reduce both the actuarial imbalance and the unfunded liability of the current system, and hence would genuinely increase the rate of return to social security. Of course, such a plan is not costless, since one must take into account what those funds would have paid for in the absence of social security reform (e.g., a tax cut or a spending increase).

76. This argument applies even if, as some would argue, there is an inexplicably large equity premium, as we saw above.

77. As we will see, the same argument applies to the money's worth estimates of trust fund investment in equities.

78. In these figures the money's worth for the IA and PSA plans is everywhere above that for the Holdtax plan, though in principle one might expect them to be coincident or else cross; further research into this question continues.

79. This linear interpolation would be exact in the case of quadratic utility.

80. We arrive at this as follows. If the household were able to achieve a 50-50 split, the last $100 switched to equity would be worth zero. The 2 percent of payroll contribution (=1/6 of wealth) into stocks moves the investor one-third of the way toward the optimum, so the last $100 of this nets him $190 (=2/3 × $285 + 1/3 × $0). Therefore the average gain for this constrained household is approximately the average of these marginal gains, ($285+$190)/2 = $237.

81. This net present value gain of $59 would correspond to a risk-adjusted internal rate of return of 3.9 percent over 30 years on a full investment into stock, versus the 2.3 percent for an unconstrained investor, and the 7 percent for the first $100 of a totally constrained investor.

82. For a discussion of possible general equilibrium effects of increased demand for equities due to holding social security assets in equities see White (1996) and Munnell and Balduzzi (1998).

83. Additional stock in the hands of constrained households means less stock and less risk in the hands of unconstrained households. The effect is likely to be that unconstrained households will likely finance investment projects that are more risky.

84. The effect of this MB investment strategy on money's worth measures—versus holding only bonds in the trust fund—is not provided in the Advisory Council report. Nevertheless, one may compare the additional revenue gleaned from moving from a trust fund consisting of 40 percent stocks under the MB plan, to one where the trust fund held half of its portfolio in equities. This alternative, dubbed the MB+ plan by the Advisory Council, has PVB/PVT ratios that are equal to or surpass those of the PSA plan for all cohorts analyzed by as much as 5–7 percent (Advisory Council 1997: 218). On the other hand, money's worth for the MB+ trajectory is not pre-

cisely comparable to that for MB plan, since other plan features are not held constant; that is, the MB+ plan also raises taxes and borrowing as does the PSA plan, and benefits are boosted as revenue rises.

85. One caveat is that money management costs would likely be somewhat lower if the funds were centrally managed, instead of held in individual accounts (Mitchell 1998). On the other hand, individual accounts would afford the advantages of additional investment choice and probably additional service not provided by the government-run system.

86. In practice it seems unlikely that benefits would be left unchanged in response to a large market drop. There are numerous instances when benefits have been reduced under both private and public defined benefit pensions, including the cut in social security benefits due to the cost-of-living delay in 1983 (for a discussion of this change see Myers 1993).

References

Abel, Andrew B., N. Gregory Mankiw, Lawrence H. Summers, and J. Richard. "Assessing Dynamic Efficiency: Theory and Evidence." *Review of Economic Studies* 56, 1 (January 1989): 1–19.

Advisory Council on Social Security. *Report of the 1994–1996 Advisory Council on Social Security.* Washington, D.C.: Social Security Administration, 1997.

Ameriks, John and Stephen P. Zeldes. "How Do Household Portfolio Shares Vary with Age?" Working Paper. New York: Columbia University Graduate School of Business, in progress.

Beach, William W. and Gareth E. Davis. "Social Security's Rate of Return." Heritage Foundation Working Paper. Washington, D.C.: Heritage Foundation, January 1998.

Beard, Sam. *Restoring Hope in America: The Social Security Solution.* New York: ICS Press, 1996.

Board of Trustees. *Annual Report of the Board of Trustees.* Social Security Administration. Washington, D.C.: USGPO, various years.

Bohn, Henning. "Social Security Reform and Financial Markets." In Steven Sass, ed., *Social Security Reform: Links to Saving, Investment, and Growth.* Boston: Federal Reserve Bank of Boston, (forthcoming) 1998.

Boskin, Michael, Laurence Kotlikoff, Daniel Puffert, and John Shoven. "Social Security: A Financial Appraisal Across and Within Generations." *National Tax Journal* 40, 1 (March 1987): 19–34.

Boskin, Michael and Daniel Puffert. "The Financial Impact of Social Security by Cohort." In R. Ricardo-Campbell and E. P. Lazear, eds., *Issues in Contemporary Retirement.* Hoover Institution Press, 1988.

Brown, Stephen, William Goetzmann, and Stephen Ross. "Survival." *Journal of Finance* 50, 3 (July 1995): 853–73.

Caldwell, Steven et al. "Social Security's Treatment of Postwar Americans." NBER Working Paper 6603. Boston: National Bureau of Economic Research, June 1998.

Diamond, Peter. "A Framework for Social Security Analysis. *Journal of Public Economics* 8, 3 (December 1977): 275–98.

———. "Macroeconomic Aspects of Social Security Reform." *Brookings Papers on Economic Activity* 2 (1997): 1–87.

Diamond, Peter and Jonathan Gruber. "Social Security and Retirement in the U.S." NBER Working Paper 6097. Boston: National Bureau of Economic Research, July 1997.

Duggan, James E., John S. Greenlees, and Gillingham, Robert. "Returns Paid to Early Social Security Cohorts." *Contemporary Economic Policy* 11, 4 (October 1993): 1–13.

Feldstein, Martin. "Would Privatizing Social Security Raise Economic Welfare?" NBER Working Paper 5281. Boston: National Bureau of Economic Research, September 1995.

———. "Transition to a Fully Funded Pension System: Five Economic Issues." NBER Working Paper 6149. Boston: National Bureau of Economic Research, August 1997.

———. "Financing Our Old Age: A New Era of Social Security." *Public Interest* 130 (Winter 1988). 1998a.

———. "A New Plan to Rescue Social Security: Savings Grace." *New Republic*, April 6, 1998. 1998b.

Feldstein, Martin and Andrew Samwick. "The Transition Path in Privatizing Social Security." NBER Working Paper 5761. Boston: National Bureau of Economic Research, September 1996.

———. "The Economics of Prefunding Social Security and Medicare Benefits." NBER Working Paper 6055. Boston: National Bureau of Economic Research, June 1997.

Forbes, Stephen. "How to Replace Social Security." *Wall Street Journal*, December 18, 1996.

Geanakoplos, John, Olivia S. Mitchell, and Stephen P. Zeldes. "Would a Privatized Social Security System Really Pay a Higher Rate of Return?" In Douglas Arnold, M. Graetz, and Alicia Munnell, eds., *Framing the Social Security Debate*. Washington, D.C.: National Academy on Social Insurance and the Brookings Institution (forthcoming) 1998.

Goss, Stephen C. "Measuring Solvency in the Social Security System." This volume.

Gruber, Jonathan. "The Incidence of Payroll Taxation: Evidence from Chile." NBER Working Paper 5053. Boston: National Bureau of Economic Research, March 1995.

Hurd, Michael and John Shoven. "The Distributional Impact of Social Security." In David A. Wise, ed., *Pensions, Labor and Individual Choice*. Chicago: University of Chicago Press, 1985: 193–215.

Ibbotson, R. and Associates. *Stocks, Bonds, Bills and Inflation.* 1996 Yearbook. Chicago: Ibbotson Associates, 1997.

Kennickell, Arthur, Martha Starr-McCluer, and Annika E. Sunden. "Family Finances in the U.S.: Recent Evidence from the Survey of Consumer Finances." *Federal Reserve Bulletin* 83, 1 (January 1997): 1–24.

Kotlikoff, Laurence J. "On the Contribution of Economics to the Evaluation and Formation of Social Insurance Policy." *American Economic Review* 79, 2 (May 1989): 184–90.

Leimer, Dean R. "The Pareto Optimality of Pay-As-You-Go Social Security Programs." Office of Research and Statistics Working Paper No. 47. Washington, D.C.: Social Security Administration, June 1991.

———. "Cohort-Specific Measures of Lifetime Net Social Security Transfers." Office of Research and Statistics Working Paper No. 59. Washington, D.C.: Social Security Administration, February 1994.

———. "A Guide to Social Security Money's Worth Issues." *Social Security Bulletin* 58, 2 (Summer 1996): 3–20.

Lumsdaine, Robin and Olivia S. Mitchell. "Developments in the Economics of Retirement." Prepared for Orley Ashenfelter and David Card, eds., *Handbook of Labor Economics*. Amsterdam: North Holland, forthcoming.

Manchester, Joyce. "Compliance in Social Security Systems Around the World." This volume.

Mehra, Rajnish and Edward C. Prescott. "The Equity Premium: A Puzzle." *Journal of Monetary Economics* 15, 2 (March 1985): 145–61.

Miron, Jeffrey A. and David N. Weil. "The Genesis and Evolution of Social Security." In Michael D. Bordo, Claudia Goldin, and Eugene N. White, eds., *The Defining Moment: The Great Depression and the American Economy in the Twentieth Century.* Chicago: University of Chicago Press, 1998: 297–324.

Mitchell, Olivia S. "Administrative Costs of Public and Private Pension Plans." In Martin Feldstein, ed., *Privatizing Social Security.* Chicago: NBER and University of Chicago Press, 1998: 403–56.

Mitchell, Olivia S. and Flavio Barreto. "After Chile, What? Second-Round Social Security Reforms in Latin America." *Revista de Analisis Economico* 12, 2 (November 1997): 3–36.

Mitchell, Olivia S., James Poterba, Mark J. Warshawsky, and Jeff Brown. "New Evidence on the Money's Worth of Individual Annuities." *American Economic Review,* forthcoming (1999).

Mitchell, Olivia S. and Stephen P. Zeldes. "A Framework for Analyzing Social Security Privatization." *American Economic Review Papers and Proceedings* 86, 2 (May 1996): 363–67.

Moffitt, Robert. "Trends in Social Security Wealth by Cohort." In Marilyn Moon, ed., *Economic Transfers in the United States.* Studies in Income and Wealth 49. Chicago: University of Chicago Press, 1984: 327–53.

Moore, Stephen. "Testimony Before the House Ways and Means Committee." Social Security Subcommittee on the Future of Social Security for This Generation and the Next, US House of Representatives. Washington, D.C., June 24, 1997.

Munnell, Alicia H. and Pierluigi Balduzzi. "Investing the Social Security Trust Fund in Equities." Working paper, Boston College School of Management, Boston, March 1998.

Myers, Robert. *Social Security.* 4th edition. Pension Research Council. Philadelphia: University of Pennsylvania Press, 1993.

———. "Money's-Worth' Analysis of Social Security Benefits: Hardly Worth the Money It's Printed On!" *Contingencies* (July/August 1996): 10–11.

Myers, Robert and Bruce Schoebel. "An Updated Money's Worth Analysis of Social Security Retirement Benefits." *Transactions of the Society of Actuaries* (1992).

O'Connell, Stephen A. and Stephen P. Zeldes. "Dynamic Efficiency in the Gifts Economy." *Journal of Monetary Economics* 31, 3 (1993): 363–79.

Panis, Constantijn W. A. and Lee A. Lillard. "Socioeconomic Differentials in the Returns to Social Security." RAND Working paper. Santa Monica, Calif.: RAND Corporation, January 1985.

Siegel, Jeremy. *Stocks for the Long Run.* New York: Irwin, 1997.

Smetters, Kent. "Investing the Social Security Trust Fund in Equities." This volume.

Steuerle, C. Eugene and Jon M. Bakija. *Retooling Social Security for the 21st Century.* Washington, D.C.: Urban Institute Press, 1994.

Technical Panel on Trends and Issues in Retirement Saving. "Final Report to the Social Security Advisory Council." In *Report of the 1994–1996 Advisory Council on Social Security.* Washington, D.C.: Social Security Administration, 1997.

Technical Panel on Assumptions and Methods. "Final Report to the Social Security Advisory Council." In *Report of the 1994–1996 Advisory Council on Social Security.* Washington, D.C.: Social Security Administration, 1997.

Thompson, Lawrence. "The Social Security Reform Debate." *Journal of Economic Literature* 21, 4 (December 1983): 1425–67.

Tobin, James. "Social Security, Public Debt, and Economic Growth." In Tobin, ed., *Full Employment and Growth*. Cheltenham, U.K.: Edward Elgar, 1996: 254–85.

Wall Street Journal, "A Big Idea." April 7, 1998: A18.

White, Lawrence J. "Investing the Assets of the Social Security Trust Fund in Equity Securities: An Analysis." *Investment Perspective*. Washington, D.C.: Investment Company Institute, May 1996.

Chapter 6
Simulating Benefit Levels Under Alternative Social Security Reforms

Gordon P. Goodfellow and Sylvester J. Schieber

HSS
526 (us)

Proposals to reform the U.S. social security retirement program can arrayed along a spectrum. At one end of the spectrum would be a continuation of the existing program, structured as it is today, financed on a mostly pay-as-you-go basis and with benefits that are redistributive based on lifetime earnings. For example, Robert Myers (1997a and b), former chief actuary of social security, advocates keeping the system essentially in its current form with some relatively minor modifications. To finance promised benefits, he would increase the payroll tax on both workers and employers by 0.30 percent of covered wages in 2015, and by similar amounts in 2020, 2025, and 2030. To the extent that further changes would be required to keep the program solvent, he advocates that the age of eligibility for benefits be increased. At the other end of the spectrum would be virtually total withdrawal of the government from playing any role in individual workers' retirement accumulation or provision.

In practice, few would advocate that the U.S. government withdraw completely from its role in assuring the retirement security of its citizens. Even the strongest advocates of individual choice in these matters are concerned about potential free-rider problems that could arise if the government did not require workers to make some provision for their own retirement needs. For example, Feldstein and Samwick (1997) proposed a system of mandatory Personal Retirement Accounts (PRAs) that would replace social security benefits. This proposal would significantly change the government's current role in securing and delivering retirement benefits, though PRA participation would be mandated by the government. This PRA system would still be supported by a safety net of welfare programs like the Supplemental Security Income system and food stamps.

Between these two end-points along the social security policy spectrum, several intermediate proposals have been suggested (see Chapter 1, this volume). These are often characterized as privatization proposals, although they include varying degrees of funding, dependence on private financial markets, and personal retirement accounts. For example, the last Advisory Council on Social Security report (1997) described the Individual Account (IA) option as one where workers would contribute 1.6 percent of covered payroll to a mandatory savings program to be administered by the Social Security Administration (SSA). As these personal accounts grew, conventional social security benefits would be curtailed somewhat. SSA would operate the mandatory savings program much like a national 401(k) plan, with a limited number of investment options across which workers could allocate their contributions and accumulating assets. At retirement, the accumulated assets would be converted to annuities. This IA proposal would give workers greater control and flexibility than the system as modified according to Myers, so it would go some distance along the privatization spectrum. Under the IA plan, however, the government would still mandate contribution rates, manage all the assets of the system including those in the personal accounts, and require the annuitization of benefits at retirement. Hence, the extent of privatization in this proposal would still be extremely limited.

A second Advisory Council proposal, dubbed the Personal Security Account (PSA) option, would require workers to invest 5 percent of covered earnings now paid to social security. This option would allow workers to manage the investment of their retirement assets with much greater discretion than under the IA plan. It would not require that PSA accumulations be annuitized (or at least not be annuitized above certain base retirement income levels). This plan calls for even larger cuts in social security benefits than the IA plan. Because the PSA proposal would give individual workers more opportunity to make personal choices, it would go further along the "privatization spectrum" than the IA proposal.

Other reform proposals can be classified along the privatization spectrum, based on their curtailment of benefits provided directly through social security and the degree of personal choice they allow workers in managing some of their own retirement accumulations. For example, the Committee on Economic Development, an association of private business executives, has a proposal positioned along the privatization spectrum between the Advisory Council's IA and PSA proposals (CED 1997). This is because it calls for greater curtailment of social security's traditional benefits than the former, but less than the latter. It also calls for a mandatory 3 percent of pay mandatory contribution that would go to a personal account. It would give workers some discretion in how their money was invested, but would require annuitization at retirement.

Proponents of social security reform frequently develop comparative analyses showing the provision of retirement benefits under current law and under the proposed reform option. Typically, the projected asset accumulations of individual workers under reform options that include personal accounts are based on historical long-term real rates of return for various classes of assets, assuming that workers would invest in "standardized" portfolios during their working careers. It is not uncommon for proponents of reform to calculate potential benefits under personal account options by assuming rates of return equivalent to historical mean or median rates of return on the assumed portfolios (see Carter and Shipman 1996; Feldstein and Samwick 1997; Advisory Council 1997).

Opponents of personal social security accounts are often critical of the projected benefits estimated to flow from such plans for two reasons. First, they argue that the stylized portfolios are not representative of likely investment patterns across the income spectrum. In particular, they suggest that lower-wage workers have largely been left out of 401(k) plans to date, have little investment experience, and might invest far more conservatively than the standardized portfolio. Second, they argue that the presentation of "typical" or average results obscures the range of outcomes that might be expected under such proposals. Both of these criticisms are examined in this chapter using a simulation model.

401(k) Participant Investment Patterns

To assess how workers direct the investment of their own retirement savings, we analyze administrative record files for 80 employer-sponsored 401(k) plans at the end of 1995. These plans are selected randomly, and hence are not necessarily representative of the universe of 401(k) plans. However, there is no reason to believe that these plans are atypical of patterns of investment behavior in plans of this sort.[1]

Our analysis of 401(k) investment patterns considers only the asset allocation patterns of employee contributions, since we are interested in workers' investment behavior. In addition, the investment options for employer contributions are more likely to be restricted to specific assets, most notably to employer stock. The analysis does not adjust workers' investment behavior to account for the fact that, in some plans, employer contributions are directed almost entirely to company stock. For this reason, we have probably understated somewhat the willingness of younger and middle-aged workers to invest in equities on their own.

The distribution of participant investments and asset holdings in these plans appears in Table 1. "Fixed income" investment vehicles account for 28 percent of total assets, which include money market funds, bonds, and guaranteed interest or stable value funds. "Balanced funds," which include a combination of bonds and corporate equities, account for another 8 percent of the assets. Assuming that the funds invested in the balanced funds in our analysis are roughly evenly split between fixed-income assets and equity assets, about one-third of the total assets in the 80 plans included here are

TABLE 1. 401(k) Assets by Type of Investment

Type of Asset	Participants with This Asset Type	Percent with This Asset Type	Total Assets	Percent of Total Assets	Average Asset Balance
Fixed income	61,102	60.2%	$538,934,914	28.3%	$ 5,314
Balanced fund	22,190	21.9	157,703,354	8.3	1,555
Company stock	25,954	25.6	309,113,664	16.2	3,048
Domestic equity	65,127	64.2	855,220,891	44.9	8,433
International equity	10,675	10.5	44,436,868	2.3	438
Total	101,417		1,905,409,691	100.	18,788

Source: Authors' calculations.
Note: The data are restricted to pay levels ≥$5,000 and balance ≥$10.

invested in fixed-income instruments, although well over half of the participants in the plans hold such assets. Sixteen percent of the assets is held in the corporate stock of the plan sponsor, and 47 percent in other equity funds. By comparison, Access Research, Inc. (1997a) estimates that 20 percent of all 401(k) assets is invested in guaranteed or stable value funds, 5 percent in money market funds, 7 percent in bonds, and 23 percent in the stock of the plan sponsor. This suggests that the distribution of assets in our dataset corresponds fairly closely with the distribution of assets across all 401(k) plans. Our sample plans average about 1,270 active participants per plan, with average participant balances of roughly $18,800. By comparison, Access Research (1997b) estimates that the average 401(k) balance in 1995 was $31,000, but their plan balances include both employer and employee financed funds, whereas ours include only the latter.

Table 2 focuses on subsets of the 401(k) participants by age, namely, those earning between $5,000 and $15,000, $25,000 and $35,000, and $60,000 and $75,000 per year. These three pay categories bracket the earnings levels designated as "low," "average," and "maximum" social security actuaries. The data indicate that higher-wage workers consistently invest a larger share of their retirement assets in equities than lower-wage workers, and younger workers consistently invest a larger share of their retirement assets in equities than their older counterparts. Table 3 summarizes equity holding patterns across age groups, and reveals that workers hold a relatively high fraction of their portfolio in stock, across all pay levels. We also show rates of equity investments developed by Dickson (1997), used for the Advisory Council's analysis of personal account accumulations and benefits under the IA and PSA proposals. Evidently, Dickson's investment portfolios assumed a more conservative asset allocation pattern than those of the 401(k) participants used in the current analysis.[2]

Dickson (1997) also suggested that annuitization requirements at retire-

TABLE 2. 401(k) Assets by Type of Investment, Plan Participant Age, and Earnings Level

	Percent of Assets by Participant Age					
	Under 21	*21–30*	*31–40*	*41–50*	*51–60*	*60+*
Annual earnings less than $15,000						
Fixed income	10.4	32.0	36.2	45.6	55.0	59.6
Balanced fund	1.7	6.4	7.8	8.7	8.6	5.9
Company stock	8.3	2.3	1.5	1.3	2.3	0.4
Domestic equity	77.5	55.2	52.4	42.5	31.9	31.7
International equity	2.1	4.1	2.1	1.9	2.2	2.3
Annual earnings $25,000 to $34,999						
Fixed income	0.0	25.6	29.7	34.7	39.1	44.3
Balanced fund	0.0	6.0	8.3	11.1	14.5	16.0
Company stock	100.0	19.8	18.1	15.7	14.0	11.7
Domestic equity	0.0	46.7	42.0	36.8	31.0	26.8
International equity	0.0	1.9	1.9	1.7	1.4	1.2
Annual earnings $60,000 to $74,999						
Fixed income	0.0	13.5	16.9	23.7	31.4	37.3
Balanced fund	0.0	8.9	10.0	8.1	7.5	7.8
Company stock	0.0	15.4	17.7	17.3	21.1	11.3
Domestic equity	0.0	57.8	53.0	48.8	38.2	42.7
International equity	0.0	4.4	2.3	2.1	1.8	0.9

Source: Authors' calculations.
Note: The data are restricted to pay levels ≥$5,000 and balance ≥$10.

ment could influence investment of assets during the working career. For instance, the PSA plan does not require annuitization of personal account distributions at retirement, whereas the IA plan would require annuitization. As a result, risk-averse individuals might invest more conservatively toward the end of their working careers if they are required to annuitize their asset accumulations at retirement, in order to guard against deterioration in the accrued value of their assets during market downturns. It is because of this latter reasoning that the stylized portfolios for IA investors were assumed to be allocated more conservatively at higher ages than those of the PSA investors.

Comparing Dickson's assumed equity investment patterns in the PSA and IA plans with the actual pattern of investment by our sample of 401(k) investors, we conclude that the earlier analysis of the IA failed to account for variations in investment behavior across earnings classes. As a result, the previous analysis of these proposals may have been biased. Specifically, the pattern of more equity investing by workers at higher earnings levels means that the distribution of investment risk and expected returns varies across earnings groups. Below we assess how differences in investment behavior

TABLE 3. 401(k) Assets Invested in Equities by Plan Participant Age and Earnings Level: Actual and Assumed Rates

	Percent of Assets in Equities by Age of Participants				
	20s	*30s*	*40s*	*50s*	*60s*
Assumed rates					
PSA assumed rate	55.0	55.0	52.0	48.0	43.0
IA assumed rate	55.0	55.0	50.0	40.0	20.0
Actual rates					
Low-wage earner	64.8	59.9	50.0	40.7	37.4
Average-wage	71.4	66.1	59.7	53.6	47.7
Maximum-wage	82.0	78.1	72.2	64.8	58.8

Sources: "Assumed rates" from Advisory Council (1997): 171.

across the earnings spectrum affect anticipated investment patterns of the alternative reform plans.

Expected Investment Returns over Time

One reason that social security privatization plans seem so promising is that the assumed rates of return on assets accumulated under the proposals significantly exceed rates of return that will be achieved under the current system. But rates of return used in these analyses are controversial for at least three reasons. The first reason pertains to the assumed differential between the long-term rates of return on financial assets and the rates of return that accrue under the current system; the second concerns the administrative costs associated with the different reform proposals; and the third relates to volatility in returns over time and variations in benefits levels resulting from such volatility. We take up each in turn.

Expected Long-Term Rates of Return Under Alternative Social Security Approaches

Many analysts contend that today's workers will earn low returns on their contributions to the social security system. As discussed by Mitchell, Geanakoplos, and Zeldes (this volume), cohorts born after 1940 expect rates of return below two percent on average. For two-earner couples, expected returns based on benefits under current law are consistently between 0.3 and 0.4 percentage points higher than they are for single workers, and for workers with higher earnings levels, projected returns are lower. For single workers whose earnings are consistently at maximum levels throughout their careers, the current law returns are consistently below 0.5 percent. Of course, these returns will not, in fact, be paid since the current social security system underfunding means that taxes must rise or benefits must fall in the future. Either of these changes portends further reductions in the rates of return, to one percent or less.

For this reason, personal account proposals that give workers the prospect of getting historical financial market returns hold out considerable promise. Carter and Shipman (1996) argue that personal account investment could earn nominal rates of return of 10.5 to 12.5 percent per year, and Feldstein and Samwick (1997) assume a real rate of 9 percent per year in simulating their PRA proposal. Dickson (1997, p. 485) estimates that "based on historical averages, the real expected equity return would be about 9.25 percent per year." The Social Security Advisory Council used 7.0 percent as its "average" expected annual real rate of return on equities, a rate that corresponds roughly to the median return on equities over the last 70 years. For government bonds, the Advisory Council assumed an ultimate long-term real rate of 2.3 percent per year.[3]

Administrative Cost Considerations

Opponents of personal account reform proposals also argue that historical rates of return cannot be realized because of asset management and record keeping costs. For example, when a mutual fund company services an IRA account, it charges roughly $30 to $35 per account per year (Dickson 1997). This may be especially problematic for millions of workers with small accounts. As an example, consider the case of a student who works 40 hours a week in the summer at a minimum wage job. Such a workers would earn roughly $2,600, generating a PSA contribution of about $130 that year. If he were charged $35 for the management of his account, the charge would amount to 27 percent of his contributions. Part-time workers who worked throughout the year would face similar or even larger administrative burdens.

There may be ways to reduce the administrative burdens on small accounts, but the administrative costs are not trivial. A few basis points can ultimately mean significant differences in retirement accumulations over the long term. For example, consider a worker who earned $30,000 in her first year out of school, starting at age 21, and whose pay grew by 1 percent over inflation each year. Assume that she contributed 5 percent of pay to a PSA-type account throughout her career and the assets earned returns at a real rate of 4 percent per year. At age 65, her accumulated balance would be 28 percent larger if she incurred investment expenses of 50 basis points (bp) per year, than if she incurred expenses of 150 bp per year (note that 100 bp is equivalent to 1.00 percent per year). The difference in the two balances at age 65 would be equivalent to 85 percent of her final year's salary.

The Advisory Council's analysis assumed that the annual administrative fees for the IA plan would be 10.5 basis points per year, and 100 basis points per year for the PSA plan. Opponents of personal account options argue that the administrative loadings would probably prove to be higher than the Council's assumed rates if either of the plans were adopted. Mitchell (1998) has looked at administrative costs in a wide range of public and private retirement systems both here and elsewhere around the world. She estimates that expense ratios for small and mid-sized 401(k) plans with an annuity product generally run at less than 100 bp if the plan offers an index equity fund, a balanced fund, a fixed income fund, and a money market fund. She estimates that a PSA-type system that could take advantage of existing 401(k) investment options might incur administrative costs of $50 to $60 per year if there were no annuities involved and an added $100 per year if an annuity option were included. Assuming a starting annual cost of $160 per year, with the administrative costs growing at the rate of growth in wages, lifetime administrative fees in a PSA plan realizing 4 percent real returns per year would be less than 30 basis points per year for a worker whose starting salary was $30,000 at age 21. For a worker whose initial pay level was $10,000 per year and whose wages grow at only 1 percent real per year, the cost would still be only 80 basis points per year. Using Morningstar data, Dickson (1997) found that overall arithmetic average of management expense for mutual funds was 122 bp per year, but the dollar-weighted average was 93 bp. This suggests that investors are sensitive to management expenses. Dickson noted that if personal accounts were invested in certificates of deposit and fixed annuities, the administrative costs would be higher. But he also noted that if administrative expenses were capped at 50 to 75 bp per year, many financial firms would still offer to manage the personal accounts under a plan modeled along the lines of the PSA plan.

Our analysis, in the next section, uses the same administrative cost rates employed by the Advisory Council — that is, 10.5 bp for the IA proposal.[4] For the PSA plan from the Advisory Council and another plan that would fully privatize social security, we use 100 bp as the annual administrative cost. This, we believe, is a conservative assumption and consistent with Dickson and Mitchell.[5]

Volatility of Returns over Time

Another concern about the rate-of-return assumptions used in many assessments of personal account proposals is that they do not recognize return volatility. For example, Figure 1 shows that the annualized total rates of return on large company stocks have varied considerably over the period 1926 to 1995. Consider the plight of a worker who hoped to retire at the beginning of 1975, and who had heavily invested in the stock market throughout his career. For such a person, inflation-adjusted returns on large-company stocks were −21.6 percent in 1973, and −34.5 percent in 1974. The net

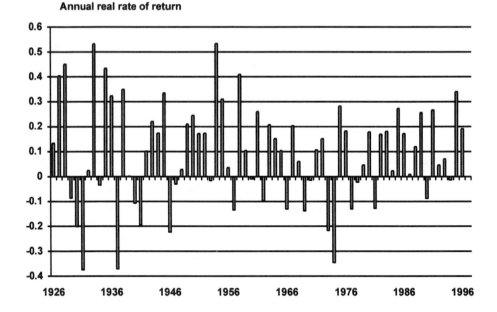

Figure 1. Annualized total inflation-adjusted rates of return on large company stocks, 1926–95. Source: Ibbotson, R. and Associates (1996).

effect of this two-year period would have been to cut in half his retirement assets held as compared to 1972. Of course, this risk is overstated to the extent that older workers tend to shift assets into fixed-income vehicles. In any event, the fact that returns do fluctuate over time suggests that a proper evaluation of alternatives must compare these risks across social security reform scenarios.[6]

Potential Variation in Benefit Levels Under Alternative Social Security Reforms

Though no one knows what the future holds, certain financial market relationships have persisted historically. For example, real returns on Treasury bills are more serially correlated than the returns on stocks. As Fischer (1983: 153) has noted, "the variance of unexpected real returns on stocks, looking ahead one month, is about one hundred times the variance of the unexpected real returns on bills." This is what makes stock investing more risky in the short term than investing in government T-bills. However, Table 4 shows that investing in stocks has yielded historical higher returns than in either T-bills or bonds, particularly over a longer holding period.

TABLE 4. Investment Performance of Stocks and Bonds by Holding Period

		Percent of Time		
Holding Period	Time Period	Stocks Outperformed Bonds	Stocks Outperformed T-Bills	Bonds Outperformed T-Bills
1 Year	1802–1992	60.2	61.3	49.4
	1871–1982	59.0	63.9	52.5
2 Years	1802–1992	64.7	64.7	53.2
	1871–1882	64.5	68.6	58.7
5 Years	1802–1992	69.5	72.7	51.9
	1871–1882	71.2	74.6	60.2
10 Years	1802–1992	79.7	79.1	52.8
	1871–1882	82.3	84.1	59.3
20 Years	1802–1992	91.3	94.2	51.7
	1871–1882	94.2	99.0	59.2
30 Years	1802–1992	99.4	96.9	46.9
	1871–1882	100.0	100.0	58.1

Source: Siegel (1994): 31.

Analysts often use historical financial market patterns to model alterna-tive investment strategies and to project future returns under various invest-ment risk/return scenarios. There are two main modeling approaches used to assess the implications of alternative investment patterns for participants in individually managed retirement accounts. The first assumes that histor-ical patterns of returns will be repeated. For example, McCurdy and Shoven (1992) compare retirement accumulations for workers who invested their retirement saving entirely in stocks over their working careers with those who invested it all in bonds. They simulate likely returns by taking 25-, 30-, 35-, and 40-year moving averages of historical returns over the period 1926 through 1989. Poterba, Venti, and Wise (1997) use a similar methodology to project potential accumulations in 401(k) plans, assuming the workers in-vested in an all-stock portfolio throughout their careers, an all-bond port-folio, or a portfolio that was half bonds and half stocks. In both cases, the evidence shows that a strategy of investing all the retirement savings in stocks consistently outperformed a strategy of investing the assets entirely in bonds.

A different projection approach uses a Monte Carlo model to draw histor-ical return rates randomly from prior periods, assigning them serially to create a wide range of potential future scenarios. Each of these scenarios is thought of as representing one possible outcome for a given investment strategy. The collection of resulting scenarios generates a probability dis-tribution of outcomes under that investment strategy, which along with the specification of preference goals allows the selection of optimal investment strategies. This approach has been used by Bajtelsmit, Johnson, and Nugent (1997) to project potential account balances and retirement benefit levels under the IA and PSA plans, and to compare them to benefits under a reform option that would essentially match the benefits promised under current law. That study did not account for administrative expenses or variations in the investment portfolios across workers' life cycles or at varying earnings levels, improvements that we think are crucial to realistic modeling of social security reform proposals.

Simulating Outcomes Under Various Social Security Reform Options

In this section we simulate three personal account plans, selected to fall at different points along the privatization spectrum discussed earlier. The first has a relatively small portion of total mandated retirement contributions in a personal account; the second has half of total retirement contributions in such an account; and the third has all contributions deposited in such an account.[7]

The first plan corresponds to the IA option developed by the Social Security Advisory Council. Here, social security benefits would be gradually scaled down to fit within the current payroll tax rate of 12.4 percent of covered payroll that finances Old-Age and Survivors Insurance and Disability Insurance (OASDI) benefits.[8] This plan mandates that workers save 1.6 percent of covered pay on top of the modified OASDI benefit, deposited into an IA account. This account would be managed by social security or its agents, giving workers limited ability to direct the investment of their accounts across broad index funds representing various segments of the financial markets.

The second plan is the Advisory Council's PSA proposal, under which disability and early survivors benefits would continue to be financed by the 2.4 percent of covered payroll that now finances those benefits, administered through the Social Security Administration. Half the remaining payroll tax (5 percent of covered payroll) would go to finance a flat floor benefit worth $410 per month (in 1996 dollars) provided to all full-career workers. This flat benefit would grow over time at the rate of growth of average wages in the economy. The remainder of the payroll tax would be invested in a PSA managed by the worker. Workers over age 55 in 1998 under this proposal would continue to participate in the existing system. Those between ages 25 and 55 in 1998 would be covered on a prospective basis under the new system. At retirement, they would receive a combined benefit based partly on their participation in the current system prior to 1998, and partly on their participation in the reformed system from 1998 onward. For those 25 years of age or younger in 1998, their full benefit at retirement would be based on their participation in the reformed system.

The third proposal we examine we call the Full Privatization (FP) plan, though disability and early survivor benefits would still be provided through the government as in the PSA proposal. Under the FP plan, the entire 10 percent of covered payroll that now goes to finance retirement benefits under the Old-Age and Survivors Insurance (OASI) program would be diverted to a personal account managed by the worker in the same fashion as the PSA plan. Consistent with the PSA transition, we assume that workers over age 55 (in 1998) would continue to be covered under the current system. Those between ages 25 and 55 (in 1998) would be covered under a combined system that would provide them a pro rata lifetime benefit based on their participation in the current system until 1998, supplemented by the benefits financed out of their FP personal account that accumulates between the beginning of 1998 and their retirement at age 65. Those workers aged 25 and under in 1998 would be fully covered by the new system.

Four birth cohorts covering people born in 1945, 1955, 1965, and 1975 are the focus of the analysis for prototypical workers with "low," "average," and "maximum" earnings levels. In each case, the simulations assume that the reform is implemented in 1998 and workers retire at age 65. As noted, we account for administrative expenses and also vary the composition of investment portfolios over the life cycle and across the wage distribution. Most of the models assume that accumulated balances in the personal accounts are converted to indexed annuities at age 65 on the same basis as in the Advisory Council's report. These annuity conversion rates do not include insurance loading factors that would be incurred if annuities were bought commercially. A final set of simulations does incorporate the cost of purchasing private annuities.

Investment portfolio allocations for the PSA and FP plan projections assume that workers at each earnings level would invest in equities at the rates shown in Table 3. For the IA plan projections, results are adjusted to account for the forced annuitization of benefits at retirement. We adjusted by the ratio of assumed IA to PSA investment in equities that was taken from the top two lines in Table 3.[9] This means that the personal account portfolios are somewhat more conservative for workers above age 40 for the IA projections than they are for the PSA and FP projections.

Monte Carlo simulations use nominal rates of return and inflation rates from a Watson Wyatt Asset Modeling system used for projecting investment scenarios for pension plan sponsors. The underlying assumptions in these simulations do not directly parallel the historical return patterns imbedded in the 1926–95 period used in the prior simulations. The expected risk-free real rate of return is significantly higher than that observed historically over the long term, 1.7 percent versus 0.6 percent. In addition, the expected risk

TABLE 5. Compound Average Returns over Selected Historical Periods

	Time Period (percent)			
	70 years 1926–1995	45 years 1951–1995	25 years 1971–1995	10 years 1986–1995
Inflation rate	3.1	4.1	5.6	3.5
Treasury bill rate	3.7	5.2	7.0	5.6
Real T-bill rate	0.6	1.1	1.4	2.1
Large-cap stock rates	10.5	12.2	12.2	14.8
Real l-cap stock rates	7.4	8.1	6.6	11.3
L-cap stock minus T-bill	6.8	7.0	5.2	9.2
Small-cap stock rates	12.5	14.5	15.5	11.9
Real s-cap stock rates	9.4	10.4	9.9	8.4
S-cap stock minus T-bill	8.8	9.3	8.5	6.3
Intermediate gov't bonds	5.3	6.4	9.0	9.1
Real interm gov't bonds	2.2	2.3	3.4	5.6
Int gov't bonds minus T-bill	1.6	1.2	2.0	3.5
Long-term gov't bonds	5.2	5.8	9.6	11.9
Real L-T gov't bond rates	2.1	1.7	4.0	8.4
L-T gov't bonds minus T-bill	1.5	0.6	2.6	6.3

Source: Ibbotson, R. and Associates (1996).

premiums for each asset class are generally lower than the observed historical risk premiums. We believe this is defensible because the capital market experience of the last 10 to 15 years suggests that the real risk-free rate has risen significantly. The rise in the real risk-free rate can be directly observd from the level of short-term interest rates — e.g., 30-day US Treasury bills as shown in Table 5 — which carry a minimum risk premium for unanticipated inflation. This measure of the real risk-free rate has averaged 1.4 percent over the last 25 years and 2.1 percent over the past 10 years, compared to 0.6 percent over the period from 1926 through 1995. Higher levels in recent years can be attributed to tight monetary policies and society's willingness or unwillingness to save at historical rates. The expected compound average return on large-capital stocks is assumed to be 9.2 percent (5.7 percent real) with a standard deviation of 17.5 percent. This compares with a historical average of 10.5 percent per year (7.4 percent real) over the 70-year period from 1926 to 1995, as shown in Table 5. Real returns are expected to be somewhat lower in this sector than the historical averages, because we are currently in one of the longest sustained bull markets in history. In addition, we believe that it makes sense to be conservative in estimating potential returns in this sector because of the concerns that some people have raised about the possible pricing effects on stocks when the baby boomers begin to liquidate their lifetime savings during their retirement period (e.g., see

Schieber and Shoven 1996). In developing the projections presented here, the expected return on small-capital stocks is 7.3 percent real versus 9.4 percent for the historical long-term rate.

While stock returns used in the simulation are somewhat lower than those actually experienced over the 70-year period 1926–95, the returns on bonds are somewhat higher than historical averages — 0.5 percent per year. This reflects the higher returns on risk-free assets in recent years and also wariness about government's ability to deal with the aging of the baby boom and their potential claims on government budgets. Although public policy-makers have made significant progress on balancing the federal budget on a current cash basis, they have not yet significantly addressed the long-term fiscal imbalances in entitlement programs. Over the last decade, unfunded liabilities calculated on an ongoing basis for social security alone have risen by several hundred billion dollars more than has the federal debt. The unfunded liabilities in Medicare have risen by even greater amounts. Until these liabilities are addressed, long-term government bond rates are likely to stay above historical long-term rates.

Model simulations generated 500 scenarios of returns for three investment vehicles over an 80-year period. The investment vehicles are equities, bonds, and short-term fixed investments best characterized as money market funds. The equity returns are based on a blend of 75 percent large-cap stocks and 25 percent small-cap stocks. The bond return is based on an assumed 50-50 blend of intermediate government and corporate bond returns, and the money market return a blend of the returns on short-term fixed-income investments. The compound average returns over the 500 simulations were 5.5 percent per year on the money market funds (1.5 percent real) with a standard deviation of 1.9 percent, 7.6 percent on the bond funds (3.6 percent real) with a standard deviation of 7.5 percent, and 10.8 percent on the stock funds (6.8 percent real) with a standard deviation of 7.5 percent.

Projection Results and Analysis

The simulations presented next use a Monte Carlo model that generates investment returns with a variance distribution consistent with U.S. historical patterns.[10]

Baseline Projections

Projections for a low-earnings worker born in 1965 appear in Figure 2. The various panels reflect the cumulative probability distribution of benefits that would be provided under the three reform plans. The top left-hand panel shows the distribution of pre-tax benefits expected under the IA: for instance, there is a 50 percent probability that expected benefits would be

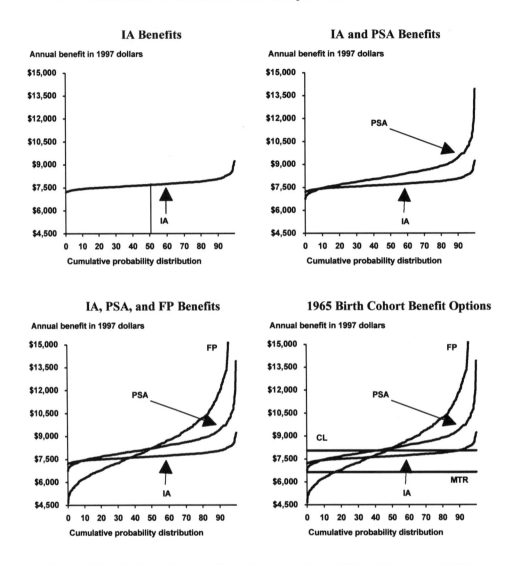

Figure 2. Distribution of expected benefit levels under the PSA and IA plans for 1965 birth cohorts, workers with low lifetime earnings. Source: Authors' calculations.

roughly $7,700. The range of benefits across the whole probability distribution goes from around $7,200 to $9,200. The top left-hand panel shows the distribution of projected pre-tax benefits under the simulated PSA plan. In this case the PSA projected benefits exceed the benefits provided by the IA plan in roughly 92 percent of the simulations: projected benefits at the 50 percent probability level are $8,200 for the PSA plan, versus $7,700 for the IA plan. At the bottom end of the probability distribution, there is some added downside risk in the PSA plan which would provide only a $6,800 benefit versus $7,200 for the IA plan. Conversely there is significantly greater upside potential with a maximum benefit under the PSA plan of around $14,000, versus $9,200 under the IA plan. Eliminating the extreme tails of the two distributions, in 95 percent of the simulated outcomes the PSA benefits fall between $7,100 and $10,500, and the IA benefits between $7,300 and $8,400. For this worker, the PSA plan would seem to offer considerable upside gain, without large added downside risk.

The bottom left-hand panel in Figure 2 adds the FP plan pre-tax benefit pattern. At the 50 percent probability level, the FP and PSA plan provide essentially the same benefit. In about half the cases, the FP benefit would be considerably above that of the PSA plan, but in the other half it would be considerably lower. The FP benefit exceeds the IA benefit in roughly 60 percent of the simulations. While the FP plan provides much greater upside potential than either of the other plans, it would do so at the cost of adding substantial downside risk for this particular worker.

All three plans may be compared to current law (CL) benefits in the bottom right-hand panel of Figure 2. Of course, current law benefits cannot be paid unless additional taxes are raised. Another reference level in the bottom right-hand panel of Figure 2 represents estimated pretax benefit that could be maintained under the current OASDI payroll tax rate. This particular benefit, called the "Maintain Tax Rate" (MTR) benefit level, is exactly equal to the benefit provided under the defined benefit element of the IA plan. As noted earlier, the MTR benefit would redistribute social security benefits somewhat differently across the earnings spectrum than current law because it would reduce benefits more for workers with higher earnings than for those at lower earnings levels. While other patterns of benefit reductions could be developed to live within the current financing rates, this is at least as good a model for comparing policy alternatives as any other.

The two horizontal lines in Figure 2 and subsequent figures can be thought of as defining the range of policy options for redefining benefits within the context of the current structure of social security. The top line assumes that all adjustments to current policy will be made on the financing side by raising revenues. The bottom line assumes that all adjustments to current policy will be made on the benefit side by reducing expenditures.

Alternative projections for workers at the low-, average-, and maximum-earnings levels are offered in Figures 3, 4, and 5 respectively, where each figure shows the results of a complete set of projections for a different birth cohorts. All benefits are shown on a pre-tax basis. All of the plans simulated assume that the reform would be implemented in 1998, so workers in the 1945 birth cohort would participate in the reformed systems between 10

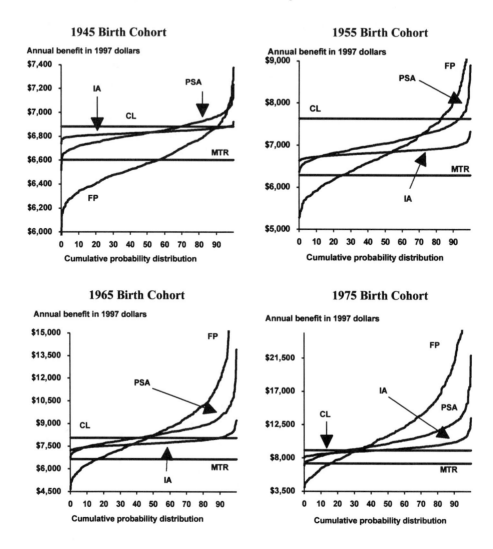

Figure 3. Distribution of expected benefit levels under the PSA and IA plans for selected birth cohorts, workers with low lifetime earnings. Source: Authors' calculations.

and 15 years prior to retirement, depending on actual retirement dates. Those in the 1955 cohort would spend roughly half their working lives in the current system and half in the reformed system. Those born in 1975 would spend virtually all of their working lives in the reformed system.

Simulations for workers with low earnings are shown in Figure 3. For the

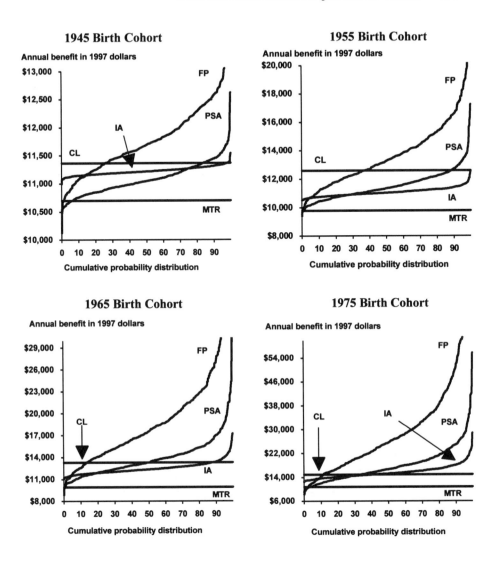

Figure 4. Distribution of expected benefit levels under the PSA and IA plans for selected birth cohorts, workers with average lifetime earnings. Source: Authors' calcuations. Note: scales on panels vary.

1945 birth cohort, the FP plan would present significant downside risk relative to either the IA or PSA, plans with very little potential upside opportunity. The variance across and between the PSA and IA plans appears considerably less than with the FP plan. For subsequent birth cohorts, the FP plan would provide somewhat greater upside opportunity, but still presents

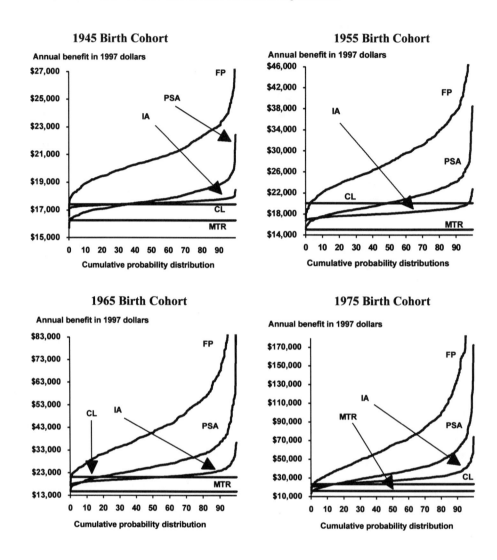

Figure 5. Distribution of expected benefit levels under the PSA and IA plans for selected birth cohorts, workers with maximum lifetime earnings. Source: Authors' calculations. Note: scales on panels vary.

considerable downside risk for workers with low earnings levels. As we will show later, these downside risks become even greater for workers with low earnings who consistently invest conservatively throughout their working lives. The PSA plan performs as well or better than the IA in about 90 percent of the simulations for the 1955 and subsequent birth cohorts. For workers with average and maximum earnings levels throughout their careers, the PSA plan would generally provide a level of benefits superior to the IA plan for all but the earliest cohorts affected by the plans. The FP plan, on the other hand, appears to create mostly upside opportunities relative to either the IA or PSA plans.

One issue not addressed in this chapter is the issue of transition costs that the various proposals would create. These are addressed at some length by the Advisory Council (1997), by Feldstein and Samwick (1997), and by Geanakoplos, Mitchell, and Zeldes (this volume). Advocates of the PSA proposed an explicit increase in the payroll tax of 1.52 percent of covered payroll plus some transitional borrowing over a 70-year period to cover these costs. Feldstein and Samwick would cover the transition costs for their proposal by a similar taxing mechanism, although their transition costs would be somewhat hidden in that they merely propose the personal account benefit be funded up to a level that matches the benefits provided by social security under current law. The point is that while the FP plan would provide a superior benefit to the PSA, IA, or current law benefit for most workers at or above average earnings levels, there may be substantial transition costs associated with the provision of such benefits.

Figures 4 and 5 support the approach that Feldstein and Samwick have taken in developing their proposal. These results suggest that there would be considerable room in the transition to a fully privatized system to use some of the current contribution rates for workers with average earnings or higher to pay transition costs for getting out of the current system. This would be accomplished by using a portion of the contributions from such workers to pay transition costs directly, leaving the remainder of their contributions to fund a personal account benefit in line with current law benefit levels. These results also suggest that there might be some flexibility to develop a redistributive mechanism on the contributory side of a fully privatized system, where workers with higher earnings levels would have some portion of their contributions redistributed to those with lower earnings. These redistributed contributions could be used by the workers with lower earnings to offset the downside risks they would suffer under a fully privatized system, as discussed above.

Benefit Projections for Conservative Investors

Simulations thus far assume that workers will invest in accordance with the patterns shown in Table 3. We believe these are reasonable assumptions on average, but some workers will be more conservative investors throughout their lives. For this reason, we have computed the fraction of workers who invested 80 percent of more of their 401(k) money in fixed income investment vehicles during 1995. The results show that while low-wage workers are somewhat more likely to invest conservatively than those with higher earn-

TABLE 6. 401(k) Plan Participants Holding 80 to 100 Percent of Self-Directed Plan Balances in Fixed-Income Assets, by Earnings Level

	Percent of Participants by Earnings Level		
Participant's Age	Under $15,000	$25,000 to $34,999	$60,000 to $74,999
20s	18.5	13.4	5.5
30s	20.3	19.4	8.4
40s	23.3	24.2	12.9
50s	32.3	28.8	15.7
60s	40.6	33.9	25.7

Source: Authors' calculations.
Note: The data are restricted to pay levels ≥$5,000 and balance ≥$10.

ings, there are also many higher-paid workers who would invest quite conservatively over their whole careers (see Table 6).

How would our results change if we assumed the worker invested all of his retirement savings in bonds over his entire working life? Results under the PSA and the IA proposals (Figure 6) are more similar to each other than in the earlier presentations, and there is a relatively smaller probability of achieving benefit levels comparable to those in current law. The downside risks are greater under the FP plan for all birth cohorts than in the earlier simulations. These results suggest that the potential beneficial effects of funding under a range of personal account plans can largely be offset by failure to diversify investments. But new financial products may be developed that could make even risk-averse individuals better off under personal account proposals than the results shown in Figure 6. For example, a product that provided a guaranteed rate of return over a specified investment period, but still allowed the investor to participate in some share of the upside benefit of higher returns if the market performs better than the return guarantee, could provide an acceptable floor for accumulations for risk-averse investors.

Table 7 shows the potential benefits that workers could achieve if they participated in such an investment program, when the real annual return on their personal account investments is 3 percent. Under the IA plan, the first three cohorts would receive benefits comparable to those under current law, and the PSA plan would out-perform current law in every case. The FP plan would provide benefits consistently 60 to 100 percent higher than the PSA plan. Part of the challenge in crafting a personal account proposal for reforming social security is to find creative ways to deal with the problems that can arise under such approaches. If future long-term financial market returns can approach the levels we have experienced over the past century, there should be considerable room to guarantee investors real

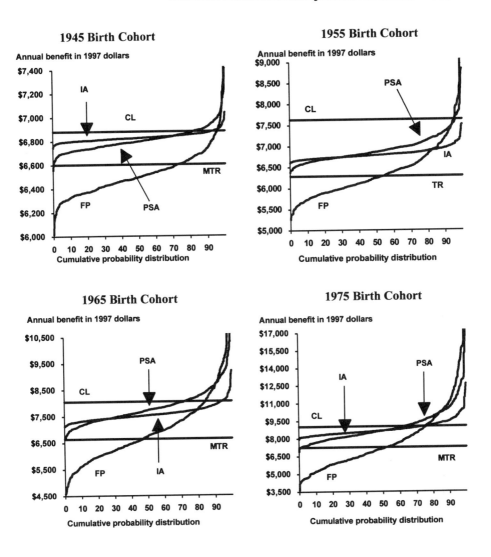

Figure 6. Distribution of expected benefit levels under the PSA and IA plans for selected birth cohorts, workers with low lifetime earnings and assuming only bond investing. Source: Authors' calculations. Note: scales on panels vary.

TABLE 7. Benefit Levels Under Alternative Social Security Reform Scenarios Assuming 3 Percent Real Returns Per Year on Individual Accounts (1997 dollars)

Birth Cohort	CL	MTR	PSA	IA	FP
Workers with low earnings					
1945	6,884	6,605	7,036	6,892	13,928
1955	7,639	6,291	7,863	7,056	14,919
1965	8,066	6,653	10,437	8,281	18,718
1975	9,060	7,273	14,890	10,410	25,300
Workers with average earnings					
1945	11,368	10,705	11,480	11,343	22,823
1955	12,618	9,802	13,030	11,502	24,532
1965	13,321	9,957	17,939	13,573	31,512
1975	14,960	10,883	26,872	17,855	44,727
Workers with maximum taxable earnings					
1945	17,439	16,258	18,638	17,794	36,432
1955	20,086	15,071	23,849	19,156	43,005
1965	21,243	14,940	35,761	23,620	59,381
1975	23,793	16,291	57,351	33,015	90,366

Source: Authors' calculations.

returns in the range of 3 or 4 percent and still leave considerable margin for the institutions that provide the vehicles.

The Tax Treatment of Benefits Under the Alternative Proposals

Thus far all of our simulations have been pre-tax, but the reform proposals differ significantly in how benefits would be taxed at distribution. For example, the Advisory Council's MB and IA plans would subject to income tax all benefits above workers' contribution amounts. The personal account benefit under the IA plan would be afforded consumption tax treatment—i.e., the contributions would be made on a pre-tax basis and benefits would not be taxed at distribution. In the case of the PSA plan, all benefits would be accorded consumption tax treatment. Benefits financed by employer contributions would be taxed when the benefit is paid because the employer contributions was a tax-deductible expense when made. Benefits financed by employee contributions would be financed with post-tax earnings and would not be subject to further income taxation when paid.

To illustrate how alternative tax treatments affect projected benefits, we assumed that 85 percent of the benefits provided through OASDI would be taxable at a 15 percent marginal rate for the MB, IA, and MTR plans. For the

PSA plan, we assumed that 50 percent of the old benefit earned prior to 1998 would be taxable and that 100 percent of the new flat benefit earned under the reform plan would be taxable at a 15 percent marginal rate. Under the PSA proposal, half the old benefit and all the flat benefit would be financed by pre-tax employer contributions. Under this proposal, the share of total benefits financed with pre-tax contributions would be accorded consumption tax treatment, which is consistent with the tax preferences accorded virtually all private employer-sponsored pension. Because half of the old OASDI benefit is financed by post-tax employee contributions, and all of the personal account benefit is financed by post-tax dollars, half the old OASDI benefit and none of the personal account benefit would be taxable under the PSA plan. Taxation of the FP benefit follows the same rules; thus 50 percent of it would be taxable at a 15 percent rate. The results of the modified benefit distributions are shown in Figure 7.

Comparing the distributions in Figure 5 with those in Figure 7 shows the differing tax effects; Table 8 summarizes the changes in the probabilities that the PSA plan will exceed the current law (CL) and IA benefits on a pre- and post-tax basis (note that the post-tax benefits are labeled CL′, IA′, and so forth in the figures and table). The differential tax effects are important. In relative terms, the effects are greater for the older cohorts than for the younger ones. While we have not extended the analysis to the maximum-wage workers, the improvement in net benefits under the PSA plan relative to the CL or IA plans would be even greater than for workers at average earnings levels.

Implications of Annuitization Fees on Benefit Levels

One of the concerns about reforming social security through creation of personal accounts is that the cost of annuitization will significantly deplete the advantages of higher rates of returns that workers can achieve through the funding of their retirement benefits. To address this concern, we developed projections that include a charge for the purchase of an annuity at retirement. Mitchell, Poterba, and Warshawsky (1999) have estimated that, on average, individual annuity policies delivered payouts valued at between 80 and 85 cents on the premium dollar paid in 1995. They found that the best plans offered at that time had payouts of slightly above 90 cents on the premium dollar. This load was used in conjunction with post-tax projections for workers with average earnings. While 10 percent is below the average prevailing now, Mitchell et al's work suggests that these markets are becoming increasingly efficient. In addition, we believe that there would be further cost pressure on these markets if the demand for annuitization increases.

Results for the PSA and FP plans including annuity loadings appear in Figure 8, labeled PSA″ and FP″. It is interesting that the pattern of PSA

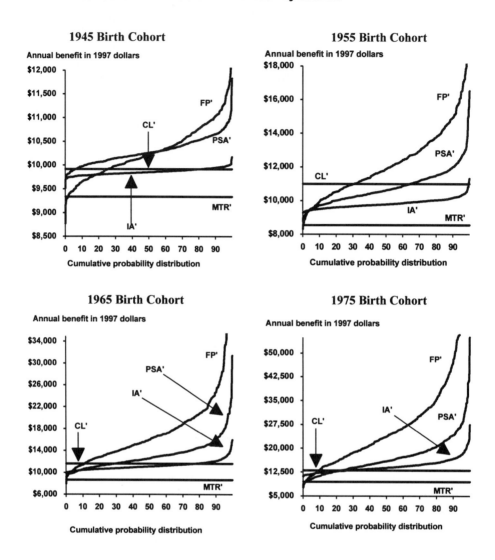

Figure 7. Projected post-tax benefit levels under the PSA and IA plans for selected birth cohorts, workers with average lifetime earnings. Source: Authors' calculations. Note: scales on panels vary.

benefits does not change much from those without annuity loadings. The reason is that at the lower end of the PSA benefit distributions, the flat benefit still provided through the OASDI program is relatively significant. Since the flat benefit is not subject to the annuity loading, the loading rate on the total benefit is significantly ameliorated. At the higher end of the

TABLE 8. Probability that PSA Benefit Exceeds the MB and IA Benefit for Worker with Average Career Earnings: Pre-Tax versus Post-Tax Computation

	P(PSA>MB)		P(PSA>IA)	
	Pre-tax	Post-tax	Pre-tax	Post-tax
1945 birth cohort	0.17	0.94	0.25	0.99
1955 birth cohort	0.12	0.34	0.72	0.95
1965 birth cohort	0.52	0.72	0.81	0.91
1975 birth cohort	0.67	0.77	0.72	0.80

Source: Authors' calculations.

distribution, the portion of the benefit financed by the personal account becomes much more significant. As this occurs, the annuity loading takes on greater significance, but it does so at benefit levels where the PSA tends to significantly outperform the other policy options, and it is not sufficient to overwhelm that improved performance.

The situation for the FP benefits is slightly different than under the PSA plan. For the 1945 birth cohort, the PSA plan would provide higher benefits than the FP plan over a larger portion of the probability distribution where annuitization costs are considered. The downside risks in the FP plan are somewhat greater as well. In the other cases, the annuitization of benefits would dampen somewhat the superiority of the FP benefit over the PSA benefit or benefits provided under the alternative policy options. The explanation for this effect is that the FP benefit would subject a larger share of total benefits to private market annuitization costs than any of the other plans. In any event, the FP plan would generally provide a superior benefit to the other options for most workers born during or after the mid-1950s.

While this analysis of annuitization costs and options could be more extensive, it suggests that some of the concerns about annuity costs relative to personal account options may be overblown.

An Alternative Perspective on Risk and Retirement Benefit Levels

Critics of personal account options point to variations in market returns over time as one of the primary reasons they oppose such plans. The implication is that personal account options include benefit risks and that the traditional defined-benefit structure of the current system does not have such risks. But this is not a fair conclusion. While the risks under the various models have a somewhat different nature and might be distributed differently, neither is free of the risk that expected levels of benefits might not be achieved for some workers. For instance, current-law benefit levels can only be achieved if taxed are raised substantially. Social security actuaries

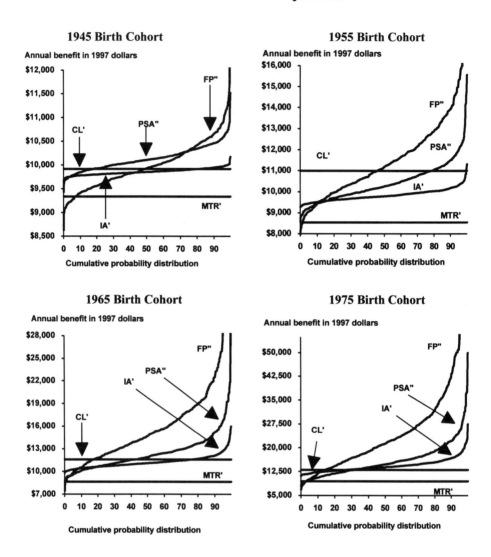

Figure 8. Projected post-tax benefit levels less annuity loadings under the PSA and IA plans for selected birth cohorts, workers with average lifetime earnings. Source: authors' calculations. Note: scales on panels vary.

estimate that the payroll tax rate would have to rise 2.5 percentage points to eliminate the current actuarial imbalance in OASDI financing and create a sufficient reserve so the trust fund balance would be stable at the end of the 75-year projection period (Goss, this volume). Conversely, personal accounts would expose workers to greater financial market risks in the accumulation of their base pensions than they now face. Personal accounts held under many reform proposals would be sensitive to the tides of those markets. It is not clear that the overall risks of a system of funded personal accounts would be any greater than they are in the current environment of unfunded political promises.[11] There is no way to cover the real deficit that exists in the current system without incurring some real costs. If the only way policymakers can get society to bear these costs is to hide them, this increases the chances that current promises will not be met. The current difference in benefit promises and financing rates in social security is so large that it is not conceivable that policymakers can conceal the cost of closing it.

One way to evaluate the tradeoffs between political and financial risks is to see what happens to the majority of people under various policy options. For example, consider the average-wage worker born in 1945 (Figure 4). Under the IA plan, required contributions would have to rise about two-thirds as much as the increase in the payroll tax required to secure current-law benefits. That is, if we raised the payroll tax today, by 1.6 percent, this takes us $2/3$ of the distance needed to eliminate the actuarial deficit and stabilize the trust fund. For the 1945 birth cohort of average workers, the MTR benefit is $10,705 in 1997 dollars, and their current-law benefit is $11,368 (under the assumptions used in developing our analytic comparisons). If an added 1.6 percent of covered payroll were raised in taxes and it was distributed on a pro rata basis relative to the differences between the current law and MTR benefits within the current benefit structure, the new expected benefit level would be $11,129 — that is, 64 percent of the way toward the current law benefit going from the MTR benefit level. Looking back to Figure 4 for the benefit projection for a worker born in 1945 and with average earnings, under the IA reform proposal there is an 81 percent probability the worker would get a benefit in excess of $11,129 under the IA plan. While it is hard to guess at what rate workers might be willing to trade political risk for financial market risk, our guess is that many workers·in the situation just described would prefer one of the personal account policy proposals to either the MTR option or one that would have them simply pay higher taxes to support the current system.

Conclusion

Social security reform plans that include a personal account are sometimes criticized because of costs and risks associated with these proposals. This chapter shows that there is considerable variability in the way people invest across the earnings spectrum, variability that should be considered when evaluating such proposals. We have also shown that administrative costs matter and that historical volatility in financial market returns would probably lead to some considerable dispersion of benefits within and across cohorts. Our analyses rest on defensible assumptions that address criticisms of earlier studies.

We find that most baby boomers will not receive their money's worth under social security for any policy option examined here, including the PSA option. Some baby boomers may have reduced benefit levels relative to current law promises, and these cuts are likely to be largest for the middle cohorts of the baby boomers. In the long term, though, our projections suggest that social security reforms including some level of personal account funding would lead to improved benefit levels for significant segments of future retiree populations. While our analysis does not consider possible potential macroeconomic effects that might arise if a personal account reform option were adopted, we are confident that higher savings rates would contribute to general improvements in worker and retiree welfare over time.

Our analysis also suggests that the greater the level of privatization and funding of the social security system under a reform plan, the greater the potential to raise benefits or reduce costs for workers in the broad middle class and higher earnings levels. Moving to a program heavily reliant on personal accounts without putting in place some form of redistribution or floor of protection at the lower end of the earnings distribution, however, would expose some workers to the risks of significantly lower benefits than they would receive under current law or alternatives that maintain some sort of floor of protection. Those exposed to these risks would be those most vulnerable to a retirement of poverty level incomes.

Our analysis of the implications of annuity costs suggests that the costs associated with private annuitization may not be as large a factor in determining the relative merits of personal account approaches to social security reform versus more traditional defined benefit approaches as previously thought. This does not mean that the issue of mandatory annuitization up to some appropriate income level is not important or worthy of consideration. Further analysis of the annuitization issues should be undertaken to improve the understanding of the potential implications of personal account reforms to social security.

Finally, we have documented the implications of financial market risks on the distribution of benefits under three specific personal account social security reform models. Those critical of personal accounts might take solace from our results showing that not everyone will come out with higher benefit levels under such policy approaches than under current social security provisions. But we assert that current law is not the appropriate standard against which to compare viable policy options. No one today is seriously suggesting that policymakers will ultimately raise taxes sufficiently to pay current promises. Until the risks associated with the unfunded political promises in the current system are factored into the analysis, there can

be no fair assessment of the relative desirability of personal account approaches to social security reform.

The authors wish to thank David Gordon and Tomeka Hill for their help in
developing the simulations presented here. We also wish to thank Olivia
Mitchell for her helpful comments, to Martin Feldstein who invited us to
present our research to a NBER conference on social security where the
comments and discussion helped us in the development of our analytical
approach, and to John Shoven for encouraging us to add a full privatization
option to our analysis. Findings, interpretations, and conclusions of this
paper represent the views of the authors and not those of Watson Wyatt
Worldwide or any of its other associates.

Notes

1. About half of the plans are administered by Watson Wyatt with the remainder
administered by another plan vendor.

2. In developing stylized portfolios, Dickson considers both 401(k) and IRA investment patterns. In his analysis, he notes that IRA investment patterns tend to be
somewhat more conservative than those for 401(k) plans and half of all IRA assets
are owned by individuals over the age of 60, whereas nearly 70 percent of 401(k)
assets are concentrated in accounts of workers between the ages of 40 and 59. He
attributes part of the difference to the distribution of assets in the two types of plans
to the age of the asset holders. He also notes that individuals tend to allocate an ever
larger portion of their assets to fixed income assets as they age. The large concentra-
tion of IRA assets among the elderly suggests that much of the IRA money is held by
people already retired. Since the focus of the current analysis is on investment
patterns of workers, we do not believe that the investment patterns in IRAs are as
relevant as those of 401(k) participants.

3. Whether these real returns are the correct ones to use is discussed by Mitchell,
Geanakoplos, and Zeldes (this volume).

4. Mitchell's analysis of TIAA/CREF suggests that this plan's costs might run 20 to
30 basis points per year with some added costs on the annuity provisions, but the IA
proposal as structured with monolithic government management of the system
might drive such cost rates down considerably. In addition, the 10.5 basis points for
IA administration is consistent with Dickson's analysis of mutual fund administration
costs. For example, in a world of 4 percent inflation with an initial annual $35 per
account administrative cost growing at the rate of inflation, with 5 percent wage
growth, and 3 percent real returns on assets over a worker's career for a worker
starting to work at age 21 and working until reaching age 65, administrative costs as a
percentage of assets managed would average 17.2 basis points per year for a worker
whose starting salary was $12,000 per year, 8.3 basis points for one with a starting
salary of $25,000, and 5.2 basis points for one at $40,000 per year.

5. Since the government could limit administrative loadings for small accounts, a
case could be made that the 100 bp we assume is an upper bound on costs.

6. This concern was partially addressed in the Advisory Council on Social Security's report by presenting alternative projections where workers were assumed to
invest only in government bonds throughout their careers, or alternatively, where

they were assumed to invest only in stocks with annual administrative costs of only 50 basis points per year. The former was assumed to provide an estimate of the potential outcome for a worker who realized relatively low career returns and the latter was considered an estimate of a high-return scenario. Under this approach, there is no way to estimate the probability of one or the other outcomes or how they might actually distribute around benefits promised by current law or some alternative level of defined benefit promise.

7. The first two proposals are described in detail in the Advisory Council's final report (1997) and the third is a variant on the second proposal.

8. Under this proposal, the scaling back of benefits would be skewed toward workers with higher lifetime earnings levels. Those at the low end of the earnings spectrum would experience relatively small reductions of their basic OASDI benefits.

9. This adjustment keeps our assumed ratio of equities to fixed-income investment equivalent to the ratio of equities to fixed-income investments in the Advisory Council's comparative analysis of the IA and PSA plans.

10. Results from additional projections are available from the authors on request.

11. Some critics of personal retirement accounts point to the potential for financial market collapse as a reason to stay with the current social security structure. Of course, a wage-based, pay-as-you-go system would also be badly affected by the collapse of financial markets.

References

Access Research, Inc. *Marketplace Update 1997*. Windsor, Conn.: Access Research, Inc., 1997.
———. "1997 Marketplace Update." Presented at the 1997 SPARK National Conference, sponsored by the Society of Professional Administrators and Recordkeepers, Washington, D.C., June 23, 1997.
Advisory Council on Social Security. *Final Report of the 1994–1996 Advisory Council on Social Security*. Vol. 1, *Findings and Recommendations*. Washington, D.C.: Social Security Administration, 1997.
Bajtelsmit, Vickie L., Richard D. Johnson, and Mistene M. Nugent. "The Impact of Social Security Reform Proposals on Individual Taxpayers." Working Paper Series No. 97-1, Department of Finance and Real Estate, College of Business, Colorado State University, 1997.
Carter, Marshall N. and William G. Shipman. *Promises to Keep: Saving Social Security's Dream*. Washington, D.C.: Regnery Publishing, Inc., 1996.
Committee on Economic Development. *Fixing Social Security*. New York: Committee on Economic Development, 1997.
Dickson, Joel. "Analysis of Financial Conditions Surrounding Individual Accounts." In Advisory Council on Social Security, *Report of the 1994–1996 Advisory Council on Social Security*, Vol. 2, *Reports of the Technical Panel on Assumptions and Methods, Technical Panel on Trends and Issues in Retirement Savings, and Presentations to the Council*. Washington, D.C.: USGPO, 1997.
Feldstein, Martin S. and Andrew Samwick. "The Economics of Prefunding Social Security and Medicare Benefits." Cambridge, Mass.: National Bureau of Economic Research, August 1997.
Fischer, Stanley. "Investing for the Short and the Long Term." In Zvi Bodie and John B. Shoven, eds., *Financial Aspects of the United States Pension System*. Chicago: University of Chicago Press, 1983.
Ibbotson, R. and Associates. *Stocks, Bonds, Bills, and Inflation*. 1996 Yearbook. Chicago: Ibbotson Associates, 1996.

McCurdy, Thomas E. and John B. Shoven. "Stocks, Bonds, and Pension Wealth." In David A. Wise, ed., *Topics in the Economics of Aging.* Chicago: University of Chicago Press, 1992.

Mitchell, Olivia S. "Administrative Costs in Public and Private Retirement Systems." In Martin Feldstein, ed., *Social Security Privatization.* Chicago: University of Chicago Press, 1998: 403–56.

Mitchell, Olivia S., James M. Poterba, and Mark J. Warshawsky. "New Evidence on the Money's Worth of Individual Annuities." *American Economic Review* (1999), forthcoming.

Myers, Robert J. Remarks presented at the session entitled "Privatizing Social Security: Changing the Implicit Grant Components," at the Allied Social Science Associations Annual Meetings, January 1997, New Orleans, Louisiana. 1997a

———. Remarks presented at a conference "Retirement Income Security in the 21st Century: Challenges Ahead," sponsored by the U.S. General Accounting Office, Washington, D.C., July 1997. 1997b

Poterba, James M., Steven Venti, and David A. Wise. "Implications of Rising Personal Retirement Saving." Presented at a Conference on the Economics of Aging, National Bureau of Economic Research, Carefree, Ariz., April 1997.

Schieber, Sylvester J. and John B. Shoven. "The Aging of the Baby Boom Generation: The Impact of Private Pensions, National Saving, and Financial Markets." Paper presented at an American Council on Capital Formation Conference, Washington, D.C., December 1996.

Siegel, Jeremy J. *Stocks for the Long Run.* Chicago: Irwin Professional Publishing, 1994.

Chapter 7
Stochastic Simulation of Economic Growth Effects of Social Security Reform

Martin R. Holmer

(us/ HSS C15 J26)

Proposals for trust fund equity investment and individually-managed invest-ment accounts under social security raise questions about the national sav-ing and economic growth effects of these reforms, as well as some of their risk implications. But current models are not structured in a way that per-mits quantitative analysis of these policy-induced growth and risk effects. This chapter describes a new model that seeks to overcome the limitations of previous models. We begin by describing this new policy simulation model and then present preliminary simulation results of the economic growth effects of current law policy. We also evaluate two "generic" social security reforms: one that increases taxes to maintain current benefits (the rising-tax reform), and a second that substitutes individual accounts for current defined benefits and increases taxes only temporarily to fund transi-tion costs (the two-tier reform). Each of these policy regimes is explored using three different simulation modes. The first simulation mode assumes that demographic and economic assumptions are deterministic and that economic growth is exogenous, as in the Trustees Report (1996) projec-tions. The second simulation mode posits deterministic assumptions, but makes growth endogenous by activating the embedded economic growth model and its links to the broader policy simulation model. Finally, the third simulation mode adds stochastic assumptions to endogenous economic growth in order to characterize economic and demographic (but not po-litical) risks.

Modeling Social Security Reforms

Our social security policy simulation model incorporates dynamic interac-tions between the population (represented with age-gender cells rather

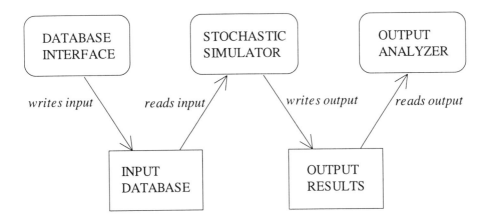

Figure 1. Modular architecture of the model. This architecture allows specialization among component programs and provides a development path to a client/server architecture that permits distributed processing of simulation runs among networked computers. Source: Holmer (1997b: 5).

than with a sample of individuals), the economy (represented in aggregate terms), and social security programs.[1] The model can analyze the implications of adding individual defined-contribution accounts to social security's existing defined-benefit OASI and DI programs, or adopting alternative asset allocation policies for the defined-benefit trust funds. It can also simulate a wide range of benefit and tax policy reforms that leave unchanged the defined-benefit structure of social security. In addition, a neoclassical economic growth model has been embedded in the broader policy simulation model so that a reform that changes national savings rates will generate a different growth path with altered earnings and asset returns. Monte Carlo methods are also used to estimate certain types of risk caused by uncertainty in social security's future demographic and economic environment, including asset returns.[2]

The model's stochastic simulation logic is encapsulated in a single computer program that reads input assumption parameters from a relational database, conducts the long-term simulation calculations for the specified policy regime under the specified demographic and economic assumptions, and writes output results to a set of text files that enable easy visualization of results or other post-simulation calculation using spreadsheets or statistical packages. The relationship between the stochastic simulator program and the other elements of the overall simulation system are shown in Figure 1. The annual recursive simulation logic of the stochastic simulator is represented in Figure 2.

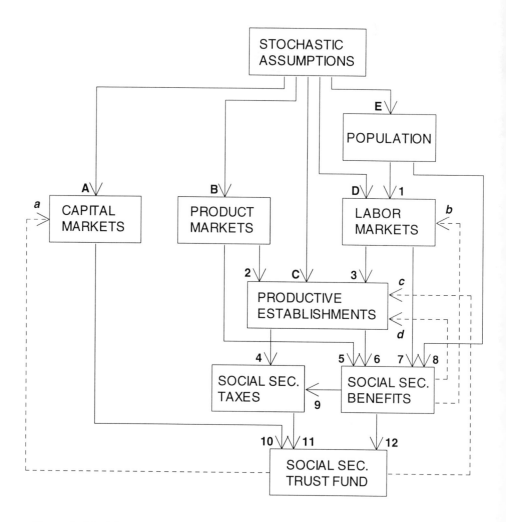

Figure 2. Modular structure of the stochastic simulator. Individual modules are represented as boxes, selected recursive linkages are marked with numbers, and lagged feedback links are marked with lowercase letters. The individual account module, which is not shown in this figure, is at the same level as the trust fund module, has the same recursive and lagged feedback links as the three social security modules. The key stochastic assumption variables include A (interest rate, corporate bond return, and equity return), B (inflation), C (productivity growth, wage-share growth, hours-worked growth), D (female and male labor force participation, unemployment), E (fertility, immigration, mortality decline, disability incidence, disability recovery). Source: Holmer (1997b: 10).

Endogenous Economic Growth

The growth model embedded in the policy simulation model is a neoclassical economic production model that assumes an exogenous rate of technological change. The logical structure of the economic growth model is specified in several equations.[3] The Cobb-Douglas production function with labor-augmenting technological change is

$$Y = A^{1-\alpha}K^{\alpha}L^{1-\alpha} = K^{\alpha}(AL)^{1-\alpha}$$

where A denotes the level of efficiency of labor input denoted by L, K denotes capital input, Y denotes real GDP, and α denotes the elasticity of real GDP with respect to capital.[4]

It is assumed that the rate of growth of physical labor input and of the level of labor efficiency (that is, the rate of labor-augmenting technological change) are exogenous to the growth model. In the broader social security policy simulation model (within which the growth model is embedded), the rate of labor input growth is determined by the population and labor market modules, whose logic is similar to that of the model used for Trustees Report projections. These modules produce growth rates in L that are exogenous to the embedded growth model, but vary in value from year to year and across stochastic scenarios. In this simplified presentation, these two exogenous rates are assumed constant. The growth path of L is specified by

$$\dot{L}/L = n$$

where n denotes the exogenous rate of growth in physical labor input and the dot notation represents a time derivative. The growth path of A is specified by

$$\dot{A}/A = g$$

where g denotes the exogenous rate of growth in labor efficiency. The assumption module of the broader policy simulation model produces values of g that may vary from year to year and across stochastic scenarios.

The growth path of K depends on the rate of capital depreciation (denoted by δ) and the rate of gross domestic capital investment as follows:

$$\dot{K} = I - K\delta$$

where I denotes gross domestic investment. To make the growth path of K endogenous to the economic growth model, the relationship between GDP and saving, and between saving and investment, must be specified. In the broader policy simulation model, the national saving rate (expressed as a fraction of GDP) is determined jointly by assumptions about private saving and government saving (surplus) in the social security program and in all other programs. Changes in social security program or individual account finances (measured from the starting simulation year) cause changes in the initial simulation year's national saving rate. And changes in the national saving rate (measured from the starting simulation year), in turn, generate changes in net foreign investment and the gross domestic investment rate (expressed as a fraction of GDP).

These saving and investment links produce a yearly value of s that is exogenous to the embedded growth model, whose investment equation is as follows

$$I = sY$$

where the gross domestic investment rate is denoted by s.

Combining equations 4 and 5 produces

$$K = sY - K\delta$$

which completes the growth path equations for the three variables in the production function specified in equation 1. The saving-investment links from the broader policy simulation model to the embedded economic growth model are discussed in more detail below along with the link from the growth model to the broader model's asset returns.

The economic growth model's constant parameters are assumed to have the following values: the capital share parameter α in the Cobb-Douglas production function is assumed to be 0.41, based on Christenson, Cummings, and Jorgenson (1980) and Dougherty (1991) as summarized by Barro and Sala-i-Martin (1995). The rate of capital depreciation δ is assumed to be 0.04, based on the average value for the 72 countries included in the Penn World Tables (Summers and Heston 1991, as reported by Binder and Pesaran 1996). The starting simulation year's gross domestic investment rate s_0 is assumed to be 0.165, based on the value used in the Brookings model (Aaron, Bosworth, and Burtless 1989). The rate in subsequent simulation years is determined by changes in social security program or individual account finances and the parameter values assumed for the saving-investment input link described below. The starting simulation year's capital-output ratio (K/Y) is assumed to be 3.11, which is the value that, under the nonstochastic Trustees Report (1996) intermediate-cost assumptions and deactivated saving-investment and asset-return links, generates an estimate of 2070 GDP equal to that of the Trustees Report intermediate-cost projection.

These baseline growth model parameter assumptions produce two steady-state results that correspond closely to the stylized facts of economic growth. First, using these baseline parameter assumptions and deactivating the saving-investment and asset-return links, the steady-state marginal product of capital implies, assuming marginal productivity pricing, a pre-tax, net-of-depreciation, real rate of return on capital equal to 9.3 percent, which corresponds to the recent U.S. empirical estimate referred to by Feldstein and Samwick (1996). And second, the annual rate of convergence to the steady state implied by the simulation is about 0.031, which is quite close to the 2 to 3 percent range suggested by recent empirical studies summarized by Barro and Sala-i-Martin (1995).

Endogenous Growth Links

The broader social security policy model and the embedded economic growth model are connected via growth model input links and growth model feedback links. The discussion above described the input links for the employment growth rate and the productivity growth rate. The input link between social security program and individual account finances and the rates of saving and investment is discussed here. Also discussed are the feedback links between the growth model and taxable earnings, and between the growth model and asset returns.

First, we describe the growth model *input link between program finances and saving and investment*. Changes in old-age and survivors insurance (OASI) and disability insurance (DI) program finances cause changes in the OASI program surplus and DI program surplus (measured from the starting simulation year and expressed as a fraction of GDP). The change in program surplus is assumed to have both direct and indirect effects on the national saving rate. The direct effect represents the national income and product accounting effect by which the change in program surplus translates directly into a change in the national saving rate (measured from the starting simulation year and expressed as a fraction of GDP). The indirect effects represent behavioral offsets to the direct accounting effect. These indirect effects are characterized by three parameters. The first is the OASI program surplus federal surplus offset rate, which expresses the assumed change in the non-OASDI federal surplus as a fraction of the change in the OASI program surplus. This offset parameter would be greater than zero if it were assumed that the federal political process would "spend" some of any increase in the program surplus. The second parameter is the corresponding federal surplus offset rate for DI program surplus changes. The third indirect saving effect parameter is the federal surplus national saving offset rate. This offset rate represents the assumption about how saving behavior in the business, household, and state and local government sectors will change in response to a change in the federal government's budget surplus. A value of zero assumes there is no change in saving, while a value of one assumes that changes in the expectations of other sectors cause saving changes that completely offset the direct effect of a change in the federal surplus on the national saving rate. The baseline values of these three parameters are 0.0 (no within-budget offsets for OASI), 0.0 (no within-budget offsets for DI) and 0.5 (consistent with Congressional Budget Office 1996), respectively.

Changes in individual account finances are also assumed to have both direct and indirect effects on the national saving rate. The direct saving effect is caused by the fact that a net surplus for all individual accounts — that is, total account contributions plus total account investment earnings minus total account withdrawals and annuity payments — contributes directly to national saving in the national income and product accounts. A change in the account surplus rate, therefore, causes a change in the national saving rate that is the same percent of GDP. A change in the account surplus rate also has two different sets of indirect saving effects caused by changes in saving behavior and tax revenue: one set associated with changes in the total amount of account contributions and investment income, and another set associated with changes in the total amount of account benefits (that is, account withdrawals and annuity payments).

Consider the first set of indirect account saving effects. A change in the total amount of required account contributions is assumed to be offset to a certain degree by a reduction in saving by other sectors of the economy. If individual accounts were mandatory, it is plausible that any increase in contributions to those accounts would lead to smaller contributions to other voluntary defined-contribution pension plans or to other household retirement savings, not only because the mandatory accounts reduced the need for other retirement savings, but also because household disposable income would be lower. In addition, because the account contributions and investment income are tax-free, governments experience an increase in lost tax revenue, which reduces their budget surpluses and the national saving rate. But the reduction in other retirement saving, to the extent that it was in tax-favored pension plans, causes a decrease in lost tax revenue.

Now consider the second set of indirect account saving effects. A change in the total amount of account benefits is also assumed to affect government tax revenues (because benefits are taxable income) and hence their budget surpluses and the national saving rate.

The total national saving effect of a change in individual account finances is the sum of this direct effect and these several indirect effects. The baseline values of the four account saving offset parameters are all drawn from a recent quantitative study of the effects of introducing large individual accounts by Howe and Jackson (1996: 23–24) and are as follows: the account contribution saving offset rate is 0.3, the (combined federal and state) income tax rate is 0.19 on account contributions and investment income, the fraction of saving offsets that occur in tax-exempt retirement saving programs is 0.5, and the (combined federal and state) income tax rate is 0.127 on account withdrawals and annuity payments.

Now that all the saving relationships associated with the input link between retirement program finances and domestic investment have been described, it remains to document the nature of the relationship between a change in the national saving rate (measured from the starting simulation year and expressed as a fraction of GDP) and a change in the gross domestic investment rate (measured and expressed in the same way). The Bureau of Economic Analysis (1996) reports that net foreign investment was about −5.3 percent of national saving during 1992. So, when the saving-investment input link is activated in the model, the starting simulation year's national saving rate is assumed to be about 0.1566, so that the domestic investment rate is 0.165 of GDP. A change of x in the national saving rate is assumed to induce a change in the domestic investment rate of $0.6x$ and a change in net foreign investment of $0.4x$, following Congressional Budget Office (1996).

Next, the growth model *feedback link to taxable earnings* is discussed. When the embedded economic growth model is activated, it determines endogenously the time path of real GDP. The establishment module of the broader social security policy simulation model contains logic that translates this level of real output into taxable earnings, a key variable for social security policy analysis. This same translation logic is used even when the growth model is deactivated and the model is operating with the Trustees Report model's logic of exogenous economic growth. So, faster (slower) growth in real output translates directly into faster (slower) growth in taxable earnings and all related social security benefits and taxes.

And finally, we describe the *feedback link to asset returns*. As the economic growth model's capital-output ratio (denoted by v and equal to K/Y) changes, the marginal productivity of capital net of depreciation (denoted by r) will change according to the equation $r = \alpha / v - \delta$. Assuming the capital markets are reasonably competitive, marginal productivity pricing implies that changes in r should induce changes in the social security policy simulation model's three asset returns. The change in r (measured from the starting simulation year) is used to induce changes in the real Treasury yield, the corporate bond spread, and the real rate of return on equities, that are proportional to the ratio of the real return and r in the starting simulation year.[5]

Growth Effects of Alternative Social Security Policies

Model estimates are presented for the economic growth effects of three social security policy regimes: (1) current law benefit and tax policy (current-law policy); (2) a defined-benefit-oriented reform that maintains current law benefits and increases future payroll taxes to achieve pay-as-you-go financing balance (the rising-tax reform); and (3) a defined-contribution-oriented reform that introduces large mandatory individual accounts, reduces defined benefits gradually, and leaves the payroll tax unchanged for 40 years to fund the reform's transition costs, and then reduces payroll taxes so that combined with the 5 percent account contribution they are at the current-law level (the two-tier reform). It should be clear that these reforms are different in specifics from those analyzed by the Advisory Council on Social Security (1997), though not dissimilar in spirit.

Estimates are produced for all three of these policy regimes using three different simulation modes: (1) the deterministic-assumption and exogenous-growth mode (abbreviated Deterministic/Exog-Growth in the tables), which is the mode used in the Trustees Report model; (2) the deterministic-assumption and endogenous-growth mode (abbreviated Deterministic/Endog-Growth in the tables), which activates the embedded economic growth model and its input and feedback links to the broader social security policy simulation model; and (3) the stochastic-assumption and endogenous-growth mode (abbreviated Stochastic/Endog-Growth in the tables), which activates the growth model and uses Monte Carlo methods to generate 1,000 stochastic scenarios that represent uncertainty in the future value of demographic and economic assumption variables as well as asset returns.

The policy simulation model's 13 major demographic and economic assumption variables are assumed to have means equal to the intermediate-cost assumptions in the Trustees Report (1996), except for the mortality decline rate. The annual rate of decline in mortality rates is assumed to have a higher mean value equal to the new Census Bureau mid-range estimate (Holmer 1997a) and similar to that recommended by the Technical Panel (1997). The equity return variable is assumed to have a mean of 10.3 percent, equal to its historical average from the late 1920s through the early 1990s.

In the deterministic-assumption mode, these 13 assumption variables and the equity return variable have a standard deviation of zero. In the stochastic-assumption mode, 10 of these 13 assumption variables are assumed to have a constant ultimate value that is drawn from a normal distribution with a mean equal to that described above and a standard deviation equal to one-fourth of the difference between the high-cost and low-cost assumption in the Trustees Report (1996). The distributions of the long-run (or ultimate) value of these 10 variables are assumed to be uncorrelated. The three other variables — the unemployment rate, inflation rate, and nominal interest rate — are assumed to fluctuate around means equal to the intermediate-cost assumptions in the Trustees Report (1996), with deviations from the long-run mean being generated by a second-order vector autoregressive process that has been estimated with historical data from the late 1920s through the early 1990s. The errors terms of these three deviation processes were found in the statistical estimation to be contemporaneously correlated. The stochastic equation for the equity return variable exhibits no autocorrelation and the standard error of the natural logarithm of the equity return is about 19 percent (Holmer 1996: 30–39).

Seven different simulation estimates appear in the tables below. The first three are average OASI cost rates and actuarial deficits (summarizing the experience over the 75-year period ending in 2070). Average cost rates are presented for both the combined defined-benefit (DB) and defined-contribution (DC) elements of OASI, if the latter exists in a policy regime, and for just the defined-benefit element of OASI. The third average estimate is the defined-benefit actuarial deficit (the negative of the summarized actuarial surplus presented in the Trustees Report). The remaining four simulation estimates are for the year 2070. The actuarial deficit (the difference between that year's cost rate and income rate) for the defined-benefit elements of OASI is expressed as a percent of taxable payroll, as are all the cost rate and actuarial deficit estimates. The remaining three estimates describe the state of the economy in 2070: real per-capita GDP (expressed in thousands of 1992 dollars), the Treasury interest rate, and the equity rate of return.

Current Law Policy

Current law policy generates in the long run a financial imbalance in the OASI program. Using all Trustees Report (1996) intermediate-cost assumptions and the deterministic-assumption/exogenous-growth simulation mode, the model produces an estimate of 1.84 percent of taxable payroll for the average actuarial deficit, which is close to the 1.85 estimate reported in the Trustees Report (1996).

OASI program finance and economic effects estimates for current-law policy in each of the three simulation modes appear in Table 1. Here, the average actuarial deficit in the deterministic-assumption/exogenous-growth simulation mode is 2.41 percent of taxable payroll, which is higher than the 1.84 percent estimate discussed above because the assumed rate of mortality decline is higher, and hence the length of retirement is longer, than assumed in the Trustees Report (1996) intermediate-cost projection. The large difference between these two estimates illustrates the critical significance of future demographic trends for the financial condition of the OASI program as it is currently designed.

When the embedded growth model and its links to the broader policy simulation model are activated, the average actuarial deficit falls (from 2.41 to 2.27) despite lower payroll tax revenue caused by lower GDP (from 49.51 to 47.87 in 2070), which is induced by the OASI deficits. The fall in the actuarial deficit is caused, in part, by the even larger decline in future initial benefit awards, which is induced by the lower level of earnings that goes along with the lower per-capita GDP. Also contributing to the fall in the actuarial deficit is the rise in the nominal interest rate (from 6.30 to 6.61 in 2070), which is caused by the growth model feedback link to asset returns. The higher interest rates produce smaller present values in the actuarial deficit calculation.

TABLE 1. Estimated OASI Program Finance and Economic Growth Effects of Current-Law Policy.

	Simulation Mode		
Simulation Estimate	Deterministic/ Exog-Growth	Deterministic/ Endog-Growth	Stochastic/ Endog-Growth
Average DB+DC Cost Rate (% taxable payroll)	13.87	13.74	14.45 (1.09)
Average DB Cost Rate (% taxable payroll)	13.87	13.74	14.45 (1.09)
Average DB Actuarial Deficit (% taxable payroll)	2.41	2.27	2.95 (1.05)
2070 DB Actuarial Deficit (% taxable payroll)	5.82	5.82	6.96 (2.92)
2070 Real Per-Capita GDP (thousands of 1992 dollars)	49.51	47.87	47.53 (5.07)
2070 Treasury Interest Rate (%)	6.30	6.61	6.72 (2.41)
2070 Equity Rate of Return (%)	10.30	10.82	11.20 (21.8)

Source: Author's calculations.
Note: See text for detailed descriptions of the current-law policy regime, the three simulation modes, and the seven estimates. Means and standard deviations of estimates are calculated using 1,000 simulation scenarios. Standard deviations are omitted in the two deterministic-assumption modes (because they are zero) and are shown in parentheses in the stochastic-assumption mode. Average estimates are for the 75 years ending in 2070.

Recognizing the effects of social security finances on the path of economic growth produces an estimate of 2070 real per capita GDP that is about 3.3 percent lower than if these effects are ignored in the exogenous-growth simulation mode. As discussed in the conclusion, this difference would be much larger if the rate of national saving were allowed to influence the rate of technological change as in many contemporary endogenous-technological-change growth models, but even a 3 percent difference is socially and politically significant.

The main conclusion from the stochastic-assumption/endogenous-growth results in Table 1 is that the future financial condition of the OASI program is highly uncertain. The mean value (over the 1,000 stochastic scenarios) of the average actuarial deficit over the 75 years ending in 2070 is 2.95 percent of taxable payroll, and the standard deviation of those 1,000 values is 1.05 percent of taxable payroll. This implies that the average actuarial deficit estimate is above 4.00 percent of taxable payroll in about 17 percent of the scenarios (and below 1.90 in as many scenarios). This mean of 2.95 percent is significantly higher than the deterministic-assumption estimate of 2.27 percent because the standard error of the 2.95 mean is only 0.03 percent (1.05 divided by the square root of 1,000). This higher mean

TABLE 2. Estimated OASI Program Finance and Economic Growth Effects of the
Rising-Tax Reform.

| | Simulation Mode | | |
| | Deterministic/ Exog-Growth | Deterministic/ Endog-Growth | Stochastic/ Endog-Growth |
Simulation Estimate			
Average DB+DC Cost Rate (% taxable payroll)	13.87	13.75	14.46 (1.10)
Average DB Cost Rate (% taxable payroll)	13.87	13.75	14.46 (1.10)
Average DB Actuarial Deficit (% taxable payroll)	0.03	0.00	0.68 (0.97)
2070 DB Actuarial Deficit (% taxable payroll)	0.02	−0.06	1.07 (2.90)
2070 Real Per-Capita GDP (thousands of 1992 dollars)	49.51	48.73	48.39 (5.17)
2070 Treasury Interest Rate (%)	6.30	6.44	6.56 (2.41)
2070 Equity Rate of Return (%)	10.30	10.54	10.92 (21.8)

Source: Author's calculations.
Note: See text for detailed descriptions of the rising-tax policy regime, the three simulation
modes, and the seven estimates. Means and standard deviations of estimates are calculated
using 1,000 simulation scenarios. Standard deviations are omitted in the two deterministic-
assumption modes (because they are zero) and are shown in parentheses in the stochastic-
assumption mode. Average estimates are for the 75 years ending in 2070.

value arises from the nonlinear effect on the average actuarial deficit of the
interactions of the stochastic assumption variables.

Rising-Tax Reform

The rising-tax policy regime maintains current-law OASI benefit policy and
gradually increases the OASI payroll tax to maintain pay-as-you-go financing
of the program. The OASI payroll tax rate remains at 10.6 percent through
2024, rises to 13.7 during 2025–2029, moves to 14.6 for the two decades
between 2030 and 2049, rises to 16.0 for 2050–2059, and then remains at
16.4 percent beginning in 2060. The long-term rise from 10.6 to 16.4 represents a tax increase of nearly 55 percent. OASI program finance and economic effects estimates for the rising-tax reform in each of the three simulation modes appear in Table 2.

The rising-tax reform's payroll tax increases have been designed so that,
in the deterministic-assumption/exogenous-growth simulation mode, the
model produces a near zero estimate for both the average actuarial deficit
(0.03) and the actuarial deficit in 2070 (0.02). There is little change in either
the program finance or economic measures for 2070 because this reform

brings the OASI program into long-run financial balance, and hence produces relatively small declines in national saving rates relative to present rates that benefit from the large current surpluses in the OASI program. Even though this rising-tax reform leaves the program in long-run financial balance, the resulting decline in national saving rates does cause a decline in real per-capita output over the next 75 years, and a rise in both interest rates and equity returns over the same period. These movements are much smaller in magnitude than those caused by current-law policy shown in Table 1.

Two-Tier Reform

The two-tier policy regime introduces a 5 percent contribution personal retirement account in 1998. Individuals are assumed to invest their account balance using a life-cycle asset-allocation strategy that calls for investing completely in equities when young and for the equity fraction to decline gradually to 23 percent beyond age 60, with the bond fraction rising. Individuals are also assumed at retirement to convert all of their account balance into an inflation-indexed annuity, which is priced assuming a 5 percent loading factor, a continuation of recent mortality decline rates, and the use of a real rate of interest calculated with an expected rate of inflation that is a moving average of recent inflation rates (Holmer 1996).

Also, as part of the two-tier reform, the defined-benefit OAI program (payroll-tax financed OASI benefits first received by those aged 60 or more) is gradually scaled back. The benefits are scheduled to decline gradually from 1999 to 2040, when initial OAI benefits would be reduced 70 percent below current-law levels. The OASI payroll tax, which is currently scheduled to be 10.6 percent during the next century, would decline, but not gradually like the benefits. The combination of the 5 percent account contribution rate and the reduced OASI payroll tax rate would be 10.6 percent beginning in 2040. But during the first four decades of the next century, the 10.6 payroll tax rate would remain in place to finance the cost of transition from pay-as-you-go financing to more fully-funded financing. In other words, the mandatory five percent account contribution would be in addition to current payroll taxes until 2040. So, during these four decades the combined tax/contribution rate would be 15.6 percent, and then after 2040 the combined rate would fall back to 10.6 percent. This simple scheme for paying the defined-contribution-oriented reform's transition cost means that those cohorts working during the first four decades of the next century will bear the cost of the transition.

OASI program finance and economic effects estimates for the two-tier reform in each of the three simulation modes appear in Table 3. This two-tier reform has been designed so that, in the deterministic-assumption/exogenous-growth simulation mode, the model produces a near zero estimate for the OASI actuarial deficit in 2070 (-0.18), which produces a

TABLE 3. Estimated OASI Program Finance and Economic Growth Effects of the Two-Tier Reform.

Simulation Estimate	Simulation Mode		
	Deterministic/ Exog-Growth	*Deterministic/ Endog-Growth*	*Stochastic/ Endog-Growth*
Average DB+DC Cost Rate (% taxable payroll)	13.52	13.33	13.87 (0.74)
Average DB Cost Rate (% taxable payroll)	8.95	8.77	9.27 (0.73)
Average DB Actuarial Deficit (% taxable payroll)	−0.69	−0.71	−0.24 (0.59)
2070 DB Actuarial Deficit (% taxable payroll)	−0.18	−0.18	0.22 (0.95)
2070 Real Per-Capita GDP (thousands of 1992 dollars)	49.51	52.03	51.57 (5.56)
2070 Treasury Interest Rate (%)	6.30	5.87	6.00 (2.40)
2070 Equity Rate of Return (%)	10.30	9.56	9.99 (21.8)

Source: Author's calculations.
Note: See text for detailed descriptions of the two-tier policy regime, the three simulation modes, and the seven estimates. Means and standard deviations of estimates are calculated using 1,000 simulation scenarios. Standard deviations are omitted in the two deterministic-assumption modes (because they are zero) and are shown in parentheses in the stochastic-assumption mode. Average estimates are for the 75 years ending in 2070.

modest long-run financial surplus (average actuarial deficit of −0.69). When the embedded growth model and its links to the broader policy simulation model are activated, the average and 2070 actuarial deficits change very little because of the offsetting deficit effects of higher payroll taxes and lower interest rates, both of which are caused by the higher level of per-capita output (up from 49.51 to 52.03 in 2070). The growth effects cause nominal Treasury interest rates in 2070 to be lower by 43 basis points, with the equity rate of return dropping by 74 basis points.

Recognizing the effects of social security finances on the path of economic growth produces an estimate of 2070 real per-capita GDP that is about 5.1 percent higher than if these effects are ignored in the exogenous-growth simulation mode. This two-tier reform produces a deterministic-assumption/endogenous-growth estimate for real per-capita GDP in 2070 of 52.03 (thousands of 1992 dollars), which is 6.8 percent above the estimate for the rising-tax reform and 8.7 percent above the estimate for current-law policy. As mentioned above, these differences would be much larger if the rate of national saving were allowed to influence the rate of technological change, as in many contemporary endogenous-technological-change growth models.

Estimates for the stochastic-assumption simulation mode indicate that the two-tier reform reduces significantly the uncertainty in the future financial condition of the OASI trust fund. The standard deviation of the 2070 actuarial deficit is less than one-third the corresponding standard deviation under current-law policy. Of course, much of this reduction is accomplished by the reform's shift from exclusive reliance on defined benefits to a heavy reliance on defined-contribution benefits. Future analysis of the variability of birth cohort replacement rates and money's worth measures will determine the overall effect of this risk transfer from the trust-funds (that is, payroll taxpayers) to beneficiaries.

Conclusion

Social security reforms that increase national saving rates can have a significant impact on the rate of economic growth, according to our simulations. The resulting higher standard of living is desirable in its own right, and also would enable society to finance future retirement income more easily.

It would seem desirable for official Social Security Administration estimates to incorporate such economic growth effects for at least two reasons. First, the magnitude of program finances relative to the size of the economy means that the program's growth effects are not insignificant. Also, official estimates already incorporate other feedback effects that are arguably smaller than the economic growth effects analyzed here. For example, the Trustees Report (1996) describes the assumed changes in the age pattern of initial benefit receipt as the normal retirement age and the delayed retirement credit rise under current-law policy. There is little rationale for including only some of social security's important behavioral effects in official estimates.

The current-law policy results presented here suggest that estimates of the program's unfunded liability (see the chapter by Steven Goss in this volume, for example) may be somewhat overstated. The overestimate is caused by the fact that most such analyses ignore the negative growth effect caused by projected social security deficits, and therefore, ignore the lower payroll taxes and the eventually lower benefit levels associated with lower national output and earnings.

The simulation results reported here are derived from an economic growth model that ignores "learning-by-doing" effects. Empirical evidence (Barro and Sala-i-Martin 1995) suggests this causes higher national saving and domestic investment rates to raise the rate of labor-augmenting productivity growth (as well as increase the capital intensity of production as in the current neoclassical growth model). Adding "learning-by-doing" effects to the growth model will increase substantially the magnitude of the long-term economic growth effects of reforms that increase the national saving rate. Recognizing endogenous productivity growth would lead to bigger declines in long-term growth under current-law policy and larger increases in future output under the two-tier reform considered here.

In addition, future research with the model will investigate the sensitivity of these economic growth results to changes in a number of behavioral parameters that are already incorporated in the model. Also, the non-political risk implications of these reforms will be estimated using policy performance measures (such as replacement rates and money's worth payback ratios) for several different birth cohorts.

Notes

1. In this sense it is similar to the model used by the Social Security Administration's Office of the Actuary to produce Trustees Report projections and reform estimates.

2. The original social security policy simulation model was developed for the 1994–96 Advisory Council on Social Security. The need to gain experience with a stochastic model that uses Monte Carlo methods of representing uncertainty was recognized by the Council's Technical Panel on Assumptions and Methods (1997). In addition to its recommendation on this matter, the Panel supported development of stochastic demographic modules. The Advisory Council also supported development of stochastic economic modules (including econometric estimation of a VAR(2) model for generating cyclical paths for three macroeconomic assumption variables: nominal interest rate, inflation rate, and unemployment rate) and program modules that enabled the model to analyze the risk implications of trust fund equity investment policies (1997). Subsequently, the Employee Benefit Research Institute has supported ongoing model enhancements and analysis. Structural defined-benefit calculation modules were added to the model as well as birth cohort experience analysis capabilities, a number of new cohort policy performance measures (such as replacement rates and money's worth returns), and an individual defined-contribution account module that allows specification of alternative life-cycle investment strategies and account balance annuitization/withdrawal options (Holmer 1996). We have also added an embedded economic growth model and linked that growth model to the broader social security policy simulation model (Holmer 1997b, c).

3. A continuous-time, differential-equation version of the growth model is presented here to simplify presentation. The implemented model is a discrete-time, difference-equation model that is logically equivalent to the one presented here.

4. This representation of technological change differs from that used in the Brookings model of social security (Aaron, Bosworth, and Burtless 1989) and in the Congressional Budget Office long-term macroeconomic model (1996). Both utilize a Cobb-Douglas production function with factor-neutral technological change. Such a factor-neutral formulation cannot generate steady-state growth behavior in the long run because it does not assume labor-augmenting technological change (Barro and Sala-i-Martin 1995). This makes a factor-neutral formulation fundamentally inconsistent with the model used in the Trustees Report for projections of current-law policy.

5. This asset return adjustment method, which is similar to that used in the Brookings model by Aaron, Bosworth, and Burtless (1989), generates changes in asset returns that are somewhat less than the change in the marginal productivity of capital net of depreciation (r). This approach differs from the feedback method

used by Congressional Budget Office (1996), in which real interest rates were assumed to rise in step with the real return on capital.

References

Aaron, Henry J., Barry P. Bosworth, and Gary Burtless. *Can America Afford to Grow Old? Paying for Social Security.* Washington, D.C.: Brookings Institution, 1989.

Advisory Council on Social Security. *Report of the 1994–1996 Advisory Council on Social Security.* Vol. 1, *Findings and Recommendations.* Washington, D.C.: Social Security Administration, 1997.

Barro, Robert J. and Xavier Sala-i-Martin. *Economic Growth.* New York: McGraw-Hill, 1995.

Binder, Michael and M. Hashem Pesaran. "Stochastic Growth." Cambridge: University of Cambridge, Department of Applied Economics Working Paper 9615, 1996.

Board of Trustees of the Social Security Administration. *Annual Report of the Board of Trustees of the Federal Old-Age and Survivors Insurance and Disability Income Trust Funds.* Washington, D.C.: Social Security Administration, 1996.

Bureau of Economic Analysis, U.S. Department of Commerce. "National Income and Product Accounts Tables." *Survey of Current Business* 78, 8 (1996): 15–77.

Christenson, Laurtis R., Dianne Cummings, and Dale W. Jorgenson. "Economic Growth, 1947–1973: An International Comparison." In John W. Kendrick and Beatrice Vaccara, eds., *New Developments in Productivity Measurement and Analysis.* National Bureau of Economic Research Conference Report. Chicago: University of Chicago Press, 1980.

Congressional Budget Office. "The Long-Term Budget Outlook." In *The Economic and Budget Outlook: Fiscal Years 1997–2006.* Washington, D.C.: USGPO, 1996.

Dougherty, Christopher. "A Comparison of Productivity and Economic Growth in the G-7 Countries." Cambridge, Mass.: Harvard University Ph.D. dissertation, 1991.

Feldstein, Martin and Andrew Samwick. "The Transition Path in Privatizing Social Security." NBER Working Paper 5761. Cambridge, Mass.: NBER, 1996.

Holmer, Martin R. "EBRI-SSASIM2 Social Security Policy Simulation Model Technical Information." Washington, D.C.: Policy Simulation Group Working Paper, 1996.

———. "EBRI Social Security Reform Analysis Project Progress Report: Phases 1 and 2." In Dallas L. Salisbury, ed., *Assessing Social Security Reform Alternatives.* Washington, D.C.: Employee Benefit Research Institute, 1997. 1997a

———. "Guide to EBRI-SSASIM2, a Social Security Policy Simulation Model." Washington, D.C.: Policy Simulation Group Working Paper, June 1997. 1997b

———. "Stochastic Simulation of Social Security Reform Growth and Risk Effects." Washington, D.C.: Policy Simulation Group Working Paper, June 1997. 1997c

Howe, Neil and Richard Jackson. "National Thrift Plan Project: Draft Final Report." Washington, D.C.: National Taxpayers Union Foundation and Center for Public Policy and Contemporary Issues, 1996.

Summers, Robert and Alan Heston. "The Penn World Tables (Mark 5): An Expanded Set of International Comparisons, 1950–1988." *Quarterly Journal of Economics* 106 (1991): 326–36.

Technical Panel on Assumptions and Methods. *Final Report of the 1994–96 Advisory Council on Social Security.* Vol. 2. Washington, D.C.: Social Security Administration, 1997.

Chapter 8
Thinking About Social Security's Trust Fund

Kent A. Smetters

H61 *HSS (us/ 526*

The U.S. Social Security Act of 1935 placed a relatively strong emphasis on individual equity: retirement benefits were designed to be closely linked to taxes paid. An individual was insured if he worked at least five years in covered occupations and earned at least $2,000 in those jobs before reaching the age 65. The first benefits were to be paid to those who turned age 65 in 1942, five years after people began to pay the social security payroll tax. The original program achieved some equity across individuals as well: benefits were calculated according to a progressive formula that gave a higher rate of return on payroll taxes paid to those with lower lifetime wages. Total benefits, however, were roughly equivalent to total payroll taxes previously collected plus interest.[1] In this way, the U.S. social security system was originally conceived to be a mostly *funded* program that deposited payroll taxes into a Trust Fund invested in special-issue government securities. Payment of benefits was limited initially to those who contributed to the system.

The funded nature of the program meant that elderly persons who were already retired at the inception of the social security system — also a group hit hard by the Great Depression — could not receive benefits because they had not contributed. Responding to this group's needs, the social security program then began its long and gradual shift to a *pay-as-you-go* system. In a pure pay-as-you-go system, there is no Trust Fund. Rather, benefits are paid with current tax receipts. This shift toward a pay-as-you-go system began with the 1939 amendments, which moved the focus away from individual equity and toward protection of the family, including dependents and survivors. The 1939 amendments also sought to provide "socially adequate" benefits, including benefits for the elderly who had paid little or nothing into the system. The 1950 and 1952 amendments substantially liberalized conditions under which people could qualify for full benefits, and provided full benefits to newly covered workers not previously covered. Later amendments increased benefits even more. By 1983, the system was almost entirely pay-as-you-go: the value of the remaining trust fund was only about $20 billion which, by one estimate, was less than 1 percent of OASI's liability at the time.[2]

The Social Security Act of 1983 (SSA83) addressed the 75-year solvency problem facing the system at that time by, among other things, increasing the payroll tax. Projected revenue collected in the following years was anticipated to exceed outlays, the extra revenue going into the trust fund. The intention of SSA83 was, in part, to create a buffer against a recession but, more importantly, to create a large enough trust fund to weather the large increase in the retiree/worker ratio as the "baby boom" generation began to retire around the year 2010. At the end of 1996, the OASI Trust Fund held $514 billion in government securities. However, the SSA83 did not go far enough to create a solvent OASI system for the long run. Under the "intermediate assumptions" of economic and demographic characteristics of the economy, as calculated by the Board of Trustees Report (1997), the Trust Fund assets will be exhausted by the end of 2029, after which full benefits cannot be paid on a timely basis without additional borrowing, an increase in tax rates, or additional revenue from elsewhere.

The existence of a social security trust fund raises several questions to be addressed in this chapter. Did the tax increase imposed in the 1983 amendments, which led to a sizable increase in the trust fund, have an economic rationale? That is, did the 1983 amendments increase national saving? And irrespective of whether the 1983 amendments increased national saving, the amendments did unambiguously increase *social security's* reserves. Should the government seek to increase these reserves even more by investing a portion of the reserves in equities? In particular, what are the pros and cons of investing some of the trust fund in corporate equities in order to delay the collapse of the fund? Another question deals with the optimal size of the trust fund. Specifically, what are the pros and cons of moving to a funded social security system by increasing the size of the trust fund? Finally, how does this option compare with *privatizing* social security, that is, moving to a defined-contribution, funded system based on individual accounts?

What Was the Rationale for the 1983 Amendments?

Mechanically, the trust fund has grown because the United States has chosen to finance benefits with earmarked taxes that exceed benefit payouts (Feldstein and Samwick 1997). *Politically*, the choice to finance benefits via earmarked payroll taxes was no historical accident. Virtually all countries with a public pension system finance benefits with earmarked payroll taxes (see Manchester, this volume). President Franklin Roosevelt's intent was to ensure that the U.S. social security program was viewed more as a retirement plan than as a handout, thereby making it harder to abandon after his presidency:

> We put those payroll contributions there so as to give the contributors a legal, moral, and political right to collect their pensions. . . . With those taxes in there, no damn politician can ever scrap my social security program. (quoted in Miron and Weil 1997: 11)

But is there a potential economic rationale for increasing the trust fund through tax increases as was done in the 1983 amendments? The answer is yes, on two counts. One rationale has to do with tax efficiency interacting with demographic considerations. Without reserves accumulating in a trust fund, the social security payroll tax would have to increase significantly in the future in order to pay for the benefits of the baby-boomer cohort. Economic theory shows that the deadweight loss resulting from distortionary wage taxation rises with the square of the tax rate, so it is more efficient to smooth payroll taxes over time instead of maintaining a strict pay-as-you-go system in which future tax rates would have to rise substantially.[3] A second motivation for funding is distributional: pre-funding future benefits reduces the tax burden on future generations. These justifications for the 1983 amendments, however, are valid only to the extent that the 1983 amendments actually increased public, or national, saving.

The 1983 Amendments, Public Saving, and Political Economy

Did the 1983 amendments increase public saving, or did the existence of additional resources in the trust fund simply create a ready source of financing for non-social security government debt? The answer to this question depends primarily on what one assumes would have happened if the bill had not been passed (the unobserved counterfactual).

Consider what I refer to as the *comprehensive* deficit created during time period t in which implicit pay-as-you-go social security debt is converted into explicit debt:

(1)
$$
\begin{aligned}
D_{t+1} - D_t = \; & [(G_t - T_t) + r_t D_t^{NS} \quad \} \text{``on-budget'' deficit} \\
& \qquad - (X_t - B_t)] \quad \} \text{social security surplus} \\
& + [(X_t - B_t) + r_t TF_t] \quad \} \text{``left pocket''} \\
& + [(D_{t+1}^S - D_t^S) \quad \} \Delta \text{ in pay-as-you-go net liability} \\
& \qquad - (X_t - B_t) - r_t TF_t] \quad \} \text{``right pocket''}
\end{aligned}
$$

Total deficit$_t$

Δ in social security's net liability $(t, t+1)$

where

B_t = social security benefits paid at time t

D_t = stock of comprehensive debt at the beginning of time t

D_t^{NS} = stock of non-social security debt at time $t = \sum\limits_{s=0}^{t-1} (1+r)^{(t-1)-(s+1)}(G_s - T_s)$

D_t^S = net liability of the pay-as-you-go portion of social security at time $t =$ present value of benefits less the present value of pay-as-you-go taxes (before Trust Fund contributions) of workers at time $t-1$

G_t = level of government spending at time t

r = interest rate on government bonds at time t

T_t = non-social security tax revenue at time t

TF_t = trust fund balance at time $t = \sum\limits_{s=0}^{t-1} (1+r)^{(t-1)-s}(B_s - X_s)$

X_t = social security tax revenue at time t

The first [•] term on the right-hand side of equation 1 is what the government reports as its official unified national deficit, equal to the primary deficit plus interest on the outstanding debt, less the social security surplus. Since social security is now technically off-budget, the total deficit less the social security surplus is referred to as the "on-budget" deficit. The second [•] term reflects the borrowing from social security that must be paid back with interest. This counts as a charge against the government budget exclusive of social security, what I have dubbed the "left pocket" of government. The third [•] term has two components. The first is equal to the growth at time t of the net liabilities of the pay-as-you-go portion of social security. The second component of the third term reflects the payback that social security—the "right pocket" of government—receives from the non-social security side of the federal government. Adding these two components gives the change in social security's total net liability. The left and right pockets cancel each other, reflecting the fact that payback of the trust fund with interest does not affect the comprehensive deficit. Nonetheless, we are still left with the social security surplus, in the first term of equation 1.

It is obvious, therefore, that an increase in the payroll tax reduces the comprehensive deficit—increasing public saving—if the other policy variables do not change. Moreover, for the purposes of estimating the budgetary impacts of specific legislation, the only reasonable approach is to hold all other laws constant. Nonetheless, some analysts believe that the passage of a particular piece of legislation could affect the political dynamics of subsequent legislation. For example, Barry Bosworth (1996: 104) questions whether it is legitimate to assume that these other policy variables remain constant when actions are taken to boost trust fund reserves. In his view, those actions could eventually be offset by changes elsewhere in the budget: "Most Americans," he argues, "are normally very surprised to learn that the surplus is being used to finance other programs, and that in most public discussions the budget deficit is defined to include the finances of social security." As shown in equation 1, an increase in payroll taxes would not increase public saving (including changes to social security's pay-as-you-go liability) if the payroll tax increase was matched dollar-for-dollar in present value with increases in promised future benefits, or other government spending, or reductions in other taxes.

Putting these pieces together, the 1983 amendments would have increased public saving (as defined above) if one assumes that (1) the government would have been willing to run a higher total national deficit in the absence of SSA83, and (2) the government did not promise to increase future benefits or fail to decrease benefits if this is what would have happened without SSA83. Excluding trust fund surpluses from the deficit measure — that is, the "on budget" deficit — could increase public saving by as much as the trust fund surplus if this policy change forced the government to reduce public spending by an equal amount. Then the new "on budget" deficit is equal to the former unified budget deficit. Bosworth argues that a focus on the "on budget" deficit would accord better with most people's perception of the deficit and could therefore increase public saving.

Some state-level empirical evidence supports Bosworth's position. To quote Bosworth (1996: 105): "[m]ost states present their budgets in ways that exclude their retirement programs, and nearly all have sought some degree of funding of those liabilities." He continues: "While the annual state retirement fund surpluses have grown steadily, to over 1 percent of GDP in the 1990s, the nonretirement budget balance has fluctuated about zero, with no clear tendency to rise or fall over time." But can we safely assume that state-level evidence is indicative of how the federal government works? Unfortunately, the answer to this question is unclear.

But whether or not the 1983 amendments increased public saving, the amendments did increase the *accounting* measure of the size of the trust fund. Should the government attempt to increase the trust fund even more by investing some of the reserves in equities? Without any change in legislation, this open-market operation would lead to a larger reported unified deficit. But, as the Technical Panel (p. 86) points out, "It is plausible, however, that if legislation allowed the Trust Funds to invest in equities, legislation could also require that the purchase of equities would not count as an expenditure and thus would not alter the measured unified budget deficit." The next section renews some of the economic, distributional, and political ramifications of investing a portion of the trust fund in equities.

Changing the Investment Strategy of the Trust Fund

The equity premium, or the average rate of return to equities above nominal short term government debt, has been historically about 6 percent (Kocherlakota 1996). This premium creates a tempting opportunity to help rescue the soon-to-be insolvent social security system by investing the large and growing trust fund in equities instead of government debt. This proposal, discussed for years, has taken on new popularity with the recent release of Social Security Advisory Council Report (Advisory Council 1997) in which several council members urged policymakers to consider this option. According to Jones (1997), switching trust fund investment policy so that equity composed 21 percent of initial wealth and 50 percent of all inflows in the stock market would extend the life of the trust fund by eight years over baseline — from the year 2029 to the year 2037 — if equity investments performed as expected.

Proponents of investing the trust fund in equities argue that this policy change could help maintain the current level of benefits in the future without increasing the payroll tax. Moreover, some of the higher returns could be plowed back into the fund to boost public and national saving. It has also been argued that a switch toward some equities would also make the government a better portfolio manager:

Currently it can be argued that the government is not performing its role as fund manager for social security as well as it might — not because of any failure on the part of those managing the system but because social security by law is allowed to invest only in the most conservative of investments: long-term, low-yield government bonds. Trustees of private pension systems and managers of state pension systems, who have the authority to invest much more broadly, would surely be castigated if they pursued such an ultra-conservative investment policy, and it can be argued that social security should have the same freedom to invest part of its funds in the broad equities market representing practically the entire American economy. (Advisory Council 1997: 83)

Arguments against investing the trust fund in equities are as old as the social security program itself. Historically, the concern was that the government would accumulate too large a share of the nation's capital stock (Miron and Weil 1997). More recent concerns have focused on the government's using its voting rights as a shareholder in a political manner. Karl Borden (1995) writes:

Allowing a fund of such magnitude to be invested by government bureaucrats is asking the government to make risk assessments in the private sector and subjects the fund to political influence. We have only to consider recent suggestions by the Clinton administration that private pension funds be required to invest a portion of their assets in "socially responsible" projects, or to consider the effects of the community reinvestment requirements the government has placed on the banking system, to realize that politicians cannot be trusted to invest fund assets with the objective of wealth maximization for fund participants. (1995: 4)

Trust fund investment discussions have also raised questions about how the risk would be assigned (Zeldes 1997). This issue was considered in broad terms by the Technical Panel of the recent Advisory Council:

A different way to think about the proposal is to realize that the risks and returns in the social security agency's portfolio [of equities] would be passed on to households, perhaps with some lag. When portfolio returns are high, this improves social security benefits or reduces social security taxes in the future; when returns are low, this approach reduces social security benefits or increases taxes in the future. . . . [Another] possibility is that Trust Fund risk will fall on as yet unborn generations, who have no opportunity to hold stocks now on their own accounts. Holding equities in the fund could give future generations exposure to current stock returns, thus improving risk sharing across generations. (*Technical Panel* 1997: 86)

Size of Trust Fund Relative to the Market

Would investing the trust fund in equities give the government too large a share of the private equities market? Hammond and Warshawsky (1996) argue that the answer is no. They consider the Maintain Benefits (MB) plan endorsed by six of the 13 members of the Social Security Advisory Council, which favors investing up to 40 percent of the trust fund in stock. This goal could be achieved by the year 2014, according to Hammond and Warshawsky. They then demonstrate that social security's share of the equities market in the year 2020 would range from 1.9 percent of all U.S. equities (assuming 9 percent real growth of all assets), to 4.9 percent (under 5 percent growth) to 27.5 percent (under -2 percent growth). They do note, however, that limited trust fund investments to a narrow index such as the S&P500 could be problematic. The value of all U.S. equities totaled about $8 trillion, but the value of the S&P500 was less than 10 percent of this value in 1996, only slightly larger than the value of the trust fund itself. Hammond and Warshawsky conclude "[p]resumably, social security equity investments would be made according to some of the broadest indexes (e.g., the broad Russell or Wilshire indexes) and would, therefore, have a limited sectoral impact."

Political Stock Choices

Whether the government would — or should — select stocks with political goals in mind is a thorny issue beyond the scope of this paper. Empirically, though, it appears that the federal government has exercised restraint from political bias when retirement assets are held in the form of individual accounts. Probably the most important example of this is the federal government's Thrift Savings Plan, the $30 billion (in 1996) defined-contribution retirement program for federal employees. The TSP offers an array of passive index funds free of political constraints.

But, the empirical case for government Trust Fund investments in equities is not all supportive. State and local governments' employees' pension funds have experienced far more political intrusions:

There have been clear instances in which political influences on some of these funds have led to misguided investments and undue losses for the funds. A number of states have guidelines for their pension funds that encourage some types of investments (e.g., investments that focus on projects or companies located in that state) and discourage other types of investments (e.g., investments in foreign companies or in companies that are extensively involved abroad or in specific countries), as compared with those that would conform to a "prudent person" fiduciary approach. Indeed, statistical studies of the annual returns yielded by state employee pension funds in the late 1980s and early 1990s have shown that the returns are significantly lower when the funds' trustees and managers are subject to greater political influence. And a number of state legislatures have raided their employees' pension funds when fiscal conditions were perceived to be tight. (White 1996: 17)[4]

In addition, investing in equities inevitably involves investing in some controversial firms. Obvious examples include tobacco stocks, foreign-owned firms, environmental polluters, and the like. Less obvious examples — but probably the most politically charged — include pornography, gambling, and abortion, as well as corporations whose chief executives are prominent advocates for partisan causes or religious organizations. These are issues that must be addressed in any proposal to invest the Trust Fund in equities.

Who Bears the Risk?

If trust fund assets are included in equities, a question arises about who bears the risk of fluctuating equity values. SSAC members favoring equity investments were clear that benefits should remain non-random:

. . . except for this change in investment policy, social security's principles and structure would remain unchanged under this approach. Social security continues as a defined-benefit plan, with the amount of benefits and the conditions under which they are paid still determined by law rather than by individual investments. . . . there would be ups and downs in returns but only very long-range trends would matter. And the assumed rate of return, while important, would be secondary to the fact that benefits would remain defined by law rather than by the relative uncertainty of individual investment decisions. (Advisory Council 1997: 86)

Hence under the MB plan, the risk associated with trust fund investment plan is passed on to future generations. Specifically, if the equity fund performs as expected, *current* workers are rewarded, in terms of future retirement benefits that are larger than those compatible with current tax rates, but *future* workers are pre-committed to absorb fully any shortfall in the trust fund below its expected value, in the form of larger taxes. Future workers are rewarded in the form of a lower payroll tax only if the equity portion of the Trust Fund performs better than expected. Putting these pieces together, future workers face an expected payoff equal to zero but with a risky tax rate. This risk allocation imposes an actuarial pay-as-you-go tax on future generations, the value of which can be assessed in a complete market setting using an option pricing approach. For example, the $3-trillion-dollar equity investment suggested by some members of the recent Advisory Council could place as much as a $9 trillion actuarial liability on future generations (Smetters 1997a).

When there are no missing financial markets, the value of the actuarial tax placed on future workers is as large as that of keeping the trust fund invested in bonds and raising the same expected revenue by increasing the payroll tax *only* on future workers (Smetters 1997a). Future generations would actually be better off, relative to this plan, if the payroll tax were increased immediately so that current workers participated in maintaining their own future level of benefits — a result that holds at any value of risk aversion. This result is ironic, given that many of those advocating trust fund investment in equities see it as a way of avoiding a payroll tax increase.

In reality, of course, financial markets are incomplete in important ways. One missing element corresponds to the inability of current and future workers to negotiate risk-sharing contracts such as futures and options contracts. Indeed, an argument for investing the trust fund in equities under these types of plans is expressed by the Technical Panel (1997: 86): "Holding equities in the fund could give future generations exposure to current stock returns, thus improving risk sharing across generations."[5] It follows that the *total* actuarial cost to future generations might be less than the explicit tax increase discussed above.

On the other hand, the total cost might actually be more than the explicit tax increase, if future workers are already exposed to a significant amount of uncertainty. The pay-as-you-go portions of the defined-benefit Medicare and social security program alone create an enormous amount of tax rate uncertainty for future workers. Indeed, the difference in combined OASDI-HI cost rates between the 1997 Trustees "low cost" and "high cost" estimates over the next 75 years is remarkably large. In particular, the 1997 Trustees estimate that supporting present-law OASDI-HI benefits would require anything from a negligible increase in the payroll tax to as much as a 30 percentage point increase! Government debt and the tax treatment of capital income also shift risk to future generations (Gale 1990; Bohn 1997a). So does the tendency of the budget deficit to increase during economic downturns, caused by a decrease in revenue (associated with linear and progressive taxes) combined with increased mandatory spending during a recession. Since the willingness of a person to accept additional correlated risk depends on the person's total portfolio of risky assets and liabilities, it follows that all risks faced by future workers — correlated and orthogonal to the risks associated with trust fund investment in equities — must be included in determining whether future workers are currently under-exposed to contemporaneous shocks. The enormous amount of risk facing future workers suggests that they might favor an explicit tax, instead of an uncertain tax that varied with equity returns. In any case, even if — very hypothetically—future workers were under-exposed to current shocks, the equity investment envisioned by some of the Advisory Council members cannot actually be beneficial to future workers. The reason is that future workers bear all the risk but face a zero expected payoff. This zero-mean gamble, therefore, decreases the expected utility of future workers in proportion to their level of risk aversion.

Another argument for trust fund investment in equities is to expose more *current* workers to equity returns (Diamond 1998). Since transaction costs associated with equity investments are rather low (Mitchell 1998), probably the best motive for doing this is paternalism (i.e., people "irrationally" under-exposing themselves to equity risk). But rational agents, who would like to offset this policy change, would be hurt due to the capital gains tax and any short-sale constraints. To prevent shifting the risk to future generations, policymakers would have to commit to reducing benefits on old people—instead of increasing taxes on young people—if equities under-performed. It is questionable whether this commitment is time consistent. Moreover, how would benefits be reduced? Although benefits could be reduced in a progressive fashion, an across-the-board reduction could be regressive. The exact politics of what would happen is unclear.

The Impact of Increasing the Size of the Trust Fund on the Economy

The issue of how to invest social security's current reserves is economically different from whether to increase the size of the reserves. The former issue pertains to how to invest existing saving, while the latter pertains to generating new saving, a process that involves tradeoffs between contemporaneous and future consumption. In light of the previous political analysis, I will assume that an increase in the trust fund cannot be counted against the on-budget deficit in calculating the government's total deficit.

Efficiency Gains

Probably the most important hurdle that any proposal designed to pre-fund social security must confront is the transition to the new system—in particular, how to continue to pay benefits to those who are already retired or near retirement while, at the same time, allowing young savers to divert some of their social security contributions to private saving accounts. Since social security is currently mostly pay-as-you-go, allowing young people to shift their social security contributions to the private capital market removes the tax revenue needed to pay benefits to the current elderly.

There are several proposals that appear to be able to pre-fund or privatize social security while making *every* generation better off. It is important to recognize, however, that these proposals are actually piggybacking on some other efficiency gain associated with tax reform (as in Breyer and Straub 1993) or from a direct arbitrage in which the government effectively borrows at a low rate and lends at a high rate (as in Altig and Gokhale 1997). Efficiency gains are unlikely to result from increased funding. The reason is that there is nothing inefficient about a transfer program that does not distort the price of contemporaneous consumption at the margin unlike, e.g., capital-income taxation. Other than changing the tax base from wages to another base, a switch from a pay-as-you-go to a funded system with recognition of all outstanding liabilities would require the same distortionary tax to service the debt as under the pay-as-you-go system.

This does not mean, however, that the payroll tax does not distort labor supply. The tradeoff involved in creating a pay-as-you-go program is that the windfall to the initial elderly comes at the cost of generating a stream of benefits whose present value is less than the present value of taxes for all future generations. The payroll tax therefore will generally be distorting. The "curse" of the pay-as-you-go system is that there is no way to reverse this distortion via pre-funding in such a way that all generations are made better off.

Macroeconomic Gains

For many reformers, efficiency gains are not the end of the story. In particular, pre-funding social security is viewed as desirable even if sacrifice is required on the part of transitional generations. And, indeed, the long-run macroeconomic impact of pre-funding social security can be quite substantial. For instance, Kotlikoff, Smetters, and Walliser (1998) demonstrate that full pre-funding of social security in their model leads to a 37 percent increase in the long-run capital stock, 4 percent increase in labor supply, 11 percent increase in output, 7 percent increase in wages, and a 19 percent decline in the cost of capital. This translates into a long-run 5 to 8 percent increase in full lifetime income, depending on the lifetime income group. Feldstein and Samwick (1997) also obtained large gains in their model.

As argued above, however, these large long-run gains are not free. Increasing the full lifetime resources of future generations requires an equal present-value reduction in the full lifetime resources of intermediate generations (Mitchell, Geanakoplos, and Zeldes, this volume). The actual utility loss on the part of transitional generations would have received from social security and the bond yield.[6] The larger this difference, the less valuable future social security benefits are to transitional generations and so losing them is less of a concession. Equivalently, a larger difference means that more of the payroll tax is effectively devoted to the windfall to the initial generations who received benefits without paying much into the system, rather than to one's own retirement benefit.

Tax Rates

Just how much would the payroll tax change in the long run, if social security were pre-funded? Feldstein and Samwick (1997) estimate that social security's current 12.4 percent payroll tax, which will need to rise to 18.75 percent in the future under present-law benefits, can eventually be replaced with only a 2 percent payroll tax invested in the capital market *if* the market performs as expected. This is because the social marginal product of capital has historically averaged a 9 percent real rate of return while the growth rate of the pay-as-you-go tax base is predicted to grow at around 1 percent during the next several decades.

Since the historic rate of return to government debt is only slightly larger than the future expected return to social security, most of the Feldstein-Samwick projected reduction in the payroll tax rate comes from exploiting the wedge between the equity premium and the historical bond yield. (The Kotlikoff, Smetters, and Walliser 1998 study also relies on this wedge.) To be sure, exploiting this wedge cannot necessarily be dismissed out-of-hand in the presence of the debate over why equity has historically delivered a 6 percent higher after-tax rate of return on average over debt (Kocherlakota 1996). In any case, to the extent that this wedge is indeed explained by risk and is therefore not exploitable, a long-run payroll tax equal to about 14.4 percent will be needed to replace the future 18.75 percent payroll tax using Feldstein and Samwick's parameter choices. (As noted above, the decline in the tax rate from 18.75 percent to 14.4 percent comes at a cost to transitional generations.) If social security were switched to a strict defined-contribution plan, a payroll tax rate less than 14.4 percent would fail to replace the current level of social security benefits on a risk-adjusted basis. If social security were kept as a defined-benefit plan, a payroll tax rate less than 14.4 percent would impose a large unfunded liability on future generations. Smetters (1997b) estimates that the Feldstein-Samwick plan would keep about seven-eighths of social security's unfunded liabilities in place if social security is kept as a defined-benefit plan.

Increasing the Size of the Trust Fund Versus Privatization

While pre-funding social security is unlikely to lead to any true efficiency gains, *privatizing* social security may. Social security remains a defined-benefit (DB) pension plan under the pre-funding approach. Privatization then involves switching from a DB plan to a defined-contribution (DC) plan. Any advantage or disadvantage that privatization has relative to pre-funding comes from this switch in pension models. This section considers several reasons why the DC model is probably superior to the DB model for providing old-age support.

Simplicity

While the assumption of full information is standard in economic theory, the effective marginal tax is actually very difficult to compute under social security. This is because the tax rate differs not only categorically (i.e., by earnings level, primary earner vs. secondary earner, etc.) but across the lifecycle as well, because the private market rate of return is higher than the rate of return to social security for most contributors (Feldstein and Samwick 1992). Moreover, people might not understand how their benefits are linked to their previous wage income in a DB plan. Indeed, the reader is encouraged to question non-economist friends and relatives about how they think that their social security benefits are calculated: answers like "I don't know" or "x fraction of my last $y \le$ three years of earnings before retiring, multiplied by z years worked" (i.e., private pension rules!) will undoubtedly be popular responses. The payroll tax therefore is more distorting than it need be—and during the prime working years—for these uninformed workers.[7]

The pure efficiency gains associated with full information can be quite large—e.g., as high as 0.6 percent of *full* lifetime income (i.e., before the purchase of leisure) or 1.5 percent of *actual* lifetime income (i.e., after the purchase of leisure)—if people perceive no marginal linkage in the current system (Kotlikoff, Smetters, and Walliser 1998). Starting from a higher perceived marginal-tax benefit linkage reduces these gains.

Privatizing social security—and, in particular, moving from a DB to a DC system—may improve efficiency to the extent that (1) people are not fully informed of their marginal tax-benefit linkage, *and* (2) a switch to a DC system improves the perceived linkage, thereby reducing the effective tax rate on labor income. Specifically, relative to social security in which the same payroll tax is used for redistribution and to pay for one's own future benefits, a DC system can disentangle these two components, and may thereby improve efficiency. These efficiency gains, though, can theoretically be achieved within the current *pay-as-you-go DB* social security system if the government is willing to inform *each person at each point in time* how an additional dollar of his payroll tax is translated into future benefits. Doing so, however, would require exposing the relatively low rate of return received by many households due to the inter-generational and intra-generational redistributing roles of social security. Switching to a private DC system therefore would have the potential advantage of making the overall tax-benefit linkage explicit without these reporting requirements.

While pre-funding social security under its current DB status would also reduce the effective tax rate of social security by bringing the rate of return to social security contributions closer to the market rate of return, this effect alone will not increase economic efficiency unless accompanied by an increased understanding of the tax-benefit linkage. Although the efficiency gains from pre-funding Social Security could be non-trivial if it led to an improvement in information, they are unlikely to be as significant as those from moving to a simpler DC system, unless the separate benefit and re-distribution roles in a funded DB system are made more clear.

Annuity Markets

To the extent that social security provides annuitization that may not other-wise exist in the private market due to adverse selection, moving to a DC plan might decrease efficiency unless at least some portion of the assets in the DC plan required to be annuitized upon retirement.[8] However, there is no reason to believe that the *full* mandated annuitization inherent in social security is optimal.[9] At least some lump-sum disbursement will be desirable for the purpose of making a bequest, giving inter-vivos transfers to children (e.g., as a down payment on a house), or holding a buffer for medical and non-medical expenses faced by beneficiaries and their heirs. While the an-nuity stream can be used to purchase life insurance in order to make a bequest, little can be done regarding the other concerns without at least some lump-sum disbursements. Moreover, on the distributional side, full mandated annuitization tends to be regressive by redistributing resources from shorter-lived poor people to longer-lived rich people, *ceteris paribus*. A DC plan, in contrast, can deal with annuitization via mandates. It is also inherently more flexible in the design of the payout options. For example, Chile allows for lump-sum withdrawals above some minimum mandated annuity level.

Risk Sharing

It is also commonly argued that a funded DB plan can better shift aggregate risk across generations. This risk shifting, however, requires that at least part of the payroll tax in a DB plan is transferred from young to old workers. This, in turn, complicates the marginal tax-benefit linkage in the DB plan. In contrast, a DC plan can do better.

At least some of the risks in the DC plan would also tend to be shifted across generations, since the government cannot credibly commit to allow-ing people to retire with few assets. Indeed, while DC plans are commonly criticized for forcing workers to bear all the risk, all actual major privatiza-tion implementations continue to provide rather generous minimum guar-antees financed on a pay-as-you-go basis.[10] A realistic DC plan, therefore, would be composed of a no-redistribution private account, along with a pure redistribution add-on tax. This separation has the advantage of a com-partmentalizing the pure distorting tax, thereby avoiding commingling redistribution with one's own retirement saving. This "twin pillars" approach has been extremely popular in Latin America (Mitchell and Barreto 1997).

In addition, the DC plan would tend to be more flexible than the DB plan in designing risk sharing. This is because the minimum benefit guarantee could be set at a lower and more reasonable level than the *fixed* benefit guarantee that might be inherent in a DB plan. While it is true that the fixed benefit guarantee passes any *excess* returns forward in time, the option value of this feature is quite small for realistic parameterizations (Smetters 1997b). The guarantee level itself is the primary issue, and a smaller minimum benefit will tend to have a much lower unfunded actuarial cost than a larger fixed benefit. Indeed, it is unlikely that the level of risk shifting that might be inherent in a funded DB plan is optimal ex ante, unless policymakers actively change benefits in addition to changing taxes in response to large shocks to equity prices. To be sure, some risk shifting across generations is desirable in order to avoid a low level of post-retirement consumption. Guaranteeing a higher level of post-retirement consumption, however, would be essentially redistributional in nature and would work in the opposite direction from reducing unfunded liabilities.

Administrative Costs

DC plans are commonly criticized as having higher administrative costs than a well-managed DB plan. Promoters of this position often point to the high transaction costs that exist in both the Chilean and UK systems. In contrast, the U.S. social security system is often argued as being remarkably efficient.

However, there are examples of very efficient full-featured DC plans in the United States. Indeed, while promoters of the high-transaction-costs argument typically consider administrative charges of around 100 basis points, a large passive index fund can, in reality, have much lower overhead fees (Mitchell 1998). Total administrative fees (excluding collection fees) of the Thrift Savings Plan, which is the DC plan for federal workers with $45 billion in assets at the end of 1996, are currently less than nine basis points (11 basis points if forfeited non-vested employer contributions are excluded). This overhead charge includes many basic services such as money management, operating and development costs of the recordkeeper's computer system, and printing and mailing of publications and participants' statements, as well as the TSP Service Office that handles its optional annuities and loan programs in addition to standard inter-fund transfers and account balance inquiries. But even nine basis points is pessimistic: the TSP fees have decreased almost monotonically from over 30 basis points in 1988, the year of the Fund's inception. In the future overhead fees could decrease to less than a single basis point, or about $1/100$ the fee assumed by promoters of the high-transaction-costs argument. The TSP avoids high administrative fees, in part, because it limits investment choice to three (soon to be four) passively-managed fund options.

While limiting choice is not necessarily efficient even if it reduces costs, restricted and regulated choice might be a desirable route to take in a privatized social security system where excessive brokerage fees resulting from uninformative advertising, wasteful competition over a homogeneous product, "account churning," and fraud are especially important issues. Limiting choice might also be desirable on moral hazard grounds in order to prevent excessive risk-taking by those whose account balances are low enough to trigger a minimum benefit. With these controls in place, it is quite possible that a DC plan could have just as low transaction costs as social security — and perhaps even lower, if choices are restricted enough so that firms are basically forced to compete on the cost side instead of on the revenue side. Achieving low costs might also require allowing each person to have only a single account in order to reduce record keeping.

Political Uncertainty and Redistribution

Some might view any inefficiency caused by redistribution within social security as simply the cost of maintaining public support for redistribution. Alternative forms of redistribution compatible with a DC model would probably gain public support, however. This is especially true of the Earned Income Tax Credit (EITC) program, which rewards people for working. Indeed, the EITC program has been expanded in recent years, even in wake of the decline in many other forms of welfare. Replacing social security's intra-generational redistribution with an EITC program can lead to non-trivial efficiency gains in the presence of borrowing constraints, especially for the poor (Smetters 1997c).

It has sometimes been argued that a DC plan might face lower political risk than a DB plan, since benefits are no longer determined by the will of policymakers. But the tax treatment of DC accounts will subject them to political uncertainty as well, so it is unclear which plan performs better here (a point emphasized in Smetters 1997b and Diamond 1998). It is true, though, that the assets in a DC plan are decentralized, a potential advantage over pre-funding. Indeed, if the government failed to take social security completely off budget, or reverted back to the current unified budget deficit measure in the future, all of the assets in the trust fund could be spent on either tax reductions or government consumption without changing either the reported trust fund balance or "deficit" measure.

Conclusion

A trust fund is an accounting device that reflects a political choice to finance social security benefits with earmarked taxes rather than with general revenue. Increasing the size of the trust fund through a payroll tax increase, like the one implemented in the 1983 amendments, leads to a smaller distortion of labor supply, relative to the policy of waiting to increase the payroll tax only when necessary to pay for benefits. An increase in the payroll tax before the baby-boomer cohort begins to retire might also be justified on distributional grounds. These arguments, however, are at least partially undermined if an increase in the size of the trust fund is offset by either dissaving in the non-social security side of government, or an increase in future benefits. Calculating a value for this offset is an important topic for future research.

We also summarize previous analyses of the merits of investing the trust fund in equities. Under such a proposal, it is unlikely that the government would own a large share of total assets in the economy. Limiting trust fund investments to a narrow index such as the S&P500, however, could be problematic, due to the small size of the funds in such an index relative to the total assets in the economy. Mixed evidence is reported on the hypothesis that politicians might manipulate stock choices for political gain. Although the federal government has resisted this temptation with retirement assets held in the form of individual accounts, the trust funds of state and local governments have experienced some political intrusions. Finally, we showed that investing the trust fund in equities under the current defined-benefit system imposes a non-trivial actuarial tax on future workers. Whether this redistribution is good or bad is a normative question outside the scope of this chapter. In theory, future generations may not be harmed very much by this transfer of risk, because no market exists allowing current and future generations to engage in risk sharing. On the other hand, a substantial amount of risk is already being transferred to future generations under baseline policy, and transferring even more risk might potentially be very harmful. Quantifying the amount of risk under baseline policy is difficult but a worthwhile avenue for future research.

Finally, we described the merits of pre-funding social security (increasing the size of the Trust Fund) and privatization (switching to a defined-contribution system). It was argued that while pre-funding social security would tend to result in few — if any — true efficiency gains, privatization might. A privatized system is more simple and more flexible. Both of these factors can result in potentially large efficiency gains. Quantitative gains from simplicity (coming from reduced labor supply distortion) are available, though potential gains associated with greater flexibility have not yet been quantified. Calculating these gains represents an important avenue for future research.

The author has received very helpful comments from Bob Dennis, Doug Hamilton, Olivia Mitchell, and Jan Walliser. The views expressed herein do not necessarily reflect those of the author and not the Congressional Budget Office.

Notes

1. A summary of major changes in the social security program is given in Kollmann (1996) and the *Social Security Bulletin* (1995).

2. The value of the OASI Trust Fund at the end of 1993 was $19.7 billion (1995 Statistical Supplement, Table 4.A1). Feldstein (1995) estimates that social security's net liability (present value of future benefits less present value of future payroll taxes across all living adults) in 1983 equaled $5 trillion using a 3 percent discount rate. For other estimates see Goss (this volume).

3. A general intertemporal tax smoothing argument was first developed by Barro (1979) and has been examined in a stochastic environment by Bohn (1990).

4. The empirical evidence referred to by White can be found in Romano (1993), Mitchell (1993), and Marr, Nofsinger and Trimble (1996).

5. Bohn (1997b) provides a rigorous treatment, as well as thoughtful cautions, on this result.

6. In fact, the low historical risk of the wages and salary base — the source of the rate of return in a pay-as-you-go social security system — relative to historical bonds suggests that an even lower rate could be used to discount social security liabilities (Smetters 1997b).

7. Technically, the payroll tax need not be fully distorting even in this case, if earnings near retirement are highly correlated with previous productivity levels.

8. Estimates of the severity of this problem are found in Friedman and Warshawsky (1990) and Mitchell, Poterba, and Warshawsky (1999). Abel (1986), however, shows theoretically, that the annuity protection that social security already provides tends to enhance the adverse selection problem in the private annuity. In recent analysis using a large-scale simulation model, Walliser (1997), shows that even if economic agents purchased a large amount of annuities due to an absence of a bequest motive, the excess of the price of an annuity above its actuarially fair value would, as a percent of the fair value, only fall from about 9 percent to 6 percent. It follows that privatization without mandates may not lead to the development of an annuity market with actuarially-fair annuities.

9. Diamond (1998) argues that the value of the "rolling annuity" (risk pooling in case of death prior to retirement) provided by social security can be quite sizable. A portion of a DC plan's assets could also be required to be forfeited upon pre-retirement death. This option would be more flexible than full annuitization.

10. These guarantees have been made explicit in every large privatization experiment, including Chile and El Salvador, the countries with the most ambitious privatization implementations to date. These countries promise to "top up" underperforming private accounts in order to guarantee a minimum level of benefits that, as a fraction of income, is equal to about the average U.S. benefit. The World Bank's privatization plan recommends a similarly sized guarantee. Australia guarantees that its pensioners will do just as well under its new system as under the old. See also Pennacchi (this volume).

References

Aaron, Henry. "Privatizing Social Security: A Bad Idea Whose Time Will Never Come." *Brookings Review* (Summer 1997): 17–23.

Abel, Andrew B. "Capital Accumulation and Uncertain Lifetimes with Adverse Selection." *Econometrica* 54, 15 (September 1986): 1079–97.

Advisory Council on Social Security. *Final Report of the 1994–1996 Advisory Council on*

Social Security. Vol. 1, *Findings and Recommendations.* Washington, D.C.: Social Security Administration, 1997.

Altig, David and Jagadeesh Gokhale. "Social Security Privatization: One Proposal." The Cato Project on Social Security Privatization, Working Paper No. 9. Washington, D.C.: Cato Institute, 1997.

Barro, Robert. "On the Determination of the Public Debt." *Journal of Political Economy* 87, 5, Part 1 (1979): 940–71.

Board of Trustees of the Social Security Administration. *Annual Report of the Board of Trustees of the Federal Old-Age and Survivors Insurance and Disability Insurance Trust Funds.* Washington, D.C.: USGPO, 1997.

Bohn, Henning. "Tax Smoothing with Financial Instruments." *American Economic Review* 80, 5 (1990): 1217–30.

———. "Risk Sharing in a Stochastic Overlapping Generations Economy." Mimeo, University of California Santa Barbara, 1997. 1997a

———. "Social Security Reform and Financial Markets." Mimeo, University of California Santa Barbara, 1997. 1997b

Borden, Karl. "Dismantling the Pyramid: The Why and How of Privatizing Social Security." The Cato Project on Social Security Privatization, SSP No. 1. Washington, D.C.: Cato Institute, 1995.

Bosworth, Barry. "Fund Accumulation: How Much? How Managed?" In Peter A. Diamond, David C. Lindeman, and Howard Young, eds., *Social Security: What Role for the Future?* Distributed by the Brookings Institution for the National Academy of Social Insurance, Washington, D.C.: 1996.

Bosworth, Barry and Gary Burtless. "Budget Crunch: Population Aging in Rich Countries." *Brookings Review* (Summer 1997): 10–15.

Breyer, Friedrich and Martin Straub. "Welfare Effects of Unfunded Pension Systems When Labor Supply Is Endogenous." *Journal of Public Economics* 50, 1 (1993): 77–91.

Congressional Budget Office. *The Economic and Budget Outlook: Fiscal Years 1998–2007.* Washington, D.C., 1997.

Diamond, Peter A. "Macroeconomic Aspects of Social Security Reform." *Brookings Papers on Economic Activity,* 1998.

Feldstein, Martin and Andrew Samwick. "Social Security Rules and Marginal Tax Rates." *National Tax Journal* 45, 1 (March 1992): 1–22.

———. "The Economics of Prefunding Social Security and Medicare Benefits." Paper presented at the NBER Meeting on Social Security Reform, August 1997.

Friedman, Benjamin and Mark Warshawsky. "The Cost of Annuities: Implications for Saving Behavior and Bequests." *Quarterly Journal of Economics* 104 (1990): 135–54.

Gale, Douglas. "The Efficient Design of Public Debt." In Rudiger Dornbusch and Mario Draghi, eds., *Public Debt Management: Theory and History.* New York and Melbourne: Cambridge University Press, 1990. 14–47.

Goss, Stephen C. "Measuring Solvency in the Social Security System." This volume.

Gramlich, Edward. "Different Approaches for Dealing with Social Security." *Journal of Economic Perspectives* 10, 3 (1996): 55–66.

Hammond, P. Brett and Mark J. Warshawsky. "Investing Social Security Funds in Stocks." Mimeo, TIAA-CREF, 1996. Forthcoming in *Benefits Quarterly.*

Jones, Thomas. "Trust Fund Investment Alternatives." In Advisory Council on Social Security, *Final Report of the 1994–1996 Advisory Council on Social Security.* Vol. 2, Washington, D.C., USGPO, 1997. 405–414.

Kocherlakota, Narayana. "The Equity Premium: It's Still a Puzzle." *Journal of Economic Literature* 44 (1996): 42–71.

Kollmann, Geoffrey. "Summary of Major Changes in the Social Security Cash Benefits Program: 1935–1996." Congressional Research Service Report for Congress, 94–36 EPW. Congressional Research Service, Library of Congress, 1996.

Kotlikoff, Laurence, Kent Smetters, and Jan Walliser. "Privatizing U.S. Social Security — A Simulation Study." In Klaus Schmidt-Hebbel, ed., *Pension Systems: From Crisis to Reform.* Washington, D.C.: World Bank, forthcoming 1998.

Manchester, Joyce. "Compliance in Social Security Systems Around the World." This volume.

Marr, M. Wayne, John Nofsinger, and John Trimble. *Economically Targeted and Social Investments: Investment Management and Pension Fund Performance.* Charlottesville, Va.: Research Foundation of the Institute of Chartered Financial Analysts, 1996.

Miron, Jeffrey and David Weil. "The Genesis and Evolution of Social Security." NBER Working Paper 5949. Cambridge, Mass.: NBER 1997.

Mitchell, Olivia S. "Public Pension Governance and Performance: Lessons for Developing Countries." Working Paper 9, Institute for Labor Market Policies, School of Industrial and Labor Relations, Cornell University, 1993.

———. "Administrative Costs in Public and Private Retirement Systems." In Martin Feldstein, ed., *Privatizing Social Security.* Chicago: University of Chicago Press, forthcoming 1998.

Mitchell, Olivia S. and Flávio Ataliba Barreto. "After Chile, What? Second-Round Pension Reforms in Latin America." *Revista de Analisis Economico* 12, 2 (November 1997): 3–36.

Mitchell, Olivia S., James Poterba, and Mark J. Warshawsky. "New Evidence on the Money's Worth of Individual Annuities." *American Economic Review* (1999), forthcoming.

Mitchell, Olivia S., John Geanakoplos, and Stephen P. Zeldes. "Social Security Money's Worth." This volume.

Pennacchi, George G. "Government Guarantees for Old Age Income." This volume.

Romano, Roberta. "Public Pension Fund Activism in Corporate Governance Reconsidered." *Columbia Law Review* (May 1993).

Smetters, Kent. "Investing the Social Security Trust Fund in Equities: An Option Pricing Approach." Technical Paper Series, Macroeconomic Analysis and Tax Analysis Divisions, Washington, D.C.: Congressional Budget Office, No. 1, 1997. 1997a

———. "Privatizing Social Security in the Presence of a Benefit Guarantee." Mimeo. Washington, D.C., 1997. 1997b

———. "Is Social Security an Efficient Way to Redistribute Resources Within Generations?" Mimeo. Washington, D.C., 1997. 1997c

Social Security Administration. Annual Statistic Supplement to the Social Security Bulletin. Washington, D.C.: USGPO, 1995.

Technical Panel on Trends and Issues in Retirement Savings. *Final Report of the 1994–1996 Advisory Council on Social Security.* Washington, D.C.: Social Security Administration, 1997.

Walliser, Jan. "Understanding Adverse Selection in the Annuities Market and the Impact of Privatizing Social Security." Technical Paper Series, Macroeconomic Analysis and Tax Analysis Divisions, Washington, D.C.: Congressional Budget Office, No. 4, 1997.

White, Lawrence. "Investing the Assets of the Social Security Trust Funds in Equity Securities: An Analysis." *Investment Company Institute Perspective* 2, 4 (1996): 1–20.

Zeldes, Stephen. "Risk in Equity Investment." Advisory Council on Social Security. *Final Report of the 1994–1996 Advisory Council on Social Security.* Vol. 2, Reports of the Technical Panels and Presentations to the Council. Washington, D.C.: USGPO, 1997: 402–4.

Chapter 9
Government Guarantees for
Old Age Income

George G. Pennacchi

Many actual and proposed social security reforms seek to privatize a country's old-age obligations by requiring that individuals contribute to defined benefit or defined contribution pension plans. But when contributions to private pension plans are mandatory, individuals may be exposed to risks that they did not face in a government-sponsored defined benefit social security system. In the case of a privately-sponsored defined benefit plan, there is the risk that the plan sponsor might default on the pension benefits promised to participants. In the case of a defined contribution plan, the primary risk is that participants' investment returns may be lower than anticipated, leaving them with inadequate wealth during their retirement years.

To make privatization reforms more attractive to the public, governments have often provided guarantees that reduce peoples' exposure to default or investment risks. Thus, there is usually an important role left for governments in mandatory-contribution privatization schemes. If social security in the United States evolves to a system based primarily on defined contribution Personal Security Accounts (PSAs), as described in Chapter 1 of this volume, it is not unlikely that government guarantees on PSA returns would also be provided. The U.S. government already guarantees the retirement benefits of participants in privately-sponsored defined benefit pension plans through the Pension Benefit Guaranty Corporation (PBGC).

In this chapter, I illustrate how the costs of various forms of pension guarantees might be estimated. These estimates can help gauge the implicit subsidies associated with particular reforms and could be incorporated into budgetary measures of government spending. Estimates of these costs might also be used to set insurance premiums paid by guaranteed private pension plans that would reduce or eliminate any government subsidies. The values of pension guarantees made by governments throughout the world are analyzed using "contingent claims analysis" (CCA), also known as "option pricing theory." Following the seminal developments by Black and Scholes (1973) and Merton (1973), a large literature in CCA has emerged. This research applies the fundamental insights of valuing options to valuing more general claims whose payments are contingent on other asset prices. In particular, CCA has been used to value many different types of government guarantees and insurance contracts, such as loan guarantees, deposit insurance, and pension benefit guarantees.

An attractive feature of CCA is that relatively few assumptions are needed to value claims. Typically, valuation requires only the assumptions that there are negligible costs to trading assets and that the equilibrium prices of these assets do not allow for riskless arbitrage. Importantly, assumptions regarding investor preferences (risk-aversion) or assets' expected rates of return are not needed. Based on this preference-free feature of CCA, Cox and Ross (1976) showed how calculating contingent claims prices could be simplified. Their "risk-neutral" valuation method was generalized by Harrison and Kreps (1979) and has become known as the "martingale pricing" approach.

The accuracy of CCA measures to value pension guarantees depends on the validity of the model's assumptions regarding the absence of trading costs and arbitrage in assets held by pension funds. Since most pension fund assets are marketable securities, particularly when a fund is a defined contribution type, trading costs are likely to be low compared to those for nonmarketable assets. The precision of CCA will improve with the degree of competition in securities markets and the lowering of securities' bid-ask spreads.

This chapter considers techniques for valuing guarantees on both defined benefit and defined contribution pensions. Previous research has focused on valuing defined benefit guarantees, perhaps because defined benefit pensions have been the dominant type of pension plan in developed countries. However, with the recent growth in social security privatization, especially in Latin America, guarantees of defined contribution pensions are becoming increasingly common.[1] The U.S. government might also decide to offer defined contribution guarantees should it adopt a PSA-based pension system. Therefore, we present a number of new results for valuing defined contribution guarantees. We also emphasizes that the martingale pricing approach can be a unifying framework for valuing all types of guarantees, both defined benefit and defined contribution. This approach may yield explicit formulas for guarantee values, or it can allow for valuation by Monte Carlo simulation. It is beyond the scope of this study to provide a detailed analysis of every possible type of government pension guarantee, but our methodology may be customized to handle specific cases.

When governments guarantee private contracts such as pension plans, adverse selection and moral hazard problems may arise. These incentive problems can be alleviated by properly structuring and pricing guarantees, and/or regulating the activities of the parties on whose behalf the guarantee is given. Discussions of these important issues can be found in a number of recent papers and, due to a lack of space, will not be repeated here.[2] Because my focus is on valuing guarantees, I often take the risk decisions of the participating parties as given. But it should be emphasized that these decisions are often linked to the guarantee's structure, pricing, or regulation.

In what follows, I first discuss the value of defined benefit pension guarantees and how the present value of premiums paid for these guarantees can be assessed. Some qualitative features of these guarantees are illustrated for typical defined benefit pension plans. Next, I discuss various types of defined contribution pension guarantees. Two types of rate of return guarantees are considered: one being a fixed rate of return guarantee and the other being a rate of return guarantee that is relative to the performance of other pension funds. I then examine a guarantee of a minimum pension level following participation in a mandatory defined contribution pension plan. Values for these rates of return and minimum pension guarantees are illustrated using typical parameter values.[3]

Defined Benefit Pension Guarantees

Defined benefit pension plans represent a majority of worldwide pension savings, and their dominance is likely to continue for the foreseeable future.[4] The liabilities of defined benefit plans more closely resemble debt claims, in contrast to defined contribution pension plans, whose liabilities are similar to those of equity claims on a security portfolio. Thus, valuing defined-benefit guarantees is similar to valuing guarantees on default-risky debt.

When a government insures a corporate sponsored pension plan, its net liability can be divided into two components: (1) its "gross" liability deriving from the loss that would occur if the sponsoring firm became bankrupt and its pension fund were underfunded; (2) the present value of the insurance premiums the government charges, as long as the firm avoids bankruptcy. We will consider the value of both components, so that by combining the two the government's net liability (subsidy) can be assessed.

In analyzing the gross value of defined benefit pension guarantees, it is useful to distinguish between pension plans that are collateralized by pension fund assets and those that are not. In most countries, defined benefit pensions are partially or fully funded by a separate portfolio of assets (a pension trust). But in some countries, notably France, Germany, and Japan, corporations need not segregate pension assets from other corporate assets for the sole purpose of backing promised retirement benefits. Rather, pension liabilities are combined with other corporate liabilities and backed only by the general assets of the corporation. Thus, for these non-segregated pension plans, pension guarantees can be valued using techniques developed to value default risky corporate liabilities.

Guarantees of Pensions Backed by Corporate Assets

Let us first consider guarantees of non-segregated plans, and then we will discuss those for pension plans backed by a separate pension fund. Merton's (1974) seminal work provided the first detailed analysis for valuing default risky corporate debt and for valuing guarantees on this debt.[5] In these models, the rate of return on firm assets is typically assumed to follow a continuous time stochastic process (diffusion process) and firm assets may be depleted by firm payments for dividends or interest payments on existing debt. Should assets be insufficient to meet a payment of one of the corporation's liabilities or fall to a level that violates a covenant, then the firm is assumed to be liquidated and its assets are divided among the firm's security holders according to pre-existing seniority rules. Thus, the schedule of the firm's payments to various security holders, along with the uncertainty of asset returns, determines when bankruptcy occurs and the residual level of assets to be split among the firm's creditors. Applying this valuation technique to a corporation having pension liabilities backed only by corporate assets would require a detailed specification of the firm's other current and future liabilities, their terms, and their relative seniority. In general, this can be a rather complicated task.

Recently, Longstaff and Schwartz (1995) have extended the work of Black and Cox (1976) to provide a relatively simple but flexible model for valuing corporate liabilities that allows for interest rate risk as well as default risk. In this model, the value of firm assets at date t, V_t, has a rate of return that follows a constant volatility diffusion process. Should assets fall to a threshold level at date T, say $V_T = \delta$, then the firm is assumed to be unable to meet its financial obligations and a corporate reorganization (bankruptcy) occurs at date T. If bankruptcy occurs during the life of a security, the security holder is assumed to receive, with certainty, a fixed fraction of the security's promised payments at the dates when these payments were originally scheduled to be paid. In other words, the security holder is issued a new security, riskless in terms of default, but with payments equal to only a proportion, say $1 - w$, of the original security's promised payments.

This model offers a greatly simplified view of the timing of bankruptcy and the recovery rates of security holders, since it does not treat explicitly how they are affected by the terms and seniority structure of the firm's individual liabilities. Whether such a simplification is justified should be evaluated on a case-by-case basis. However, if this framework is adapted to a firm having pension liabilities, the pension guarantee could be valued using similar formulas. Should bankruptcy occur, the government insurer would be responsible for the proportional loss, w, of each future pension payment. The government's liability at bankruptcy would then be w times the value of the pension benefits at that date. Of course, the likelihood of bankruptcy as specified by the relative initial value of firm assets, V_t, versus the bankruptcy point, δ, is critical for determining the present value of this guarantee.

Guarantees of Pensions Backed by a Pension Fund

Let us now consider the value of pension guarantees when a pension fund, segregated from other corporate assets, collateralizes pension liabilities. This is the most common type of defined benefit plan, and can be found in countries such as Canada, the Netherlands, the United Kingdom, and the United States. A number of studies have applied contingent claims techniques to value this type of pension guarantee,[6] usually assuming that the term to maturity of the pension insurance is known. In other words, the models assume a non-random date at which the firm's pension plan could be terminated and, if it were underfunded, the insurer would experience a claim. This is a convenient assumption since it allows guarantees to be valued in a manner similar to that of a standard European put option (Merton 1997). In practice, however, a government insurer experiences a possible claim when the sponsoring firm enters bankruptcy, and this date is likely to be highly uncertain. Thus, in practice, it is clear that the value of a pension guarantee depends on both the financial condition of the insured pension fund, and the financial condition of the fund's sponsoring firm.

Research by Marcus (1987) departs from this literature by acknowledging that plan termination dates may be random. His formula for the value of a pension guarantee models the insurer as having a forward contract on the pension fund's assets, with the forward price equal to the fund's liabilities, and a maturity date contingent on the bankruptcy of the sponsoring firm. More recent work (Pennacchi and Lewis 1994; Lewis and Pennacchi 1997) has revised the Marcus analysis to model the guarantee as a contingent put option rather than a contingent forward contract, the difference being that, in practice, a government does not obtain a positive payment when a firm with an overfunded pension plan fails. The guarantee is then analogous to a put option on the pension fund's assets, with an exercise price equal to the pension fund's liabilities, and a contingent maturity date determined by the sponsoring firm's bankruptcy.

The general approach taken in this literature specifies continuous-time stochastic processes for the sponsoring firm's (corporate) assets, V_t, the sponsoring firm's (corporate) liabilities, D_t, the pension fund's assets, F_t, and the pension fund's accrued vested liabilities, A_t. In general, these four processes will be correlated, and their expected growth rates will be affected by the assumed behavior of the sponsoring firm and the demographic structure of the participants in the pension plan. For example, V_t depends not only on the random change in the return on the firm's assets but also on any net payouts from the corporation's assets made by the firm. Similarly, the process followed by F_t depends on the random rate of return on the pension fund's investments, and also on the firm's new contributions to the pension fund less any benefits paid to retirees. Finally, A_t depends on the random change in value of the fund's current vested benefits (due to changes in market interest rates), and also on the amount of new benefits granted to workers and retirees less any benefits paid to retirees (Marcus 1987).

Given this framework, we can now specify the payment required by a government guarantor should a pension claim arise. At date T, the government is assumed to be liable for the amount $L_T = \max(0, A_T - F_T)$, where T is defined as the first time that V_T falls to a level δD_T, and where $0 < \delta \leq 1$. $1 - \delta$ is the firm's level of negative net worth when bankruptcy occurs.[7] The contingent payment by the government has the structure of a put option, but with the maturity date T of the option being stochastic, coinciding with the bankruptcy of the sponsoring firm. The martingale pricing can be applied to calculate the present value of this government guarantee, L_t. This approach is equivalent to other CCA methods (Kocic 1996) and so requires only the assumption that equilibrium security prices not allow for arbitrage opportunities.[8]

The basic idea of the martingale approach is that the value of a government's guarantee can be computed as the expected payment made by the government, discounted at the risk-free rate of interest, where the expected payment is that which would occur if all assets had an expected rate of return equal to the risk-free rate.[9] Specifically, if we let r_s be the continuously compounded, short-maturity, risk-free interest rate at date s, then the present value of the government's guarantee can be calculated as $L_t = E_t^*$ $[\exp(-\int_t^T r_s ds)\ L_T]$. Here $E_t^*[\bullet]$ is the date t expectation of the discounted payment assuming all assets have an expected rate of return at date s equal to the risk-free rate, r_s.[10] Note that a world where the average rate of return on all assets equaled the risk-free rate would be one where all investors were risk-neutral. Hence, the martingale approach often reduces to what is referred to as "risk-neutral pricing." However, it should be emphasized that this approach does not explicitly assume universal risk-neutrality. In fact, it does not require any specific assumption regarding investor preferences. The association with risk-neutrality is only a computational technique that leads to the unique arbitrage-free value for the government's guarantee.

Loosely speaking, the martingale approach gives the correct value for L_t because of two erroneous assumptions whose effects cancel each other out, resulting in a correct valuation. One incorrect assumption is that all assets have an average rate of return equal to the risk-free rate, that is, there are no "risk premia" in asset rates of return. This implies a "risk-neutral" expectation of L_T that differs from the "true" expectation of L_T, leading to the first error. The other incorrect assumption is that this risky payment should be discounted at the risk-free rate rather than a discount rate that includes a risk premium, leading to a second error. Because both the first and second "errors" involve a failure to account for risk premia, the first error "understates" the expected growth of L_T by the risk premia while the second error "overstates" the discount factor applied to L_T by the risk premia. Mathematically, these two errors cancel, leading to a correct valuation formula. Importantly, because this computational technique does not require specification of the actual risk premia of the assets in the economy, no assumptions regarding the signs or magnitudes of risk premia are needed.

Computing the expectation of the discounted value of the government's payment does require specific assumptions regarding the firm's rate of net payouts from corporate assets, the rate of net contributions to the pension fund, and the rate of net new pension benefits. An explicit solution can be derived for the case in which these rates are constants (Pennacchi and Lewis 1994; Lewis and Pennacchi 1997). Guarantee values for this case will be illustrated shortly. However, when firm payouts, pension fund contributions, or pension benefit growth rates are more general functions of the four variables, V_t, D_t, F_t, and A_t, the expected value of the government's discounted payment can be computed using a Monte Carlo technique. This involves simulating a large number of risk-adjusted sequences of the variables in a manner similar to Boyle (1977). The average value of the discounted payments generated by this Monte Carlo simulation will converge to the theoretical expected discounted payment of the government. When carrying out the Monte Carlo simulation it is easiest to assume that the firm's payouts, pension fund contributions, and net pension benefit increases occur at discrete dates, such as the end of every month or year (Cooperstein, Pennacchi, and Redburn 1995). Between these payout and contribution dates, the risk-adjusted processes for the variables are simulated excluding these payout or contribution effects.

We do not present estimates of defined benefit guarantees using such a simulation technique here, but it should be noted that prior work has used Monte Carlo simulation to value defined benefit guarantees. Estrella and Hirtle (1988) estimate the value of the U.S. PBGC guarantees by simulating stochastic processes for pension fund assets and the assets of the sponsoring firm. They do not value cashflows using a martingale approach, but instead assume that the expected real rate of return on pension fund assets is a constant 2.5 percent per year while the expected real rate of return on firm assets is 1 or 1.5 percent, depending on the firm's past growth performance. In addition, they assume a constant real interest rate and discount PBGC payments for terminated pension plans at a real 2.5 percent rate.

One could debate whether these expected return and discount rate assumptions are reasonable. Further, these assumptions are unnecessary if one values pension guarantees using martingale pricing, which requires only the no-arbitrage assumption. In addition, the martingale approach easily allows for stochastic interest rates, a potentially important consideration given the relatively long duration of pension fund liabilities. Thus, it is important to emphasize that ad hoc assumptions can usually be avoided and interest-rate uncertainty can be incorporated by following the martingale approach. This point is applicable to a simulation model currently being developed by the PBGC itself, known as the Pension Insurance Management System (PIMS). This is a highly detailed model which, in its current form, calculates the PBGC's expected future cashflows needed to resolve terminated pension plans. As with Estrella and Hirtle (1988), PIMS could be modified to incorporate stochastic interest rates and to calculate the present value of the PBGC's cashflows by applying martingale pricing techniques.

Valuing Premiums Paid for Pension Guarantees

We now consider how the present value of premiums received by a government pension insurer can be computed so that its net liability can be determined. While we consider the value of contingent insurance premiums given a rate structure similar to that paid by PBGC-insured pension plans, this valuation technique could be modified for other types of rate structures.

Valuing future premiums paid to the PBGC is a nontrivial problem because premiums are contingent on future levels of pension underfunding as well as the solvency of the sponsoring firm. Consider the premium to be received by a pension insurer in some future year, τ. If the sponsoring firm is solvent, this insurance premium is assumed to consist of a flat rate premium per current participant, denoted p_0, and a two-part variable premium equal to a proportion, p_1, of the amount of pension underfunding, and subject to a cap or maximum variable payment per participant of κ. For example, the PBGC sets a flat premium of p_0 = \$19 per participant plus a variable rate premium of p_1 = \$.009 per \$1 of current underfunding up to a maximum variable payment of κ = \$53 per participant. (This maximum variable payment, κ, is currently being phased out.)

Maintaining the notation A_τ and F_τ as the pension fund's accrued liabilities and assets in future year τ respectively, let us also define e_τ as the number of participants in the pension fund during year τ and $P_\tau(t)$ as the value at date t of the premium income to be received by the PBGC in year τ. Then, assuming the solvency of the sponsoring firm, the premium income received at date τ takes the form $P_\tau(\tau) = e_\tau p_0 + p_1 \max(0, A_\tau - F_\tau) - p_1 \max(0, A_\tau - F_\tau - e_\tau \kappa / p_1)$. The last two terms can be viewed as put options written on the pension fund assets, the first having an exercise price of A_τ and the second having an exercise price of $A_\tau - e_\tau \kappa / p_1$.

Given the four processes describing the pension fund's and the corporation's assets and liabilities, we again apply the martingale approach to value this contingent premium income. Similar to the previous analysis for valuing the government's gross liability, the current (date t) value of the premium income anticipated in future year τ can be computed as the "risk-neutral" expectation of the discounted premium received, that is, $P_\tau(t) =$

$E_t^*[\exp(-\int_t^\tau r_s ds)\ P_\tau(\tau)]$. Summing this expression over all future years τ equals the value of all future premium income to be received by the government. For general assumptions regarding the firm's rate of net payouts from corporate assets, the rate of net contributions to the pension fund, and the rate of net new pension benefits, $P_\tau(t)$ can be calculated using the Monte Carlo simulation technique described in the previous section, where firm payouts, pension contributions, and new benefit increases occur at discrete dates. For the special case in which the payout rate, contribution rate, and the rate of new benefit increases are constants, Lewis and Pennacchi (1997) have derived an explicit formula for the value of this premium income. The next section illustrates the behavior of this premium value, along with the value of the government's gross liability for this particular case.

Comparative Statics for Defined Benefit Guarantees

For parameter estimates characterizing typical U.S. pension plans, Figures 1 and 2 graph the value of the government's gross liability as a percentage of pension liabilities, $100 \times L_t/A_b$, and its net liability (assuming no cap on premiums) as a percentage of pension liabilities, $100 \times [L_t - P_\tau(t)]/A_t$.[11] Figure 1 graphs these values as a function of the firm's net worth for the case of a 30 percent underfunded plan and for the case of a 30 percent overfunded plan. In both cases, the difference between gross and net liabilities rises with firm net worth, reflecting the higher present value of premiums to be paid by the more solvent firms. As expected, gross and net liabilities are much less for the overfunded plan that the underfunded plan, and government liability for underfunded plans rises as the firm's net worth falls. Interestingly, however, the government's liability for overfunded plans falls as the firm's net worth falls. The intuition for this result is that should a firm with an overfunded plan fail, the government will bear no loss and have no further exposure to this pension plan.

Figure 2 shows insurer gross and net liabilities as a function of pension fund's funding ratio, for a firm whose net worth is 10 percent of its corporate liabilities, and for a firm with a 100 percent net worth-liability ratio. In both cases, liabilities rise as pension funding falls. In addition, the difference between gross and net liabilities rises with declines in pension funding, reflecting the assumed premium rate structure that charges higher premiums to firms with greater underfunding. However, note that government liabilities are higher for low-net-worth firms when pensions are underfunded, but the reverse occurs when pensions are overfunded. The intuition is similar to that reflected in Figure 1: a firm with high net worth having a moderately overfunded plan may pose a larger liability than would a firm on the brink of bankruptcy with the same pension overfunding. The high net worth firm is likely to remain in operation longer, increasing the probability that its pension fund will become underfunded in the future.

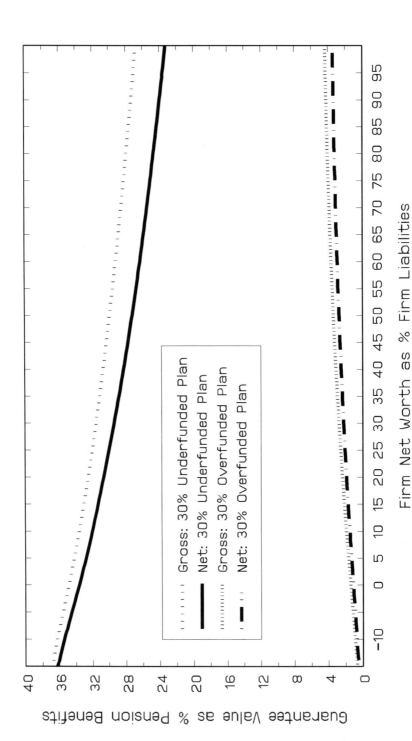

Figure 1. Value of gross and net pension guarantees by firm net worth. Source: Author's calculations.

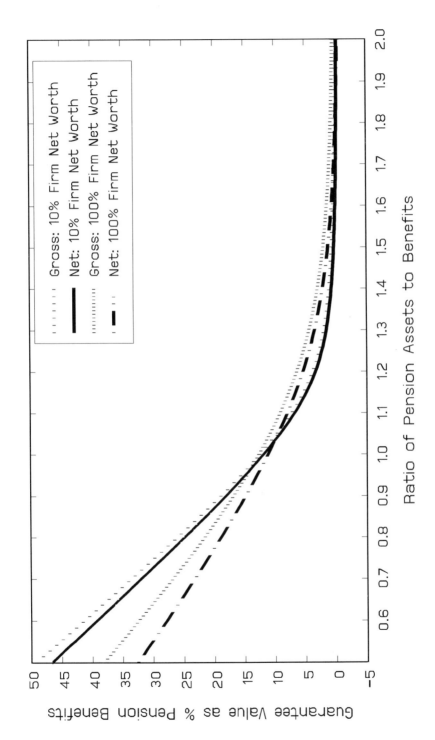

Figure 2. Value of gross and net pension guarantees by pension funding level. Source: Author's calculations.

Defined Contribution Pension Guarantees

Defined contribution pension plans are sometimes afforded government guarantees on rates of return. These guarantees can be valued by recognizing their similarity to so-called "exotic" options such as "forward start options," "options to exchange one asset for another," and "options on the minimum of two risky assets."[12] We begin by considering a relatively simple fixed minimum rate of return guarantee, similar to one provided by Uruguay. We then consider a minimum rate of return guarantee that is a function of the average rate of return earned by all pension funds, such as that provided by the government of Chile.

A Minimum Fixed Rate of Return Guarantee

Uruguay permits both private and public pension funds, known as "Asociaciones de Fondos de Ahorro Previsional" (AFAP).[13] In the case of public AFAPs (but not the private AFAPs), the government guarantees to pension fund participants a minimum annual real rate of return of 2 percent. Thus, a public AFAP which earns less than 2 percent during a given year would require a government transfer to make up the difference.

Applying martingale pricing methods, Pennacchi (1997) obtains an explicit formula for the value of these annual rates of return guarantees, making use of the similarity between these guarantees and an annual series of forward start options. A forward start option is an option that is paid for now, but whose exercise price is set equal to the contemporaneous value of the underlying asset at some future date prior to the maturity date of the option.[14] The analogy between a rate of return guarantee and a forward start option is that a (continuously compounded) rate of return on an asset over some future interval, say from date t_1 to time t_2, needs to be computed based on two future asset values: $\log[F(t_2)] - \log[F(t_1)]$, where $F(t)$ is the value of the (pension fund) asset at date t. In general, the t_1 beginning date of the rate of return is in the future, so $F(t_1)$ is unknown and analogous to the unknown beginning exercise price of the forward start option.

Valuing the government's rate of return guarantee makes of a weighted annual series of "at-the-money" Black and Scholes type (1973) put options, where the weights are proportional to the assumed growth in net new contributions to the pension fund (Pennacchi 1997). If an individual annual guarantee has any value and the real growth rate of the pension fund is non-negative, the value of the annual series of guarantees can be shown to grow without bound as the number of future years for which this guarantee is made increases. Clearly governments should be very cautious in providing such a guarantee, particularly to funds anticipated to grow substantially.

A Minimum Relative Rate of Return Guarantee

In Chile, private pension funds known as "Administradora de Fondos de Pensiones" (AFPs) are required to earn an annual real rate of return that is a function of the average annual real rate of return of all private pension funds. If R_a is the (ex-post) average annual rate of return earned by all AFPs, then each AFP must earn at least $\min(R_a-\alpha, \beta R_a)$ where $\alpha = .02$ and $\beta = \frac{1}{2}$. Thus, if R_a turns out to be ≥ 4 percent, each AFP must earn at least $\frac{1}{2}R_a$, while if R_a turns out to be ≤ 4 percent, each AFP must earn at least $R_a - 2$ percent. All AFPs are required to hold capital (a guarantee fund) of at least 1 percent of the value of its pension portfolio, invested in the same security portfolio as that of its pension fund. If the fund's return is less than $\min(R_a-\alpha, \beta R_a)$, it must make up the difference from its capital and replenish its capital within 15 days. The AFP's license will be revoked if it fails to do so. Thus, given an AFP capital ratio of $c = .01$, the government is exposed to loss following an AFP that earns less than $\min(R_a-\alpha, \beta R_a) - c = \min(R_a-\alpha-c, \beta R_a-c)$.

The Chilean-style government guarantee for an individual AFP is analogous to an annual series of options to exchange the individual AFP's pension assets for the minimum of two other risky assets. A formula for the value of this guarantee takes the form of an annual series of bivariate normal distribution functions.[15] As one might expect, the value of this relative rate of return guarantee is sensitive to the standard deviation of the individual AFP's rate of return as well as the correlation between the individual AFP's return and the average return of all AFPs.

Figure 3 plots the annual cost of this Chilean-style guarantee as a percentage of the current value of the pension fund assets, $100 \times L_t/F_t$. This is done for different assumed correlations between individual AFP and average AFP returns. The guarantee value is shown for three cases: when the individual AFP standard deviation equals, is twice, or is one-half that of the average of AFPs. As would be expected, the value of the guarantee falls as the correlation rises. Interestingly, when the standard deviation of the individual AFP's return exceeds that of the average of AFPs (which should be the case for the typical AFP since individual risk is diversified by averaging), then even when the correlation is perfect, the guarantee has positive value. Currently no premium is charged to cover this government insurance in Chile.

Valuing Minimum Pension Guarantees for Defined Contribution Plans

This section considers the value of a minimum pension guarantee for a participant in a mandatory defined contribution pension system, where a fixed proportion of a worker's wage is assumed to be contributed to a pen-

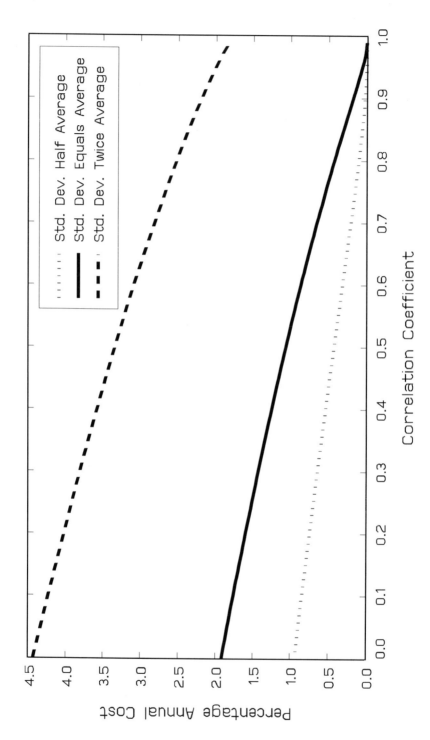

Figure 3. Value of relative rate of return guarantee by correlation between individual and average AFP. Source: Author's calculations.

sion fund that earns risky returns. Previous studies estimating the value of this guarantee for the case of Chile include work by Wagner (1991) and Zarita (1994). Wagner values this guarantee by simulating its annual cost when the demographics and maturity of the pension system are at their steady state values. The model calculates this cost under different assumptions regarding the real rate of return on pension fund assets and the level of the minimum pension guarantee. Contingent claims techniques are used by Zarita with a model that explicitly allows for a stochastic rate of return on pension fund assets, so that a worker's accumulated pension savings at retirement is random. When a worker's saving at retirement is less than the cost of an annuity providing the minimum pension, the government is assumed to make a payment to cover the difference. The risk-neutral expected value of this government payment is calculated using a Monte Carlo simulation of the worker's risky pension investment assuming a deterministic level of wage contributions each period and a constant real interest rate.

Our approach is similar to that of Zarita (1994) but includes three important extensions. First, in addition to allowing pension returns to be stochastic, we also allow a worker's real wage, and thus his monthly pension contribution, to follow a random process. The evolution of real wages is also assumed to influence the minimum pension set by the government when the worker retires. Second, real interest rates are assumed to follow a stochastic process. This is potentially important since retirement annuity values are a function of real interest rates. Also valuing the government's guarantee requires that real interest rates discount the government's guarantee payments and, in general, these payments are systematically related not only to asset returns and wage levels, but also to the real interest rate. Third, we model the government's payments for a minimum pension in a more realistic manner. Upon reaching retirement, a retiree may have a choice regarding his benefit payments. If he has sufficient pension savings, he may choose to close his pension account and use his savings to purchase a lifetime annuity that provides a benefit at or above the minimum pension. Alternatively, he can maintain his pension account and receive benefits by a scheduled withdrawal of funds from his account. For a retiree with an account balance insufficient to purchase a minimum pension annuity, a scheduled withdrawal of funds is required. The maximum amount that a retiree can withdraw each year is determined by a government schedule that depends on the retiree's current pension account balance and the value of a lifetime annuity, where this annuity is calculated using the government's "technical" interest rate. If and when a retiree's pension account balance is exhausted, the government guarantees that it will pay him the minimum monthly pension for the remainder of his life.

As discussed in Turner and Wantanabe (1995) and Smalhout (1996), a worker who attains retirement age with a pension balance slightly above or equal to the price of a minimum pension annuity will have an incentive to not purchase an annuity, but will instead choose the scheduled withdrawal option. By choosing this scheduled withdrawal, he will receive free longevity insurance at the government's expense. Should he live longer than expected, the government provides him with a minimum pension. If, instead, he dies sooner than expected, his heirs will inherit the balance of his pension account. Thus, in some states of the world, he received a government subsidy that would not occur if he had immediately purchased a lifetime annuity. Hence, for someone reaching retirement with moderate to small pension savings, who is the individual most likely to require minimum pension assistance, it is more realistic to assume a scheduled withdrawal of pension funds. Unlike Zarita (1994), our model explicitly considers the scheduled withdrawal option.

The full model, detailed in Pennacchi (1997), is based on three random processes: the rate of return on pension fund assets, the growth in real wages, and the change in the short term real interest rate. These three processes may be correlated. The short-term real interest rate determines the term structure of real yields (Vasicek 1977). An additional minor source of uncertainty is the individual's mortality. The probability of death at each age is assumed to be uncorrelated with economic variables and is taken from Chile's official life table. A hypothetical male worker is assumed to begin making pension contributions at age 20 and, should he live until the retirement age of 65, begin a scheduled withdrawal of his pension savings at the maximum level allowed by law. The worker's mandatory monthly contribution equals 10 percent of his randomly evolving wage and is invested in his pension fund earning a random rate of return.

At retirement, the maximum that can be withdrawn each month is calculated following the actual Chilean government formula, described in Diamond and Valdés-Prieto:

Every twelve months, the fixed real amount that will be withdrawn in each of the following twelve months is calculated. This amount is $P = F/UC$, where F is the current balance in the individual account and UC is calculated from the official life table and a technical interest rate (TR), and it is essentially the reserve needed to finance an annuity that pays $1 a month when investments yield TR. The return TR in turn is calculated according to a formula fixed by law. This formula specifies that, for AFP i, TR_i for year $t = 0.2 *$ (average of past real returns of Fund i during past five years) $+ 0.8 *$ (average of implicit rates of return on all real annuities sold in calendar year $t-1$). (1994: 290)

Our model follows this formula exactly, except that in calculating TR we approximate "the implicit rate of return on all real annuities sold in calendar year $t-1$" with the date t real yield on a nine-year zero-coupon indexed bond, since Diamond and Valdés-Prieto (1994) report that the duration of newly issued annuities is approximately nine years. Thus, during the individual's retirement period, the amount withdrawn is a function of the last five years' returns of the individual's AFP (affecting TR), the current randomly evolving real yield on a nine-year bond (affecting TR), the individual's age (affecting UC), and the individual's pension fund balance (which is affected by past withdrawals and pension fund asset returns).

The above formula's "maximum" withdrawal is, however, truly the maximum *only* if it exceeds the government's minimum pension level. If not, the amount withdrawn is equal to the minimum pension. This occurs until the retiree's pension account is exhausted, should he live that long. After the account balance is exhausted, the government pays the minimum pension until the end of the retiree's life.

The minimum pension is set at the discretion of the government, and it depends on a number of political and economic factors. For simplicity, our model assumes that the minimum pension at the beginning of an individual's retirement follows the formula: minimum pension = ¼*(average wage at start of individual's working life)*(growth in the individual's real wages over his working life)*½. This assumed formula reflects the likelihood that the government will tend to raise the minimum pension should real wages (and the standard of living) rise. Since Turner and Wantanabe (1995) report that the minimum pension is approximately 25 percent of the average wage and because our model assumes that the individual's real wage will almost double over his 45 years of work (1.5 percent average annual growth), the formula represents a minimum replacement rate of approximately 25 percent.[16]

To value this guarantee, the martingale approach is used to transform the model's three random processes into risk-adjusted counterparts, so that the value of the guarantee can be computed as the expectation of the government's discounted minimum pension payments. This expectation is calculated using a Monte Carlo simulation, where contributions or withdrawals from the individual's pension fund account occur each month. Parameter values typical of Chile were selected (see Pennacchi 1997). Guarantee values are calculated for the use of a 20-year-old male beginning wage earner starting with a zero pension fund balance. Mortality is based on the Chilean life tables for male annuitants. Normalizing an average Chilean monthly real wage at 100 as of the time this individual begins work, we find that the average level of the minimum pension set by the government (according to the formula discussed above) at the worker's retirement date was 44.7.

Figure 4 graphs the present values of the minimum pension guarantee for this 20-year-old worker, using alternative initial monthly wages ranging between 10 and 100.[17] The value of this guarantee ranges from 251.8 for an individual with an initial monthly wage of 10, to 5.8 for an individual with an initial monthly wage of 100. The shape of the relationship is convex, as one might expect given the put option-like nature of this guarantee. Also plotted in Figure 4 is the individual's age at which his pension fund account would be depleted, should he live that long. This ranges from age 72.1 for an initial

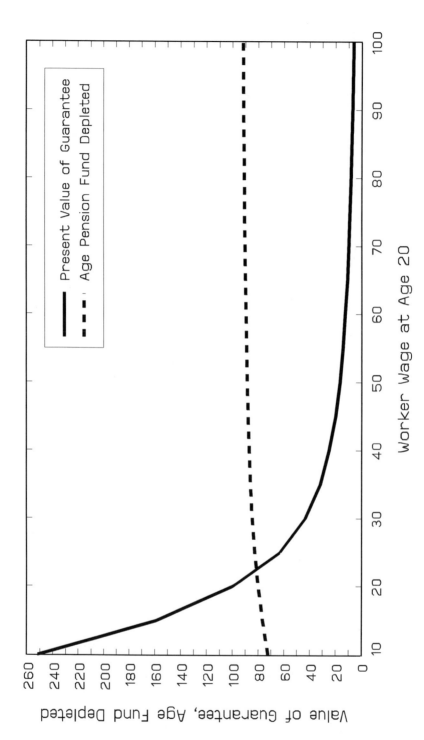

Figure 4. Minimum pension guaranteed by initial wage level. Source: Author's calculations.

wage of 10, to age 91.8 for an initial wage of 100. Note that this age profile has a concave shape: higher initial wage increase the time before the pension account is depleted, but less than proportionally. While higher initial wages tend to result in proportionally higher accumulated pension savings at retirement, the government's scheduled withdrawal formula allows greater pension withdrawals for individuals with higher savings. Thus the withdrawal schedule tends to dampen the effect that greater retirement savings have on the age at which pension funds are depleted.

Conclusion

Social security privatization programs frequently require that workers contribute to defined benefit and/or defined contribution pension plans. Relative to government-sponsored defined benefit social security systems, these privately-sponsored pension plans subject individuals to default risk (in the case of defined benefit plans) or investment risk (in the case of defined contribution plans). To make privatization reforms politically attractive to the public, governments have typically offered guarantees that reduce individuals' exposure to default or investment risks. Should the United States privatize a substantial portion of its pension obligations using a PSA-type approach, government guarantees of pension plan performance might be a real possibility.

Our analysis illustrates how the martingale pricing approach, also known as the risk-neutral valuation method, can be applied to value such pension guarantees. This methodology then permits the computation of risk-based insurance (guarantee) premiums. Requiring that riskier pension funds, and possibly riskier individuals, pay higher insurance premiums could help control adverse selection and moral hazard behavior. It would reduce the subsidies and the economic distortions associated with government guarantees. The potential for reducing such distortions through risk-based premiums may ultimately change the type of pension system that a government chooses to adopt.

The ability to price guarantees can also allow government budgets to be measured on a market-value basis. A government's total liability from providing guarantees can be calculated by aggregating the values of individual guarantees. This aggregation requires detailed data on the economy's individual pension plans, pension funds, and/or worker demographics. Such an exercise is beyond the scope of this chapter, but the analysis presented here provides a foundation for obtaining a more accurate indicator of government fiscal policy.

The author is grateful for comments and guidance by William Murphy, Krishna Ramaswamy, Hector Salazar, Salvador Valdés-Prieto, Nicholas Souleles, and especially Olivia Mitchell.

Notes

1. Mitchell and Barreto (1997) and Queisser (1995) describe Latin American pension reforms. More general discussions of pension systems are given in Mitchell (1994), Davis (1996), and Turner and Wantanabe (1995).

2. See Bodie and Merton (1993), Pesando (1996), and Smalhout (1996).

3. To simplify the exposition, details of the methods and formulas for valuing guarantees are not presented, but these can be found in Pennacchi (1997).

4. For example, several governments, including those of Great Britain and Italy, are currently promoting private pensions as a solution to their over-dependence on government-provided retirement benefits. Their reform proposals presume that private pensions will be mainly of the defined benefit type.

5. An excellent review of this and subsequent work appears in Merton (1990).

6. A partial list includes Treynor (1977), Langetieg, Findlay, and da Motta (1982), Marcus (1987), Bodie and Merton (1993), and Hsieh, Chen, and Ferris (1994). Lewis and Cooperstein (1993) use the approach in Marcus (1987) to estimate the current exposure of the PBGC.

7. Note that this modeling of bankruptcy is similar to that of Longstaff and Schwartz (1995). In general, the analysis is valid when δ is any positive number, though it is best interpreted as being less than or equal to 1.

8. A more detailed and technical discussion of martingale pricing can be found in Duffie (1996).

9. This risk-free rate of interest can be stochastic, so that interest rate risk can be explicitly modeled. See Lewis and Pennacchi (1997) or Pennacchi (1997) for details.

10. The risk-free discount factor is given by $\exp(-\int_t^T r_s ds)$, where $\exp(\bullet)$ is the exponential function.

11. This analysis draws on Lewis and Pennacchi (1997).

12. For a description and analysis of these exotic options, see Hull (1997).

13. See Mitchell (1996) for a discussion of pension system reform in Uruguay.

14. In other words, the option's exercise price is set so that it is "at-the-money" at some prespecified future date prior to the option's maturity date.

15. See Pennacchi (1997), who builds on results in Margrabe (1978), Stulz (1982), and Johnson (1987).

16. One component of the lifetime growth of an individual's real wage is likely to reflect increased (economy-wide) average productivity, while another component should reflect the individual's increased productivity due to greater experience and seniority. Thus, it is reasonable to expect that an individual's lifetime real wage growth will exceed the economy-wide average. For this reason, the formula includes a final factor of one-half. The result is that our simulations give an average minimum pension at the individual's retirement date equal to 44.7 percent of the initial average real wage, implying that, on average, there is a slightly less than doubling (from 25 percent) of the minimum pension.

17. A GAUSS program that calculates the guarantee values in Figure 4 is available from the author upon request.

References

Black, Fischer and John Cox. "Valuing Corporate Securities: Some Effects of Bond Indenture Provisions." *Journal of Finance* 31 (1976): 351–68.

Black, Fischer and Myron Scholes. "The Pricing of Options and Corporate Liabilities." *Journal of Political Economy* 81 (1973): 637–59.

Bodie, Zvi and Robert C. Merton, "Pension Benefit Guarantees in the United States:

A Functional Analysis." In Ray Schmitt, ed., *The Future of Pensions in the United States*. Philadelphia: Pension Research Council and University of Pennsylvania Press, 1993: 194–234.

Boyle, Phelim. "Options Pricing: A Monte Carlo Approach." *Journal of Financial Economics* 4 (1977): 323–38.

Cooperstein, Richard L., George G. Pennacchi, and F. Stevens Redburn. "The Aggregate Cost of Deposit Insurance: A Multiperiod Analysis." *Journal of Financial Intermediation* 4 (1995): 242–71.

Cox, John and Stephen Ross. "The Valuation of Options for Alternative Stochastic Processes." *Journal of Financial Economics* 3 (1976): 145–66.

Davis, E. Philip. "An International Comparison of the Financing of Occupational Pensions." In Zvi Bodie, Olivia S. Mitchell, and John A. Turner, eds., *Securing Employer Based Pensions: An International Perspective*. Philadelphia: Pension Research Council and University of Pennsylvania Press, 1996.

Diamond, Peter A. and Salvador Valdés-Prieto. "Social Security Reforms." In Barry P. Boxworth, Rudiger Dornbusch, and Raul Laban, eds., *The Chilean Economy: Policy Lessons and Challenges*. Washington, D.C.: Brookings Institution, 1994.

Duffie, Darrell. *Dynamic Asset Pricing Theory*. Princeton, N.J.: Princeton University Press, 1996.

Estrella, Arturo and Beverly Hirtle. "Estimating the Funding Gap of the Pension Benefit Guaranty Corporation." *Quarterly Review*, Federal Reserve Bank of New York (Autumn 1988): 45–59.

Harrison, Michael and David Kreps. "Martingales and Arbitrage in Multi-Period Securities Markets." *Journal of Economic Theory* 20 (1979): 381–408.

Hsieh, Su-Jane, Andrew H. Chen, and Kenneth R. Ferris. "The Valuation of PBGC Insurance Using an Option Pricing Model." *Journal of Financial and Quantitative Analysis* 29 (1994): 89–99.

Hull, John. *Options, Futures, and Other Derivative Securities*. Third ed. Englewood Cliffs, N.J.: Prentice Hall, 1997.

Johnson, Herbert. "Options on the Maximum and Minimum of Several Assets." *Journal of Financial and Quantitative Analysis* 22 (1987): 277–83.

Kocic, Aleksandar. "Numeraire Invariance and Generalized Risk Neutral Valuation." *Advances in Futures and Options Research* 9 (1997): 157–73.

Langetieg, T. C., M. C. Findlay, and L. F. J. da Motta. "Multiperiod Pension Plans and ERISA." *Journal of Financial and Quantitative Analysis* 17 (1982): 603–31.

Lewis, Christopher and Richard Cooperstein. "Estimating the Current Exposure of the Pension Benefit Guaranty Corporation to Single-Employer Pension Plan Terminations." In Ray Schmitt, ed., *The Future of Pensions in the United States*. Philadelphia: Pension Research Council and University of Pennsylvania Press, 1993. 247–76.

Lewis, Christopher and George G. Pennacchi. "Is Federal Pension Insurance Fairly Priced?" Working Paper, University of Illinois, 1997.

Longstaff, Francis A. and Eduardo S. Schwartz. "A Simple Approach to Valuing Risky Fixed and Floating Rate Debt." *Journal of Finance* 50 (1995): 789–819.

Marcus, Alan. "Corporate Pension Policy and the Value of PBGC Insurance." In Zvi Bodie, J. Shoven, and D. Wise, eds., *Issues in Pension Economics*. Chicago: University of Chicago Press, 1987.

Margrabe, William. "The Value of an Option to Exchange One Asset for Another." *Journal of Finance* 33 (1978): 177–86.

Merton, Robert C. *Continuous-Time Finance*. Oxford: Basil Blackwell, 1990.

———. "An Analytical Derivation of the Cost of Deposit Insurance and Loan Guarantees: An Application of Modern Option Pricing Theory." *Journal of Banking and Finance* 1 (1997): 3–11.

————. "On the Pricing of Corporate Debt: The Risk Structure of Interest Rates." *Journal of Finance* 29 (1974): 449–70.

————. "Theory of Rational Option Pricing." *Bell Journal of Economics and Management Science* 4 (1973): 141–83.

Mitchell, Olivia S. "Retirement Savings in the Developed and Developing World: Institutional Structure, Economic Effects, and Lessons for Economies in Transition." In Avril Van Adams, Elizabeth King, and Zafiris Tzannatos, eds., *Labor Market Policies for Managing the Social Cost of Economic Adjustment.* Washington, D.C.: World Bank, 1994.

————. "Social Security Reform in Uruguay: An Economic Assessment." Pension Research Council Working Paper 96-20, The Wharton School, University of Pennsylvania. 1996.

Mitchell, Olivia S. and Flávio Ataliba Barreto. "After Chile, What? Second-Round Social Security Reforms in Latin America." *Revista de Analisis Economico* 12, 2 (November 1997): 3–36.

Pennacchi, George G. "Government Guarantees for Old Age Income: A Detailed Analysis." Pension Research Council Working Paper 97-10, The Wharton School, University of Pennsylvania. 1997.

Pennacchi, George G. and Christopher Lewis. "The Value of Pension Benefit Guaranty Corporation Insurance." *Journal of Money, Credit and Banking* 26 (1994): 735–53.

Pesando, James E. "The Government's Role in Insuring Pensions." In Zvi Bodie, Olivia S. Mitchell, and John A. Turner, eds., *Securing Employer Based Pensions: An International Perspective.* Philadelphia: Pension Research Council and University of Pennsylvania Press, 1996.

Queisser, Monika. "Chile and Beyond: The Second-Generation Pension Reforms in Latin America." *International Social Science Review* 48 (1995): 23–39.

Smalhout, James H. *The Uncertain Retirement.* Chicago: Irwin, 1996.

Stulz, Rene. "Options on the Minimum or Maximum of Two Assets." *Journal of Financial Economics* 10 (1982): 161–85.

Treynor, Jack L. "The Principles of Corporate Pension Finance." *Journal of Finance* 32 (1977): 627–38.

Turner, John A. and Noriyasu Wantanabe. *Private Pension Policies in Industrialized Countries: A Comparative Analysis.* Kalamazoo, Mich.: W.E. Upjohn Institute for Employment Research, 1995.

Vasicek, Oldrich A. "An Equilibrium Characterization of the Term Structure." *Journal of Financial Economics* 5 (1977): 177–88.

Wagner, Gert. "La seguridad social y el programa de pension minima garatizada." *Estudios de Economia* 18 (1991): 35–91.

Zarita, Salvador. "Minimum Pension Insurance in the Chilean Pension System." *Revista de Analisis Economico* 9 (1994): 105–26.

Chapter 10
Means Testing Social Security

David Neumark and Elizabeth Powers

J26   (05)
J14
H55

Worldwide population aging has brought into sharp focus several controversial features of social security systems. For instance, it is often thought that the "contributions" a worker makes to the social security system are not clearly and positively linked to the benefits ultimately received.[1] Indeed, the complexity of the benefit calculation in the U.S. social security system makes it unlikely that most workers understand the relationship between their next dollar of payroll tax contributed and their ultimate benefit. This may explain why many younger workers express the belief that the present system is unsustainable and they will receive no retirement benefit. When workers believe that most or all of their social security payroll deduction is net tax, this has work disincentives. In turn, such disincentives may hurt economic growth and impose efficiency costs on the economy (Kotlikoff and Sachs 1997; Feldstein 1997). Another potential growth-inhibiting feature of large unfunded social security systems is their pay-as-you-go nature. It is often argued that such a system supplants self-financed retirement saving with intergenerational transfers, thereby reducing the capital stock (Kotlikoff 1979). A further criticism of a pay-as-you-go system is that it has generated excessive redistribution from younger to older cohorts (Kotlikoff 1992; Auerbach et al. 1992).

Despite these criticisms, most experts acknowledge that there is one goal many public pension systems around the world have achieved: they have prevented many elderly households from sliding into poverty. In the United States, the poorest 40 percent of elderly and disabled households receive 80 percent of their income from social security, and social security benefits lift 6 percent of the population above official poverty lines (Aaron 1997). Consequently, there is little support for eliminating public retirement income support systems entirely, at least in the United States and other developed nations. On the other hand, if reforms are required, many believe that cutting benefits for the relatively affluent would be a useful way to achieve system solvency. In this chapter we explore the pros and cons of converting social security from a universal entitlement program to a program based on individual need in old age: that is, "means-testing" social security benefits.

If social security benefits were fully means tested, then a retiree's benefit would be reduced in accordance with his post-retirement income, as well as his (real and/or financial) asset holdings. Partial means tests might reduce benefits as income rose, but could ignore assets (or vice versa): alternatives might take only some components of income or assets into account when determining benefits. For example, the Concord Coalition advocates a social security "affluence test" that would cut benefits 10 percent for retired households with income between $40,000 and $49,000, and would increase the reduction by 10 percentage points for each additional $10,000 of income, to a maximum of an 85 percent reduction in benefits.[2] This approach is a dramatic departure from the current system, in which benefits depend positively on past income, while (aside from the "retirement test," discussed below) they are taxed lightly, if at all. A means-tested program might also act as a "safety net" or "bottom tier" of a multi-tier retirement system, for example, in conjunction with a defined contribution public system (Mitchell and Zeldes 1996).[3]

Examining the Current System

It is natural to ask whether the present social security system already incorporates any means-test-like features, since expansion of such features could afford a natural way to create a broader means-tested system. Before 1990, social security benefits in the United States were reduced by $1 for every $2 of earned income above an exempt amount. Recently, benefits have been reduced at a more generous rate of $1 for every $3 of earned income.[4] A penalty on labor income, or "retirement test," is clearly necessary for a system intended as a retirement income support, whether it is means-tested or not. That the retirement test is not intended as a means test is evident from the fact that no other types of income directly reduce social security benefits. Since 1983, some retirees' benefits have been subject to the federal income tax; the proceeds are returned to the Old Age Survivors and Disability Insurance (OASDI) trust fund. But fewer than a quarter of all beneficiaries pay this tax, and only the most affluent retirees "return" a significant share of their benefits. Only at household income categories exceeding $50,000 does the tax burden exceed 10 percent of benefits received.[5] Further, asset holdings do not affect benefits at all, except to the extent that asset income or realized capital gains might ultimately contribute towards the application of the federal tax to social security benefits.

For these reasons, we believe it is safe to say that a social security program in which benefits were targeted to needy recipients through a means test would look quite different from today's system. The simplest imaginable system would be similar to the Supplemental Security Income (SSI) program that has two separate tests, one for income and the other for assets (we discuss this program at length below). If income exceeds a given amount, no benefits are received. If income is below the limit but positive, benefits are reduced (perhaps dollar-for-dollar). If assets exceed a fixed limit, no benefits are received (alternatively, a benefit reduction rate might be applied to the excess).[6] This simple scheme could be made more complex by applying different limits or benefit reduction rates to different types of earnings (for instance, treating earned income more harshly to preserve something like a "retirement test"); or by exempting some assets (like an owner-occupied home).

A more sophisticated scheme would unify the treatment of income and assets. By applying a formula to annuitize wealth stocks (i.e., to convert a stock of wealth into an equivalent income flow), benefit reduction formulas could be applied to wealth as they are to income.[7] If society expects recipients to expend all resources prior to their death, then the entire stock of real and financial wealth might be subject to the annuitizing formula. Again, however, one could apply different weights to different types of income and annuitized wealth, or possibly exclude some assets from the annuitization formula.

The primary debate in the United States has been over whether moderate changes that preserve the existing social security system will do, or whether a privatized or partially privatized system would be superior. The argument over whether the gains from a privatized system are real or illusory is fairly complex (Mitchell and Zeldes 1996). The relative merits of means testing, on the other hand, appear straightforward. Most obviously, means testing, by restricting who can receive benefits, or by offering only small benefits to all but the "neediest" elderly, could dramatically shrink the size of the social security system, and hence enable the payroll tax to be greatly reduced. It is the distortionary impact of this tax (an inefficiency that increases with the square of the tax) that is viewed as the most troublesome component of the current system by many (Kotlikoff and Sachs 1997; Feldstein 1997). If it caused the social security system to shrink dramatically, means testing would greatly reduce the redistribution from younger to older generations that has been the subject of so much recent criticism. In particular, even under a pay-as-you-go system, means testing would halt redistribution from current workers with moderate lifetime incomes to the currently-affluent elderly. Finally, benefits would be determined by actual post-retirement resources and not by one's earnings history, so that benefits intended to help low-income households would not be paid to well-off retirees.

One drawback of means testing is its potential negative impact on saving. That is, when social security benefits depend in some way on one's level of financial assets (or the income these assets produce during retirement), some people might choose not to save, or to save very little. This view has been extremely influential in the current debate and appears to have precluded serious discussion of a means-tested reform option. For example, in an appendix to the report of the Bipartisan Commission on Entitlement and Tax Reform (1995), several experts endorsed the statement that "Means testing would tax . . . saving by cutting Social Security as income from private saving increases, conveying the message: Don't save or we will punish you for your frugality by denying you Social Security" (112). Similarly, the Technical Panel (1997) reported to the recent Advisory Council on Social Security that it "opposed means-testing social security benefits on the basis of other retirement income or accumulated wealth. To avoid loss of social security benefits, some workers might reduce their own retirement saving or persuade employers to shift compensation from pension contributions to earnings. Either response would lower savings and private retirement incomes" (6).

Equally damaging to the means testing case is the fact that new work disincentives may be created by a means test. Should social security benefits in a means-tested program be reduced or restricted on the basis of asset holdings at retirement, this would discourage the additional work needed to finance retirement savings in "ordinary" (non-tax-favored) savings, or in defined contribution private pension schemes. Income testing of benefits may also discourage work, per se. If social security benefits are reduced or eliminated when post-retirement income increases, then defined benefit pension payments or annuitized income from defined contribution plans would reduce public benefits. Depending on the exact rules of a means-tested program, workers might have an incentive to retire early. This is because additional private pension benefits might be partially or completely offset by reduced public benefits, and could even disqualify retirees from receiving any public benefits.

These possible negative effects of a means-tested social security policy may or may not outweigh its benefits. Despite the fact that means testing has been so resolutely rejected in the current debate, there is actually little direct evidence on the possible magnitude of the potential adverse effects. In the next section, we briefly discuss the current scant evidence on the likely impact of means testing public retirement income programs, and then present new evidence on the potential labor supply distortions from a means test, based on evidence from the United States.

Previous Evidence on Means Testing

An extensive literature seeks to estimate the effects of changing various parameters of the social security system on saving and labor supply behavior, relying on variation in program parameters across individuals to identify the effects of interest (e.g., Gustman and Steinmeier 1984, 1986, 1991; Burtless and Moffitt 1985). This literature may be fruitfully applied to assessing changes to the existing system that preserve its basic structure, but it is less relevant to the means testing debate.[8]

One of the few rigorous analyses of the means-testing option appears in Feldstein (1987), who argued that "a means-tested program with benefits set at the optimal level may induce some utility-maximizing workers to save nothing. Although their resulting consumption in retirement would then be less than they would have chosen without a social security program, the utility value of the extra consumption during working years more than offsets the reduced consumption during retirement" (470). An overlapping generations model is employed to investigate the circumstances under which society would be better off under a universal pay-as-you-go system than a targeted (means-tested) pay-as-you-go system. In this model, workers receive earnings when young, and no income when old, but may save from first period income if they wish. Feldstein considers a particularly simple means test, where only zero-savers can collect benefits in old age. Not surprisingly, he finds that the relative advantages of a means-tested system depend critically on the responsiveness of private saving to the disincentive created by the means test. He concludes that an income test is the right "means" to use, but this finding relies on the assumption that income is exogenous. If it were not, one would expect efficiency losses to result from an income test as well.

Evidence from other countries is also germane. For instance, Australia's social security system has been means tested since its inception in 1909, although the design of the means test has varied greatly over the years.[9] The system's initial design was simple, with separately applied income and asset tests. In the 1960s, the asset and income means tests were "merged." A 10 percent rate of return was imputed on assets over a disregard level, and this imputed return was added to other income and affected benefits through the income test. Controversy over the treatment of assets culminated in the asset test being dropped altogether in 1976; by 1985, however, an asset test was reintroduced in an effort to rein in program costs.[10] Under the new rules, the participation rate dropped to 65 percent of people of pensionable age, from 74 percent in 1983. Currently the Australian old-age benefit reflects an average wage replacement rate of only around 20 percent. Therefore, while many elderly families in Australia receive some benefit despite the means tests (the all-time high was 78 percent in 1978), the "full" benefit is low, and many receive even lower benefits due to the means test.

The notion that asset tests could discourage saving had been a concern of Australian policy makers since the system's inception. For example, the asset test was already liberalized to exempt the home in 1912, because of the view that "taking it into account penalized thrift and discouraged home ownership" (Schultz et al. 1991: 224). However, the controversy continued. "During the postwar years . . . the main argument voiced against means testing related to the impact [on] . . . the propensity of individuals to save. Means testing was seen as a major disincentive to saving. It was argued that there was little point in saving for retirement if, upon reaching the age-pension eligibility age, the retiree was denied a pension because of the means test" (225). The income test has also been frequently changed. Over the years gifts from children, asset income, and capital gains income have all been the subject of policy changes.

Considering this lengthy and varied experience with means testing, the lack of econometric evidence on the effect of means testing on Australians' work and retirement saving patterns is somewhat surprising. One explanation may be that the system's complex and inconsistent treatment of various types of income and assets is perceived to create a greater problem with "tax avoidance" than with changes in real activity like work and consumption. For example, when assets were not tested prior to 1986, retirees apparently shifted wealth into no- or low-interest accounts to escape the income test.[11] Loopholes probably affected the post-retirement composition of assets or income more than the real pre-retirement behavior that generated the resources in the first place.

An Alternative Approach to Studying Means Testing

In the remainder of this chapter we attempt to draw inferences about the potential behavioral responses to means testing social security by examining the effects of the United States Supplemental Security Income (SSI) program for the aged. Here we offer evidence on the effects of an income- and asset-tested retirement program on the pre-retirement labor supply of potential recipients. In our analysis, we exploit the state-level variation in SSI benefits to estimate the effects of SSI on labor supply. We use data on male-headed households from waves 4 and 5 of the Survey of Income Program Participation (SIPP), covering individuals in the 1983–1986 period, to estimate the effects of state SSI supplements via a difference-in-difference approach that controls for variation in labor supply behavior across states and across different types of individuals. In related work (Neumark and Powers, forthcoming) we examine the effect of variation in SSI benefits on saving of those approaching the age of eligibility for benefits, finding that higher benefits reduce pre-retirement saving among likely program participants.[12]

In our view, the SSI program for the aged has many parallels to the type of means tested social security program that might emerge from social security reform process. Part of the SSI program provides payments to the poor elderly (aged 65 and over).[13] The federal government sets eligibility criteria and benefit levels for the federal component of the program. The federal government also specifies maximum benefit levels for couples and individuals, which are reduced by income from other sources, including social security retirement and disability benefits. (The first $20 per month of non-means-tested transfer income, the first $65 of earned income, plus one-half of remaining earnings, are disregarded in reducing SSI benefits.) Thus, other sources of retirement income influence both eligibility for SSI and the size of potential benefits. Financial resources also affect eligibility. For example, as of 1985 (corresponding roughly to the time period covered by our data) individuals with over $1,600 in countable assets, and couples with over $2400 in countable assets, were ineligible.[14] In 1984 there were 1.55 million persons receiving SSI payments who were eligible because of age (Committee on Ways and Means 1995).[15]

Though the federal government sets eligibility criteria and benefit levels, states may also supplement federal SSI benefits. For example, in January 1985 the maximum federal monthly benefit was $325 for an individual, and $488 for a couple. The highest state benefit was in California, with a maximum combined monthly benefit of $504 for an individual and $936 for a couple.[16] In December 1985 the average federal monthly benefit paid was $146 for individuals and $232 for couples, and the average state supplements were $97 and $257, respectively, with 39 percent of SSI recipients receiving state supplements (Kahn 1987).

Empirical Analysis

To derive empirical estimates, we use a sample of male heads of households drawn from the SIPP, which when weighted serves as a nationally-representative sample of households.[17] Households are interviewed every four months (each four-month interval is referred to as a "wave") for two to three years. Most questions are asked retrospectively about the previous four months. This paper uses the first (1984) panel of the SIPP, covering the period from October 1983 through July 1986.

Several measures of labor force activity are used as dependent variables for the analysis. A binary employment variable is used that equals one if the individual reports positive hours of work in the first month of wave 4. Actual hours of work in that month are also studied. We also examine effects on years of covered social security employment (a variable collected in a special wave 5 topical module), which provides a longer-term perspective. Finally, because family labor supply and the wages earned by each family member may influence post-retirement income and wealth, we also examine some results regarding the possible impact of the SSI program on monthly family earned income in wave 4; this also gives us a convenient measure of aggregate total family labor supply.

Descriptive statistics for the sample of men aged 40–64 for whom we estimate labor supply effects appear in Table 1. Of this group, 83 percent of the group is employed in wave 4, and weekly hours of work average 37. Average years of covered social security employment are just under 23 years for this group, and average monthly family earnings are $2,628. Each house-

TABLE 1. Descriptive Statistics and Determinants of SSI Participation

	Descriptive Statistics, Male Household Heads Aged 40–64	Probit for SSI Participation, Male Household Heads Aged 65+
Employed, wave 4	.83	—
Hours, wave 4	37.03 (19.45)	—
Years of covered Social Security employment, wave 5	22.88 (13.80)	—
Family earnings, wave 4	2628.39 (2107.47)	—
Maximum state SSI supplement >20% of federal benefit	.20	.022** (.007)
Maximum SSI benefit, individual	365.49 (58.43)	—
Maximum SSI benefit, couple	566.00 (137.83)	—
Currently authorized for food stamps	.04	.019 (.013)
Years authorized for food stamps	.06 (.65)	.015** (.003)
Less than high school	.26	.05** (.01)
Some college	.17	−.01 (.02)
College graduate	.24	−.004 (.02)
Black	.08	.024** (.009)
Never married	.03	.04** (.01)
Divorced/widowed/ separated/spouse absent	.11	.007 (.007)
N	4560	1787

Source: Authors' calculations, 1984 SIPP. Column 1 reports means, with standard deviations in parentheses. Maximum SSI benefit is combined federal and state, obtained from the 1985 Green Book (Committee on Ways and Means 1985), and is based on current marital status. Classification of states providing supplements higher than 20 percent of the federal benefit is based on whether the supplement for either an individual or a couple exceeds this amount. Column 2 reports partial derivatives of the participation probability, with standard errors based on probit coefficients in parentheses; SSI benefits are measured in hundreds of dollars. High school graduates are the reference category. ** indicates statistically significantly different from zero at the 5-percent level, and * at the 10-percent level. All estimates are weighted.

hold is assigned a maximum state SSI benefit based on household composition (whether the household is comprised of an individual or a couple) and state of residence. For the empirical analysis, we create a variable that equals one for observations in states in which the benefit exceeds 20 percent of the federal maximum (for either individuals or couples), and zero for states that do not supplement the federal benefit; we exclude observations from the intermediate states.[18] In addition to the high benefit states, states such as Hawaii, Maine, Oregon, and Utah paid very low supplements. Twenty percent of our sample resides in states with state SSI supplements exceeding 20 percent of the federal benefit.[19] Average maximum combined (federal and state) benefits are $365 for individuals, and $566 for adults.

Demographic variables in the analysis include race (black or non-black), marital status (married spouse present, never married, and ever married), and education (less than high school, high school graduate, some college, and college graduate). As explained below, we also require estimates of the probability of participation in SSI at or after age 65. We obtain these estimates by studying the determinants of SSI participation among those aged 65 or over, based on participation of the male at any time during wave 4.

We are interested in estimating the effects of the potential receipt of SSI benefits on various labor supply measures, denoted Y. Two factors influence the potential value of SSI benefits: the level of the benefits, and the likelihood of receiving them. Thus, for example, we might expect a person with characteristics associated with low permanent income (such as low education), in a state with high SSI benefits, to experience the greatest labor supply disincentives. In contrast, a white, married college graduate is extremely unlikely to be eligible for SSI, whether he resides in a state with high or low benefits. Thus, to estimate the effects of SSI, we focus on variation in labor supply behavior associated with high SSI benefits for those with a relatively high likelihood of eligibility.

We therefore begin by identifying exogenous characteristics associated with likely future SSI receipt. By studying workers over age 65, we can identify characteristics associated with a high likelihood of SSI participation. We then distinguish among workers under age 65 based on these characteristics, defining a dummy variable "Part" to equal one for likely participants (based on a chosen threshold for the estimated probability of participating upon reaching age 65), and zero otherwise.[20]

Perhaps the simplest test for effects of SSI on labor supply would be to estimate a regression equation of the form:

(1) $Y = \alpha \cdot \text{Part} \cdot \text{Age4049} + \beta \cdot \text{Part} \cdot \text{Age5059} + \gamma \cdot \text{Part} \cdot \text{Age6064}$

   $+ \delta + \eta \cdot \text{Age5059} + \theta \cdot \text{Age6064} + X\psi + \epsilon,$

where the age variables are dummy variables for the indicated ranges, and the sample includes individuals aged 40–64. The matrix X includes demographic controls. This can be thought of as a "federal experiment"; state benefit levels are not used to introduce variation among likely participants in incentives to go on SSI. For reasons discussed below, we do not rely on this test, but it is useful in understanding the empirical procedure we use.

The estimates of α, β, and γ indicate differences in labor supply between individuals likely to be eligible for SSI, and those unlikely to be eligible. For example, γ measures the behavioral difference between 60–64-year-olds likely to be eligible and those unlikely to be eligible ($Y|_{Part=1,Age6064=1}$ − $Y|_{Part=0,Age6064=1}$), and ($\gamma − \alpha$) measures the difference in the change in Y from ages 40–49 to ages 60–64 between likely participants and non-participants ($[Y|_{Part=1,Age6064=1} − Y|_{Part=1,Age4049=1}] − [Y|_{Part=0,Age6064=1} − Y|_{Part=0,Age4049=1}]$).[21] If SSI reduces the labor supply of likely participants, we should find at least one of two effects: $\gamma < 0$, because likely participants are predicted to work less; or ($\gamma − \alpha$) < 0, because the work disincentive on likely participants becomes more evident as they approach the age of eligibility for SSI.

One might also expect, a priori, that estimates of γ and ($\gamma − \alpha$) — rather than β and ($\beta − \alpha$) — are of greatest interest and are more likely to reflect disincentive effects because, for a number of reasons, the influence of SSI should be strongest for workers nearing the age of eligibility. First, given stochastic influences on earnings and wealth, older workers can form better predictions of post-retirement income. Second, workers may pay more attention to the potential receipt of SSI benefits as they approach the age of eligibility (paralleling findings in Mitchell 1988). We therefore focus on estimated effects for individuals aged 60–64, but also report effects for those aged 50–59.

There are competing reasons to prefer using estimates of γ and of ($\gamma − \alpha$) (and similarly for β) to draw inferences about the effects of SSI. One reason to prefer estimates of γ is because ($\gamma − \alpha$) is identified from differences in behavior across cohorts, which requires the assumption of constant behavior across cohorts, or at least that cross-cohort differences are the same across states; in contrast, identification of γ does not require such assumptions. On the other hand, looking at ($\gamma − \alpha$) effectively uses workers aged 40–49 in the state as a control group, because it identifies the effects of SSI from changes in the behavior of 60–64-year-olds relative to this group. There may be state-specific differences in behavior of likely participants in a state regardless of their age, stemming from economic conditions, tax policy, or other income-support programs. As a consequence, changes in behavior with age, rather than levels, may provide more reliable information. We report both types of estimates, but focus more on the changes with age captured in ($\beta − \alpha$) and ($\gamma − \alpha$).

Of course, while estimates of α, β, and γ, in equation 1 could represent the effects of the SSI program, the estimates are based on a rather tenuous identifying assumption — namely, that in the absence of the program the labor supply behavior of men (or families) with characteristics associated with SSI participation would be the same as those of other men. That is, the group for which Part = 0 (for example, highly educated men) serves as the "control group" for the estimation of the effects of SSI. It is well known, however, that age profiles of labor supply differ systematically with variables such as education, marital status, and race. This may arise because health is correlated with these characteristics, or because they affect optimal retirement decisions. In addition, if likely participants are most dependent on current income for consumption, a comparison with unlikely participants would bias the results against finding negative effects of SSI benefits on labor supply. Because the variables that determine Part are systematically related to labor supply for reasons that may have nothing to do with SSI, estimation of equation 1 will lead to biased estimates of the effects of SSI.

   The empirical strategy we follow instead, therefore, is to exploit state-level variation in the provision of SSI benefits. Individuals in states *without* state supplementation of SSI benefits, but *with* characteristics associated with SSI receipt, serve as a much more compelling control group with which to compare the behavior of individuals in states *with* state supplementation and *with* characteristics associated with SSI receipt. At the same time, state-specific labor supply profiles may also differ in ways that are correlated with SSI benefits. Therefore, we want to identify the effects of SSI from *relative differences* between the behavior of likely participants and unlikely participants in supplement and non-supplement states, effectively using the unlikely participants to control for these state differences. For example, older high school dropouts (who are much more likely to be SSI participants) may work less, or decrease their labor supply more as they age, compared with more-educated workers. But the difference-in-difference framework only infers an effect of SSI if the difference between the labor supply of older high school dropouts and older more-educated workers is larger in states that supplement SSI than in states that do not.

   An intuitive way to think about the approach is to imagine dividing the sample into states that generously supplement SSI, and states that do not supplement SSI. We then estimate equation 1 only for the subset of states that do not supplement SSI, and a similar equation

(2) $Y = \alpha' \cdot \text{Part} \cdot \text{Age4049} + \beta' \cdot \text{Part} \cdot \text{Age5059} + \gamma' \cdot \text{Part} \cdot \text{Age6064}$
$+ \delta' + \eta' \cdot \text{Age5059} + \theta' \cdot \text{Age6064} + X\psi + \epsilon'$

for the states that supplement SSI. Estimates for these two subsamples provide the relevant difference-in-difference estimates. For example, focusing on 60–64-year-olds, γ' and γ each measure the difference in behavior between likely and unlikely participants within a particular type of state (i.e., high and low supplement states). Here γ serves as the "baseline" difference in behavior of those with characteristics associated with participation in SSI, and therefore $(\gamma' - \gamma)$ captures the effect of SSI supplements on the labor supply of likely participants. Similarly, $(\gamma' - \alpha') - (\gamma - \alpha)$ captures the effect of SSI on changes in labor supply with age, based on the difference in behavior between likely and unlikely participants in high supplement states versus low supplement states.

Note that, as discussed above, this framework allows the age profile of labor supply for a whole state population (captured in δ, η, and θ, or δ', η', and θ') to differ for states that do and do not supplement SSI. This is potentially important to control for biases that might arise from a relationship between policy and other sources of variation in the level or age profile of Y in a state (e.g., if states in which older individuals have a higher propensity to work also tend to offer more generous SSI supplements). Rather than estimate equations 1 and 2 using separate state samples, we obtain difference-in-difference estimates from an interactive specification estimated for the pooled sample of states:

(3) $Y = \alpha \cdot \text{Part} \cdot \text{Age4049} + \beta \cdot \text{Part} \cdot \text{Age5059} + \gamma \cdot \text{Part} \cdot \text{Age6064} + \delta + \eta \cdot \text{Age5059}$

$\quad + \theta \cdot \text{Age6064} + \alpha' \cdot \text{Part} \cdot \text{Age4049} \cdot \text{Supp} + \beta' \cdot \text{Part} \cdot \text{Age5059} \cdot \text{Supp}$

$\quad + \gamma' \cdot \text{Part} \cdot \text{Age6064} \cdot \text{Supp} + \delta' \cdot \text{Supp} + \eta' \cdot \text{Age5059} \cdot \text{Supp}$

$\quad + \theta' \cdot \text{Age6064} \cdot \text{Supp} + X\psi + \epsilon$

where "Supp" is a dummy variable for states with generous SSI supplements. In this specification the estimate of γ' is the difference-in-difference estimate of the effect of SSI on Y for those aged 60–64, and the estimate of $(\gamma' - \alpha')$ measures the effect on the change in Y from ages 40–49 to ages 60–64.[22,23] The pooled regression lets us easily assess the statistical significance of our difference-in-difference estimates, since the estimates are obtained from a single estimation.

Results for SSI Participation

The probit estimates for SSI participation among men aged 65 or older appear in column 2 of Table 1. One would expect that more generous SSI benefits also increase the likelihood of participation; this is confirmed in the table, as the estimated coefficient on the generous state SSI supplement variable is positive (.022) and strongly significant. Education, race, and marital history variables are also strongly associated with SSI participation. High school dropouts are significantly more likely than high school graduates to be SSI participants, with a differential of 5 percentage points. Black and never-married men are also considerably more likely to be on SSI. Finally, to capture unobservables related to low permanent income, and possibly also unobserved heterogeneity in the propensity to participate in income-support programs, information on food stamp enrollment is included in the probit; the number of years authorized, in particular, is strongly positively associated with SSI participation.[24,25]

We use these probit estimates to generate predicted probabilities of participation in SSI for those aged 40–64, which are used in turn are used to construct the variable Part that is used in labor supply models like equation 3. For most of the specifications we estimate, we define Part to equal one when the predicted probability is at or above the 90th centile of the distribution of the predicted probabilities, and zero otherwise. Based on the proportion of participants among those aged 65 and over, approximately one-half of those above this centile should end up on SSI. Selecting which threshold to use presents a trade-off. On the one hand, a high threshold isolates the effects of SSI on those who are most likely to participate, for whom labor supply disincentives may be stronger. On the other hand, those with higher probabilities may need to work more to finance current consumption, since they tend to be poor, or may initially work sufficiently little that disincentive effects are difficult to detect. We therefore also present evidence based on higher and lower thresholds.

Results for Labor Supply

Before proceeding to investigate the impact of SSI on labor supply, we present estimates of the age profiles for the alternative dependent variables measuring labor supply for our sample of men aged 40–64 in Panel A of Table 2. The equations in each column also include controls for education, race, and marital status. For each of the four dependent variables — employment, hours, years of covered social security employment, and family earnings — there are substantial declines with age, particularly for those aged 60–64. The decline in years of covered social security employment with age must reflect cohort effects, because it is a cumulative measure of labor supply.

In Panel B of Table 2, we proceed to the difference-in-difference estimates of equation 3 to estimate the effects of SSI on labor supply.[26] The first two rows contain estimates of β' and γ' for the various dependent variables. Recall that these coefficients measure the differences — for individuals at ages 50–59 and 60–64 respectively — between the behavior of likely participants and unlikely participants in states with generous SSI supplements, using the difference in behavior between likely and unlikely participants in non-supplementing states as a "control." In all four columns the estimate of γ' is negative, consistent with the hypothesis that the pre-retirement labor supply of older likely participants in generous states is relatively lower. However, none of these estimates are significantly different from zero. There is even less evidence of negative labor supply effects from the estimates of β', which are positive and significant in the 5- or 10-percent level for the three direct labor supply measures.

TABLE 2. Estimates of Age Profiles and Difference-in-Difference Estimates of Effects of SSI on Labor Supply, 90th Centile of Participation Probabilities Used to Define Likely SSI Participants, Male Household Heads Aged 40–64

Estimator	Employed Probit	Hours Tobit	Years of Covered Soc. Sec. Employment	Family Earnings Tobit
A. Age profiles of labor supply measures				
Age 50–59	−.10**	−5.90**	2.76**	−152.69**
	(.01)	(.70)	(.54)	(69.91)
Age 60–64	−.27**	−21.12**	−6.25**	−1526.84**
	(.01)	(.91)	(.70)	(90.73)
B. Difference-in-difference estimates of Effects of SSI				
Effect of SSI on 50–59 year-olds (β')	.093*	12.14**	6.70**	78.24
	(.055)	(4.04)	(3.08)	(390.48)
Effect of SSI on 60–64 year-olds (γ')	−.062	−5.38	−3.03	−36.22
	(.071)	(5.92)	(4.55)	(567.95)
Effect of SSI on 50–59 year-olds relative to 40–49 year olds ($\beta' - \alpha'$)	−.074	.21	3.59	−1067.38*
	(.083)	(5.69)	(4.32)	(551.44)
Effect of SSI on 60–64 year-olds relative to 40–49 year olds ($\gamma' - \alpha'$)	−.229**	−17.31**	−6.14	−1181.84*
	(.095)	(7.17)	(5.48)	(689.67)
Log likelihood	−1122.9	−11554.1	−10659.4	−23432.0

Source: Authors' calculations, 1984 SIPP. There are 4560 observations in Panel A, and 2940 observations in Panel B. See Table 1 for details. Specifications in Panels A and B also include dummy variables for education, race, and marital status. Specifications in Panel B correspond to equation (3) in the text. The specifications also include dummy variables for age (50–59 and 60–64), a dummy variable for states with maximum benefits for either individuals or couples exceeding 20% of the federal benefit, interactions between the "high supplement" variable and age dummy variables (for ages 50–59 and 60–64), and interactions between the age dummies for all ranges (40–49, 50–59, and 60–64) and a dummy variable for "likely participants." The coefficients reported in the table are from the variables interacting age, "high supplement," and "likely participant." The "likely participant" dummy variable is define to equal one for observations for which the predicted probability of participation in SSI, using the estimates from column 2 of Table 1, exceeds .0799, which is the 90th centile of the weighted distribution of estimated probabilities. Observations from states that supplement SSI, but with supplements below 20%, are excluded. ** indicates statistically significantly different from zero at the five-percent level, and * at the 10-percent level. All estimates are weighted.

We also report estimates of $(\beta' - \alpha')$ and $(\gamma' - \alpha')$, which describe the changes relative to individuals aged 40–49. In this case, there is considerably stronger evidence of labor supply disincentive effects of SSI. In particular, the estimated drop-offs from ages 40–49 to 60–64 are statistically significant at the 5-percent level for employment and hours, and at the 10-percent level for earnings. Furthermore, looking at the drop-offs from ages 40–49 to 50–59, two of the four estimates are negative (one significant at the 10-percent level), and there are no longer significant positive effects. This evidence, and the differences compared with the estimates of β' and γ', suggest that state-specific differences in labor supply mask life-cycle changes induced by SSI.[27]

There is a potentially important source of misspecification in the Panel B estimates. This arises because states with high SSI supplements also offer relatively generous benefits in other transfer programs, including, of course, SSI for the disabled. These programs may be available not only to those eligible for SSI for the aged, but also to younger men, in particular the disabled. As a consequence, we may see labor supply effects among those below age 65 that are a response to programs other than SSI for the aged. To better isolate the incentive effects of SSI for the aged, and in particular to eliminate spurious relationships that may arise through relationships between disability and income-support programs available to the younger disabled, we re-estimate the equations from Panel B of Table 2 excluding from the sample individuals with any self-reported work-impairing disability.

Estimates for this subsample appear in Panel A of Table 3. The results for ages 60–64 are now more fully consistent with the labor supply disincentive effects of SSI. As before, the estimates of $(\gamma' - \alpha')$ are negative, and estimates for employment and hours are both significant at the five-percent level. For this sample, though, the estimates of γ' are also negative, and significant at the 5- or 10-percent level for employment and hours. In contrast, the estimates of β' are no longer positive and statistically significant. Thus, once we exclude individuals whose behavior is most likely to be influenced by other programs whose generosity is potentially correlated with supplemental state benefits for SSI for the aged, state-specific differences in labor supply measures at all ages are less important, and the estimated effects of labor supply are more similar whether or not we use the 40–49-year-olds as a control group.[28]

Next, we consider problems that arise in measuring features of state SSI programs. In particular, as mentioned earlier, some states choose to administer their own programs, in which case they can set their own eligibility criteria. Therefore we further restrict the sample to include only the subset of states with federal administration of SSI, to ensure that we are looking at states with federal administration and therefore identical benefit formulas and asset rules (see Appendix Table A1). This is potentially important because in states with policy features that differ from the federal ones, one can

TABLE 3. Difference-in-Difference Estimates of Effects of SSI on Labor Supply, Excluding Individuals with Work-Impairing Disability, and States with State-Administered SSI Programs, Male Household Heads Aged 40–64

	Employed	Hours	Years of Covered Soc. Sec. Employment	Family Earnings
A. Excluding individuals with work-impairing disability				
Estimator	Probit	Tobit	Tobit	Tobit
Effect of SSI on 50–59 year-olds (β')	.013 (.05)	6.10 (3.93)	2.31 (3.00)	−312.87 (436.36)
Effect of SSI on 60–64 year-olds (γ')	−.118* (.07)	−12.96* (6.24)	−4.94 (4.79)	−107.44 (693.68)
Effect of SSI on 50–59 year-olds relative to 40–49 year olds ($\beta' - \alpha'$)	−0.63 (.08)	1.17 (5.49)	4.52 (4.18)	−1131.49* (611.21)
Effect of SSI on 60–64 year-olds relative to 40–49 year olds ($\gamma' - \alpha'$)	−.194** (.09)	−17.88** (7.33)	−2.73 (5.61)	−926.06 (815.46)
B. Also excluding states with state-administered SSI programs				
Effect of SSI on 50–59 year-olds (β')	.031 (.06)	8.84 (5.06)	6.71 (4.04)	−464.10 (553.54)
Effect of SSI on 60–64 year-olds (γ')	−.132* (.08)	−12.13 (7.49)	−3.23 (6.01)	−4.84 (820.36)
Effect of SSI on 50–59 year-olds relative to 40–49 year olds ($\beta' - \alpha'$)	−.073 (.10)	3.15 (7.43)	5.24 (5.93)	−1581.19* (822.08)
Effect of SSI on 60–64 year-olds relative to 40–49 year olds ($\gamma' - \alpha'$)	−.236** (.12)	−17.82* (9.24)	−4.70 (7.40)	−1121.93 (1019.90)

Source: Authors' calculations, 1984 SIPP. There are 2478 observations in Panel A, and 1284 observations in Panel B. Specifications correspond to those in Panel B of Table 2. See notes to Table 2 for additional details.

be eligible for the state but not the federal benefit, or vice versa,[29] making it difficult to identify the appropriate maximum benefit level. As reported in Panel B of Table 3, the estimates are very similar to those in Panel A. In particular, the estimates of γ are negative for each of the labor supply measures (and significant at the 10-percent level for employment). The estimates of $(\gamma' - \alpha')$ are negative and significant at the 5- or 10-percent level for employment and hours. Given the considerable reduction in the sample size, coupled with little change in the point estimates, our last analysis reverts to the sample in Panel A of Table 3.

The evidence to this point indicates that generous supplemental state SSI benefits reduce the labor supply of older men. In any difference-in-difference estimation, it is instructive to ask which differences identify the effect. In particular, in our case we estimate the effects of SSI from the difference between the labor supply of likely participants and unlikely participants in high supplement states, relative to the same difference in low supplement states. Thus, the estimates of γ' can be identified largely from a difference in labor supply between likely participants in the two types of states ("main effects"), largely from a difference in labor supply between unlikely participants in the two types of states, or some combination. Similarly, the estimates of $(\gamma' - \alpha')$ can be identified largely from differences in the drop-off in labor supply from ages 40–49 to ages 60–64 among likely participants in the two types of states ("main effects"), or more from differences among unlikely participants. Whether or not the estimates reflect main effects does not render the empirical procedure valid or invalid (if it did, there would be little reason to use difference-in-difference estimation), but may bear on the interpretation of the estimates. In particular, researchers are more likely to place confidence in the results if they show up in the main effects, and are not driven primarily by differences in behavior among unlikely participants in high and low supplement states, which could arise from omitted state-specific influences on the behavior of unlikely participants.

Table 4 provides evidence on this question, by reporting the decomposition of the difference-in-difference estimates into the differences in behavior for the likely participants and the differences for the unlikely participants. Especially for the direct employment and hours labor supply measures, most (65 to 78 percent) of the estimated effects come from the comparison between the likely participants. Indeed, for employment and hours the estimates of the differences in the drop-off from ages 40–49 to 60–64 between likely participants in the two types of states are statistically significant at the 5- or 10-percent level.[30]

Conclusion

Means testing of social security is one way to resolve the pending social security imbalance, but it has been largely dismissed as a real policy alterna-

TABLE 4. Decompositions of Difference-in-Difference Estimates of Effects of SSI on Labor Supply

	Employed	Hours	Years of covered Social Security employment	Family Earnings
Levels, 60–64				
a. Likely participant, high supplement state - likely participant, no supplement state	−.07	−8.03	−2.76	627.11
b. Unlikely participant, high supplement state - unlikely participant, no supplement state	.04	3.04	1.60	616.13**
Difference-in-difference estimate (a. − b.)	−.11	−11.06*	−4.36	10.97
Percentage of estimate from likely participant comparison	.65	.73	.63	—
Difference, 60–64 vs. 40–49				
a. (as above)	−.15*	−14.13**	−1.69	−597.13
b. (as above)	.05	4.08	1.74	315.53
Difference-in-difference estimate (a. − b.)	−.20**	−18.20**	−3.42	−912.66
Percentage of estimate from likely participant comparison	.75	.78	.49	.65

Source: Authors' calculations, 1984 SIPP. Estimates are based on the specifications and sample in Panel A of Table 3, although excluding the demographic controls. See notes to Tables 2 and 3 for additional details.

tive. This chapter gathers some existing evidence and offers new information required to evaluate how such policy might influence behavior. We draw inferences about the potential consequences of means testing social security by studying the effects of SSI for the aged, which currently operates as a sort of means-tested retirement program. State-level variation in generosity of supplemental SSI payments is used to identify the effects of SSI on labor supply as men approach the age of eligibility for the program, studying a sample of male household heads. We find evidence that SSI discourages work among men nearing the age of eligibility, as one might anticipate given the way the SSI program penalizes post-65 income and assets. While the relevance of these results for a social security program would depend on the exact parameters of a means-tested program, we believe that our evidence implies that the cautious approach that has been taken in the past to the means-testing option is justified.

These results must be used cautiously both as evidence on the effects of SSI, and as evidence on the likely consequences of means testing social security. With respect to the evidence on the effects of SSI, we emphasize that these are the first estimates of which we are aware of the effects of SSI on pre-retirement labor supply, and additional analyses should be done using other data sets. With respect to using our findings regarding SSI to infer the likely consequences of a means-tested social security program, there are three issues that must be kept in mind. First, it is always possible that any new program might be sufficiently different from SSI that our results would not generalize. Second, if the alternative to the means-tested program — for example, a partially-privatized component of a two-tier program — either operates or is perceived to operate very differently from the current social security system, behavioral responses to a means-tested program might differ from the responses to SSI that we estimate. Finally, the SSI program serves a poor population, whereas social security, even if means tested, would be likely to continue to serve a higher-income population for which behavioral responses might differ.

The authors thank Kathleen Beegle for outstanding research assistance and Olivia Mitchell for helpful comments. Neumark gratefully acknowledges support from NIA grant K01-AG00589.

Notes

1. For some U.S. workers (e.g., relatively low-earning spouses in two-earner families) it is literally true that an additional dollar of payroll tax contributed will not increase the old-age benefit at all.

2. The Concord Coalition advocates "affluence testing" all entitlement programs, not just social security.

3. In the 1970s, Milton Friedman proposed means testing social security (Friedman and Cohen 1972).

4. The exempt amount for couples was $13,500 in 1997.

5. The base of the tax includes one-half of social security income. The source for the 1995 figures is Congressional Budget Office projections reported in the 1994 Green Book (Committee on Ways and Means 1994).

6. The Concord Coalition plan is thus an income-tested, but not asset-tested, scheme.

7. This is akin to the current federal approach to education finance, where a portion of parents' annuitized wealth holdings is added to their incomes to determine how much of their child's education they are expected to finance.

8. The recent social security "privatization" literature reflects this problem, tending to rely more on theoretical and simulation methods, as well as discussion of privatization schemes in other countries, most notably Chile. See for instance, Altig and Gokhale (1996), Arrau and Schmidt-Hebbel (1993), Feldstein (1995), Gustman and Steinmeier (1995), Kotlikoff (1995), Mitchell and Zeldes (1996), and Pennacchi (this volume).

9. The historical information in this section is drawn from Schultz et al. (1991).

10. By the standards of U.S. private saving, these asset limits were fairly high at $76,300 (in 1985 U.S. dollars) for couples who owned homes; and $150,000 for couples who rented (housing equity is excluded from the asset test).

11. The asset test was reintroduced in 1986 in large part as a response to the popular belief that this type of "evasion" was widespread.

12. Powers (forthcoming) examines the impact of the asset test applied in the AFDC program. Hubbard, Skinner, and Zeldes (1995) use a simulation model to assess the impact of asset tests associated with U.S. welfare programs collectively.

13. Unlike social security, there is no early retirement option in the SSI program. However, the SSI program also provides benefits to the blind and disabled irrespective of age, and is also linked to a health care program, Medicaid. We do not consider these components of the program in this paper.

14. Kahn (1987) discusses the definition of countable assets, and McGarry (1996) provides more details regarding the SSI program.

15. Zedlewski and Meyer (1989) estimate that about 30 percent of the elderly poor receive SSI benefits.

16. If states choose to administer the SSI program, they are also free to set their own eligibility criteria such as asset limits. However, many (but not all) states use the federal criteria (Social Security Administration 1985).

17. The SIPP actually identifies "householders," who are the individuals in whose name the home is owned or rented (also referred to as "reference persons"). In the case of a married couple owning a house jointly, either the husband or wife can be listed as the householder. The data set documentation provides no guidance as to who is classified as the householder in the case. To avoid selecting males who might be less likely to be classified as heads of household based on other criteria, we selected only records on male householders. In fact, the majority of those receiving SSI for the aged are single women (Kahn 1987), because of the greater life expectancy and lower earnings of women.

18. A continuous benefits measure would use all of the available information. On the other hand, all we know about individuals prior to age 65 is the maximum benefit available, not the benefit they would actually receive. In addition, the maximum SSI benefits reported in the Green Book (Committee on Ways and Means) are subject to error for some states. For three states (Minnesota, Vermont, and Washington) benefit levels vary by location, and the maximum reported is for metropolitan areas rather than a statewide level. Since none of these states is classified as paying benefits exceeding 20 percent of the federal level, this measurement problem does not result in misclassification when this particular threshold is used. Regardless of these considerations, the qualitative results are similar using a continuous measure of maximum benefits (including all states), or — as in the reported results — distinguishing states with generous supplemental benefits from states that do not supplement benefits. Appendix Table A1 discusses state supplemental benefit patterns.

19. We suspect that trivially small supplements have no effect on behavior. This was confirmed in unreported results using a zero threshold for the supplement dummy variable, for which the estimated effects were weaker but qualitatively similar than those reported in the paper.

20. We also experimented with using a continuous measure of the estimated probability of participation; the results were similar to those reported below.

21. The notation $Y|\ldots$ means the expectation of Y conditional on the information that follows the $|$.

22. For example, the difference-in-difference parameter capturing the effect of generous state SSI supplementation on the level of Y for likely participants aged 60–64 is

$$(Y|_{Supp=1,Part=1,Age6064=1} - Y|_{Supp=1,Part=0,Age6064=1})$$
$$- (Y|_{Supp=0,Part=1,Age6064=1} - Y|_{Supp=0,Part=0,Age6064=1})$$
$$= (\gamma + \delta + \theta + \gamma' + \delta' + \theta' - \delta - \theta - \delta' - \theta') - (\gamma + \delta + \theta - \delta - \theta) = \gamma'.$$

23. In principle, we could also use variation over time in state supplemental bene-fit levels, and hence use the earlier observations on likely participants in a state as a "control group." However, variation over time in state supplements is minimal, with many states staying fixed (nominally) from year to year, and most states having only small changes over longer periods (Committee on Ways and Means, various years).

24. Because the variable measuring years of food stamp receipt may reflect both age effects and cohort effects, we do not remove the effect of age on this variable in estimating the probability of participation for those under age 64 based on the probit estimates. That is, a 60-year-old with 10 years on food stamps might not have lower permanent income or a lower propensity to enroll than a 50-year-old with the same number of years on food stamps, if cohort effects have boosted food stamp usage among younger cohorts.

25. Because we assume financial resources are endogenous with SSI participation, we do not include them in our estimation of participation probabilities. Not surpris-ingly, financial resources are strongly negatively correlated with SSI participation (McGarry 1996).

26. Some care must be exercised in interpreting the estimates of β', γ', $(\beta' - \alpha')$, and $(\gamma' - \alpha')$ as effects of SSI on labor supply. Because supplemental benefit levels may influence participation, an indicator of the benefit levels was included in the participation equation. In principle, then, a change in benefit levels could also change the classification of an individual as a "likely participant." Because we do not allow such changes in estimating the effects of SSI, the estimates must be interpreted conditional on this classification not changing. Such an interpretation is likely to be valid for most of the observations in the data set, with the exception of those initially on the border line between being classified as a likely or unlikely participant.

27. In Appendix Table A2, we report estimates of the same specifications using the 75th and 95th centiles of the estimated probabilities of participation, rather than the 90th. As expected if the disincentive effects are stronger for more likely participants, the estimated effects of SSI are weaker when the 75th centile is used, and stronger when the 95th centile is used. This holds true for the estimated effects for 60–64 year olds. Using the 75th centile (in Panel A), the signs of the estimated effects are generally the same as for the 90th centile — in the direction of labor supply disincen-tive effects — although the estimated effects are not statistically significant. On the other hand, using the 95th centile yields uniformly larger estimated effects, with the estimates of $(\gamma' - \alpha')$ statistically significant at the 5- or 10-percent level for the three direct labor supply measures. However, the standard errors are quite a bit larger than when the 90th centile is used. Thus, results using the 90th centile are used in the remainder of the paper.

28. The restriction to those without a work-impairing disability reduces the sample size by 462. When we deleted an additional 83 observations with transfer income from any means-tested program, the results were very similar.

29. McGarry (1996) notes that this occurs frequently.

30. The estimates come from the same specification and sample used in Panel A of Table 3, although dropping the demographic controls because they are so strongly associated with use of SSI (see Table 2). As the second-to-last row in each panel of Table 4 shows, the difference-in-difference estimates were little changed by dropping the demographic controls.

APPENDIX TABLE A1. State SSI Supplemental Maximum Benefits, 1985

State	Individuals	Couples	>20% of Federal Benefit	Federally-Administered
Alabama				
Arizona				
Arkansas				Yes
California	179	448	Yes	Yes
Colorado	58	278	Yes	
Connecticut	172	119	Yes	
Delaware				Yes
Washington, D.C.	15	30		Yes
Florida				
Georgia				Yes
Hawaii	5	9		Yes
Illinois	35	34		
Indiana				
Iowa				Yes
Kansas				Yes
Kentucky				
Louisiana				Yes
Maine	10	15		Yes
Maryland				Yes
Massachusetts	129	202	Yes	Yes
Michigan	27	40		Yes
Minnesota	35	66		
Missouri				
Montana				Yes
Nebraska	61	89		
Nevada	37	74		Yes
New Hampshire	27	21		
New Jersey	31	25		Yes
New York	61	76		Yes
North Carolina				
North Dakota				
Ohio				Yes
Oklahoma	60	120	Yes	
Oregon	2			
Pennsylvania	32	49		Yes
Rhode Island	54	102	Yes	Yes
South Carolina				
Tennessee				Yes
Texas				
Utah	10	20		
Vermont	53	97		Yes
Virginia				
Washington	38	37		Yes
Wisconsin	100	161	Yes	Yes

Source: 1985 Green Book and Kahn (1987). Sample is restricted to states individually identified in the SIPP. The maximum federal benefits were $325 for individuals, and $488 for couples. Classification in column 3 is based on maximum benefit for either an individual or a couple. In California and Wisconsin, the cash value of food stamps is included in the supplement (Zedlewski and Meyer 1989). For a small number of individuals living with non-recipients or ineligible spouses, the maximum benefit is reduced.

APPENDIX TABLE A2. Sensitivity Analysis for Estimated Effects of SSI in Panel B of Table 2, Alternative Definitions of Likely SSI Participants, Male Household Heads Aged 40–64

Estimator	Employed Probit	Hours Tobit	Years of Covered Soc. Sec. Employment Tobit	Family Earnings Tobit
A. Using 75th centile of participation probabilities				
Effect of SSI on 50–59 year-olds (β')	.04 (.05)	5.04 (3.26)	1.56 (2.48)	−254.33 (314.18)
Effect of SSI on 60–64 year-olds (γ')	−.05 (.06)	−3.37 (4.57)	−2.03 (3.49)	−180.88 (435.30)
Effect of SSI on 50–59 year-olds relative to 40–49 year olds ($\beta' - \alpha'$)	−.01 (.07)	1.57 (4.54)	3.61 (3.45)	−670.18 (437.26)
Effect of SSI on 60–64 year-olds relative to 40–49 year olds ($\beta' - \alpha'$)	−.01 (.08)	−6.83 (5.62)	.02 (4.28)	−596.73 (537.00)
Log likelihood	−1129.8	11562.7	−10663.8	−23436.4
B. Using 95th centile of participation probabilities				
Effect of SSI on 50–59 year-olds (β')	.09 (.07)	10.94** (5.44)	4.72 (4.19)	−53.79 (534.45)
Effect of SSI on 60–64 year-olds (γ')	−.09 (.10)	−14.10 (8.66)	−13.34** (6.70)	−672.82 (849.79)
Effect of SSI on 50–59 year-olds relative to 40–49 year olds ($\beta' - \alpha'$)	−.08 (.11)	−1.79 (8.27)	2.37 (6.32)	−747.88 (805.22)
Effect of SSI on 60–64 year-olds relative to 40–49 year olds ($\gamma' - \alpha'$)	−.26* (.14)	−26.84** (10.72)	−15.69* (8.24)	−1366.91 (1046.52)
Log likelihood	−1119.4	−11551.9	−10655.9	−23428.7

Source: Authors' calculations, 1984 SIPP. There are 2940 observations in Panels A and B. The 75th centile of participation probabilities (as well as the 80th and 85th centiles) is .0381; the 95th centile is .0962. See notes to Table 2 for additional details.

References

Aaron, Henry J. "A Bad Idea Whose Time Will Never Come." *Brookings Review* (Summer 1997): 17–23.

Advisory Commission on Intergovernmental Relations. *Significant Features of Fiscal Federalism.* 1988 edition. Vol. 1. Washington, D.C.: USGPO, 1987.

Advisory Commission to Study the Consumer Price Index. *Toward a More Accurate Measure of the Cost of Living: Final Report.* Washington, D.C.: USGPO, 1996.

Altig, David and Jagadeesh Gokhale. "A Simple Proposal for Privatizing Social Security." *Economic Commentary.* Cleveland: Federal Reserve Bank of Cleveland, May 1, 1996.

Arrau, Patricio and Klaus Schmidt-Hebbel. "Macroeconomic and Intergenerational Welfare Effects of a Transition from Pay-as-You-Go to Fully Funded Pensions." Washington, D.C.: Policy Research Department, World Bank 1993.

Auerbach, Alan J., Jagadeesh Gokhale, and Laurence J. Kotlikoff. "Social Security and Medicare Policy from the Perspective of Generational Accounting." *Tax Policy and the Economy* 6 (1992): 129–45.

Bipartisan Commission on Entitlement and Tax Reform. *Final Report to the President.* Washington, D.C.: Superintendent of Documents, 1995.

Bosworth, Barry and Gary Burtless. "Population Aging in Rich Countries." *Brookings Review* (Summer 1997): 10–15.

Burtless, Gary and Robert A. Moffitt. "The Joint Choice of Retirement Age and Postretirement Hours of Work." *Journal of Labor Economics* 3, 2 (April 1985): 209–36.

Committee on Ways and Means. *Overview of Entitlement Programs, Green Book.* U.S. House of Representatives, Washington, D.C.: USGPO, various years.

Diamond, Peter A. "Proposals to Restructure Social Security." *Journal of Economic Perspectives* 10, 3 (1996): 67–88.

Feldstein, Martin. "How Big Should Government Be?" *National Tax Journal* 50, 2 (1997): 197–213.

———. "Would Privatizing Social Security Raise Economic Welfare?" NBER Working Paper 5281. Cambridge, Mass.: NBER, 1995.

———. "Should Social Security Benefits Be Means Tested?" *Journal of Political Economy* 95, 3 (1987): 468–84.

Friedman, Milton and W. Cohen. *Social Security: Universal or Selective?* Washington, D.C.: American Enterprise Institute, 1972.

Gramlich, Edward M. "Different Approaches for Dealing with Social Security." *Journal of Economic Perspectives* 10, 3 (1996): 55–66.

Gustman, Alan L. and Thomas L. Steinmeier. "Privatizing Social Security: First Round Effects of a Generic, Voluntary, Privatized U.S. Social Security System." NBER Working Paper 5362. Cambridge, Mass.: NBER, 1995.

———. "Changing the Social Security Rules for Work after 65." *Industrial and Labor Relations Review* 44, 4 (July 1991): 733–45.

———. "A Structural Retirement Model." *Econometrica* 54 (1986): 555–84.

———. "Modeling the Retirement Process for Policy Evaluation and Research." *Monthly Labor Review* 107, 7 (July 1984): 26–33.

Hubbard, R. Glenn, Jonathan Skinner, and Stephen P. Zeldes. "Precautionary Saving and Social Insurance." *Journal of Political Economy* 103 (1995): 360–99.

Kahn, Arthur L. "Program and Demographic Characteristics of Supplemental Security Income Recipients, December 1985." *Social Security Bulletin* 50, 5 (May 1987): 23–57.

Kotlikoff, Laurence J. "Privatization of Social Security: How It Works and Why It Matters." NBER Working Paper 5330. Cambridge, Mass.: NBER, 1995.

————. *Generational Accounting.* New York: Free Press, 1992.

————. "Testing the Theory of Social Security and Life Cycle Accumulation." *American Economic Review* 69 (1979): 396–410.

Kotlikoff, Laurence J. and Jeffrey Sachs. "It's High Time to Privatize." *Brookings Review* (Summer 1997): 16–22.

McGarry, Kathleen. "Factors Determining Participation of the Elderly in SSI." *Journal of Human Resources* 31, 2 (Spring 1996): 331–58.

Mitchell, Olivia S. "Worker Knowledge of Pension Provisions." *Journal of Labor Economics* 6, 1 (1988): 21–39.

Mitchell, Olivia S. and Stephen Zeldes. "Social Security Privatization: A Structure for Analysis." *American Economic Review* 86 (May 1996): 363–67.

Neumark, David and Elizabeth Powers. "The Effect of Means-Tested Income Support for the Elderly on Pre-Retirement Saving: Evidence from the SSI Program in the U.S." *Journal of Public Economics,* forthcoming.

Powers, Elizabeth T. "Does Means-Testing Welfare Discourage Saving? Evidence from a Change in AFDC Policy in the United States." *Journal of Public Economics,* forthcoming.

Schultz, James H., Allan Borowski, William H. Crown, and Shinya Hoshino. *The Economics of Population Aging: The "Graying" of Australia, Japan, and the United States.* New York: Auburn House, 1991.

Social Security Administration. "The Supplemental Security Income Program for the Aged, Blind, and Disabled: Characteristics of State Assistance Programs for SSI Recipients." Washington, D.C.: U.S. Department of Health and Human Services, 1985.

Technical Panel on Trends and Issues in Retirement Savings. *Final Report of the 1994–96 Advisory Council on Social Security.* Washington, D.C.: Social Security Administration, 1997.

Zedlewski, Sheila R. and Jack A. Meyer. *Toward Ending Poverty Among the Elderly and Disabled Through SSI Reform.* Washington, D.C.: Urban Institute Press, 1989.

Chapter 11
Social Security and Employer Induced Retirement

Robert M. Hutchens

Northrop Grumman . . . recently offered early retirement incentives to long time employees like me. So I took them up on it and enjoyed all of January off. Never having had that much time to myself since High School (College vacations spent in an aeroplane factory) I really enjoyed it and recommend it to anyone else with that option. [My wife] is still too young however, so I am back as a contract employee for another 6 months and hoping to get them to let me work part time, the ideal situation. (http://www.ddg.com/nemesis/95.MAR.html)

Employers play an important role in the retirement behavior of older workers. When business deteriorates and workforce reductions are requisite, employers like Northrop Grumman often ask older workers to lead the exodus. More broadly, in setting wage levels and pension parameters, employers can influence a worker's attitude toward retirement. Since changes in social security policy can similarly affect attitudes toward retirement, one would think that changes in social security policy could influence employer behavior toward older workers. This chapter uses a simulation model to explore potential links between the social security program and employer efforts at encouraging workers to retire. The simulations are built on an implicit contract theory of unemployment insurance (Hutchens 1995, 1996). In essence I treat social security as a special form of unemployment insurance limited to people age 62 and older, one that is financed out of taxes with no experience rating.

   A large economic literature argues that such a system will affect the way in which employers respond to periods of slack demand.[1] In a manner consistent with that literature, I first describe a simulation framework that allows a conventional unemployment insurance system to affect employers' propensity to initiate separations. Next I introduce a type of social security system into the model, and examine how separation probabilities change by age. Additional simulations show how changes in the parameters of the social security system affect behavior. At the outset it is important to be clear about the limitations of this exercise. The simulations do not constitute empirical evidence, but are instead best viewed as rough estimates of the potential magnitude of anticipated economic effects. Also, the analysis is built on a simplified version of the social security system. As such, the results remain suggestive; they cannot be viewed as hard data in support of policy.

Theoretical Framework

This section introduces an implicit contract model of how government transfers influence employer behavior. We first sketch an implicit contract model of unemployment insurance and temporary layoffs, and then discuss links between social security and employer initiated separations.[2]

Consider an economy with many firms and homogeneous workers. Workers obtain income for consumption by entering into a one-period contract with a firm. Workers are assumed to be risk averse, so they seek contracts that minimize income fluctuations. When employed, each worker earns wage w and obtains utility $U(w(1-t))$, where t is a payroll tax.[3] When not employed, the worker obtains utility $U(c + b + z)$, where c is government unemployment insurance, b is a private payment from the firm, and z is the consumption value of leisure and home production. Letting p represent the probability that the worker is employed, the worker's expected utility under the contract is:

$$EU = pU(w(1-t)) + (1-p)U(c+b+z).$$

For simplicity, the model assumes each firm employs a single worker. Firms compete for workers by offering contracts that maximize profit while economizing on income risk to workers. For a contract to be acceptable to workers, expected utility under the contract must be greater than or equal to that available in alternative jobs and activities. Letting EU^* represent this alternative expected utility, we have:

(1) $$EU \geq EU.^*$$

Firms also pay taxes. Like the workers, firms are assumed to pay a payroll tax equal to t. As developed below, the payroll tax can be used to finance social security. In addition, the firms pay taxes to finance unemployment insurance. Since unemployment insurance benefits are experience rated, the cost to the firm of providing unemployment insurance c is ec, where e is an experience rating tax rate with $0 \leq e \leq 1$. When e is less than one, the firm does not bear the full cost of the government-provided unemployment insurance, and experience rating is imperfect. In this case the subsidy per worker is $(1 - e)c$.

At the time the contract is negotiated, the employer is uncertain about the future state of product demand and thereby the worker's marginal product, θ. The value of θ is only revealed after the contract is signed, but before work begins. When it is revealed, we assume it becomes public knowledge. (There is no asymmetric information in this model.) Assume that θ is distributed $f(\theta)$. As such, given the realized value of θ, the contract specifies $w(\theta)$, $b(\theta)$, and $p(\theta)$.

An employer's expected profit when negotiating the contract can then be written:

(2) $$\Pi = \int_{-\infty}^{+\infty} \{(\theta - w(\theta)(1+t))p(\theta) - (b(\theta) + ec)(1 - p(\theta))\}f(\theta)\,d\theta.$$

In other words, for a realized value of θ, the firm's profit is the sum of (i) the marginal product (θ) minus wage costs ($w(\theta)(1+t)$) multiplied by the probability of employment $p(\theta)$, and (ii) the private payments to non-workers ($b(\theta)$) and the cost of unemployment insurance (ec) multiplied by the probability of nonemployment ($1-p(\theta)$). Expected profit is the expected value of this sum (i plus ii) over all feasible values of θ. Given the profit function, the firm's problem is to offer a contract that maximizes the present value of expected profit (Π) subject to two constraints: $p(\theta)$ lies between zero and one, and expected utility under the contract is no less than that in jobs elsewhere in the market (EU*).[4] We write this problem as

$$\max_{w(\theta),b(\theta),p(\theta)} \Pi \text{ subject to } EU = EU^* \text{ and } 0 \le p(\theta) \le 1.$$

This problem is easily analyzed when the payroll tax t is zero.[5] In this case, the resulting contract has two key features. First, the firm provides complete insurance. Wages paid to the employed and private payments to the non-employed are set so that marginal utilities are the same for all realized values of θ. Given the assumed utility function, and letting an asterisk denote optimal levels, this implies that for all values of θ:

(3) $$w^* = b^* + c + z.$$

Second, the employment probability, $p^*(\theta)$, follows the following simple rule:

(4)
$$\text{If } \theta \ge z + (1-e)c \text{ then } p^*(\theta) = 1,$$

$$\text{If } \theta < z + (1-e)c \text{ then } p^*(\theta) = 0.$$

In other words, the worker is employed (and receives wage w^*) if the revealed value of θ is greater than or equal to the value of "externally financed consumption" ($z + (1-e)c$). Otherwise, the worker is not employed and receives b^* from the firm and c from the government.

In this simple world without asymmetric information, workers are indifferent between employment and nonemployment. The contract insures that they have the same utility regardless of their work status. Moreover, an increase in government unemployment insurance (c) results in a dollar for dollar reduction in private payments to nonworkers (b^*). The firm makes these private payments in order to protect workers from income fluctuations. When the government provides this protection, then the firm cuts back, paying an experience rated tax of e for each dollar of government benefits.

One interesting result of equation 4 is that neither wages nor private payments enter into the employment decision. That is a fundamental difference between this model and a labor supply model. Wages and private payments (such as pensions) are endogenous transfer payments that have nothing to do with the employment decision. Employment is strictly a function of the worker's marginal product and externally financed consumption. Also, given equation 4, the probability that the worker is employed depends on both his realized marginal product and the level of externally financed consumption. Specifically, a higher government subsidy to non-employment (a higher level of $(1-e)c$) results in more nonemployment. Consequently, when experience rating is complete ($e = 1$) and the subsidy is zero, the worker is employed if and only if the realized marginal product in the firm exceeds the consumption value of home production z.

The model becomes more complex with positive payroll taxes. We assume the payroll tax is shared between employer and employee, but it is not levied on private payments to the nonemployed. Hence, an increase in "t" has two effects. First, it raises employer wage costs, and thereby creates incentives to shift compensation away from earnings and toward those private payments. Second, the tax reduces a worker's utility when employed relative to utility when not employed. Both effects reduce the probability of employment.[6]

Now, what does this have to do with social security and older workers? We know that companies do make payments to nonemployed older workers in the form of pensions, early retirement window plans, and severance pay. Moreover, these payments are often made with an eye toward available government benefits; pensions are typically integrated with social security so that private benefits fall when a person becomes eligible for government benefits (see Gregory, this volume). That behavior is thoroughly consistent with the model.

The model also implies that social security should affect separations in a manner similar to unemployment insurance. We have strong evidence that imperfectly experience rated unemployment insurance increases the likelihood of temporary layoffs during periods of slack demand. Since social security benefits are not experience rated, they could similarly increase the likelihood of employer induced retirements during periods of slack demand.[7]

Evidence

This section provides partial support for the model just described. Specifically, we show that the U.S. social security program is used as a form of unemployment insurance, and that employer behavior is influenced by government assistance to older workers.

Unemployment Insurance Receipt at Age 62

One way to test the structure just described is to examine whether unemployment insurance receipt increases around the time that workers become eligible for social security benefits. In order to preserve worker utility in an implicit contract setting, the firm must compensate laid off workers. Unemployment insurance is likely to be a part of that compensation, especially when UI experience rating is imperfect. If social security tends to increase employer induced separations, then we should also observe an increase in unemployment insurance receipt around the time that workers become eligible for old age benefits. At that time, employers essentially compensate separated workers with a combination of social security, unemployment insurance, and, perhaps, pension benefits.

Hutchens (1996) used 1975 Current Population Survey data to show that the probability of UI receipt increased sharply around age 62, particularly for the lower skilled employee. In 1975 most workers in the U.S. could simultaneously receive both unemployment insurance and social security benefits. This evidence then suggests that social security does, in fact, increase employer induced separations.

Employer Behavior and Expansions of Government Assistance to Older Workers

Turning to international evidence, we find at least two cases where the payment of government transfers to older workers caused employers to reduce older workers' employment. One was the Austrian extension of unemployment benefit duration in 1988, and the second was the West German "59er" plan.

The Austrian case, documented in Winter-Ebmer (1996), arose from the 1998 extension of the duration of unemployment insurance benefits from 52 to 209 weeks. This extension only applied to workers over age 50 who lived in specific counties of Austria. Moreover, to be eligible, a worker had to be involuntarily unemployed: that is, the unemployment had to arise from a layoff and not be the result of a quit or a misconduct discharge. Comparing older affected workers with a "control group" consisting of both younger workers and older workers in non-selected counties, Winter-Ebmer demonstrates that this policy change not only increased the duration of unemployment receipt for older workers in the selected counties, but also increased the *incidence* of unemployment insurance receipt. Specifically, older workers eligible for the extended benefits entered the unemployment insurance program at a rate 11 percentage points higher than the controls. From the perspective of the above theory, what is particularly interesting is that the government transfers flowed to the workers, not the employers, yet it was the employers who changed behavior.

A similar phenomenon occurred in the West German "59er" program. Under this program, when an employer's economic prospects were sufficiently bleak, the West German government permitted workers to receive government supplied early retirement benefits (unemployment insurance and public pensions) at age 59, and more recently, at age 57. Workers could not simply apply for the benefits; rather, their employers had to seek coverage under the program and then designate specific workers for early retirement. And that is exactly what happened. Although the benefits flowed to the workers, case studies indicate that employers often used the program to shed older employees (Naschold et al. 1994; Casey 1989).

Some U.S. Workers Seem to Use Social Security as a Form of Unemployment Insurance

Additional evidence is offered by Rust (1990), who examines the lag between the age at which workers apply for benefits and the age at which they first receive OASI payments for six months or more. He finds a two-year delay among the set of applicants that eventually received OASI payments. Rust then goes on to say that

the majority of workers who apply for benefits at age 62 and continue working are either low-wage/income workers whose total annual earnings at ages after 62 are not significantly higher than the earnings test level or are a smaller group of workers who apparently initially intended to quit working at age 62 but experienced adverse financial problems or encountered a particularly attractive job opportunity that prompted them to return to work. (1970: 374)

From the perspective of the above theoretical framework, one would like to know how often these workers returned to work with their pre-application employer. Unfortunately, Rust does not address that question.

Evidence from several other countries also indicates that social security recipiency rates trace a pattern similar to unemployment insurance over the business cycle. Specifically, old age program recipiency rates increase during recessions and decrease during expansions (Rebick 1994).

Although the latter results on the business cycle as well as Rust's findings might be explained with a standard labor supply analysis (whereby workers choose their hours of work in order to maximize personal utility), the first two elements of evidence do not fit easily into that framework. Rather, the

evidence suggests that employers are actively involved in retirement decisions, a conclusion consistent with the implicit contract explanation discussed above.

Setting Up the Simulations

One might question whether the economic incentives inherent in the U.S.
social security program are strong enough actually to induce workers and
firms to use social security as a form of unemployment insurance. Moreover,
one would like to know whether policy changes could have important behavioral effects. Simulation provides a useful tool for exploring such issues.
This section expands the previous model in order to simulate the effects of a
structure similar to the U.S. social security program. The simulations begin
with a model of the unemployment insurance system that yields an incidence of layoffs that is consistent with that empirical evidence. The social
security program is then introduced into the model, with social security
treated as a form of unemployment insurance available after age 62. The
simulations then indicate how the introduction of this social security plan
affects the incidence of employer-initiated separations. Given that, one
can go on to examine how changes in the social security program affect
behavior.

   This section begins with a description of the model used in the simulations. It then discusses how social security is parameterized, a discussion that
includes a necessary but lengthy examination of actuarial adjustments. The
section closes with a description of other parameters used in the simulations, as well as the initial "benchmark" runs.

The Model

To generalize our earlier discussion, we assume that workers live for several
periods and thus enter into multiperiod contracts with a single firm. There
is no mobility between firms in this model once the contract is signed; the
worker either is employed by the contracting firm or spends time in "nonemployment." To keep things relatively simple, all of the workers are assumed to reach their 65th birthday on January 1, 1995. To simplify survival
rates, we also assume that all the workers in this cohort are males (obviously,
similar simulations could be performed for women), and all financial variables abstract from inflation.

   As before, workers are either employed or not employed, and they evaluate well-being with the utility function $U(\bullet)$ (where $U' > 0$, $U'' < 0$). In
the multiperiod case expected utility in period j is specified as $EUj =$
$p_j(w_j(1-t)) + (1-p_j)U(b_j+g_j+z_j)$, where

   p_j is the probability that the worker is employed in period j,
   w_j is the worker's wage in period j,

t is the payroll tax,

b_j is the private payment from the firm to the worker in period j,

g_j is either social security or unemployment insurance, and

z_j is the consumption value of leisure and home production in period j.

To simplify the exposition, we assume that a period lasts for one year and that period j is synonymous with age j. Workers live for a maximum of J periods (or years). On their 25th birthday they enter into employment contracts that stretch from that day until death. Mobility costs are such that once workers have accepted the contract, they remain with the firm until retirement. In consequence, viable contracts must yield lifetime utility that equals or exceeds that in alternative jobs and activities. We write this constraint as

$$(6) \qquad \sum_{j=1}^{J} \beta^{j-1} \lambda_j EU_j = EU(S)^*,$$

where λ_j is the fraction of the birth cohort surviving to age j given that they have survived to age 25 (since no one lives past J, $\lambda_J = 0$),

β is the worker's discount rate, and

EU* is the expected utility in alternative jobs and activities.

Government transfer payments in period j (g_j) take the form of either unemployment insurance or social security benefits. Unemployment insurance benefits (denoted c) can be received in all periods of the contract. Social security benefits (denoted v) can be received only after age 62. For the present analysis, social security benefits are set at the same value (v_0) for all people over 62 and are only available to nonworkers. Actuarial adjustments and rules governing simultaneous receipt of social security and unemployment insurance are dealt with below. Thus, $g_j = c + v_j$, where $v_j = 0$ for $j = 25\text{–}61$, and $v_j = v_0$ for $j = 62\text{–}J$. Government taxes are as before. Unemployment insurance benefits are in part financed through experience rating; the cost to the firm of an unemployment insurance benefit c is ec, where e is an "experience rating" tax rate, with $0 \le e \le 1$. The firm and the worker also each pay a payroll tax t on wage income.[8]

Once again the firm's goal is to maximize profits over the length of the contract. The firm's technology is, however, somewhat different. A worker with skill level S has two possible marginal products: $S\,\theta(H)$ or $S\,\theta(L)$, with $\theta(H) > \theta(L) \ge 0$. Let θ_j represent the state of demand for the firm's product in period j. At the time the worker and firm enter into the contract, they are uncertain about both the worker's skill level and future values of θ_j. Let the probability that $\theta_j = \theta(H)$ be $q_j(\theta(H))$ and the probability that $\theta_j = \theta(L)$ be $q_j(\theta(L)) = 1 - q_j(\theta(H))$. The state of demand ($\theta_j$) is revealed at the beginning of period j, at which point it becomes public knowledge.

With regard to skill level, assume that the worker and firm only know the expected value of the worker's skill level at the time that the contract is negotiated. The actual value of S is drawn from the distribution $f(S)$ in the first year of the contract, and remains at that level until age 70. One could think of S as similar to an index of the quality of the worker-firm match. Although outsiders cannot observe it, and neither the worker nor the firm knows its value when the contract is signed, match quality affects the worker's productivity in the firm. In order to simplify the simulations, we assume that worker's skill drops to zero after age 70 as does marginal product within the firm. While the firm maintains its contractual commitment to pay pensions to workers after age 70, it no longer employs these workers.[9]

Let $w(\theta_j)$, $b(\theta_j)$, $p(\theta_j)$ represent the value of the wage, the private payment, and the employment probability respectively for the two possible values of θ_j in year $j = 25, J$. Then the firm's expected profit in year j from a worker with skill S who has survived to year j can be written:

$$(7) \qquad \Pi_j = \sum_{\theta_j=\theta(L)}^{\theta(H)} q(\theta_j)\{(S\theta_j - w(\theta_j))p(\theta_j) - (b(\theta_j) + ec)(1 - p(\theta_j))\}.$$

As before, the firm's problem is to offer a contract that maximizes the present value of expected profit subject to two constraints: $p(\theta_j)$ lies between zero and one, and expected utility under the contract is no less than that in jobs elsewhere in the market (EU*). Now, however, the contract must be written over the J years of the worker's potential lifetime. The discount rate (β) used by the firm is assumed to be the same as that used by the worker. Thus, the optimal contract sets $w(\theta_j)$, $b(\theta_j), p(\theta_j), j = 25- 69$, and b_j, $j = 60-J$ so as to solve the problem,

$$\max\int_S\{\sum_{j=25}^{70} \lambda_j\beta^{j-25}\Pi_j\}f(S)\,dS + \sum_{j=70}^{J} \lambda_j\beta^{j-25}b_j,$$

subject to

$$\sum_{j=25}^{J} \lambda_j\beta^{j-25}EU_j = EU* \quad \text{and} \quad 0 \leq p(\theta_j) \leq 1.$$

Although this looks daunting, it has essentially the same solution as the simpler model above. Once again, when $t = 0$ the firm provides complete insurance against income fluctuations, implying,

$$w_i* = b_i* + g_i + z_i = w_j* = b_j* + g_j + z_j, \text{ for } i, j = 25, J,$$

where * denotes optimal levels. Thus, as above, consumption when employed (w_j*) equals consumption when not employed ($b_j* + g_j + z_j$). In this model, however, the equality holds both within and across all periods of the contract.

The probability of employment in this model is also quite similar to that developed previously. When $t = 0$, a worker is employed if the worker's marginal product $(S\,\theta_j)$ exceeds that worker's "externally financed consumption" when not employed $(v_j + (1-e)c + z_j)$. As payroll taxes are raised, employment falls (because the marginal product is less likely to exceed $v_j + (1-e)c + z_j + 2w_j*dt$).

Social Security and Actuarial Reductions

For the purpose of our simulations, a simplified version of the U.S. Old Age Insurance (OAI) program is assumed. In the actual system, a worker's benefits are determined by four factors. The first factor is the Primary Insurance Amount (PIA). The PIA is a function of the worker's average indexed monthly earnings in covered employment. Roughly speaking, workers with higher lifetime earnings tend to have a higher PIA. For these simulations, it is assumed that all workers have a PIA of $10,000 per year or $833.33 per month. Recall that the workers are employed under an identical contract, and all receive the same wage when working. The second factor affecting real world social security benefits is the recipient's family. Workers with the same PIA may receive different social security benefits because of differences in marital status or number of dependents. To simplify matters, this is left out of the simulations. All the workers in this model are single with no dependents.

A third factor influencing benefits is the beneficiary's current earnings. At present, an age 62 beneficiary with annual earnings about a certain exempt amount has benefits reduced by $1 for each $2 in earnings. These numbers change with age, and beneficiaries who are age 70 and older are exempt from the earnings test. For purposes of the simulations, it is assumed that nonemployed workers receive their full social security benefit, and that employed workers earn too much to receive benefits; all of the employed workers' benefits are taxed away by the earnings test. Current earnings can also alter the worker's average indexed monthly earnings, and thereby both the PIA and the level of benefits. Since our model assumes that workers receive the same annual wage each year they work, this effect is ignored here.[10]

Finally, social security benefit levels depend on the age at which the worker begins receiving benefits. Currently workers obtain benefits equal to the full PIA if they elect to receive social security at age 65. Workers who elect to receive social security benefits prior to age 65 receive reduced benefits. By returning to work, however, early retirees can increase their monthly benefit due to benefit recomputation. Consider, for example, a male who receives social security benefits for one year following his sixty-second birthday, returns to work, and fully retires at age 65. If his earnings at age 63 and 64 are above the earnings test, then his benefit at age 65 will be 93.4 percent (100% − 12 months × 5⁄9 of 1%) of the full social security benefit. Another adjustment is made for people who elect to receive benefits after their 65th birthday, called the delayed retirement credit.

TABLE 1. Social Security Benefits Are Not Actuarially Neutral for Workers Who Expect to Work After They Become Beneficiaries

	Annual Social Security Benefit at Selected Ages					Present Value of Benefits at Age 62
	62	63	65	70	75	
Person A Expects to receive benefits after age 63 and:						
Receives benefits at age 62	$8,000	$8,000	$8,000	$8,000	$8,000	$117,951
Does not receive at age 62	$0	$8,667	$8,667	$8,667	$8,667	$119,114
Person B Expects to not receive benefits from age 63 through 69 and:						
Receives benefits at age 62	$8,000	$0	$0	$11,433	$11,433	$97,115
Does not receive at age 62	$0	$0	$0	$12,250	$12,250	$95,480

Source: Author's calculations.

As a result of these rules, expected work behavior plays a fundamental role in any assessment of the effect of actuarial adjustments. Alternatively stated, as a result of these rules, the penalty for receipt of social security benefits in year j depends crucially on expected work behavior in year $j+1$, $j+2$, and so forth. A worker who is laid off at age 62 and receives social security early retirement benefits pays a penalty in the form of lower future benefits. If, however, that individual returns to work, this penalty can be effectively postponed until age 70. And in the present context, because of discounting and the probability of death, a postponed penalty is a reduced penalty.

Table 1 illustrates this point; it shows that by returning to work, a worker can effectively postpone and thereby reduce the penalty associated with early retirement. At age 62, workers A and B are observationally identical males with the same social security earnings record and the same benefit entitlement. Moreover, both experience a layoff on their 62nd birthday, and both contemplate receipt of social security benefits at age 62. The only difference between the two is that worker B expects to return to work while worker A does not. More precisely, regardless of what happens at age 62, worker A expects not to work and to receive social security benefits from age 63 to death. In contrast, worker B expects to work from age 63 through age 69, and then fully retire on his 70th birthday.

Now, consider the social security benefits received by worker A. If he initiated receipt at age 62, worker A would receive $8,000 in social security benefits in that year and annually for the rest of his life. At a 2 percent real discount rate and given the survival rates of males born in 1930, the present value of this stream of benefits is $117,951. However, if he postponed receipt to age 63, due to actuarial adjustments his annual benefit would rise to $8,667, yielding a present value of $119,114. In other words, by retiring at 62 instead of 63, the worker loses $1,163 (= $119,114 − $117,951). Had he foregone receipt at age 62, he would have obtained higher expected lifetime social security benefits.

Next, consider the social security benefits received by worker B, who like worker A would receive $8,000 in social security benefits if he initiates receipt at age 62. Unlike worker A, worker B expects to return to work and not receive social security benefits from age 63 through 69; in consequence, his annual social security benefit at age 70 will be $11,433. If worker B receives benefits at age 62, receives no benefits from 63 through 69 and then receives benefits again from 70 until death, the present value of his benefits at age 62 (computed with the same assumptions applied to worker A) is $97,115. If, however, worker B decided to not receive benefits at age 62, he would raise his social security at age 70 to $12,250. This higher benefit at age 70 and zero benefit at age 62 translates into a present value at age 62 of $95,480. Thus, worker B gains money by collecting social security benefits at age 62. He gains $1,635 (= $97,115 − $95,480). In contrast to worker A, had worker B forgone receipt at age 62, he would have obtained lower expected lifetime social security benefits.

Note that like worker A, worker B pays a penalty for receiving benefits at age 62. For both people the penalty takes the form of lower annual benefits. The key difference between A and B is that B works from age 63 to 70 and thereby postpones the penalty until age 70. Due to discounting and survival probabilities, a penalty postponed is a penalty reduced. Thus, it would be thoroughly rational for worker B to use social security as a form of unemployment insurance. Since he expects to be reemployed, person B increases his lifetime benefits if he receives social security during his age 62 hiatus from work. The gains from current receipt are well in excess of the cost of future penalties from actuarial reductions.[11]

It follows that for purposes of the simulations, the cost of actuarial reduction must be evaluated as a function of the worker's expected future employment. That is possible in this model. We can determine the probability of a high or low realization of θ for future periods, and from that derive the future employment probabilities. This derivation is not, however, a simple matter. The appendix lays out the details of how the cost of actuarial reductions is programmed into the simulations.

Why does the firm in this paper care about actuarial reductions? After all, the firm is maximizing profits. If receipt of social security benefits at age 62 implies lower benefits for a worker at age 80, why does the firm care? The answer is that the firm is maximizing profits subject to a worker's lifetime expected utility constraint. If actions taken at age 62 reduce the worker's expected social security benefits at age 80, then those actions affect the firm's profit, since the contract will require offsetting private pension payments at age 80. Thus, in this model firms fully internalize the effect of social security actuarial adjustments when they make their separation decisions. There is no opportunistic behavior by firms.

Other Parameters in the Model

Table 2 presents the parameter values assumed for the first set of simulations. Most of these parameters are explained above, but e, c, and β deserve further discussion. The UI program parameters e and c are set at .7 and $3,500 respectively. The value for e comes from Table 10 of Topel (1985). Since c is an annual benefit, it is computed as the product of $250 (the approximate average state maximum weekly benefit in 1995) and 14 weeks (the approximate average weeks of unemployment insurance receipt for UI recipients over the 1980s and early 1990s).[12]

The discount rate, β, is set at .04. Since this is the discount rate that both firms and workers use in evaluating the future, one could reasonably argue that the rate should be set at the level used by firms for purposes of capital budgeting. When the firms in this paper place older workers into nonemployment, they bear risk. Due to actuarial adjustments in the social security system, they are gambling that future demand shocks (which affect the worker's future employment) and mortality outcomes are such that the

TABLE 2. Parameters Used When Calibrating the Model

Variable	Symbol	Assumed Value
Value of θ at its high realization	$\theta\,(H)$	1.3
Value of θ at its low realization	$\theta\,(L)$	.7
Consumption value of home production	z	$16,000
Unemployment insurance benefit	c	$3,500
Social security benefit at age 65	v_o	$10,000
Serial correlation parameter in the error equation $q_j(H)=(1-\alpha)\,u_j+\alpha q_{j-1}(H)$	α	0
Experience rating parameter	e	.7
Payroll tax rate	t	.075
Earnings	w	$26,000
Fraction of birth cohort surviving to age j given survived to age 25	λ_j	Derived from Felicitie Bell et al. (1992), Table 6
Distribution of skills	$f(S)$	Uniform from $23,900 to $38,900.
Discount rate for both worker and firm.	β	.04

Source: Author's calculations.

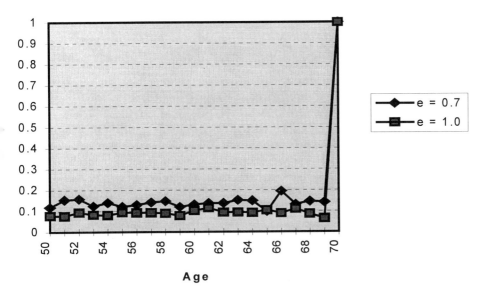

Figure 1. Percent not employed by age: calibrating the model with two values of the experience rating parameter. Source: Author's calculations.

money saved by sending the worker home today will not result in losses in the future. Given that, they would arguably evaluate these decisions using the discount rate applied to other risky ventures. Surveys of corporate capital budgeting practices find that firms use real annual discount rates that range from zero to 13 percent (Boudreau 1983: 566).

The simulations are calibrated to yield results for unemployment insurance that are similar to Topel's results on the effects of experience rating.[13] Specifically, the model is calibrated so that raising the experience rating parameter from .7 to 1.0 (and thereby eliminating the subsidy due to imperfect experience rating) reduces the annual rate of nonemployment from .14 to .10.

Figure 1 illustrates the results of the "benchmark" simulations.[14] This is a graph of the nonemployed as a percent of the population by age for ten runs of the simulation model. Each run involves drawing new random variables for the ten firms (each of which employs five workers). Note that in the absence of social security, the simulations yield roughly the same percentage of nonemployed people from age 50 to 70. That is as expected, since both home production (z) and skill (S) are the same for all ages. Note also that at age 70, all workers become nonemployed. That is because by construction, skill levels equal zero from age 70 until death.

Simulation Results

Figures 2–5 introduce a social security program into the calibrated model. In a program with no actuarial adjustment, Figure 2 shows that early retirees receive the same annual benefit as late retirees. As expected, the model produces an abrupt jump in nonemployed workers at age 62; the nonemployment rate rises from .14 to .50 for workers age 62 or older. Since social security is not experience rated, it acts like a particularly generous form of unemployment insurance. The simulations indicate that this type of unemployment insurance would have dramatic effects on employer behavior.

We introduce actuarial adjustments to social security benefits in Figure 3. The higher line indicates the effect of imposing an early retirement penalty of $\frac{5}{9}$ of 1 percent per month and a delayed retirement credit of $\frac{3}{8}$ of 1 percent per month. Roughly speaking, this is the contemporary system. Clearly such adjustments matter at ages 62 and 63, dramatically reducing nonemployment at these ages. After age 65, however, they have little effect (compare Figure 3 with Figure 2), and despite these adjustments, nonemployment rates from age 62 on are well above those in the absence of social security (Figure 1).

The lower line in Figure 3 indicates the effect of the benefit adjustment scheduled to be implemented in the year 2008. Here the normal retirement age is 66, the annual penalty for early retirement from age 62 to 65 is .0625 percent per year, and the delayed retirement credit is 8 percent per year. The simulations again indicate that these changes could significantly alter the level of nonemployment. Indeed, the level of nonemployment at ages 62–65 is almost at the same level as with no program. The simulations imply major shifts in employer behavior.

Figure 4 presents a simulation of the effect of reducing the payroll tax for people over 62 from .15 to .10. A lower payroll tax should raise employment by reducing the propensity for employers to move workers from employment to nonemployment. The higher line indicates the effects of the contemporary system; this is identical to the higher line in Figure 3. The lower line indicates the effect of the reduced payroll tax. While the reduced tax succeeds in raising employment at ages 62–65, it also decreases employment at older ages. That decrease is due to actuarial adjustments in the social security program. An increase in the probability of work at ages 62–65 translates into higher social security benefits between ages 66 and 69, which then reduces the probability of work at these later ages.

The effect of financing social security out of a consumption tax rather than a payroll tax is shown in Figure 5. Such a tax places a smaller burden on earned income (payments made when people are working), and a larger burden on nonearned income like social security benefits, unemployment insurance benefits, and pensions. In order to raise the same revenues as the 15 percent payroll tax, consumption would have to be taxed at a rate of

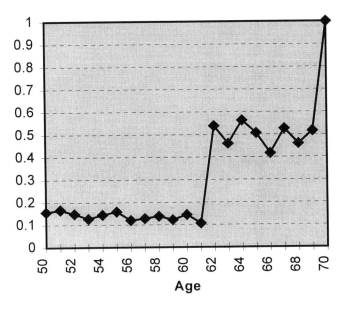

Figure 2. Percent not employed by age: social security with no actuarial adjustment. Source: Author's calculations.

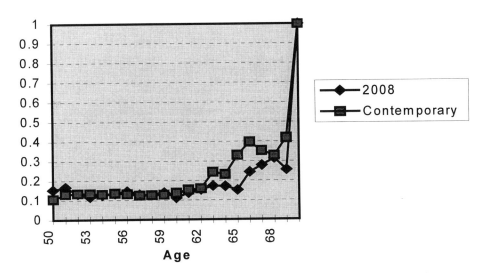

Figure 3. Percent not employed by age: social security with contemporary and 2008 actuarial adjustment. Source: Author's calculations.

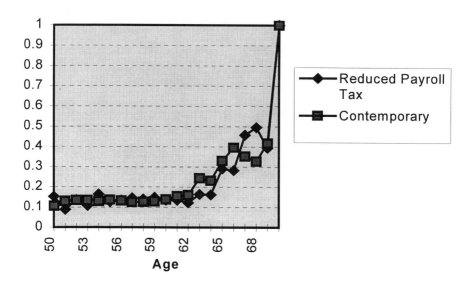

Figure 4. Percent not employed by age: reduced payroll tax bor workers over age 62.
Source: Author's calculations.

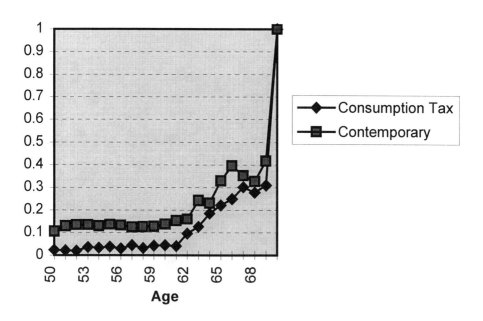

Figure 5. Percent not employed by age: replacing payroll tax with consumption tax.
Source: Author's calculations.

approximately 9.2 percent.[15] For purposes of the simulation, that is translated into a tax of 9 percent on all forms of income; thus the consumption
tax reduces the tax on earnings from 15% to 9% and raises the tax on
nonearned income from 0% to 9%. In Figure 5 the higher line once again
represents the 1995 social security system. The lower line represents the
effect of the consumption tax. The change in financing does, indeed, lead
to an increase in employment at all ages.

Conclusion

Previous research shows that firms respond to adverse demand shocks by
laying off the young and encouraging retirement of the old, and the unemployment insurance program influences these employer responses. Our
research has suggested that social security may have a similar effect on
employer efforts at inducing early retirement.

Our simulation model explores the potential magnitude of this social
security effect. The simulations assume that employers make all retirement
decisions, and that their response to social security is similar to their previously documented response to unemployment insurance. The main result
is that social security could well have a significant effect on employer behavior. Moreover, the pattern of results is sensitive to changes in actuarial
adjustments and alternative financing mechanisms.

Interesting policy questions arise if we view social security as a form of
unemployment insurance. In particular, this perspective leads one to question the use of payroll taxes that fall exclusively on earnings. In the implicit
contract model used here, a payroll tax causes the employer to both shift
compensation from earned to nonearned income (e.g., pensions), and to
increase the probability of nonemployment. This effect could be particularly important for older workers, and it may be useful to consider policies
that reduce such incentives.

A consumption tax is one salient alternative to the payroll tax. Since it falls
on all forms of income, a consumption tax (such as a value added tax)
would not cause employers to shift compensation from earned to nonearned income. It follows that one way to increase the employment of older
workers would be to introduce a small consumption tax on the full population, and simultaneously reduce payroll taxes for workers over 62. Revenues
from the consumption tax could be assigned to the social security Trust
Fund and thereby offset losses from the reduced payroll tax. Indeed, the
consumption tax could be set so as to increase total revenues and thereby
address the long run financial problems of the social security system.

The debate within the recent Advisory Council on Social Security provides another way to think about this paper's policy implications. As described in Chapter 1 of this volume, the Council examined three alternative
proposals for keeping the system in long-run actuarial balance while im-

proving money's worth ratios for younger cohorts. It is interesting to ask how viewing the current social security program as a form of unemployment insurance fits into the debate over these three alternatives.

All three alternatives might be used by workers as a form of old-age unemployment insurance. For example, under the MB alternative, if benefits and taxes were structured so that the program effectively subsidized early receipt, then firms might seek to use the program as a form of unemployment insurance. One might argue that this is less likely for the IA and PSA option. If the individually controlled accounts essentially paid a lump sum benefit (or an actuarially fair annuity) once a person reached a certain age, then — at least in the above model — these accounts would not affect an employer's propensity to induce early retirement. However, both options IA and PSA have components that differ from simple IRA-type accounts (e.g., both provide a minimum benefit to retirees). If such benefits are actuarially unfair (and that seems quite likely in a minimum benefit program), then the incentives examined in this paper could persist for some groups of workers. Thus, under all three alternatives, social security could still be used as a form of unemployment insurance.

It is possible that by reducing incentives to use social security as a form of unemployment insurance, the government could both increase work in the older population and reduce the long-run government budget deficit. Indeed, to the extent that these incentives cause socially inefficient separations, there may exist tax and benefit changes that reduce deadweight losses and shrink the long run deficit without affecting the well-being of either workers or retirees. But a complete discussion of optimal changes and resulting effects on the long run deficit requires additional empirical information on how the social security system influences employer behavior. The simulations presented here suggest that these behavioral effects may be important.

Appendix

This appendix provides details on how actuarial adjustments were analyzed in the simulation model. As noted in the text, people who elect to receive social security benefits before their 65th birthday receive reduced benefits, while people who elect to receive benefits after their 65th birthday receive a delayed retirement credit.

For purposes of the simulation, these rules are operationalized as follows. Let, the annual social security benefit for an individual age A who has worked N years after his 62nd birthday be written as $G(A, N)$, where both A and N are integers. Thus, people who take "normal" retirement at age 65 after working all three years between age 62 and 65 have an annual social security benefit of $G(65,3)$. Given this, for all $62 \leq A \leq 70$ and $0 \leq N \leq A - 62$, let

$$G(A,N) = \beta G(65,3)$$

where

$$\beta = (1 + .06666*(N-3)) \text{ if } N \le 3,$$

$$\beta = (1 + .04500*(N-3)) \text{ if } N > 3.$$

Thus, people who begin receiving social security retirement benefits at age 62 receive a benefit equal to 80 percent of their age 65 "normal retirement" benefit ($G(62,0) = .8G(65,3)$). If they work one year between their 62nd and 65th birthdays (with earnings such that they get zero benefits due to the retirement test), their benefit at age 65 is $G(65,1) = .866*G(65,3)$. Alternatively, if they work four years between their 62nd and 68th birthdays, their benefit at age 68 is $G(68,4) = 1.045*G(65,3)$. A minor complication in this is that if a worker begins receipt at age 62 (say) and then works prior to age 65, benefits are not recalculated until age 65. This too was incorporated into the simulations.

When firms in these simulations decide whether to employ a worker who is age 62 or older, their calculations must include an assessment of expected social security benefits. Employment in the current period not only means forgone social security benefits in the current period, but also higher social security benefits in the future. For purposes of these simulations it is necessary to develop an algorithm for calculating the present value of those future benefits.

Since the workers in this model are no longer employed after their 70th birthday, it is straightforward to compute the present value of social security benefits after that point in time. Consider a worker who, at the time of his 70th birthday, has worked $N(70)$ of the eight years between his 62nd and 70th birthday, where $N(70)$ is an integer between 0 and 8. From that day forward the worker receives a social security benefit of $G\{70,N(70)\}$. Let $B\{70, N(70)\}$ denote the present value of those benefits:

(A.1) $$B\{70, N(70)\} = \sum_{i=70}^{110} (1/(1+r))^{i-70}(l_i/l_{70}) G\{70,N(70)\}$$

where

l_i is the fraction of the birth cohort surviving to exact age i, l_i/l_{70} is the probability of surviving to age i given survival to age 70, and r is the rate at which the firm discounts future costs and benefits.

Now, consider a worker who just celebrated his 69th birthday, having worked $N(69)$ years since turning 62, where $N(69)$ is an integer between 0 and 7. If he is employed over the next year (and does not, in consequence, receive social security benefits) the present value of his social security benefits is

$$((l_{70}/l_{69})/(1+r))*B\{70, N(69)+1\}.$$

If he is not employed over the next year (and consequently receives social security benefits) the present value of his social security benefits is

$$G\{69,N(69)\} + ((l_{70}/l_{69})/(1+r))*B\{70, N(69)\}.$$

Of course, in deciding whether to employ the worker, the firm must take into account this difference in the expected present value of social security benefits. The firm's decision rule on the 69th birthday (after θ is revealed) would be to employ the worker if his value of marginal product exceeds the value of his externally financed consumption, where the value of externally financed consumption is,

(A.2) $z + G\{69,N(69)\} - ((l_{70}/l_{69})/(1+r))*(B\{70, N(69)+1\}-B\{70, N(69)\})$

The final term in this sum is the expected present value of additional social security benefits that result from an additional year of work at age 69 and $N(69)$. This is subtracted from the age 69 social security benefit ($G\{69,N(69)\}$) because the worker essentially forgoes these additional benefits if he does not work at age 69.

At this point it is useful to compute $B\{69,N(69)\}$, the expected present value of social security benefits at age 69 and $N(69)$ before θ is revealed. To do this, one must determine the probability that the worker is employed at age 69 and $N(69)$. But this is just the probability that $S\theta(69)$ exceeds the sum in (A.2). Let $p(\theta(69))$ represent that probability. Since $\theta(69) = \theta(H)$ if $q_{69}(H) \geq .5$ and $\theta(L)$ with if $q_{69}(H) < .5$, and the distribution of q is generated from a uniform distribution, that probability can be computed. Then

$$B\{69, N(69)\} = p(\theta(69))((l_{70}/l_{69})/(1+r)) B\{70, N(69)+1\}$$
$$- (1-p(\theta(69)))(G\{69,N(69)+ ((l_{70}/l_{69})/(1+r))B\{70, N(69)\}).$$

Now, consider a worker who just celebrated his 68th birthday, having worked $N(68)$ years since turning 62, where $N(68)$ is an integer between 0 and 6. If he is employed over the next year (and does not, in consequence, receive social security benefits) the present value of his social security benefits is

$$((l_{69}/l_{68})/(1+r))*B\{69, N(68)+1\}.$$

If he is not employed over the next year (and consequently receives social security benefits) the present value of his social security benefits is

$$G\{68,N(68)\} + ((l_{69}/l_{68})/(1+r))*B\{69, N(68)\}.$$

The firm's decision rule on the 68th birthday (after θ is revealed) would be to employ the worker if his value of marginal product exceeds the value of his externally financed consumption, where the value of externally financed consumption is

(A.3) $z + G\{68,N(68)\} - ((l_{69}/l_{68})/(1+r))*(B\{69, N(68)+1\}-B\{69, N(68)\}).$

This is obviously similar to (A.2). One can then follow the above algorithm to compute $B\{68,N(68), \ldots, B\{62,0\}$.

Given an individual who is age A_0 with years of work N_0, the simulation program first computes $B\{70,N(70)\}$ for all feasible values of $N(70)$. Given that it computes $B\{69,N(69)\}$ for all feasible values of $N(69)$, and so forth back to $B\{A_0,N_0\}$. The worker is then employed if his value of marginal product exceeds $z + G\{A_0, N_0\} - ((l_{A_0}+1/l_{A_0})/(1+r))*(B\{A_0+1, N(A_0)+1\} - B\{A_0+1, N(A_0)\}).$

The author wishes to thank without implicating Gary Fields, Michael Leonesio, Olivia Mitchell, and Steven Sandell for helpful comments and discussions about this chapter.

Notes

1. See for example, Feldstein (1976) and Topel (1983, 1984, 1985).
2. This model has antecedents in Feldstein (1976), Topel (1984), Wright and Hotchkiss (1988), and Burdett and Wright (1989), and is related to the models in Hutchens (1995, 1996).
3. Assume that and $U' > 0$ and $U'' < 0$.
4. No constraints are placed on the range of wages or pensions, thereby permitting contracts where workers make payments to firms.
5. The Lagrangian for this problem is

$$L = \Pi + \int_\theta [\lambda\{EU - EU^*\} + \{\alpha(\theta)(1 - p(\theta)) + \beta(\theta)p(\theta)\}]f(\theta)\,d\theta$$

where λ, $\alpha(\theta)$, and $\beta(\theta)$ are Lagrange multipliers with $p(\theta) < 1$ implying $\alpha(\theta) = 0$ and $p(\theta) > 0$ implying $\beta(\theta) = 0$. The resulting first order conditions are

$$L_{w(\theta)} = -(1+t)p(\theta) + \lambda(1-t)U'(w(\theta)(1-t))p(\theta) = 0,$$

$$L_{b(\theta)} = -(1-p(\theta)) + \lambda U'(b(\theta)+c+z)(1-p(\theta)) = 0,$$

$$L_{p(\theta)} = \theta - w(\theta)(1+t)+b(\theta)+ec + \lambda[U(w(\theta)(1-t))-U(b(\theta)+c+z)] - \alpha(\theta) + \beta(\theta) = 0.$$

These equations must be satisfied for each θ. A similar problem is analyzed in Hutchens (1995).
6. More rigorously, an expansion of the first order condition for the employment

---

probability around the point $t = 0$ yields the following modification of the employment rule in equation 4:

$$\text{If } \theta \geq z + (1-e)c + 2w^*dt \text{ then } p^*(\theta) = 1,$$

$$\text{If } \theta < z + (1-e)c + 2w^*dt \text{ then } p^*(\theta) = 0.$$

Thus, an increase in the payroll tax ($dt > 0$) results in a lower employment probability.

7. Of course, these ideas do not apply to all jobs. Implicit contracts are most likely to arise in situations where a firm and its workers are engaged in repeated interactions over a long period of time, and, in consequence, an implicit contract model of layoffs (or retirements) can only apply to a subset of jobs. Also, the model assumes that employers make all separation decisions, ignoring the reality of employee-initiated separations. Future research should integrate the complex reality of employer-initiated and employee-initiated retirements into a single framework.

8. There is no guarantee that these taxes yield a balanced budget. Any shortfall is made up through a head tax that is assessed when the cohort is born.

9. Of course, age 70 is arbitrary; alternatives would be age 80 or 90. The more interesting and realistic case of gradually diminishing skill is beyond the scope of the present analysis.

10. Recomputation involves nominal earnings (as opposed to indexed earning) after age 60. Thus, the effect of recomputation is complicated. At least one source argues that this effect is in reality usually small. See Steuerle and Bakija (1994: 218).

11. See Rust (1990: 374) for a similar analysis.

12. Note also that α equals zero in the table. Since $q_{ij}(H)$ is the probability of a high realization of θ, and $q_j(L)$ is the probability of a low realization, where $q_j(L) = 1 - q_j(H)$, let $q_j(H) = (1-\alpha)u_j + \alpha \, q_{j-1}(H)$, where u_j is a uniformly distributed error on the unit interval, and $0 \leq \alpha \leq 1$. This specification permits simulations with serially correlated demand shocks. If $\alpha = 0$, $q_j(H)$ is simply a uniformly distributed error term that is independent across periods. If, however, α is greater than zero, $q_j(H)$ is a uniformly distributed error term that exhibits serial correlation. That is useful; it allows one to simulate the effect of demand shocks that influence behavior over more than one period. Since $\alpha = 0$ in all simulations, sensitivity to serial correlation is not explored here.

13. Using CPS data from 1977–81, Topel (1985) finds that elimination of the subsidy due to imperfect experience rating would reduce the monthly unemployment rate from .0516 to .0376. Since the annual rate of unemployment in the March 1978 Current Population Survey was .158, and since the average monthly rate in 1978 was .060, for purposes of the simulation I multiply these numbers by 2.63 = 15.8/6.0. Leon and Rones (1980), Table 1 indicate that the average monthly unemployment rate in 1978 was 6.0. Young (1980), Table 5 indicates that the incidence of unemployment in calendar 1978 was 15.8.

14. Since all workers are born on the same day and have the same expected skill level, the simulations proceed as follows.

1. Just before the workers' 25th birthday, the firm enters into identical lifetime contracts with five workers. Once the ink is dry on the contracts, skill level is revealed. As indicated in Table 2, this is operationalized by drawing five random numbers from a uniform distribution with a lower bound of $23,900 and an upper bound of $38,900.

2. Each year the firm draws an error term from a uniform distribution. As discussed above, the distribution of the error is of the form, $q_j(H) = (1-\alpha)u_j +$

$\alpha q_{j-1}(H)$, where u_j is a uniformly distributed error on the unit interval, and $0 \leq \alpha \leq 1$. If $q_j(H) > .5$ then $\theta_j = \theta(H)$. Otherwise $\theta_j = \theta(L)$.

3. Letting S_i, $i = 1,5$ denote the skill level of the five workers, the firm employs a worker if the value of the worker's marginal product $(S \theta_j)$ exceeds the worker's "externally financed consumption" when not employed $(v_j + (1-e) c + z_j + 2 w_j dt)$.

4. Workers who are not employed receive unemployment insurance if under age 62, social security benefits if over 62, and private payments. Note that workers who receive social security benefits do not receive unemployment insurance benefits.

15. Payroll tax collections for OASDHI in 1994 were $446.3 billion, and personal outlays (disposable income minus savings) were $4,826.5 billion. To raise $446.3 billion, a consumption tax would have to tax personal outlays at a rate of $446.3/4,826.5 = .092$.

References

Bell, Felicitie C., Alice H. Wade, and Stephen C. Goss. *Life Tables for the United States Social Security Area, 1900–2080*. Washington, D.C.: Social Security Administration, Office of the Actuary, August 1992.

Boudreau, John W. "Economic Considerations in Estimating the Utility of Human Resource Productivity Improvement Programs." *Personnel Psychology* 36 (1983): 551–76.

Burdett, Kenneth and Randall Wright. "Unemployment Insurance and Short-Time Compensation: The Effects on Layoffs, Hours per Worker, and Wages." *Journal of Political Economy* 97, 6 (December 1989): 1479.

Casey, Bernard. "Early Retirement: The Problems of 'Instrument Substitution' and 'Cost Shifting'." In Winfried Schmaehl, ed., *Redefining the Process of Retirement: An International Perspective*. Berlin, Heidelberg, New York, London, Paris, Tokyo, Hong Kong: Springer-Verlag, 1989.

Feldstein, Martin. "Temporary Layoffs in the Theory of Unemployment." *Journal of Political Economy* 84 (October 1976): 937–58.

Gregory, Janice M. "Possible Employer Responses to Social Security Reform." This volume.

Hurd, Michael D. "Research on the Elderly: Economic Status, Retirement, and Consumption and Saving." *Journal of Economic Literature* 28, 2 (June 1990): 565.

Hutchens, Robert M. "Social Security Benefits and Employer Behavior: Evaluating Social Security Early Retirement Benefits as a Form of Unemployment Insurance." Cornell University Working Paper, July 1995.

———. "Social Security, Unemployment Insurance, and Employer Induced Early Retirement." Cornell University Working Paper, July 1996.

Leon, Carol Boyd and Philip L. Rones. "Employment and Unemployment During 1979: An Analysis." *Monthly Labor Review* (February 1980): 3–10.

Naschold, Frieder, et al. "The Transition from Working Life to Pensioned Retirement in the Federal Republic of Germany." In Frieder Naschold, and Bert de Vroom, eds., *Regulating Employment and Welfare: Company and National Policies of Labor Force Participation at the End of Worklife in Industrial Countries*. New York and Berlin: Gruyter, 1994.

Rebick, Marcus. "Social Security and Older Workers' Labor Market Responsiveness: The U.S., Sweden, and Japan." In Rebecca M. Blank, ed., *Social Protection Versus Economic Flexibility: Is There A Trade-Off?* Chicago and London: University of Chicago Press, 1994.

Rust, John. "Behavior of Male Workers at the End of the Life Cycle: An Empirical

Analysis of States and Controls." In David A. Wise, ed., *Issues in the Economics of Aging.* Chicago: University of Chicago Press, 1990.

Steuerle, C. Eugene and Jon M. Bakija. *Retooling Social Security for the 21st Century: Right and Wrong Approaches to Reform.* Washington, D.C.: Urban Institute Press, 1994.

Topel, Robert H. "Experience Rating of Unemployment Insurance and the Incidence of Unemployment." *Journal of Law and Economics* 27, 1 (April 1984): 61–90.

———. "On Layoffs and Unemployment Insurance." *American Economic Review* 73, 4 (September 1983): 541–59.

———. "Unemployment and Unemployment Insurance." *Research in Labor Economics* (Greenwich, Conn.: JAI Press) 7 (1985): 91–135.

Winter-Ebmer, Rudolf. "Benefit Duration and Unemployment Entry: Quasi-Experimental Evidence for Austria." University of Linz, Austria, 1996.

Wright, Randall and Julie Hotchkiss. "A General Model of Unemployment Insurance With and Without Short-Time Compensation." *Research in Labor Economics* 9 (1988): 91–131.

Young, Anne McDougall. "Work Experience of the Population in 1978." *Monthly Labor Review* (March 1980): 43–47.

III
Political and Practical Considerations Regarding Social Security Reform

Chapter 12
Compliance in Social Security Systems Around the World

Joyce Manchester

J26

H55

H26

(selected countries)

How can social security programs best be structured to encourage participation while at the same time promoting the goals of old-age insurance within an efficient and equitable system? If workers do not perceive the need to pay into the government-sponsored pension system to provide financial stability in old age, and if the tax authority cannot persuade them of the desirability of doing so, evasion can result. Tax collection agencies will then collect less revenue than they should, tax rates must be higher with corresponding labor market effects, and some people will not have adequate resources in old age. In addition, the economy may suffer efficiency losses because people adjust their behavior to escape paying the tax. National saving may be depressed and development of financial markets may lag, with deleterious effects on growth.

This chapter examines the problem of noncompliance in social security systems from the perspective of the economy, the individual, and the tax administrator. We then present evidence on the extent of noncompliance in the United States, Germany, and a range of developing countries. Several lessons emerge that could inform the policy debate in the United States. We conclude with suggestions for social security reform targeted to the problem of evasion, some of which are pertinent to the proposals offered by the recent Advisory Council on Social Security.

Evasion in Social Security Programs

The term "tax evasion" can be broadly defined to include tax avoidance as well as flagrant refusal to abide within the law. In the context of social security programs, examples of evasion include sheltering part, but not all, of income from payroll tax, avoiding the tax by not working or by working in the informal sector, or retiring early so as not to pay the tax. In each case, workers or their employers change behavior in response to the social security program. Such behavioral changes instigated by the tax system result in some loss for the economy. Economists refer to such a loss as an "efficiency loss," since resources are no longer put to their best use. Hence tax avoidance as well as tax evasion imply that the economy does not produce as much as it could otherwise.

In general, tax evaders face some risk of being identified and fined, and the economy also suffers from the revenue loss. In some cases, evaders may still benefit from public services provided by the government, such as national defense, highways, and education. In the case of social security, however, evaders may be shut out from the system, or may only receive partial social benefits in their old age. Though such treatment may be deserved, a young working person may not look far enough ahead to realize the consequences of not participating in the system today. In other words, evasion within social security systems can have more serious consequences for individuals than evasion within the general tax system.

The structure of social security systems sometimes invites evasion, though not always intentionally. Social security programs usually levy payroll taxes on earnings at a constant rate, up to a maximum level of earnings and with no exemptions. Generally, social security taxes are not levied on non-wage compensation (e.g., health insurance, provision of a car, subsidized cafeteria lunches) or capital income, and most countries allow the self-employed either to decide the amount of their contribution or to contribute on a voluntary basis. On the expenditure side, social security old-age benefits generally take the form of a flat amount plus an amount proportional to past earnings. Conventional defined-benefit formulas typically provide benefits based on the number of years of contribution and the average wage over the last few years before retirement. When the last few years of work matter for the benefit received, or when a spouse's employment history has little bearing on eventual benefits, people may change their behavior to avoid the payment of contributions.

Why Be Concerned About Evasion?

Evasion is a problem for the economy at large, for the individual, and for a nation's tax administration system. Eliminating evasion completely might not be desirable even if it were possible, but many countries would enjoy greater production, faster growth, and better protection for their elderly populations if they increased compliance in their social security systems.

The Economy-Wide Perspective

Noncompliance or evasion leads to three negative effects for the economy at large. First, evasion results in lost revenues and larger distortions in labor markets, because higher tax rates are needed to get the same revenue. The economy produces less than its potential because people work less, apply for disability pensions more readily, and retire early. These problems are currently serious for many Central and Eastern European countries. Second, when the informal sector is less productive than the formal sector, aggregate output is reduced as well. Evidence from several Latin American countries supports this view. And third, national saving may be lower than under full compliance because most workers who evade probably cannot or will not save on their own. More discussion on each point follows.

Labor market distortions and efficiency losses. Analysts identify two components of the loss in well-being, or "deadweight loss," associated with distortions in labor markets due to payroll taxes. First, a distortion arises when individuals do not understand the link between social security contributions and benefits (Auerbach and Kotlikoff 1987). For example, complex benefit rules and differences among individuals in the implicit rate of return on contributions may lead workers to disregard the link between their contributions and anticipated benefits. At the extreme, people may treat the payroll tax as a pure tax for which nothing is received in return. In this case, a shift to "notional accounts" that are individual accounts but still under the pay-as-you-go framework could eliminate the deadweight loss. Under a tax system that combines lump-sum taxes and notional accounts, individuals would perceive no net tax at the margin, though the rate of return could be very low.

The second component of deadweight loss concerns the loss in well-being that occurs when contributions to the social security system earn the rate of growth of the economy in a pay-as-you-go system, rather than the higher market return on capital in a privatized system. Feldstein and Samwick (1996) argue that current benefits in the U.S. social security system could be paid for with a contribution rate of only 1.96 percent of payroll, rather than the current 12.4 percent, if contributions were invested at the private market rate of return rather than in the pay-as-you-go system. Hence the deadweight loss from social security arises from the extra 10.44 percentage points of the payroll tax. Feldstein and Samwick estimate this deadweight loss to be equivalent to 2.5 percent of earnings, or about 1 percent of GDP. After accounting for the transition costs involved in pre-funding a new privatized system, the deadweight loss of social security is calculated to be worth 1.57 percent of taxable payroll, or about 0.6 percent of GDP.

This sort of calculation would not necessarily apply to regions of the world in which large informal labor markets operate. Here, high payroll taxes induce informal-sector work where social security taxes are not collected. In such cases, spendable income and future retirement benefits obtained from working in the formal sector must be compared with spendable income (including possible penalties if detected) and lack of retirement benefits obtained from working in the informal sector. Both of these must be compared with the rewards to leisure. Hence the economic problem becomes much more complicated and depends, for example, on how people respond to the risk of being fined if caught evading the tax (Cowell 1985; Slemrod 1996).

Output losses. Evasion can result in output losses for the economy directly if the informal sector is less productive than the formal sector, due to a lower capital/labor ratio in the former. Evidence from developing countries suggests that formal sector production is, in fact, more capital-intensive than production in the informal sector (Corsetti 1994; Schmidt-Hebbel 1996). The distribution of firms according to factor intensities ranges from large and highly capital-intensive formal-sector enterprises in manufacturing, mining, and utilities, to the urban street vendors and the rural small landholders who work with little or no capital and often represent the core of the informal economy. For example, an average formal-sector worker in Peru works with US$30,000 of capital, but informal sector workers have capital worth only $1,000 (Castiglia, Martinez, and Mezzera, cited in Schmidt-Hebbel 1996).

Markedly different capital-labor ratios by sector imply that factor reallocation from the labor-intensive informal sector to the capital-intensive formal sector in response to reducing the tax wedge of social security taxes would reduce wages and increase interest rates in the economy at large. Lower wages and higher interest rates would benefit retired cohorts and hurt future generations. However, such an effect seems to be offset empirically by future efficiency gains arising from shifting resources toward the formal sector, augmented by possible efficiency gains in capital markets and pension system management. Evidence suggests that the efficiency gain accruing to all generations may be very large because managerial and technical skills seem to be disproportionately concentrated in formal production sectors of developing economies. Significant further efficiency gains due to pension reform could be reaped from capital-market deepening and adopting a pension system with tax-benefit linkage managed by the private sector, as argued by the recent literature on pension reforms (World Bank 1994; Corsetti 1994; Holzmann 1997).

Saving effects. If social security contributions represent forced saving (i.e., individuals would not save the mandated proportion of earnings unless compelled to do so), then aggregate saving falls occurs when individuals evade the social security tax. This saving effect is easy to see when the social security system is funded. In a defined contribution pension scheme in which individuals are required to save 10 percent of their earnings in an individual account, for example, aggregate saving is less when workers evade the contributions unless they save at least as much on their own. But low-income workers in the informal sector would likely not save as much independently. Hence aggregate saving falls and future growth of the economy may be depressed as a result of evasion.

One exception to the negative relationship between evasion and aggregate saving might occur in a purely pay-as-you-go system, in which participants save less for retirement because they expect social security to provide benefits. The pay-as-you-go nature implies that no accumulation of funds takes place within the social security system, because current contributions are spent on current benefits. Those who do not participate would likely save more for retirement on their own, so aggregate saving could be greater when evasion occurs. Partial offset would occur, however, because participants would have to pay a higher contribution rate to make up for the reduction of revenue from the evaders, and some of that higher contribution would have gone to increased private saving if payroll taxes had been lower.

Even in a pay-as-you-go system, however, noncompliance may reduce aggregate saving if the incentives of the program induce strategic behavior. For instance, some social security programs require beneficiaries to contribute for a minimum number of years to qualify for a pension. Workers who participate in the formal sector for the minimum number of years, and then evade payroll taxes for the remainder of their working lives, may receive the same level of benefits as those who remain in the formal sector. Those minimum benefits are financed out of higher payroll taxes on participants, again reducing national saving. In a second example of strategic behavior, a second earner in a married couple may not need to contribute to social security at all to qualify for benefits. In the United States, for example, the second earner receives 50 percent of the first earner's benefit without contributing. Evasion by these second earners, who may choose to work in the informal sector or to conceal their earnings from the tax authority, again requires higher payroll taxes on participants to provide benefits for all eligible individuals.

Solvency effects. Evasion can also have consequences for the long-term viability of a social security system. In a pay-as-you-go system, evasion leads to higher contribution rates for those who do contribute. Consequent increased distortions in labor markets lead to even more evasion. Eventually, such a system could collapse. In a defined contribution system with individual accounts, however, retirees receive only the value of their contributions (plus earnings) over their working years. Those who do not contribute cannot later claim benefits, thereby lessening the financial strain on the system.

The Participant's Perspective

From the participant's perspective, the question is whether the promise of old-age benefits from the social security system warrants making contributions when young (Bailey and Turner 1997). Those who have a high discount rate, meaning that they value a dollar of consumption today more highly than a dollar of consumption in the future, and those who are myopic and simply do not concern themselves with the future, may choose not to contribute to the social security program. Those with little or no confidence in the tax administrator or the government may choose not to participate as well. Those who do not perceive a link between contributions today and benefits tomorrow or who see better rates of return elsewhere may find preferred uses for their dollars. High inflation may erode promised benefits, reducing credibility in the system. And an individual with a low life expectancy may conclude that the annuity provided by social security is not a good deal. As a result, some of these individuals will be vulnerable in old age due to lack of full participation at younger ages. High penalties if caught or strong aversion to breaking the law may deter some from evading the system.

The problem of noncompliance is not limited to developing countries. In the United States, 42 percent of all returns had some understatement of taxable income in 1979 (Slemrod and Bakija 1996). When asked about their past tax compliance behavior, about one-quarter of taxpayers responded that they failed to comply at some point within the past five years. Because of tax evasion, some people pay less tax than they should, and everyone else pays more.

Of course, what matters for labor supply and the decision to stay in the formal labor market is the marginal tax rate on total compensation, not just the marginal tax rate arising from the payroll tax on wages received. Total compensation includes employee benefits such as health insurance and pension benefits as well as payroll taxes paid by the employer. Since such benefits are excluded from tax in many countries, the "effective" marginal tax on total compensation is often much less than the statutory tax rate on wages. For example, in Albania the statutory payroll tax rate in 1979 was 31.7 percent, while the effective payroll tax rate was just 19.5 percent; in Croatia, the tax rate was 22 percent, but the effective rate was just 12.4 percent (Andrews and Rashid 1996).

Moreover, the payroll tax is only one component of the total marginal tax on earnings. The overall tax wedge includes employees' and employers' social security contributions as well as personal income taxes and consumption taxes. Calculating social security contributions and income taxes by applying tax rules to the level of earnings of an average production worker, the average overall tax wedge for European OECD countries was 63.1 percent, while the average for Australia, Canada, Japan, the United Kingdom, and the United States was 39.8 percent (OECD 1993).

The Tax Administrator's Perspective

Tax administration plays a crucial role in influencing attitudes toward tax evasion and enforcing the rules. An agency's ability to collect taxes depends on organization, institutional infrastructure, and operations, including access to sufficient financing. But it also depends on cultural factors, economic conditions, and legal mandates (Vazques-Caro and Reid 1992). When the employer withholds payroll taxes directly, managing those transactions becomes important and depends heavily on record-keeping by employers.

Countries have adopted different strategies to facilitate and monitor taxpayer compliance and to collect the information required by a social security system. In Argentina, for example, the banking sector acts as the tax collector and reports to the government tax administrator. In Germany, by contrast, social security taxes are collected by the public health system and transferred to the public pension insurance institutions. Then the public pension institutions conduct on-site supervision of both the health system and employers to determine whether contributions were collected correctly. In Lithuania, the revenue and data collection systems for social insurance taxes and income taxes are separate. In the United Kingdom and Ireland, revenue collection occurs in one agency, while separate agencies have responsibility for inspection and enforcement. In the United States, the Social Security Administration is charged with identifying those who are delinquent in paying contributions. But the Internal Revenue Service has responsibility for collecting taxes, auditing taxpayers, and enforcing payment.

Insight from the theoretical literature. Economic studies of tax compliance use principal-agent models to model the interaction between the taxpayer and the tax collector (Reinganum and Wilde 1985). In this framework, a tax collector (the principal) is allowed to act strategically, basing its audit rules on the information it receives from taxpayers (the agents). At the same time, audit policies of the tax agency affect taxpayer reporting decisions, with higher audit probabilities generally leading to less evasion. Groups that are audited most heavily may nevertheless show the highest rates of evasion, despite the deterrent effect of audits, because the tax collector has information identifying those groups as likely evaders.

Other studies focus on the fact that not all evasion is detected, and that not all taxpayers respond to incentives to evade (Feinstein 1991). Auditors differ in their ability or willingness to determine the size of the "true" tax base, and taxpayers may be differentially able to disguise their "true" tax liability. Federal income tax evasion in the United States was estimated to be almost 2 percent of GDP in 1991 (Alm 1996), but econometric analysis suggests that only about one-half of tax evasion is detected (Feinstein 1991).

Beyond the financial incentives influencing taxpayer reporting decisions emphasized in the economics literature, other factors play an important role and have been studied in the sociology, psychology, and legal literatures on tax compliance (Cowell 1990). Improving a tax agency's public image and its treatment of taxpayers may go a long way toward increasing compliance. Hence explaining different behavior across countries may not be possible by looking at financial incentives of the social security system alone.

Often evasion is intertwined with the problem of bureaucratic corruption in tax administration (Schleifer and Vishny 1993). One analysis finds that a rise in the tax rate produces lower net revenue, when some proportion of the auditors are corrupt and enforcement costs are nonzero. In this case, it may actually be more cost effective for the government to lower audit probabilities and allow some cheating (Gang, Goswami, and Sanyal 1996). If corruption is low enough, however, revenues garnered from capturing people cheating may exceed those from choosing an audit structure in which everyone declares their true income.

How Bad Is the Problem of Tax Evasion?

Evidence from a few developed and developing countries highlights specific tax evasion problems under existing social security programs.

Developed Countries

On the whole, evasion is not believed to be a major concern in the United States, although the growing presence of self-employed individuals may alter that perception in the future. In 1987, the tax gap for social security and Medicare taxes, meaning the amount that was not paid, was estimated at $34 billion in 1997 dollars, or 0.5 percent of GDP (see Table 1). Unpaid taxes among the self-employed accounted for 65 percent of the total. The overall noncompliance rate for U.S. social security and Medicare taxes, defined as the aggregate amount of the tax liability not paid voluntarily as a percentage of the "true" tax liability, was 11.0 percent in 1987. The noncompliance rate was just 4.5 percent for social security and Medicare taxes paid through employers (FICA taxes). In 1997, the employment tax gap was estimated at $50 billion (Internal Revenue Service 1993).

Among the 10 percent of workers who are self-employed, however, the noncompliance rate is much higher, at about 55 percent in 1987. Such a high noncompliance rate among the self-employed suggests that evasion is an issue for social security even in the United States, and the IRS admits that the estimates may be underestimates of the "true" tax gap. One reason the estimates may be too low is that there is an unknown number of nonfilers of all types of employment tax returns. Another reason is that people may underpay the self-employed social security tax.

Available evidence indicates that U.S. noncompliance may be concentrated among women workers. The proportion of working women reporting self-employment earnings rose from 3 percent to 7 percent between 1975 and 1992, and now represents more than 4 million women (Social Security Administration 1995). The proportion of working women who reported being self-employed on the job held longest during the calendar year grew from 4.1 percent to 6.7 percent between 1975 and 1990 (Devine 1994). Self-employed women tend to be middle-aged, with about two-thirds of them

TABLE 1. Estimates of the Social Security and Medicare Tax Gaps and
Noncompliance Rate, 1987 and 1997

	1987	1997
Gross tax gap (billions of 1997 $)	34.1	49.7
FICA	12.0	18.1
Reporting gap	4.1	7.6
Remittance gap	7.7	10.5
SECA		
Reporting gap	22.1	31.6
Noncompliance rate (percent)	11.1	10.3
FICA	4.5	4.2
SECA	55.7	58.7
Net tax gap (billions of 1997 $)	28.8	42.5
FICA	6.8	11.1
SECA	22.1	31.4

Source: Internal Revenue Service (1993). These are Alternative I estimates, based on the
"recommendations" of IRS examiners. Alternative II estimates, based on amounts eventually
assessed, are slightly smaller. The gross tax gap is the aggregate amount of that year's tax
liability that is not paid voluntarily and timely. The noncompliance rate is the gross tax gap as a
percentage of "true" tax liability. The net tax gap is the amount of the gross tax gap remaining
after IRS enforcement activities. FICA refers to the Federal Insurance Contributions Act mandating social security and Medicare taxes for employees who work for employers. SECA refers
to the Self-Employment Contributions Act, mandating social security and Medicare taxes for
self-employed workers.

between the ages of 30 and 54 in 1992, compared with 55 percent of all
working women in this age group. One in 10 employed women over the age
of 35 was self-employed in her main job in 1990. Moreover, self-employed
women tend to be clustered around the low end of the income distribution.
More than three-quarters of those women reported earnings of less than
$18,000 in 1992, and more than half reported earnings of less than $8,400.
Fully 75 percent of women who were self-employed in their main job were
married with a spouse present, meaning that if they paid the full 12.4 percent self-employment tax for social security, but planned on collecting benefits through a spouse, their full contribution was likely to be viewed as a pure
tax (Feldstein and Samwick 1996).

By contrast, evasion does not appear to be an important problem in the
German pension system. This is the result of a tight network and cross-check
system connecting the databases of the Tax Authorities, the Labor Office,
and the health, unemployment, and pension insurance system (Queisser
1996). Even minor employment contracts not subject to social insurance
contributions are registered to verify total earnings per person and insurance exemption. Social insurance coverage is also seen to be in the in-

terest of employees, particularly because family members are covered by government-provided health insurance at no extra charge. Since social insurance coverage is comprehensive, workers are automatically enrolled in pension and unemployment insurance as well. Contributions are collected by approximately 1,200 statutory sickness funds and then transferred to the respective pension insurance institutions. The sickness funds are reimbursed by the pension system for collection costs. Public pension institutions conduct on-site supervision of both sickness funds and employers to determine whether contributions are collected correctly. About one-fifth of all German employers were audited in 1994, and only 5 percent of employers were found to have contributed less than the mandated contributions.

Germany does face a serious financing problem in its social security program because so many people retire early or qualify for disability benefits at an early age. Hence a large discrepancy exists between the system dependency ratio and the population dependency ratio. While these early retirees and disabled persons are generally not labeled evaders, because they are acting within the law, the conditions for qualifying for early benefits may have to be changed to preserve the long-run viability of the system.

Developing Countries

In many developing countries, the ratio of pension system contributors to the size of the total labor force is 40 percent or less (see Table 2). Informal labor markets play a prominent role in these economies, and the structure of labor markets often leads to frequent unemployment or underemployment. Low compliance rates in the face of aging populations imply high contribution rates for those who remain in the system, and may portend shrinking benefits for those who expect to receive old-age support.

Measuring social security evasion in developing countries, however, is tricky business. Some analysts point to the ratio of the number of people who currently contribute to the pension system relative to the number of people who participate in the pension system, meaning that they have contributed at one time. However, many countries do not require the self-employed, those temporarily unemployed, or students to contribute to the system. For example, the ratio of active pension contributors to system participants is only around 50 percent in Chile, suggesting that many people are avoiding contributions by working in the informal system (Campbell 1994). But Chile does not require the self-employed, military personnel, and several other categories of working-age individuals to contribute. A careful study of evasion in Chile found that over 95 percent of those required to contribute to the Chilean pension scheme do so (Chamorro 1992). Such high compliance may in part result from a careful system of cross-checks that includes car dealers and other retailers. Nevertheless, it remains true that people may join the informal labor market to avoid paying

TABLE 2. Ratio of Public Pension Scheme Contributors to the Labor Force in Major
World Regions, Late 1980s to Early 1990s

	Percent
OECD countries	93.9
Latin America and Caribbean	38.3
Middle East and North Africa	41.3
Asia	23.5
Sub-Saharan Africa	6.4

Source: World Bank (1994), Table A.4. Note: Unweighted averages.

TABLE 3. System Dependency Ratios and Demographic Old Age Dependency
Ratios, 1992

	System Dependency Ratio	*Demographic Old Age*
Czech Republic	49	32
Hungary	59	36
Poland	49	28
Russia	46	31
USA	31	30
Switzerland	43	34

Source: Vittas and Michelitsch (1995). Note: The system dependency ratio is the number of
pensioners, including widows, orphans and disability pensioners, divided by the number of
contributors. The demographic old age dependency ratio is the number of people 60 years and
over divided by the number ages 20 through 59.

the contribution to the pension system. The share of the informal sector in
Chile is estimated to be about 18 percent of gross domestic product (GDP)
and has grown to more than half of GDP in some Latin American countries
(Loayza 1994).

Countries with only small percentages of working age people contributing to the social security system face increased revenue pressures both now
and in the future. For example, in Romania, half of the working age population contributes to the social security system, while 75 percent of the working age population is employed (Andrews and Rashid 1996). As a result, the
revenues flowing into the social security system are not as high as they might
be. And as these non-participants age, some of them will require public
assistance. The magnitude of the problem is suggested by the divergence
between the system dependency ratio and the demographic old age dependency ratio (see Table 3). In Hungary, for example, the ratio of pensioners
to contributors is 59 percent, although the ratio of people age 60 and over to
the working age population is just 36 percent.

Two diverse ways of dealing with this problem are illustrated by Chile and
Argentina. In Chile, all elderly people are eligible to receive a minimum

level of social assistance that is means tested, whether they have contributed to the pension scheme or not. Those who have contributed to the pension system for at least 20 years are guaranteed a more generous minimum pension, since the government will "top off" the individual's pension account. Both the social assistance and the minimum pension are financed out of general revenues, where the tax base is more broadly based than the payroll tax. In Argentina, by contrast, the elderly receive a flat benefit only if they have contributed to the pension system for a minimum of 30 years. Those who have contributed less than 30 years get social assistance only. Flat benefits are financed out of the payroll tax, implying that the tax burden falls disproportionately on groups with lower earnings.

Brazil illustrates the important role that policy reform and central record-keeping can play in reducing evasion. In the early 1990's, Brazil's pay-as-you-go scheme offered rather generous benefits for both pensioners (after just 6 years of affiliation, increasing to 15 years in 2012) and disabled persons (after only one year of affiliation), replacing between 75 and 100 percent of the individual's average salary (World Bank 1995). Contribution rates to support the social insurance system in 1992 were as high as 45 percent. On top of the payroll tax, the tax rate on corporate profits was about 50 percent, of which 10 percent went to the social security system. In part as a response to these conditions, half the labor force worked in the informal sector, but over half of the labor force qualified for pensions. In some parts of Brazil, applicants for benefits need only supply self-maintained evidence of annual contributions to the social security system, leaving open the real possibility of counterfeit credentials. It is therefore hardly surprising to see a large discrepancy between the social insurance dependency rate (40 percent) and the population dependency rate (15 percent). Moreover, a recent crackdown on fraudulent receipt of benefits in the state of Rio found that 10 percent of benefits were paid to dead beneficiaries. Central record-keeping would enhance participation in the system and rein in undeserved benefit payouts. In addition, moving to a system in which contributions over a longer working period are more closely linked to benefits would encourage participation in the system.

Recent experience in the Ukraine demonstrates how structural change in the economy can sometimes wreak havoc with a national pension system. Following the fall of the Soviet empire, GDP in the Ukraine fell 45 percent and real wages fell to about 37 percent of their 1990 levels. Prior to 1990, evasion in the government-sponsored pension system did not exist, since the state-owned enterprises paid the 32.5 percent contribution to the state and workers complied with their one percent contribution. As real wages dropped and firms began to focus on maximizing profits, however, the old-age pension system came under great strains. Pension fund revenues declined sharply, while the number of beneficiaries rose. According to a 1995 household survey, more than one-third of Ukrainian respondents allocate time to occupations best seen as informal, including working on land plots (Fallon, Hoopengardner, and Libanova 1996; Riboud and Chu 1996).

The prevalence of informal sector activity together with retirement at early ages imply that the pension system in its current form is not sustainable in the Ukraine. Men can receive a full pension at age 60 if they have worked 25 years in covered employment, and women can receive a full pension at age 55 if they have worked 20 years in covered employment. Those without the requisite number of years in covered employment but older than the normal retirement age can receive a social pension, equal to 18 percent of the average wage. But these promises probably cannot be kept: the system dependency ratio (the ratio of pensioners to contributors) is now about 120 percent, while the population dependency ratio (those age 60+ divided by those age 20–59) is just 49 percent. In addition, the share of employment in the formal sector (now 60 percent) may continue to decline for three reasons. First, as financing shortages have hit the system, pension benefits have been so compressed that the link between contributions and benefits is now extremely weak. Second, high payroll taxes encourage employers and employees to evade tax payments. Third, expansion of self-employment and the private sector as state-owned enterprises shrink will probably increase the size of the informal sector. Simulations suggest that the current pension system would be sustainable only if the share of the formal sector were to remain constant (Riboud and Chu 1996), but this is unlikely, so major changes will be needed in the structure of the Ukrainian pension system.

Concern about working women who are self-employed is not unique to highly industrialized countries, as illustrated by Turkey. In that country, women comprise 12.5 percent of self-employed workers, whereas they represent just 10.2 percent of workers employed by others, not including civil servants (Bag-Kur Statistical Yearbook 1994). Large percentages of self-employed women outside the social security system may mean less saving for the economy today, and more dependence on social assistance for these women in retirement.

Will Changing Incentives Cause People to Change Their Behavior?

A key question that must be answered when seeking to reduce pension system evasion is whether people would move out of the informal sector and start paying contributions if the pension scheme were to be reformed. Little direct evidence to answer this question is available, though related information appears promising. Research in Brazil recently found that, regardless of gender or age, an increase in payroll taxes reduced the probability of contributing to the social insurance system (World Bank 1994). If these elasticities also work in the other direction, then reducing payroll tax rates should increase contributions to social security. For workers age 30 to 39, the responsiveness was substantial (elasticities of one for both men and women).

Other experience also suggests ways to reduce tax evasion. For example, India undertook an extensive overhaul of its income tax system in 1985–86. Prior to the reform, taxes on individuals were based on a schedule with eight tax brackets and a maximum marginal tax rate over 61 percent. After the reform, the number of tax brackets was reduced to four and the maximum marginal tax rate was reduced to 50 percent. At the same time, the tax base was broadened by limiting tax concessions in the areas of individual saving, business investment, and depreciation provisions. Following the reform, revenue gains were attributed to the induced decrease in tax evasion (Das-Gupta and Gang 1996). But tax evasion declined as a response to both rate reduction and more assiduous income-tax enforcement. Conversely, tax evasion appeared to be relatively insensitive to reform efforts. This implies that base-broadening efforts should be complemented by reforms designed to strengthen tax administration and raise enforcement capacity. Reforms of the tax base had less effect on the tax base of upper income groups compared with lower income groups, due to the increased propensity of upper income groups to use tax shelters.

Recent experience on tax reform efforts in Argentina is less promising. Contribution rates for social security were cut 16 percent at the end of 1995, but no change in evasion was observed in the year immediately following the change; in fact, revenues fell by approximately 16 percent. Some observers explain this behavior by noting that many workers may have seen the lowered contribution rate as temporary, because the pension system is running such large deficits. Whether the decline in contribution rates will have a noticeable impact on evasion after several years remains to be seen.

Options for Curbing Evasion in Social Security Programs

Reducing evasion in social security programs around the world has been discussed in several recent contexts (World Bank 1994; Mitchell and Fields 1995; James 1997). One proposal is to make the pension system itself more efficient, equitable, and better administered. A mandatory pension program for all workers would avoid the problems of adverse selection inherent in a voluntary system, and would take advantage of the benefits of forced saving for individuals as well as the economy. Overly generous benefit levels risk imposing unreasonable contribution rates on workers. Recognizing that the link between benefits and contributions must be clear to all workers, defined contribution plans are more transparent than defined benefit plans, but notional accounts or other accounting devices could have similar incentive effects. Pension benefits paid only to those who have paid into the system for a given number of years and only after a certain age encourage participation. Both the number of contributing years and the age limit should be chosen with care to fit the structure of labor markets and the demographic characteristics of the country. The laws regarding disability benefits must be designed carefully to avoid easy access to disability benefits in lieu of qualifying for pension benefits. To protect those who do not qualify for the pension plan, a single anti-poverty program should apply to all individuals.

In addition, it must be recognized that some developing or transition countries may choose to exempt large segments of the working population from the mandatory scheme for social security, perhaps because enforcing compliance among the informal sector is too difficult. Nevertheless, in this event, both the economy and the exempted individuals will miss out on some important benefits. The economy will not reap the rewards of a higher saving rate that leads to more investment and greater output. Individuals outside the system will be at the mercy of politicians to provide a minimum level of social assistance in their old age, with benefits derived from general tax revenues or debt finance. This too imposes an extra burden on the next generation of workers.

Along with social security policy reforms must come better tax administration and enforcement to encourage confidence in the system, transparency in its operations, functional independence, and financial accountability (Reid and Mitchell 1995). Fewer people and businesses would evade, no doubt, if record-keeping were more mechanical. Less corruption would probably result if employers' records had to undergo the scrutiny of cross-checks and audits.

Some controversial social security reforms would target the problem of evasion in specific groups. First, sharing the contributions of married couples rather than granting an automatic spousal benefit would remove the incentive not to pay social security taxes on the lower-earning spouse's earnings. In systems that award benefits based on earnings or contributions, whether they be notional accounts systems or defined contribution plans, the earnings or contributions of married couples could be combined in a single account and then split evenly at the time of retirement. This type of "earning sharing" or "contribution sharing" for married couples would alleviate the pure tax on the earnings of second earners in systems that automatically award benefits to wives based on the husband's earnings history. Such a scheme would also go a long way toward providing benefits for part-time workers or stay-at-home parents who take care of the family while the other spouse works outside the home. Particularly in a country such as the United States where divorce rates are so high, earning sharing would mean that women would be less likely to end their lives in poverty.

A second potential reform might be to levy lower payroll tax rates on workers under age 25. This could reduce the temptation for employers to hire younger people "off the books" while they are in entry jobs and receiving training. Because the payroll tax is generally set as a flat rate, it represents a large percentage of the low wages typically received by these younger workers. Implementing such a policy in developing countries could reduce the size of the informal sector, and even in developed countries, reduced payroll taxes for younger workers could enhance youthful compliance and set the stage for compliance throughout their working years.

A third idea is to have governments match tax contributions for workers with wages under a minimum level, rather than setting a single contribution rate across all workers. The Mexican government contributes one peso per day to the accounts of all contributors, and the Czech Republic has a small matching scheme as well. To target low-wage workers, governments might contribute one-quarter of the payroll tax for workers at the minimum wage, and one-eighth of the payroll tax for workers at 1.25 times the minimum wage, phasing out to no matching contribution at 1.5 times the minimum wage. Encouraging people to participate in the social security system could be less expensive for the government than covering all of social assistance for nonparticipants in their old age and could dramatically reduce evasion.

Finally, some countries have chosen to establish separate social security systems for the self-employed with lower contribution rates; of course, retirement benefits are commensurably lower as well. The rationale for such treatment is that the self-employed sometimes perceive that they are unduly burdened with both halves of the payroll tax, though most evidence indicates that the employer share of payroll taxes is borne by the employee in the form of lower wages (Gruber 1995).

Conclusion

Social security evasion occurs when participants perceive taxes paid will generate little or no payoff in the future. It also occurs when workers value extra pay today more heavily than future benefits in retirement, and when they can earn better rates of return by investing by themselves in private markets. In these cases, the social security tax becomes distortionary, and people try to avoid or evade paying the contribution. Social security administrators face a difficult task, particularly when they lack the resources and/or the political will to detect and punish noncompliance, yet they are responsible for paying promised benefits. Corruption and fraud among tax administrators and tax collectors are also sometimes problems.

No single policy prescription will eliminate evasion in all social security programs. But careful design can encourage participation in the system, thereby helping to assure long-term solvency of the system, desirable effects on saving, labor supply and output, and popular support. Encouraging compliance is an important concern for social security reform in the United States. Serious enforcement and the attitude of taxpayers and administrators also play important roles. But striving for a balance between enforcement and tolerance is essential. Public as well as private costs of enforcement must be weighted against other policy goals such as fairness, efficiency, and transparency. Maintaining credibility in the government social security program depends on the willingness of taxpayers to forgo wages today to receive benefits in the future.

The author gratefully acknowledges support from the World Bank, where she was a Visiting Fellow while writing an earlier version of this chapter. The views expressed are those of the author alone and not those of the Congressional Budget Office or the World Bank. The author would like to thank Olivia Mitchell as well as Anita Schwarz, David Lindeman, Estelle James, Kent Smetters, Jan Walliser, and many others involved in pensions at the World Bank for helpful discussions.

References

Alm, James. "Explaining Tax Compliance." In Susan Pozo, ed., *Exploring the Underground Economy*. Kalamazoo, Mich.: W. E. Upjohn Institute, 1996: 103–28.

Andrews, Emily S. and Mansoora Rashid. "The Financing of Pension Systems in Central and Eastern Europe: An Overview of Major Trends and Their Determinants, 1990–1993." Technical Paper 339. Washington, D.C.: World Bank, 1996.

Auerbach, Alan and Laurence Kotlikoff. *Dynamic Fiscal Policy*. Oxford University Press, 1987.

Bag-Kur (Social Security Organization of Self-Employed Persons) *Statistical Yearbook*. Turkey. 1994.

Bailey, Clive and John Turner. "Contribution Evasion and Social Security." Geneva: International Labour Office, 1997.

Campbell, G. R. "Chilean Government Worried by Pension Fund Noncompliance." *IBIS Review* (September 1994): 14–17.

Chamorro, Claudio. "La cobertura del sistema de pensiones chileno." Dissertation, Santiago: Catholic University of Chile, 1992.

Corsetti, Giancarlo. "An Endogenous Growth Model of Social Security and the Size of the Informal Sector." *Revista de Analisis Economico* 9, 1 (1994): 57–76.

Cowell, Frank A. *Cheating the Government: The Economics of Tax Evasion*. Cambridge, Mass.: MIT Press, 1990.

———. "Tax Evasion with Labour Income." *Journal of Public Economics* 26 (1985): 19–34.

Das-Gupta, Arindam and Ira N. Gang. "Decomposing Revenue Effects of Tax Evasion, Base Broadening and Tax Rate Reduction." New Brunswick, N.J.: Rutgers University, mimeo, September 1996.

Devine, Theresa. "Characteristics of Self-Employed Women in the United States." *Monthly Labor Review* 117, 3 (March 1994): 20–34.

Fallon, Peter, Tom Hoopengardner, and Ella Libanova. "Poverty and the Ukrainian Labor Market." Washington, D.C.: World Bank, mimeo, 1996.

Feinstein, Jonathan. "An Econometric Analysis of Income Tax Evasion and Its Detection." *RAND Journal of Economics* 22, 1 (1991): 4–35.

Feldstein, Martin and Andrew Samwick. "The Transition in Privatizing Social Security," NBER Working Paper 5761. Cambridge, Mass.: NBER, 1996.

Gang, Ira N., Omkar Goswami, and Amal Sanyal. "Corruption, Tax Evasion and the Laffer Curve." New Brunswick, N.J.: Rutgers University, mimeo, February 1996.

Gruber, Jonathan. "The Incidence of Payroll Taxation: Evidence from Chile." NBER Working Paper 5053. Cambridge, Mass.: NBER, 1995.

Holzmann, Robert. "On Economic Benefits and Fiscal Requirements of Moving from Unfunded to Funded Pensions." Saarbrücken: University of the Saarland, mimeo, January 1997.

Internal Revenue Service. "Federal Tax Compliance Research: Gross and Net Employment Tax Gap Estimates for 1984–1997." IRS Publication 1415-E (Rev.10-93). Washington, D.C., 1993.

James, Estelle. "Pension Reform: Is There an Efficiency-Equity Trade-Off?" Washington, D.C.: World Bank. Paper prepared for Conference on Inequality: Reducing Growth in Latin America's Market Economies, January 1997.

Loayza, Norman V. "Labor Regulations and the Informal Economy." Policy Research Working Paper 1335. Washington, D.C.: World Bank, August 1994.

Mitchell, Olivia S. and Gary S. Fields. "Designing Pension Systems for Developing Countries." Washington, D.C.: World Bank, Poverty and Social Policy Department, mimeo, September 1995.

OECD. *The OECD JOBS STUDY: Evidence and Explanations Part II, The Adjustment Potential of the Labour Market.* Paris: OECD, 1993.

Queisser, Monika. "Pensions in Germany." Policy Research Working Paper 1664. Washington, D.C.: World Bank, October 1996.

Reid, Gary J. and Olivia S. Mitchell. "Social Security Administration in Latin America and the Caribbean." LAC Report 14066. Washington, D.C.: World Bank, 1995.

Reinganum, Jennifer F. and Louis L. Wilde. "Income Tax Compliance in a Principal-Agent Framework." *Journal of Public Economics* 26 (1985): 1–18.

Riboud, Michelle and Hoaquan Chu. "Pension Reforms and Growth in Ukraine: An Analysis Focusing on Labor Market Constraints." Washington, D.C.: World Bank, mimeo, October 1996.

Schleifer, Andrei and Robert W. Vishny. "Corruption." *Quarterly Journal of Economics* 108, 3 (1993): 599–617.

Schmidt-Hebbel, Klaus. "Pension Reform, Informal Markets and Long-Term Income and Welfare." Paper presented at a World Bank conference on "Pension Systems: From Crisis to Reform." Washington, D.C., November 21–22, 1996.

Slemrod, Joel. "A General Model of the Behavioral Response to Taxation." Ann Arbor: University of Michigan, mimeo, May 1996.

Slemrod, Joel and Jon Bakija. *Taxing Ourselves: A Citizen's Guide to the Great Debate over Tax Reform.* Cambridge, Mass.: MIT Press, 1996.

Social Security Administration. *Social Security Bulletin Annual Statistical Supplement 1995.* Washington, D.C.: USGPO, 1995.

Vazques-Caro, Jaime and Gary Reid with Richard Bird. "Tax Administration Assessment in Latin America." LAC Report 13. Washington, D.C.: World Bank, January 1992.

Vittas, Dmitri and Roland Michelitsch. "Pension Funds in Central Europe and Russia." Policy Research Working Paper 1459. Washington, D.C.: The World Bank, May 1995.

The World Bank. *Averting the Old Age Crisis: Policies to Protect the Old and Promote Growth.* New York: Oxford University Press, 1994.

———. "Brazil: Social Insurance and Private Pensions." Report No. 12336-BR. Washington, D.C.: The World Bank, 1995.

Chapter 13
Possible Employer Responses to Social Security Reform

Janice M. Gregory

HSS
J26 /05/

A recent survey of chief financial officers of the largest companies, organizations, and local governments in the United States found that 68 percent reported that concerns about social security had already begun to change the way they communicate to employees about their benefit plans. About a third of them felt that their concerns about social security were already driving plan design. Fewer than one-fifth were indifferent to concerns about social security solvency (Watson Wyatt Worldwide 1997).

These survey results show that many of the changes being considered to address the financial imbalances in the United States social security system will alter the utility of retirement plans sponsored by employers for their employees, and they will also trigger changes in the design of these plans. Enacting social security reforms without sufficient consideration of how such actions will affect employer-sponsored plans could severely disrupt employers' ability to design plans that meet their business needs. It could also harm irreparably millions of workers whose retirement security relies on income from both social security and employment-based retirement savings.

With limited exceptions, employer-sponsored plans presume that plan participants will receive social security benefits. This presumption can be illustrated by comparing the design of private sector employer plans with plans designed for those state and local government employees who have been excluded from social security coverage. For example, among medium and large *private* establishments in 1994–95, plan formulas affecting 51 percent of defined benefit plan participants were integrated with social security. By contrast, among *public* (state and local government) defined benefit plans, only 4 percent of participants were in plans with integrated formulas. The amount of final earnings replaced by the employer pension typically is higher in those state and local government plans where the employees are not covered under social security than it is in plans where employees are covered. Approximately half of state and local government plans provide automatic cost-of-living increases after retirement, whereas private sector plans rely almost entirely on ad hoc increases, if any post-retirement increase in supplied at all (EBRI 1995).

It is not surprising that most employer-sponsored plans assume receipt of social security benefits, inasmuch as growth of the employer-sponsored retirement system parallels the maturation of the social security program. The social security program was enacted in 1935, and, by 1940, approximately 17 percent of private sector full-time workers enjoyed pension coverage (PWBA 1992). Today, almost all workers are covered under the social security program, while approximately half of the civilian workforce also participate in employer-sponsored retirement plans (EBRI 1994a).

Most employer-sponsored plans assume a social security program structured much like the current one. Although social security has changed since its creation six decades ago, its basic outline has remained the same. Annuity payments are made to retired workers and/or the worker's dependents and survivors, and the size of the payments is based on covered earnings and weighted to replace a greater portion of lower earnings. Social security benefits were not indexed until 1972, but periodic increases in benefit levels before that time approximated the effects of increases in real wages and inflation indexing. The wage replacement rate at retirement under the social security program was 40 percent for an average wage worker in 1940 (Myers 1993) and is only slightly higher today (Board of Trustees 1997). Thus, the U.S. social security program has provided a secure and stable base upon which the employer-sponsored pension system grew.

In addition, employers whose employees are covered under the social security program pay one-half of the social security payroll tax and view this tax, and the benefits it provides, as part of the retirement portion of their compensation package for employees (Graham 1994). To the extent that an employer's business circumstances restrict the amount of resources that profitably can be allocated to compensation, increased social security taxes — or, for that matter, any other increased cost to the employer as a result of social security reform — will result in reductions in other components of the compensation package, including employer sponsorship of and contributions to retirement plans.

Since it is as yet unclear how the social security programs will be changed, it is impossible to discuss with precision how employer-sponsored plans will be adjusted. But it is imperative to increase understanding of the interaction between the social security program and employer-sponsored plans. The goal of this chapter is to establish a framework that can be used to identify the questions that must be asked, and the research that must be undertaken, to identify more clearly the likely interaction between employer-sponsored plans and proposals to reform the social security program. We first outline the role of employer-sponsored plans in providing retirement income to employees and explain how retirement plans are linked closely to the business needs of the plan sponsor. Next we examine features of employer-sponsored plans that social security reform will influence, including interfering with the employer's business purposes in sponsoring a plan, adding to the plan's cost, and triggering a change in the plan design. Reforms that interfere with the employer's business purposes in sponsoring a plan and reforms that add to the cost of compensation may cause some employers not to offer a retirement plan, while others would reduce their plans as they turn to more efficient means to meet their business goals in a competitive environment. Reforms that trigger changes in a plan design, if not imposed precipitously, may have a lesser effect on plan sponsorship and on the amount of retirement income employees accumulate through employer-sponsored plans, but may raise other important questions.

Our hope is that this discussion and future research will help clarify which common features of employer-sponsored plans will be most at risk under specific social security reform proposals. As support coalesces around one or more options for social security reform, policymakers may then also take steps to address the problems that proposed reforms will engender in employer-sponsored plans.

Role of Employer-Provided Plans in Providing Retirement Security

Pensions provide the largest source of retiree income, other than social security, for the middle three quintiles of the elderly population (Quinn, this volume). Moreover, pensions constitute a larger source than income from assets. Survey responses indicate that many current workers expect that funds provided through employer-sponsored pension or savings plans will be their *most* important source of income when they retire. Over half of all workers surveyed in 1996 responded that funds provided through employer-sponsored savings plans would be their most important source of retirement income (EBRI 1996b). This compares with 23 percent who gave a prominent role to personal savings or investments, 10 percent who named social security, and 15 percent who named other sources as their most important source of retirement income.

These expectations of future retirees have at least some foundation in fact. In 1974, approximately one-quarter of retired families received benefits from employer plans; by 1988, 40 percent of retired families received such payments. By 2018, when the baby boom cohort will be moving rapidly into retirement, it is expected that over 75 percent of retired families will have pension income (EBRI 1997a). "Retired families" in this estimate are defined as married couples living together where at least one spouse is age 55 or over, and nonmarried persons age 55 and older.[1]

While current worker expectations that pensions will provide more of their retirement income than social security may or may not be realized, it is true that employer-sponsored plans have been more efficient than individual arrangements, such as IRAs, in accumulating retirement income for workers. Several factors account for this (ERIC 1996). First, employer-sponsored plans often act as a form of automatic savings. Benefits automatically accrue in most defined benefit plans, and employer contributions benefit all employees under many profit-sharing plans. Second, under employer-sponsored defined benefit plans, participants are sheltered from risks that can reduce individual retirement savings. The employee, once vested, is virtually guaranteed whatever benefit he or she has earned under the plan. The employer bears full responsibility for payment of the accrued benefit regardless of whether there are assets in the trust to pay the benefit. Should the employer become bankrupt, the Pension Benefit Guaranty Corporation (PBGC) assumes payment of the promised benefit (up to certain limits). Third, under most defined benefit and defined contribution plans, participants receive the benefit of a professional investment manager. Even in plans where each participant directs the investment of the funds in his or her account, the plan generally allows each participant to allocate his or her account only among designated professionally managed investment funds and index funds. Fourth, plans that allow participants to make contributions through payroll deduction programs make decisions to save less painful and regular savings more likely to occur. Fifth, employees who contribute to employer-sponsored individual account plans (e.g., 401(k) plans) often reap an immediate enhancement of their investments through an employer matching contribution. Finally, participants in employer-sponsored participant-directed individual account plans are more likely to have free access to information and assistance (e.g., decision guides or benefits forecasting software) that enable them to make better informed investment decisions.

While employer contributions to a retirement plan clearly are a boost to employee savings, employer-sponsored plans that offer individual saving opportunities have proven to be more successful in enticing people to save than individual saving initiatives. In 1992, for example, of the approximately 57 million individuals eligible to make deductible contributions to an IRA, only 6 percent (3.6 million) took advantage of this savings opportunity. Even during the period 1981–86, when IRAs were universally available, the maximum number of tax returns claiming an IRA deduction was only 16.2 million, in 1985. By contrast, in 1993, there were 106 million civilian non-agricultural wage and salaried workers in the U.S., of whom 25 million (24 percent) made contributions to employer-sponsored 401(k) plans, even though 401(k) plans are not universally available throughout the workforce (ERIC 1996). Moreover, 401(k) plans attracted participants at earlier ages. While approximately 29 percent of the contributors to both IRAs and

401(k) plans were age 41–50, 53 percent of the 401(k) participants were age 40 or under, compared with 38 percent for IRA contributors.

Even if most workers' benefits were enhanced under social security reform, as some proposals claim will occur, that advantage would be largely erased if those reforms also caused employees to save less elsewhere or caused employers to reduce or eliminate their retirement plans. Thus, if reforms are enacted that cause reductions in pension income, the retirement expectations of many current workers might not be realized.

Business Purposes of Employer-Sponsored Plans

In the United States, employers offer pensions voluntarily to achieve business purposes. These plans are seen as effective management tools to attract and retain high-quality employees, to motivate employees, and to facilitate the departure from the employer's workforce of older employees who either cannot or do not desire to continue working. In recent years, it is also clear that the impact on employees due to the downsizing and reorganizing of many U.S. companies was dramatically reduced through the flexible use of early retirement options under employer-sponsored pension plans (ERIC 1996).

At present, retirement plans provide employers a cost-effective means of providing compensation to employees. Under the current tax structure, retirement plans can represent a significant component of compensation at a cost to the employer that is lower and less immediate than direct cash payments to employees. They also offer employees delayed taxation on their compensation.

An employer can design a retirement plan to further its business and workforce goals. There are traditional defined benefit or profit sharing plans. But employers also are turning to a growing number of new plan designs such as target benefit plans, age-based profit-sharing plans, cash balance plans, pension equity plans, floor offset plans, or retirement bonus plans. The most popular "new" plan by far is the 401(k) plan.

If the employer's business strategy is to use a few experienced and seasoned employees to manage and direct a workforce of primarily young, entry-level people, the employer may offer a target benefit plan or an age-weighted profit-sharing plan. Either can provide a quick buildup of benefits for older employees while minimizing costs for younger employees. If the business requires a constant inflow of new employees, however, the employer may turn to a plan such as a cash balance plan that provides an easily portable benefit, one that does not build up disproportionately larger benefits as the employer's age and service increase, and one that will not penalize employees for leaving (KPMG 1996). Financially stable employers who want to encourage a stable workforce may encourage employee investment in employer stock. Employers who rely on a steady turnover in their workforce may not. Young start-up companies, strapped for cash, may rely primarily on stock ownership plans or salary-reduction 401(k) plans designed not to require any employer contributions. Many employers who can afford to do so use a mixture of plans to meet various business goals. Most major employers sponsor not only a traditional defined benefit plan but also a 401(k) plan with an employer match, as well as stock option plans and other types of retirement and savings vehicles.

Each substantive social security reform proposal must be compared in detail to the present social security program in terms of benefit adequacy, benefit equity, financial stability, and impact on the economy. Such proposals also must be analyzed to determine how each will affect various employer-sponsored plan designs and, more specifically, how the proposed change in the social security program might disrupt the ability of each design to meet its business objectives. Once reform is enacted, each employer sponsoring a plan or plans will ask those questions — and will modify its plans accordingly.[2] The majority — 73 percent — of chief financial officers of major U.S. enterprises responding to a survey have already expressed concern that social security problems could undermine companies' ability to retire workers on an orderly basis in the future (Watson Wyatt Worldwide 1997).

Effects of Social Security Program Reforms on Employer-Sponsored Plans

If employees do not believe they have accumulated sufficient resources to meet their retirement income expectations, they are not likely to retire. This will have profound effects for the pension system as well as for the employment market. If social security benefits were significantly reduced and/or the program's cost to employers significantly increased, then employers must divert compensation dollars away from their initial goals and toward retirement, must encourage employees to increase their reliance on personal savings, must manage workforce size and cost through increased use of downsizing, or must rely on some combination of these options. This is true regardless of the type of retirement plan(s) the employer now sponsors. Given the intensely competitive nature of today's world-wide business climate, it is not likely that employers will be able to absorb changes in the social security program by increasing overall compensation costs. Rather, several possible outcomes might be envisioned.

Integration of Employer-Sponsored Plan Benefits with Social Security Benefits

Under current law, private sector employers may take the availability of social security benefits into account in their benefit plan formulas. The rationale for integration, or, more correctly, "permitted disparity," rests on the employer payment of one-half of the social security payroll tax and on the fact that social security benefits are weighted toward lower wage levels. In medium and large private establishments, half of defined benefit plan participants (over 8 million workers) were in integrated plans in 1995. Thirty-seven percent were in plans integrated through a step-rate excess formula and about 14 percent were in offset plans (EBRI 1995). Social security integration is, however, more widespread than this figure would indicate. The figure excludes employees of small firms who participate in integrated pension plans. Some defined contribution plans also are integrated with social security benefits. In addition, even where the benefit structure may not be integrated with social security, the employer may use permitted disparity in meeting the nondiscrimination rules of the Internal Revenue Code. Finally, as stated earlier, virtually all employer-sponsored retirement plans assume their participants will receive social security benefits under a structure similar to the current program. Thus, while discussions of integration tend to focus on plans whose formulas are formally linked in some way to social security benefits, in the broadest sense almost all plans are integrated.

The effect of changes in social security benefits on integrated plans—and on the recipients of benefits from those plans—will vary according to the type of integration used. In many plans, the rate of employer-provided contributions or benefits for compensation below a certain dollar level is less than the rate of employer-provided contributions or benefits for compensation above that level. These are commonly called "excess" plans, and they are the most common form of integration today. Excess formulas can be used in traditional defined benefit plans or in defined contribution plans. Similar results can be obtained in flat-rate (generally union) plans, in profit-sharing plans, in money purchase plans and other plan designs. The dollar level that divides the higher and lower rates can be social security covered compensation (which is the average of the social security taxable wage bases in effect for each of the previous 35 years), the social security taxable wage base, or an arbitrary dollar amount (Canan 1997). The difference between benefits or contributions above and below this integration level is strictly limited by law—hence "permitted" disparity.

Benefits provided to employees under an excess plan will not be automatically adjusted when the social security defined benefit is changed, even if the social security benefit is dramatically reduced. Such plans might be subject to employee demands for higher pensions if employees felt they did not have enough money to retire. Changes to the taxable wage base will, however, affect the vast majority of excess plans, which typically rely on either covered compensation or the taxable wage base as their integration point. Increases in the taxable wage base will reduce the number of employees receiving benefits above the integration level. Social security reform that both reduced the defined benefit and increased the taxable wage base might intensify pressure on these plans, unless employees, especially middle income employees, think they will accumulate enough retirement savings through other means.

Under an offset plan, the pension benefit is adjusted, within the limits imposed by Internal Revenue Code, for the expected value of the employee's social security benefit. If that expected value is changed through social security reform, the pension benefit may be adjusted automatically to compensate for the change, unless the plan is amended. Depending on how the social security reform provisions are constructed, such a result also could occur even if the overall expected value of the social security benefit was not changed, but a portion of the benefit is shifted to a defined contribution system. Under such proposals, permitted disparity might be limited to the portion of the social security benefit still funded and paid as a defined benefit.

Reducing the dollar amount of the offset without an attendant reduction in plan benefits would be prohibitively costly for most employers. Most analysts conclude that the adjustments in the pension benefits probably would not affect low or high income employees so much as they would affect middle income employees.[3] Reduced integration that raised the pension benefits of lower-income employees might be offset by changes that slowed future accruals under the pension plan. Employees at the high end of the scale probably would derive more of their retirement income from non-qualified plans. Because middle-income employees are likely to derive a greater portion of their retirement income from the employer's tax-qualified plans than are either the lower-income employees or very-high-income employees, they have the most to lose if pension benefits are reduced to offset the costs of integration changes.

Finally, statistics are not available on the number of plans that do not integrate their contributions or benefits with social security but that use permitted disparity in meeting the Internal Revenue Code nondiscrimination rules. If the ability to integrate were reduced in any way, however, it is safe to assume that a number of these plans also would have to adjust their plans in order to accommodate the changes at an acceptable cost.

"Bridge" Benefits

Many individuals retire before they begin receiving social security benefits, and some plans provide special benefits that "bridge" the gap between actual retirement and commencement of social security payments, currently age 62 for reduced benefits and age 65 for full benefits.

Most social security reform proposals advocate, at a minimum, speeding up the scheduled increases in the social security normal retirement age from 65 to 66 and then 67. Others would also increase the age for social

security early retirement, now scheduled to remain at 62, albeit with benefits at a reduced level, when the normal retirement age increases.

Plans that provide bridge benefits to age 65 would suffer direct and dramatic cost increases under any of these proposals. Plans that currently
bridge to age 62 could come under pressure to extend their payments as
age-62 social security benefits decrease and workers want to continue to
retire early but to delay commencing their social security benefits to a later
age. Workers who retire early and do not have access to bridge payments
might draw down balances in their 401(k), IRA, or other savings accounts
before social security and annuitized pension payments commence, reducing disproportionately the funds they might need later as a protection
against inflation and other contingencies.

Under any future trends and policies, significant numbers of workers will
continue to retire early. For proposals providing for social security individual savings accounts, this raises the question of whether and under what
conditions an individual should have access to such an account before the
early or normal retirement ages specified under the social security program.

Guaranteed Minimum Benefit Levels

Some defined benefit pension plans provide more than one benefit formula, and the employee receives whichever benefit is greatest. In many
cases, one of the formulas will be a minimum or guaranteed benefit level. If
social security benefits are reduced, some employers may incur a greater
outlay for such floor or minimum benefits and may need to curtail them to
contain costs. Depending on the extent of the reductions in the social
security benefits, however, employers offering such benefits could face pressure to increase them. Whether the employer can sustain or expand such
benefits, or whether the employer will reduce the floor on minimum benefit
levels, will depend on their cost and on whether such actions are in concert
with the employer's business objectives.

Administration of Social Security Defined Contribution Accounts

Currently 145 million workers contribute to the social security program
each year (Board of Trustees 1997). If social security defined contribution
accounts were established, a system would have to be devised to collect the
contributions from or on behalf of workers and to allocate each contribution to the appropriate investment(s). While social security reforms that
change the integration of pensions with social security benefits can have a
dramatic impact on many employer-sponsored retirement plans, creation of
social security defined contribution accounts potentially could affect all employers whether the employer currently sponsors a retirement plan or not.[4]

Under current law, employers remit social security payroll taxes to the government through a single transfer of funds based on their total payroll up to the social security wage base. How often payments are made depends on the size of the employer, and funds can be deposited as often as daily. However, employers report the wages of individual employees only after the end of the year.

Under a revised social security program that included individual savings accounts, it would be necessary to determine whether employers still will be able to remit all social security contributions through a single transfer, or whether they will be required to remit separate transfers for each employee. It will also be necessary to determine whether transfers will occur on the current schedule (i.e., as often as daily), or whether transfers for the defined benefit portion will occur on one schedule and transfers for the defined contribution portion on another. In addition the employer will need to know where to send the money for the defined contribution portion — to the Internal Revenue Service, to a new social security defined contribution office, directly to investment funds set up by the government or a quasi-governmental body, or directly to investment funds in the general economy.

Over 40 percent of civilian workers currently work at an establishment that does not sponsor a retirement plan for any of its employees (EBRI 1995). Of those who do work for establishments with retirement plans, many of those plans may be funded solely through employer contributions that occur on a quarterly or, more frequently, only on an annual basis. Thus, many employers have no experience whatsoever in handling employee contributions to a retirement plan or in processing contributions as frequently as occurs under a 401(k) plan. Additional administrative requirements on the employer also will reduce the amount of money available to provide other employment-based benefits or compensation for employees.

The simplest, least intrusive, and least costly method for employers would be to require the employers' contributions to be made according to procedures as close to current law as possible, to have the government allocate cash to each worker's individual account, and to have the worker tell the government directly how to allocate his or her account among available investments. The most complicated, intrusive, and costly scenario for employers would be to require the employer to transmit individual account contributions to any fund the employee designated on a daily basis (which would be more rapid than that required under current law for 401(k) deposits). The amounts of these deposits could in many cases be less than the cost of administration (see Pozen and Kimpel, this volume).

Each of these scenarios raises a host of important problems and questions. An individual account system that relied primarily on current schedules of wage reporting and on government administration would minimize burdens on those sponsoring plans for their employees, but employees might find the process unacceptably slow unless the government established a new mechanism for handling the individual accounts. Currently, individual wages are not reported until after the close of the year, and it takes the Social Security Administration approximately another year to post that information to individual wage records (NASI forthcoming).

A system that relied primarily on employers to make the deposits to the employee's investment account might be quicker in getting cash into the individual's account, but it could also be so expensive that employees might find other parts of their compensation reduced. It could also be a compliance nightmare. The IRS currently tracks whether money deposited to the government matches taxes owed, but it does not track people's earnings records (and thus is not now equipped to track whether deposits made on behalf of an individual actually are made to that individual's account). The Social Security Administration currently tracks individual earnings records, but is not well positioned to determine whether individual taxes paid match with earnings records. Moreover, while the current system under which social security individual earnings records are accumulated has a low reported error rate, each year, about 2 percent of W-2 reports (or about 4.5 million out of 223 million reports filed) cannot be matched with any individual social security file (NASI forthcoming). Deposits made by an employer to investment accounts in the open market could pose the most widespread compliance issues to the government, since it would be difficult to verify that payments actually had been made and that the money was being invested according to acceptable fiduciary standards. Such a system could result in significant and burdensome reporting requirements on employers.

Responsibility for informing the individual worker of the status of his or her social security account is also a significant issue. This important job would be extremely difficult to accomplish through employers, since the information would have to be transferred each time an employee changed jobs and since a significant percentage of employees hold more than one job simultaneously or during any given year.

While these are only some of the possible problems and questions, they are sufficient to show that establishing social security defined contribution accounts without serious study of the administrative issues involved could have adverse effects on employers, on the sponsorship of employer pension plans, on the government, and, of course, on the millions of individuals who will depend on those accounts for a significant portion of their retirement security. Often overlooked and viewed as inconsequential, administrative issues may prove to be some of the more complicated and intractable in social security reform. They should be "forethought" — not an afterthought.

Impact of Social Security Defined Contribution Accounts on Employee Saving

Very little empirical microeconomic research exists regarding what motivates employees to save in a pension plan. Thus, if social security individual savings accounts are created (whether in addition to current social security benefits or in lieu of a portion of those benefits), the impact that such accounts will have on whether employees save money elsewhere is unknown. Will employees be motivated to increase their savings in 401(k) and other plans as they see their account balances increasing in their social security account? Or will they assume that the social security account will be sufficient and decrease their other retirement savings? If the defined benefit portion of the social security benefit is substantially reduced, will employees be motivated to save more on their own, or will they decide the goals are unreachable and save less? Will they be more aggressive in their investment choices, or will they be more risk-adverse?

Employees' responses to these questions will affect the employer's ability to manage its workforce and the employer's decisions on whether and what types of plans to offer. Employers could incur difficulties in meeting non-discrimination rules for their qualified plans if lower-paid employees decrease their savings. Employers may also alter their commitment to offer savings plans at all. On the other hand, if employees are motivated to increase their savings, more employers might decide to sponsor retirement plans for their employees.

Employee Access (or Lack of Access) to Retirement Saving Accounts

Most studies that are optimistic about the retirement prospects of the baby boom cohort assume that the individual keeps all of his or her retirement savings until retirement (EBRI 1994b). Retirement prospects change dramatically if there is too much "leakage" from the system. Allowing access to savings to meet current financial emergencies may be necessary, however, before employees with few other financial resources will be able to participate. Moreover, removing savings from a retirement plan in order to invest in a college degree (for one's self, not one's children) or to purchase a house may enhance the individual's ultimate retirement income.

Proposals to establish social security savings accounts generally require mandatory participation at specified levels. Thus, participation is not an issue. Access to money in those accounts is an issue, however, and the answers provided for a new social security program will have ramifications for savings programs sponsored by employers. For example, if employees are required to contribute additional funds to a social security savings account to which they have no access until they reach the social security retirement age, employees could pressure employers and policymakers to provide greater access to savings in employer-sponsored plans such as 401(k) plans. Employees also could reduce their savings in restricted plans and increase their savings in plans (such as after-tax savings plans) that have fewer restrictions.

If the result is less overall private and pension savings retained until retirement (a possibility, not a foregone conclusion), then many workers will face delayed retirement and a reduced standard of living in retirement.

Education of Employees About Retirement Savings

Many experts agree that future retirees must assume more responsibility for accumulating the assets that they need to retire. Education is central to helping workers meet that responsibility.

Employer-provided education programs have significantly increased the incidence of employee saving. In one survey, among those who have had "a great deal" of assistance in retirement planning from their employers, 62 percent had already done a "fair amount" or a "lot" of retirement planning (Towers Perrin 1991). Among those who received little or no employer planning assistance, 41 percent had already planned for retirement. Among survey respondents who had not saved for retirement, 32 percent said they could not afford to do so, but only 19 percent of respondents receiving a great deal of employer assistance said they could not afford to save money.

Almost three-quarters (71 percent) of current workers participating in some type of salary reduction retirement savings plan, such as a 401(k) or 403(b) plan, say their employer has provided them with educational material or seminars about the plan. Among those with such resources available, the vast majority (81 percent) used the material or attended the seminars (EBRI 1997d). Participants who were provided educational materials that estimated the income needed for retirement appeared to increase the portion of their savings allocated to equity investments (EBRI 1996a).

In addition, when an employee receives a distribution that is eligible for a rollover to an IRA or other qualified plan (and thus the money could continue to be preserved in a tax-deferred fund for retirement), the plan is required to give the employee an explanation of the rollover rules. But serious education about retirement requires sustained effort; a technical explanation of the rollover rules at the time a distribution is made is not likely to enlighten many employees.

As social security reforms are considered, questions that should be asked include: To what extent will proposed changes to the social security program increase or hinder the education of employees about the need to save? If the new social security program has a defined contribution component, will the government undertake an education program for participants, and what impact will the government program have on the effectiveness of employers' programs?

Age of Retirement and of the Workforce

In the coming decades, employers will have to adjust to an older workforce. In the decade from 1990–2000, the number of workers aged 45 to 54 is expected to increase by over 50 percent while the number of workers aged 25 to 34 is expected actually to decline by 10 percent (Schieber and Graig 1994). The median age of the U.S. population was 28 in 1970, is 33 today, and will climb to 39 by 2010 (Select Committee on Aging 1992). Whether an older workforce will translate into later retirements is a different question, however.

Most social security reform proposals include an increase in the social security normal retirement age. Only recently has information begun to be compiled concerning how often reduced social security benefits for earlier retirement will actually induce workers to delay their retirement.[5] The trend in recent decades clearly has been for male workers to retire at earlier rather than later ages (EBRI 1997a). Certain plan designs may shelter employees from the effects of rising retirement ages so that employees will have no motivation to delay retirement. Employees have access to 401(k) and IRA savings without penalty beginning at age 59½, and those who accumulate sufficient assets in a defined contribution plan to retire early may do so. Moreover, under some offset plans, benefits under the plan may increase as early retirement benefits under social security decrease so that, for the employee, there is no change in economic status.

If increases in the social security normal retirement age do not induce more workers, particularly male workers, to delay their retirement, pressure on employer-sponsored pensions to provide greater early retirement subsidies will increase. If employers can neither meet the demands for increased early retirement subsidies nor accommodate large numbers of older employees in their workforce, employees will be forced to rely more on individual savings.

Plans That Do/Do Not Provide Additional Accruals Indefinitely

Under some employer-sponsored plans, benefits continue to accrue as long as the individual continues to work for the employer. Under other plans, benefit accruals cease at some point, generally after a certain number of years of service. In addition, in many plans, factors such as early retirement subsidies may make it more advantageous to retire at one age than at a later age.

As the normal retirement age under the social security program rises, pressure may be brought to bear on pension plans that limit accruals, either to uncap the limits (thus encouraging employees to work to later ages) or to provide benefits to bridge any gap between the age at which plan participants typically attain the plan's maximum accrual and the age for retirement under the social security program. Employers will have to decide on a course of action.

Replacement Ratio Targets

Despite recent downward trends, the majority of individuals who participate in employer-sponsored retirement plans still rely on a defined benefit plan for their primary benefit. In 1993, a defined benefit plan was the primary plan for 56 percent of active participants. The number of individuals who rely on defined benefit plans as their primary plan has remained relatively constant at between 25 and 30 million since 1975 (EBRI 1995). Under such plans, employers can predict with some certainty what employees can expect to receive in terms of replacement of their wages.

For these employees, social security reforms that reduce benefits will have an adverse effect on their ability to attain the overall (social security benefits plus pension benefits) income replacement ratio envisioned in their employers' plans. Reforms that shift benefits to defined contribution accounts will make attainment of a desired replacement ratio less certain.

Indeed, as account balances in defined contribution plans have increased, employers have had an increasingly complicated job determining when employees will accumulate sufficient resources to retire. This is especially true where the defined contribution plan is a 401(k) plan or other plan where participation is triggered by employee contributions. In these cases, attainment of a desired replacement ratio is affected not only by the rate of return on investments in an employee's account but also by whether most employees participate in the plan and, for those who do participate, the level and regularity of their contributions.

Concerns are expressed that individuals who do save fail to invest their savings aggressively enough to produce the returns needed to support an adequate retirement income. In one survey, 39 percent of the respondents who participated in 401(k) savings plans did not know how their plan dollars were allocated among asset classes. Among those who did know how their plan dollars were allocated, one-third had no money at all invested in stocks, including 31 percent who were under age 30 (Towers Perrin 1991). But other studies present a more hopeful picture, including one study that analyzed the investment behavior of 36,000 participants in 24 defined contribution plans. This study revealed that almost 60 percent of the aggregate assets were in fixed-income options. However, when the data were further analyzed by age of participant, the high percentage of assets in fixed-income options was primarily attributable to older workers who were nearing retirement and who also had larger account balances. Younger workers in the study had a higher percentage of assets in equity funds (Clark and Schieber 1998). More detailed recent studies present a varied picture *within* age groups. One analysis of investments under three large 401(k) plans revealed that between 17 and 41 percent of younger participants (aged 20–29 and 30–39) had no equity investments whatsoever, while others in these same age groups had placed more than 80 percent of their investments in equities (EBRI 1996c). A similar analysis also would have to be conducted, of course, on investment choices made if social security individual accounts were enacted.

Provision of Disability and Survivor Protection

The current social security program provides substantial, and often over-looked, survivor and disability protection. A 27-year-old married couple with two small children, where both parents earned average wages, had over $300,000 in social security survivor protection and $207,000 in social se-curity disability protection in 1997. Altogether, the social security program provided about $12 trillion in life insurance protection in 1997, an amount exceeding the combined face value of all private life insurance policies in force. Of the 44 million persons receiving benefits each month, 3 million were children under age 18, mostly children of deceased workers, and 5 million were disabled adults (Advisory Council 1996).

Any change in social security benefits that reduced the life and disability protections currently offered also will have an effect on employer plans. Most employers provide some life insurance protection to their employees, and many who provide pensions also provide disability benefits. The disabil-ity benefits are almost always offset by receipt of social security disability pay-ments. While these effects may not be as dramatic as changes affecting retire-ment payments, they still must be examined carefully before determining that they are not of major consequence. Of course, the effect of reductions in social security survivor and disability protection would be very dramatic for the individuals who otherwise would have received such payments.

Plans That Are Over/Under-Funded

For defined benefit plans, the ability of the plan sponsor to accommodate reductions in social security benefit payments with increases in pension payments, or to provide additional protections against social security bene-fits that may fluctuate in value (e.g., from social security individual ac-counts), will be influenced to some degree by the status of the plan's fund-ing before such changes are effective. A plan that enters such a transition heavily overfunded obviously will have a wider range of financially viable options available to it than a plan that enters such a transition already strapped for cash, or even than a plan that is adequately funded but incur-ring substantial annual funding requirements.

However, several factors may impede the ability even of heavily over-funded plans to accommodate changes in social security benefits. One is that repeated changes in the tax laws over the past two decades have substantially reduced the ability of defined benefit plans to fund adequately for their long-term obligations and/or have reduced allowable contributions to defined contribution plans.

Prior to 1982, periodic revisions in the law generally were intended to increase retirement savings by liberalizing the tax treatment of individual and employer-sponsored plans. This practice produced long-term national savings and dramatically increased retirement savings but reduced current revenues to the federal government. Legislation enacted in 1982 reversed this trend, and at least eight other laws enacted since 1982 imposed even more limits on qualified plans.[6] As Congress struggled to reduce the burgeoning federal deficit it looked increasingly to retirement plans to increase current revenues to the government.

Some policymakers have begun to express the view that the trend of previous years should be reversed. For example, legislation[7] enacted in 1997 increases a critical funding cap that applies to many defined benefit plans. Analysis shows that such funding restrictions merely delay funding for working baby boomers, ensuring that companies will be faced with increasing funding requirements in the future precisely when they may also be facing the effects of social security reforms (ERIC 1996).

Other limits constraining the benefits that can be paid from tax qualified plans have a similar, but less often highlighted, effect. An employer designs its plans to meet business purposes and to provide employees with the resources, in combination with social security benefits, to replace enough of their wages in order that they will be able to retire. When this goal is not met through the employer's qualified plans, then employees may receive supplemental benefits from nonqualified plans. As Congress repeatedly narrowed the range of retirement income that can be supplied from qualified plans, reliance on nonqualified plans boomed. Benefits from nonqualified plans are not funded; they are paid out of the employer's available cash when the employee retires. Unless the limits on qualified plans are increased now, the demand for nonqualified payments will increase dramatically in the future, strapping the employer's future cash flow at precisely the same time that increased funding may be required for qualified plans and social security reforms may be taking effect.

The deferred tax treatment afforded qualified plans is a very cost-effective way for the government to help finance the retirement needs of American workers. The relationship between current tax expenditures and future tax receipts is evident in the impact of pre-funding of retirement benefits on the current tax expenditure attributable to private sector plans. Over the 1995–1999 period, only 29 percent of the pension tax expenditure is attributable to private sector plans. By contrast, 57 percent of the expenditure is attributable to federal (non-military), state, and local government employee plans, and 15 percent is attributable to military plans (Joint Committee on

Taxation 1995). The private sector figure is low today relative to the expenditure attributed to public sector plans in part because today's private sector retirees are paying taxes on benefits financed by funds for which the deferral of taxes occurred in previous years.

Design and Administration of Plans During a Transition Period

Much discussion has already ensued regarding transition requirements if social security reform results in significant changes in the social security benefit structure. Little or no discussion has occurred about the transitional effects of such changes on an employer's workforce and plans.

Employers sponsoring plans will face enormous challenges of their own during any transition period. They must design and simultaneously administer plans suitable for older employees who may be grandfathered under the current social security system, for middle-aged employees under one or more transition systems, and for younger employees under a new social security system. All the problems and costs of design, administration, and employee education will be, at a minimum, tripled. Employers who change their plans to meet changing business objectives do so after careful study and intensive employee education. In this case, employers will be dealing with changes that may or may not be coherent in terms of the company's business needs.

Conclusion

Employer plans have proved to be a reliable, effective, and efficient way to provide workers participating in those plans important tools to prepare for retirement. Employees expect to rely on these plans in the future for a greater portion of their retirement security than has been the case in the past. The design of those plans and the role they will play in the future can change from current expectations, however, because of the effects of social security reform.

The most immediate impact of social security reform will be on both the explicit and implicit integration of pension benefits with social security benefits and the administrative and other issues that arise if individual savings accounts are established under social security. Over the long term, the design of employer retirement plans will shift to accommodate the new social security program, business needs, costs, and employee desires. This paper has examined some of the possible changes that could occur in employer plans. As support coalesces around one or more approach to social security reform, each should be examined for possible impact in the areas studied in this paper. Only then can one determine whether the new combined system will meet societal goals of providing retirement income to individuals, since neither the social security system nor the pension system were designed as stand-alone retirement programs.

Views expressed in this paper are those of the author and do not represent the views of the author's employer.

Notes

1. The data assume that lump sum distributions are preserved until retirement and that income is paid in the form of an annuity.

2. Once the effect of a given social security reform proposal on current employer-sponsored plan designs is understood, we must additionally ask whether the new combined system is likely to meet societal goals of providing retirement income to individuals, since neither the social security system nor the pension system have been designed as stand-alone retirement programs. However, this larger question is left for a later discussion. In addition, employers may urge a particular form of social security reform because they think that it will further general business purposes, such as increasing international competitiveness, even though the reform may require extensive renovation of their own employee benefit plans. A discussion of this point is premature at this time, since most businesses are only beginning their study of the issue.

3. For example, see Select Committee on Aging (1992). Graham (1994) reports that, for employees earning $35,000 or more, pensions available from integrated plans are greater than those from non-integrated plans.

4. Here we focus on administrative issues that arise from the employer point of view. The government would face many other issues as well. For an examination of many of those issues, see the NASI study, in progress.

5. A 1997 EBRI/Gallup survey begins to build a base upon which to examine the potential impact of future changes in the social security retirement age (EBRI 1997b). For a survey of studies conducted prior to the 1983 amendments to the social security program see Special Committee on Aging (1982).

6. For a list of laws containing provisions that reduced amounts that could be contributed to or paid from tax-qualified plans, see ERIC (1996).

7. The Taxpayer Relief Act of 1997, PL 105-34, increases the 150 percent of current liability funding limit to 170 percent over a period of years.

References

Advisory Council on Social Security. *Report of the 1994–1996 Advisory Council on Social Security*. Washington, D.C.: Social Security Administration. 1997: 1–33, 89.

Board of Trustees of the Federal Old-Age and Survivors Insurance and Disability Trust Funds (Trustees). *1997 Annual Report*. Washington, D.C.: 105th Congress, 1st Session: House Document 105-72, April 1997.

Canan, Michael J. *Qualified Retirement and Other Employee Benefit Plans: 1998 Practitioner Edition*. St. Paul, MN: West's Employment Law Series, West Publishing Co., 1997.

Clark, Robert L. and Sylvester J. Schieber. "Factors Affecting Participation Rates and Contribution Levels in 401(k) Plans." In Olivia S. Mitchell and Sylvester J. Schieber, eds., *Living with Defined Contribution Pensions*. Philadelphia: Pension Research Council and University of Pennsylvania Press, 1998: 69–97.

Employee Benefit Research Institute (EBRI). *EBRI Databook.* Third Edition. Washington, D.C.: Employee Benefit Research Institute, 1995.

———. *EBRI Databook.* Fourth Edition. Washington, D.C.: Employee Benefit Research Institute, 1997. 1997a

———. "Employee Benefits, Retirement Patterns, and Implications for Increased Work Life." *EBRI Issue Brief* 184. Washington, D.C.: Employee Benefit Research Institute, April 1997. 1997b

———. "Employment-Based Retirement Income Benefits: Analysis of the April 1993 Current Population Survey." *EBRI Issue Brief* 153 (1994): 1. 1994a

———. "A Framework for Analyzing and Comparing Social Security Policies." *EBRI Issue Brief* 183: 17. Washington, D.C.: Employee Benefit Research Institute, March 1997. 1997c

———. "Participant Education: Actions & Outcomes." *EBRI Issue Brief* 169. Washington, D.C.: Employee Benefit Research Institute, September 1996. 1996a

———. "The Reality of Retirement Planning Today: Lessons in Planning for Tomorrow." *EBRI Issue Brief* 181: 8. Washington, D.C.: Employee Benefit Research Institute, January 1997. 1997d

———. *Retirement in the 21st Century . . . Ready or Not.* Washington, D.C.: Employee Benefit Research Institute, 1994: 43–46. 1994b

———. *Results of the 1996 Retirement Confidence Survey.* Washington, D.C.: Employee Benefit Research Institute, 1996. 1996b

———. "Worker Investment Decisions: An Analysis of Large 401(k) Plan Data." *EBRI Issue Brief* 176: 7. Washington, D.C.: Employee Benefit Research Institute, August 1996. 1996c

ERISA Industry Committee (ERIC). *Getting the Job Done: A White Paper on Emerging Pension Issues.* Washington, D.C.: ERIC, 1996.

Graham, Avy D. "Coordinating Private Pensions and Social Security." *Monthly Labor Review.* Washington, D.C.: U.S. Department of Labor, March 1994.

Joint Committee on Taxation. "Estimates of Federal Tax Expenditures for Fiscal Years 1996–2000." Washington, D.C.: United States Congress, JCS-21-95, September 1995.

KPMG Peat Marwick LLP. *Retirement Plan Redesign for the 21st Century: The Basics.* Washington, D.C.: KPMG, 1996.

Myers, Robert J. *Social Security.* 4th edition. Philadelphia: Pension Research Council and University of Pennsylvania Press, 1993.

National Academy of Social Insurance Panel on Privatization of Social Security (NASI). "Setting Up Individual Social Security Accounts." Washington, D.C.: NASI. Forthcoming.

Pension and Welfare Benefit Administration (PWBA). *Trends in Pensions 1992.* Washington, D.C.: U.S. Department of Labor, 1992: 75.

Schieber, Sylvester J. and Laurence A. Graig. *U.S. Retirement Policy: The Sleeping Giant Awakens.* Washington, D.C.: Watson Wyatt Worldwide, 1994: 15–16.

Select Committee on Aging. *Congressional Symposium on Women and Retirement.* Washington, D.C.: U.S. House of Representatives: Comm. Pub. No.102-897: 87, 1992.

Special Committee on Aging. *Linkages Between Private Pensions and Social Security Reform.* Washington, D.C.: USGPO, 1982: 19–20.

Special Committee on Aging. *Aging America, Trends and Projections.* Washington, D.C.: USGPO, 1991: 6.

Towers Perrin. *Preparing for Retirement.* New York: TPFC, 1991.

Watson Wyatt Worldwide. *Questioning the Future of Social Security and Medicare: Results of the 1997 CFO Survey on Government Entitlement Programs.* Bethesda, Md.: Watson Wyatt Worldwide, 1997.

Chapter 14
An Actuarial Perspective on How Social Security Reform Could Influence Employer-Sponsored Pensions

Christopher Bone

HSS (U)

J26

J32

The U.S. retirement income system has often been described as a three-legged stool, with the three supports of the stools being social security, employer-sponsored retirement plans, and individual savings. In this analogy, significant changes in the length or strength of one leg of the stool may require changes in the other legs. Yet, to date, actuarial analysis of proposed social security reforms have focused primarily on how the proposed changes would affect the social security program as a stand-alone entity.[1] This chapter reviews the actuarial implications of social security reform for the second leg of the stool — retirement plans sponsored by employers.

We approach this topic by focusing on two areas where actuaries typically are called to assist plan sponsors in determining plan design. These are the pension expense that employers will recognize as a result of a particular plan design, and the lifetime pension benefit of retired former employees expressed in terms of replacement of pre-retirement disposable income (the benefit planning function). To address these issues, we begin by categorizing plans by sponsor and benefit design type. These categories are used as a framework for evaluating the pension expense an employer may incur and the types of benefit changes that might occur under a range of different social security reforms. This allows preliminary analysis of the speed and direction of employer responses to different social security reform alternatives. Such analysis may permit policymakers to begin to review the effects of social security reform proposals on the combined government and employer-provided retirement security system.

Key Items of Actuarial Analysis

Most employer-sponsored retirement plans are designed around the concept of replacing pre-retirement income in retirement (Allen et al. 1988).

Given the amount of income replacement provided by social security to certain groups of employees, most plan sponsors therefore, implicitly or explicitly, consider the level and timing of social security benefits in designing retirement benefit plans. For a sponsor of a retirement program that supplements social security, key actuarial implications of social security reform will be the cost to the sponsor of the revisions to social security and the effect of changes on the behavior of plan participants. Cost to the sponsor may arise in several areas, for example, as payroll taxes or in the cost of the sponsor's plan. Cost issues of primary concern are:

- Who pays — employees through payroll taxes or a broader group through use of income tax revenues?
- How much are the costs/savings to the plan sponsor?
- When do costs increase/decrease?
- Is the cost recorded at a different time than the cash flow?

Anticipated behavioral changes will be evaluated by plan sponsors in terms of the interaction of projected workforce requirements with changes in individual incentives to work. Many plan sponsors design plans to accomplish certain workforce management goals. To continue to achieve these goals, "designed" plans may require modification in different ways as a result of behavioral effects of a particular proposed reform.

Categorizing Plans and Sponsors by Benefit Design Philosophy and Sponsor Type

In evaluating the differential impact of actuarial feedback effects from social security reform, many alternative categorizations could be investigated. We find it useful to categorize first by sector of employment and then by plan type and benefit design philosophy. This categorization allows us to follow the various alternative regulatory schemes that govern plan sponsors' reporting of expense for retirement programs. The ability to determine expense implications for various plans may give further insight on sponsor reactions when we subsequently proceed to outline alternatives for reform and likely reactions among plan sponsors.

The range of different types of plan sponsors by type includes: public sector employers; large private sector employers; small private sector employers; not-for-profit employers; and employers who participate in multiemployer pension plan arrangements. Different regulatory, accounting, and functional environment factors apply to plan sponsors of different types and tend to focus attention on differing measures of pension cost. Furthermore, both government and private sector sources of data on plan sponsors often focus only on members of a particular sector or on plans of a particular variety.[2]

Measuring Pension Cost in Different Sectors

Measurement of pension cost is a confusing issue, as evidenced by the multiple and mutually inconsistent measures of liabilities and costs required for a private sector defined benefit plan in the current regulatory environment (McGill et al. 1996). Moreover, the confusion does not stop with private sector plans. Similar types of cost (e.g., pension costs reported on financial statements) are inconsistently reported across sectors of employment. Thus a similar plan and workforce may generate different reported pension expense if the sponsor is a public-sector rather than a private-sector employer.

Given the wide disparity of cost rules and of their application, there may be a temptation to dismiss the importance of these inelegant rules to influence plan sponsor decisions. Unfortunately, these conflicting and confusing rules have significant implications for the plan sponsors' ability to access capital markets, to budget and raise cash, and to avoid regulatory costs. Understanding the rules under which a particular plan sponsor operates may have significant bearing on the sponsor's likely reaction to proposed changes in social security.

These differences in cost incidence and determination apply primarily to defined benefit plans. By contrast, defined contribution plans bring with them a certain simplicity, in that the cost of a defined contribution plan, regardless of the entity sponsoring the plan, is almost always equal to the amount of cash dedicated to funding the plan for that year. Because of the substantial additional guarantees and subsidies available within their structure, defined benefit plans present a complex set of rules that vary by entity type and size as discussed below.

Public sector plans. In the past, governmental plan accounting for defined benefit plans was typically recorded on a basis equal to the cash contribution to the plan for the plan year. Contributions were usually based on a projection of future liabilities and assets, but sometimes ignored certain promised benefits or even used legislated "rules of thumb." New accounting rules that are effective for fiscal periods beginning after June 15, 1997, require governmental employers to report pension plan expense on the basis of accruing for all promised benefits, using assumptions and funding methods appropriate for an ongoing plan (GASB 27 1994). However, for many plans, it is anticipated that contributions will be equal to the recorded expense. Most governmental plans use a contribution measure that is anticipated to be level over time (usually a level percentage of covered salaries; see PPCC 1996). Many governmental plans have opted out of social security coverage and so perhaps could be assumed relatively immune to changes in social security were it not for two issues: (1) the persistent proposals to include all new public sector employees under social security (Advisory Council 1997), and (2) the overlap in benefits caused by employees who, by changing jobs and employment sector, move in and out of employment covered by social security.

Large private sector employer plans. Under private sector accounting standards, pension cost is determined using a projected cost per year of service concept. Assumptions used to measure cost are a blend of those embedded in annuity purchase rates and rates based on the likely experience of the specific plan in question. Cash contributions are determined primarily based on expected asset returns of the plan and other assumptions specific to the plan, subject to the constraints of the Employee Retirement Income Security Act (ERISA) and the Internal Revenue Code. The actual contribution amounts typically vary significantly from expense reported under the accounting standards. Most large private sector employers appear to make decisions regarding plan changes primarily based on the effect on accounting cost, rather than the effect on contributions.

Small private sector employer plans. While smaller private sector plan sponsors are often covered by the accounting and contribution rules that apply to larger private sector entities, contribution requirements may have a greater role in determining changes in benefit policy than accounting rules. For many smaller entities, particularly those that are not publicly traded, pension accounting rules are not viewed as particularly relevant or providing useful information. Contribution requirements are subject to the constraints of ERISA and the Internal Revenue Code as for large private sector plans.

Not-for-profit employer plans. These plans may be governmental entities (e.g., certain hospitals and colleges), in which GASB rules apply, or may instead be entities which are subject to private sector accounting constraints and many of the requirements of ERISA. Particular care is often taken in this sector to match expense with contributions. Thus, as with small and governmental plans, contributions are the primary focus on which a decision is likely to be made.

Multiemployer plans. Sponsors of multiemployer plans are typically a union or a joint employer/union association. Under most accounting regimens, cost is recorded on the books of the employer of the covered participants on the basis of the required cash contribution (based on a projected view of liabilities and ERISA constraints). In certain circumstances, where there is a significant likelihood that an employer might withdraw from a multi-employer plan, liabilities measured on a plan termination basis may be required to be reflected on the books of the employer (FASB 87, 1985). These liabilities are typically measured on the basis of annuity purchase rates, similar to the basis that applies to the accounting for large private sector pension plans. As such, they can be significantly affected by short-term changes in the level of interest rates.

The categorization above reveals a convergence on two views. One is an accounting paradigm that applies primarily to large private sector entities and some small private sector employers and employers that participate in multiemployer plans. This paradigm is based on a notion of pension cost per year of service and pension liabilities measured in a way that reflects some portion of the cost to purchase annuities. This view of cost affects decisions about changes in pension benefits due to social security reform for large private sector employers and may affect smaller private sector employers or participants in multiemployer plans. Most other sponsors will look primarily at how benefit changes affect current cash contributions. For defined benefit plans, this second "contribution-based" view will be based on projected liabilities and best estimates of future asset returns; these contributions are often expressed as a level cost as a percentage of pay.[3]

Categorization by Type of Plan

Before proceeding to discuss plan sponsors' reactions to alternative social security reform proposals, it will also be useful to establish the varieties of plans and the alternatives for measuring expense under these plans and for using these plans to affect employee behaviors.

Defined contribution plans. Defined contribution plan design typically follows one or more of the following design philosophies: the plan functions as a mechanism for gainsharing, with contributions to accounts tied fairly directly to profitability or share price (e.g., an Employee Stock Ownership Plan); the plan provides access to tax deferred savings opportunities (e.g., a 401(k) plan with no employer matching of contributions); the plan is driven by an employer target for amount of benefit at retirement; or the plan provides an opportunity to save with direct financial encouragement provided by the employer (e.g., a plan where the employer matches employee contributions up to a certain percent). Differences in philosophy regarding the plan's function and aims may lead plan sponsors to different responses to changes in social security reforms. For instance, plans that are viewed by sponsors as gainsharing mechanisms may regard increases or reductions in social security benefits as not significantly affecting the primary purpose of the plan, and so make no changes in the plan; but plans driven by target income replacement will need to reexamine plan design if social security benefits are changed.

Defined benefit plans. Defined benefit plans have a variety of plan features allowing the sponsor to affect worker decisions regarding continued employment versus work with another employer or retirement. These features include: vesting rules, retirement subsidy provisions, variation in the accrual of benefit as a function of service, etc. By their nature, defined benefit plans tend to reflect employer targets and an explicit or implicit model of planning for scheduled retirement and so are likely to be adjusted in response to changes in the level of benefit provided by social security.

Unfunded non-qualified plans. Common in large private sector employers for the top executive group, these plans can be either defined contribution or defined benefit plans. Of note is the distinction for these plans between cash flow (contributions) and accrual of expense. Furthermore, these plans do not enjoy the exemption from FICA tax that funded tax qualified plans do. Participants in these programs are typically earning more than the maximum earnings subject to payroll tax for social security benefits. Thus, proposals to remove the cap on earnings subject to payroll tax (already in effect for the Medicare portion of taxes) have an effect on the cost of these plans.

Responses of Employer-Sponsored Plans to Alternatives for Social Security Reform

Having established categories of plan sponsors and reviewed alternative broad categories of plan design, we ask how these different types of plans and sponsors would be affected by alternatives for social security reform. The following section analyses component parts of social security reform proposals that are incorporated in or have been discussed by various proponents of changes to social security.

Increases in FICA Tax Rates

One proposal for putting social security back into long-range balance would be through an immediate increase in the payroll tax rate. Alternatively, rather than collecting increased taxes now, increases in the tax rate could be deferred and brought into effect as the difference between social security system revenues and benefit payments narrows.

For a plan sponsor designing a retirement program that is supplemental to social security, a key design parameter is the target living standard in retirement provided by the program. This is addressed by examining the level of replacement of earnings income needed to provide the same disposable personal income after retirement. This replacement standard changes in response to marginal income tax rates (Palmer 1994). Since earnings income is subject to social security payroll taxes, but annuities and investment income are not, a higher payroll tax reduces the percentage of pre-tax earnings that the combination of social security, employer pensions and personal savings must provide. In short, income that was taxed away during employment need not be replaced in retirement. Hence, even without any planned increase in social security *benefits*, an increase in social security *tax rates* may lead to declines in the amount of scheduled private pensions, as pension plan designers react to anticipated lower pre-retirement standards of living. It is likely that some employers will change their pension programs to realize these savings so as to offset any increase in cost due to increases in tax rates. Alternatively, employers might recover the cost of increases in taxes directly, by granting smaller increases in wages than would otherwise have been given; the savings due to reduced replacement income would then serve to reduce the amount of employee savings required in order to reproduce pre-retirement living standards.

Defined contribution plans. If tax rates are increased, these rate increases can be expected to raise employer costs and thereby reduce profitability for private sector employers. But, over time, the tax increases may be anticipated to be passed on to employees in lower wage rates or in decreases in benefits so that total compensation remains constant and profitability is restored. This scenario assumes that outside constraints (e.g., mandated wage rules) do not enter into the calculation. Thus for defined contribution gainsharing plans, social security reform through increased payroll tax rates appears unlikely to reduce long-term allocations to profit sharing plans. Gainsharing type plans are also least likely to be viewed by the sponsor as retirement target arrangements, and so may remain significantly unaffected by increases in social security payroll tax rates.

However, in defined contribution plans for which a primary function is to provide employees with access to tax-deferred savings, actual rates of savings in these plans could well decrease. As higher payroll taxes reduce workers' take-home pay, people may be less willing and less able to save.

Finally, employers with target benefit plans may be anticipated to revise the plans to reflect lower saving needed to replace pre-retirement pay. These revisions are likely to occur over time as sponsors periodically evaluate their total benefit packages, rather than immediately upon the change in tax rates. Matched savings plans will also be reviewed by plan sponsors in light of the lower required replacement ratios generated by the new taxes. Of course, any decrease in propensity or ability to save may generate a need for proportionately greater matching if employer workforce management goals are to be met, so that whether employer matching will rise or fall is not immediately clear. Under the nondiscrimination rules of the Internal Revenue Code, employer responses will be further affected by the need to ensure that the amount of income deferred by non-highly compensated individuals is sufficiently close to the amount deferred by highly compensated individuals. This last effect could force some employers to reevaluate plan designs immediately. Hence, if policymakers are to avoid significant disruption in defined contribution plans at the point of a *social security* payroll tax increase, changes in the nondiscrimination rules that apply to *employer-sponsored* defined contribution plans must be considered.

Defined benefit plans. Defined benefit programs, by their nature, tend to target a defined replacement income, and thus reductions in replacement income required to maintain pre-retirement standards of living will probably be factored into the design of these plans. However, there will be no particular urgency to the issue, since anticipated benefit reductions would be a relatively small percentage of the retirement benefit, and the increase in payroll tax does not, of itself, require amendment of the pension plan.

Hence, any changes would probably be accomplished as a part of a periodic benefit program review, rather than immediately upon the change in rates. Many defined benefit plans require routine updating to keep benefit levels in line with increases in pay levels; for these plans, the change to reflect lower replacement ratios could readily take the form of delaying updates to the plan formula. Benefit cost decreases under the reform are likely to spread over an extended period, for both projected contribution amounts and accounting costs.

Increases in Social Security Taxable Earnings Base

Another alternative for reforming the social security program would be to remove the cap on earnings subject to tax and to instead subject all earnings to tax (as in the Medicare Hospital Insurance program). This would engender some additional level of social security benefits, but, due to the highly progressive social security benefit formula, the cost to social security of increased benefits would be more than offset by increased tax collections.

As with tax-rate increase proposals, an increase in the maximum amount of taxable earnings would reduce the replacement ratios required to maintain pre-retirement standards of living. The decrease in the required replacement ratio would only apply to higher paid individuals, since the decrease in pre-retirement disposable income applies only to income expected to exceed the projected pre-retirement maximum taxable earnings base under current law. Hence, one might anticipate that retirement plan designers would decrease marginal replacement ratios as income increases.

A review of the regulatory structure that governs many employer-sponsored plans confirms the likelihood of and suggests some immediacy to changes that reduce the relative retirement income replacement ratios for higher paid individuals. Rules designed to prevent private pension plans from unduly favoring highly paid individuals apply to private sector (and most not-for-profit) organizations. These rules are often complied with, to some extent, by public sector entities. Under these rules, allowance is made for the provision of greater benefits to highly paid individuals due to the fact that social security taxes are only assessed on earnings up to (and social security benefits are only calculated based on) the maximum social security taxable earnings. In essence, for defined contribution plans, the current configuration of the rules recognizes the employer portion of the OASDI social security tax as equivalent to a pension contribution; employers are effectively allowed to continue that level of contribution to a defined contribution plan, providing that certain other rules are met.[4] Rules with comparable intent (but greater complexity) apply to defined benefit pension plans, providing for a level of "permitted disparity" in the provision of benefits to higher-paid individuals. It is anticipated that these special exemptions for anticipated disparity would be eliminated if the underlying feature of social security (i.e., the cap on taxable earnings) is removed. Complete data on the extent to which current plan designs rely on permitted disparity to pass nondiscrimination tests are not available (particularly since plans need not explicitly adjust benefit levels to integrate with social security to rely on permitted disparity), but clearly it characterizes a majority of the defined benefit plan universe (Olsen et al. 1977).

An initial reaction to the combination of a decrease in marginal required replacement ratios and the elimination of permitted disparity may be to assume that the two offset. But, barring a restructuring of the benefit plan, elimination of permitted disparity would increase benefits provided to all employees on earnings less than the social security earnings base, including employees earning less than the earnings base for whom no change in required income replacement has occurred. If the pension plan is restructured to bring benefits for lower-paid individuals back to the same levels as in effect before the elimination of permitted disparity, the reduction in the combined social security and private pension benefit for higher-paid individuals will exceed the reduction generated in the required replacement rate. This is due to the progressive nature of the social security benefit calculation. For the most highly paid individuals, this effect is further exacerbated by the cap on pensionable wages that can be used in determining benefits under qualified (funded) pension plans. This cap, which generally may be assumed to apply to many of the individuals at a plan sponsor with ultimate authority to approve changes in plan design, may force an employer with relatively egalitarian retirement income provisions to design a separate plan solely for the provision of benefits to the highly paid. Such a nonqualified plan would likely be at least technically unfunded, and cannot cover a broad spectrum of employees. These plans, covering only a few decisionmakers, are of course inexpensive when compared with costs of providing benefits to all employees. Given the cost incentives to rework plans if permitted disparity is eliminated, it is likely that employers will respond quickly to amend plans in the event that payroll taxes are applied to all earnings. It would not be surprising if increasing numbers of employers shifted primarily to nonqualified plans for senior executives and reduced the employer role in the provision of pensions for other workers.

Reductions in Social Security Cost of Living Adjustments (COLA)

Other proposals to reform social security have focused on benefit decreases rather than tax increases. Among these are proposals to reduce the indexation of the benefit by indexing to the Consumer Price Index minus some arbitrary fraction (e.g., CPI − 0.5%). Alternatively, only a portion of the benefit might be indexed (e.g., only the benefit up to the poverty level, or only the amount of benefit received up to the median benefit level).

For sponsors reviewing replacement ratios, a reduction in social security benefits leads to an increase in the amount that must be provided by employer or employee monies in order to maintain pre-retirement living standards in retirement. However, any widespread change in the indexation of social security benefits may be anticipated to lead to rethinking of what it means to provide a pre-retirement standard of living in retirement. Clearly, the individuals' circumstances change during retirement, and the maintenance of the pre-retirement living standard is unlikely to be exact even at the point of retirement. Will employers change the planning basis to one of maintenance of the level of real disposable income at retirement? Will employees show increased interest in indexed annuities or the ability to manage assets (and so explicitly take steps to guard against inflation risk)? Cost implications of this type of policy change would only apply as plans are amended, for most of the categories of plans and sponsors that we have discussed. Thus, changes to reflect these considerations are likely to occur on a gradual basis without significant immediate disruption of the employer plan arena.

Public sector defined benefit plans. While the implications of a reduction in COLA are likely to be reflected relatively slowly for most types of plans, special considerations may apply to public sector plans. Indexed retirement benefits are much more prevalent in these plans (PPCC 1996), and immediate taxpayer pressure on benefits may be anticipated, if indexation of public sector pensions is more generous than for social security benefits.

Means Testing of Social Security Benefits

Means testing proposals call for curtailing or taxing away social security benefits for those with incomes or assets exceeding certain levels. Clearly a means test would represent a tax on income from savings that, while perhaps not quite a "cliff," certainly presents a very sharp incline.

As with other reductions in social security benefits, a means test increases the amount of retirement income that must come from employer and employee funds to maintain a specified pre-retirement living standard, for the individuals whose benefits will be affected. However, the actual mechanism by which means testing is affected may significantly modify choices about ways to provide retirement income. For instance, means testing might codify a preference for stable (annuity) income by establishing rules that favor annuities compared to asset pools that yield investment income.

Furthermore, the steepness of the implied tax on savings may tend to accelerate any trend to provide sharply different benefits for decision-makers (assumed likely to be subject to any means test) versus rank-and-file employees. Thus, means testing may further increase the number of non-qualified plans that provide retirement benefits only for the top echelon of employees. Other employees may be covered under a plan that (in conjunction with benefits calculated under social security) provides adequate income to the lowest paid and fails to replicate pre-retirement living standards for employees in the middle earning ranges.

Increases in Retirement Age

A number of reform advocates have recently suggested a partial solution to the social security system's problems by raising the age at which unreduced social security benefits are paid. Proposals include increasing the normal retirement age to age 70, or indexing it to increases in longevity. Other proposals would change the age at which early retirement benefits are first paid.

Changes to the age of retirement clearly affect the underlying basis of planning for retirement by plan sponsors, in that most plans, regardless of sector of employment, feature an accumulation of capital or of retirement benefits. If the date of commencement is to be delayed, then the accumulation per year can safely be reduced. But the retirement age for social security benefits is not necessarily closely linked to retirement ages used by plan sponsors in designing retirement plans for their own employees. Instead, employer retirement planning models typically reflect employer perceptions of workforce needs. To the extent that the social security retirement age proposals reflect the actual availability of an active, productive older workforce, employers may be expected to respond to the same trends in worker productivity by raising pension plan retirement ages in tandem with social security. But, to date, employers continue to sponsor early retirement incentives in defined benefit plans that encourage retirement well before the age of earliest retirement under social security, even as increases in social security normal retirement age are scheduled to begin under existing law.

Defined benefit plans. Certain defined benefit plans integrate early retirement benefits very closely with social security through the use of supplemental retirement benefits that are payable until social security retirement age (either early or normal) is reached. Under these plans, an increase in social security retirement age could serve to extend the duration of these supplemental retirement benefits. Thus, an increase in the age of normal or early retirement under social security could have severe cost implications for these plans, leading sponsors of the plans to immediately revisit the plan design.

Invest Social Security Trust Assets in Private (Domestic) Equities

Recent proposals have advocated investing some of the social security trust funds in equity investments. Under this model, the government would passively purchase domestic securities, presumably through index funds. Increases in the funds available for investments in domestic equity securities would potentially be significant, raising questions about the degree of governmental control of private equity, the leveraging of passively held index investments, and the power of entrenched management. If the federal deficit is no longer partially financed by the excess of social security taxes over benefit payments, there may be effects on interest rates as well.[5]

The proposal would appear likely to increase short-term demand for equities and so raise values of current equity investments. However, interest rates or taxes might also rise as the federal government financed (or reduced) the deficit by raising additional monies. In balanced portfolios, the effect of rising interest rates on bond prices would tend to offset gains due to additional demand for equities. Over the longer term, there remain unanswered questions about the equilibrium of interest rates versus returns on equities.

Defined contribution plans. In and of itself, this reform does not change the underlying benefit structure of the social security program and so would not necessarily induce demand-driven changes in defined contribution plans. However, to the extent that long-term rates of return are increased or decreased, changes in contribution rates may be required to assure adequate retirement income under the new investment paradigm. Such changes are likely to be very slow, as investors and plan sponsors first wait for data to verify the change in investment returns and then modify plans as part of a review of total benefit packages.

Large private sector defined benefit plans. A narrowing of the spread between equity returns and bond interest rates may have little effect on portfolios and therefore on the long-term contribution requirements and returns of most defined benefit plans. However, for plans governed by private sector accounting rules, there can be a significant effect on reported cost. For these plans, liabilities are determined on the basis of a mixture of annuity purchase rate assumptions and of assumptions germane to anticipated plan experience. In essence, this forces the determination of liabilities using a discount rate equal to a long bond interest rate, rather than discounting at the anticipated rate of return on the investments. The net effect is to set a pattern of high costs for immature plans, followed by low or even negative costs as the plan matures. A decrease in the spread between equity rates of return and long bond interest rates would decrease this effect over the long term. However, over the near term, large private sector plans would probably see significant reductions in reported pension expense, if the interest rate used to determine expense were to rise.

Privatization in IRA-Like Accounts

Some analysts propose to reserve a portion of social security taxes, or increase taxes, to fund investment in individual defined contribution social security accounts. These accounts would serve as mandatory IRA-type investments. Through the individual account mechanism, the issue of government investment in private sector equities is to some extent finessed, although the issue of replacing a significant source of funds for current deficit financing remains.

The proposed reform shares many features with the proposal to invest social security trust fund assets in equities. It would likely have a similar effect on short-term demand for equities and on interest rates. Identical questions arise about shifts in the long-term equilibrium of interest rates vs. returns on equities. The added item of interest is the clear similarity between the privatized accounts and existing defined contribution plans. At least one proposal (CED 1997) has argued that plan sponsors might directly credit defined contribution plan allocations against the new privatized accounts, so long as the accounts meet certain restrictions. By allowing employers to credit contributions directly to existing defined contribution plans against the new taxes, net savings in the economy are not increased with respect to employees of employers that sponsor existing plans. It is possible, although speculative, that employers who do not currently offer defined contribution plans might be encouraged to offer such a plan as an addition to the required mandatory IRA account. Another concern regarding these accounts is that employers might be forced to step in and increase benefits if returns are poor. However, the similarity of mandatory IRA accounts to current defined contribution plans argues that this risk is no different from that already borne by employers whose retirement programs include a combination of defined contribution and defined benefit plans.

The proposal also shares many features with an increase in social security tax rates. However, in addition to the reduction in required replacement ratios as a result of lowered pre-retirement disposable income, mandatory IRA's may be anticipated to generate additional benefits. Thus, the resulting reduction in employer-provided benefits is likely to be much more significant than for the payroll tax increase alone. For employers with both a defined contribution and a defined benefit plan, this reaches its logical conclusion in the proposal to directly offset defined contribution plan contributions against mandatory IRA contributions.

Conclusion

The degree to which social security reforms determine changes in employer-sponsored retirement plans will depend on the regulatory environment and the desire of plan sponsors to affect retirement decisions of their own workforce. Preliminary analysis indicates that increases in social security tax rates are most likely to affect defined contribution plans, due to the interaction of decreased ability to save by lower-paid individuals with the nondiscrimination rules for defined contribution plans. The immediate effect may be limited, however, for plans that are not currently close to failing these tests. The effect of removing the limit on earnings subject to payroll taxes would be to require immediate redesign of the majority of private sector, defined benefit plans (and presumably some defined contribution plans as well). This is due to the anticipated elimination of permitted disparity rules at the time the cap on taxable earnings is removed. In conjunction with the progressive nature of the determination of the social security benefit, this could accelerate the trend to a two-tier system of unfunded pension plans for the top-paid group, and a funded plan which is adequate for the lower-paid and inadequate for employees in the middle.

Increases in retirement ages are anticipated to have long-term design implications for sponsored plans; short-term cost increases may be limited to plans that provide early retirement supplements. Similarly, reductions in social security cost-of-living adjustments appear to affect the plan sponsor retirement system gradually, save for the potential for more rapid changes to indexation provisions of public sector plans. Means testing raises many unanswered actuarial issues and could require large and immediate changes in sponsored retirement plans.

Proposals to change the investment policy pursued by the Social Security Administration affect not only benefit design costs but also near-term financial cost drivers, particularly for large private sector plans. These changes could generate large reductions in reported pension (and retiree medical) costs. Longer-term increases in sponsor cost would emerge if this policy were to decrease long-term returns in equity investments. The establishment of mandatory IRA-type accounts would argue for similar effects on markets, but also puts participant benefits at risk if equity markets fail to perform. This adds additional risk that employers will need to increase benefits in a future market downturn, but not to any greater extent than that currently faced by sponsors who rely on a combination of defined contribution and defined benefit plans in designing a retirement program.

If we are to derive a retirement income security policy for all individuals, it is imperative that social security reforms be evaluated not solely for their effects on social security benefits, but also with respect to their effects on employer-sponsored retirement plans, and the desire and ability of employees to save on their own behalf. This chapter uses a preliminary assignment of plans into categories by sector of employment and by type of plan to allow better understanding of the cost drivers and the benefit models underlying plan sponsors' reactions to different reform proposals. Use of similar methodology with alternate methods of categorizing plans (e.g., collectively bargained status) may lead to additional insights and should be pursued. Finally, all proposals put forward to date use a combination of the types of social security reforms discussed; applying the above type of analysis to actual proposals would require careful evaluation of the interaction of the various reforms.

Notes

1. For areas of relative actuarial agreement with respect to the effects of social security reform proposals on the social security program, see the monograph series on various reform issues produced by the American Academy of Actuaries.

2. A discussion of employer data sources useful in policy modeling appears in Citro and Hanushek (1997).

3. Placing employers in categories is at best approximate, and meant to describe the regulatory paradigm that receives primary focus. Certain sponsors within a sector may behave more like sponsors within other sectors because of business circumstances such as regulatory environment. For instance, many utilities once focused primarily on cash contribution requirements, as do smaller private firms, because of the importance of regulatory accounting rules (FASB 71, 1982).

4. These additional rules include a restriction that the rate of employer contribution for monies contributed to a plan based on compensation in excess of social security Earnings Base be no more than double the rate of contribution to the plan due to compensation up to the social security Earnings Base. Rules on nondiscrimination testing are contained in Sections 401, 410 and 414 of the Internal Revenue Code and the various regulations provided under the authority of these sections. Specific rules regarding the ability to integrate employer plans with the provisions of social security are included in Sections 401(a)(5) and 401(1).

5. Of course, as the excess of social security taxes over benefit payments is anticipated to become zero and then turn negative over time, the loss of this source of deficit financing is inevitable.

References

Advisory Council on Social Security. *Final Report of the 1994–1996 Advisory Council on Social Security.* 2 vols. Washington, D.C.: Social Security Administration, 1997.

Allen, Everett, Joseph Melone, Jerry Rosenbloom, and Jack VanDerHei. *Pension Planning—Pensions, Profit-Sharing, and Other Deferred Compensation Plans.* 6th ed. Homewood, Ill.: Irwin, 1988.

American Academy of Actuaries Committee on Social Insurance. "Sorting Through Proposals on Social Security and Medicare." *Contingencies* 7, 6 (1995): 32–36.

———. "Privatizing Social Security." *Contingencies* 8, 4 (1996): 24–30.

Committee for Economic Development. *Fixing Social Security.* Washington, D.C.: CED, 1997.

Citro, Constance and Eric Hanushek. *Assessing Policies for Retirement Income—Needs for Data, Research, and Models.* Washington, D.C.: National Academy Press, 96–111, 1997.

Financial Accounting Standards Board. *Statement No. 71, Accounting for the Effects of Certain Types of Regulation.* Stamford, Conn.: FASB, 1982.

———. *Statement no. 87, Employers' Accounting for Pensions.* Stamford, Conn.: FASB, 1985.

Governmental Accounting Standards Board. *Statement No. 27, Accounting for Pensions by State and Local Governmental Employers.* Norwalk, Conn.: GASB, 1994.

McGill, Dan, Kyle Brown, John Haley, and Sylvester J. Schieber. *Fundamentals of Private Pensions*. 7th ed. Philadelphia: Pension Research Council and University of Pennsylvania Press, 1996.

Olsen, Kelly, Jack VanDerHei, and Dallas Salisbury. "A Framework for Analyzing and Comparing Social Security Policies." *EBRI Issue Brief* 183. Washington, D.C.: Employee Benefits Research Institute, March 1997.

Palmer, Bruce A. "Retirement Income Replacement Ratios: An Update." *Benefits Quarterly* (Second Quarter 1994).

Public Pension Coordinating Council. *1995 Survey of State and Local Government Employee Retirement Systems*. Chicago: PPCC, 1996.

Chapter 15
An Organized Labor Perspective on Social Security Reform

David S. Blitzstein

HSS (US)
526
550

Organized labor has participated in the Advisory Council on Social Security process from the very beginning. The famous 1937–38 Council which designed the U.S. social security system included Sidney Hillman of the Amalgamated Clothing Workers and Philip Murray of the United Mine Workers. Organized labor has had representation on all of the Advisory Councils over the years, a requirement put into the law in 1956. On this last round, three representatives of organized labor were members of the 1994–96 Advisory Council.

These three labor members of the 1994–96 Advisory Council, along with three other Council members, supported the Maintain Benefits (MB) proposal. Labor members of the Council were in agreement with organized labor's support of social security's long-term guiding principles. These are to ensure a system that provides universal coverage with benefits that are an earned right and benefits that are wage-related. Also, we believe social security should remain a system based on compulsory contributions, and one that is self-financed. Finally, we maintain that social security should be a system that is redistributive for purposes of setting adequate benefits, a system that is not means-tested, a system that is portable and wage-indexed, and one that provides inflation-protected benefits. Organized labor has been a strong advocate of social security since its inception, and has actively promoted its expansion of coverage and benefits from 1935 to the present.

Over the years, organized labor has leveraged its support for social security by developing a strategy to promote private pensions through collective bargaining. Led by the success of the United Mine Workers and the United Auto Workers in the late 1940s, unions began to negotiate pension pre-funded defined benefit (DB) pension plans. The auto workers, in a brilliantly orchestrated campaign called "Too old to work, too young to die," deliberately integrated their pension proposals with social security benefits in an effort to encourage employers to support expanded social security benefits. In the early days, the combined negotiated benefit of $100 a month was a fixed amount, so any increase in social security reduced the company's financial obligation. As social security benefits increased over time, unions tended to drop these integration provisions (Fraser 1990). However, social security benefits are still a major factor in determining union bargaining policy as it relates to negotiating adequate retirement benefits.

Despite organized labor's council members' support for the MB plan, it is important to state that this proposal of the Advisory Council does not represent the AFL-CIO's official position on social security. This is because the AFL-CIO's governing executive council is in the process of updating and refining its stance on social security policy. For this reason, my objective is to critique some of the social security privatization proposals and to discuss the role of social security from a national perspective. This discussion is based on my experience representing organized labor as a pension negotiator and acting as a trustee of several multiemployer pension funds.

The Emergence of the Privatizers

The last Advisory Council marks a political watershed. Its report is the first by an Advisory Council in 60 years that failed to support unanimously the social insurance principles of the system's founding fathers. This is also the first council report in which a group of members formally recommended a partial privatization of the social security system. Even the 1982–83 National Commission on Social Security Reform, a group convening during the height of the Reagan era, rejected privatization in the face of a system financial crisis of an immediate nature (rather than a future one, such as we face now).

What is interesting about the current debate is its timing. It is surprising that privatization has gained a national audience now, just as the social security system is in the process of building historically large surpluses to pay for the baby boom generation's retirement.

The roots of this movement may be traced to the 1983 amendments. As Paul Starr noted a decade ago, pay-as-you-go (PAYGO) financing was the bane of privatization because it was nearly impossible to undo (Starr 1988). That is, all privatization proposals run into immediate trouble because of the "double payment problem." This arises as a transition cost to pay for current retirees while shifting active workers over to an individual account (IA) system. According to Starr, a PAYGO system is locked in, except for the periods when it is accumulating large surpluses and taxpayers are paying partly for their own retirement. Starr refers to this period as privatization's "demographic opportunity," and it would seem that such a period is occurring now. For those of us who oppose privatization, we are in the "danger zone," but most of us do not even know it. In essence, the Advisory Council's individual account proposals are an effort to privatize the social security "surplus," diverting some portion of this surplus into private accounts that would otherwise begin accumulating in a publicly held reserve to pay for part of the costs of the baby boom generation.

Pay-as-you-go financing has been a controversial subject since the adoption of social security. Not surprisingly, and true to Starr's forecast, supporters of privatization identify PAYGO financing as the "central problem with social security." They characterize PAYGO financing as "an income transfer system . . . rather than a retirement savings mechanism" (Advisory Council 1997: 103).

There is a deep historical irony in this debate over social security financing, since the fact is that social security in the United States was initially conceived as a partially funded system. The legislative decision to move toward a PAYGO system was negotiated in the 1939 amendments by conservative Senator Arthur Vandenberg, who feared that large social security surpluses would legitimize federal deficits or government control over private firms (Starr 1988). In short, the privatizers can thank one of their own for the transition cost dilemma.

One must admire the political acumen of Franklin Delano Roosevelt in creating a social security financing structure that has endured over 60 years. In my view, the political stability of the social security program is rooted in its lack of dependence on the federal budget. This provided the system with a cloak of political inviolability. But this too was almost not the case. Again, in another historical irony, the 1937–38 Advisory Council report envisioned an equal contributory role by the federal government. But this financing option was defeated.

Understanding Social Security's Long-Range Deficit

Looking ahead, it is clear that the subject of the social security long-range deficit of 2.19 percent of payroll requires more attention and understanding. The deficit, described in the 1996 Trustees Report, is at the crux of the Advisory Council report and the current debate over the solvency of the system. Interestingly, all three Council factions failed to analyze the deficit or its root cause.

One problem is that the social security system actually is projected to run surpluses indefinitely under the actuary's "low-cost" scenario. I raise this point because the "intermediate cost" scenario used by the Advisory Council relies on several questionable assumptions. For instance, it seems unreasonable to assume that economic growth will average only 1.8 percent over the next 20 years, a rate lower than any comparable period in the United States history. The "intermediate scenario" assumes that growth slows even further in later years, until the economy's growth rate is less than half of the

2.8 percent rate experienced over the last 20 years. Similar concerns can be raised about the conservative projections for future fertility and immigration rates (Baker 1996). One could readily argue that these key assumptions do not make sense in light of America's rebounding economy and tight labor markets.

A further concern about social security's projected deficits is prompted by a statement buried on page 163 of the Advisory Council Report. This Appendix, an insightful analysis describing actuarial experience of the Trust Fund since 1983, explains the source of the system's financial problems (Advisory Council 1996: 163–64). To many, this discussion will be surprising. Consistent with my earlier comments about overly conservative demographics, the actuarial report shows that demographic assumptions over the last 12 years have actually reduced, not increased, the social security deficit by 0.83 percent of taxable payroll. Moreover, the beneficiary/worker ratio has not changed since 1983 and has not contributed to the estimated long-range deficit. The actuarial report concludes that this fundamental ratio was fully taken into account in the 1983 financing provisions, so, contrary to popular opinion, demographics are not driving the social security long-range deficit.

Instead, other factors must be taken as causing the long-range deficit:

1. The shifting estimating period, accounting for 0.55 percentage points of the deficit.
2. The disability assumptions, accounting for 0.70 percentage points of the deficit.
3. Method changes, adding 0.93 percentage points to the deficit, and
4. Economic assumptions, accounting for 0.79 percentage points of the deficit.

Within the economic assumptions, the most important adverse experience was the steep decline in real wage growth from 1.5 percent to 1.0 percent, which by itself accounted for 0.50 percent of the deficit. Clearly, wage growth and social security's payroll tax financing system are inextricably linked. I believe that policymakers should be talking about the destructive wage stagnation of the 1980s and 1990s in light of social security's long-range financial balance, rather than social security privatization.

Defined Benefit (DB) Versus Defined Contribution (DC)

Organized labor believes that it is unacceptable to reduce social security's defined benefit plan design through partial privatization. Under the Personal Security Account (PSA) proposal, somewhat over 60 percent of the average worker's benefit would be based on a defined contribution account, and slightly less than 30 percent under the individual account proposal. It is disingenuous for supporters of privatization to profess their support in the Council report for the "four-tier" retirement program resting on a compulsory social security system, when in fact their proposals act to replace the key DB foundation of the system (Advisory Council 1997: 17). The hallmark of the current social security DB plan is that it provides predictable income protection from the hazards of old age, disability, and death.

A major objection to privatization is that defined contribution (DC) accounts do not guarantee benefits. That is, the value of future DC benefits is determined by the capital market, which is inherently risky. In addition, there is always a risk of retirees having to purchase an annuity during a market downturn, and being forced to accept sharply reduced income. The reality is that social security privatization will not abolish the business cycle. Ultimate DC benefits are uncertain and not accurately quantifiable. Comparisons of replacement ratios, internal rates of return, and money's worth are of limited use when comparing benefits in a DB world, but are misleading when examining DC accounts.

Problems arising from movement to a DC format are exacerbated by social security's current inflation protection of benefits. To my knowledge, Wall Street does not broadly offer private investments that are guaranteed to keep up with future inflation. A dramatic expansion of government indexed inflation bonds in a privatization scenario would only shift the risk of inflation back to Washington (Advisory Council 1997: 17). Growing life expectancies also challenge the DC paradigm. The PSA group's proposed annuity voluntarism adds an additional layer of risk to privatization.

Equity Rates of Return: The Privatizer's False Solution

A common theme embraced by all Advisory Council proposals is the investment of trust fund or privatized assets in private equities. This is a dramatic departure from past financing practices of the social security system, and one with unpredictable macroeconomic consequences on interest rates, the federal deficit, the price of equities, and the rate of return on equities. We should note that the MB group did not advocate the near-term enactment of the equity investment proposal until further study was conducted.

What is also troubling about investing a portion of social security trust funds in equities is its potential deception and distortion of the real issues. It reminds me of my collective bargaining experience with employers who think they can fund their pension plans solely on investment returns without cash contributions. It's the false belief that you can "invest" your way out of a funding problem. I would submit that a bear market like the one in 1974–75 would end the privatization debate. Furthermore, Baker's study (1977) addresses some of the inconsistencies of the investment assumptions used by the Advisory Council. He questions the compatibility of projecting a real 7.0 percent annual return for stocks extrapolated from past historical performance, with annual economic growth over the next 75 years at least two percentage points below what it was over the past 75 years. According to Baker, in order for stocks to continue to generate a 7 percent annual return under the trustees' assumptions of economic growth, price-to-earnings ratios would have to soar to an unheard-of 34 to 1 in 2015, and an absurd 485 to 1 in 2070 (Baker 1997). So much for investing our way into actuarial balance.

In the case of social security, equity investing and its superior rates of return have become the new panacea for policymakers, offering a way to avoid or reduce payroll tax increases. Whether it is politically correct or not, policymakers should not exclude payroll tax increases from their list of strategic options. Our social security taxes are still competitive with comparable industrial competitors, and gradual increases would not destabilize America's economic prowess.

The Privatizer's Agenda and Private Sector Pensions

After reading the Advisory Council report, it dawned on me that those who support individual accounts do not discuss how these would dovetail with the private-sector employer-sponsored retirement system. In fact, I would argue that social security privatization may result in replacing private sector pensions with IRA and Keogh-type accounts. Social security as it has been developed in the United States is the antithesis of privatization, promoting economic protection through a pooling of community resources. By contrast, privatization aims to separate the individual from the larger community. It is just as likely that privatization will separate the individual from the corporation or the union.

Historically, the social security program and the private pension system developed side by side. Social security did not "crowd out" the private retirement system as some theorists expected. Far from displacing private pensions, the social security program may have institutionalized the need for private retirement income. Unfortunately, private pension coverage has stagnated in the United States in the last two decades. This failure of private pension coverage to expand may have further emboldened the privatizers.

Organized labor strongly supports the current three-tier retirement income system. We believe that a social contract exists among the government, employers, workers, and retirees. In this way, organized labor rejects the anti-community message of privatization.

We can still return to the origins of our three-tier national retirement policy. We believe evolution is still under way, that policy mistakes have been made that can be corrected, and that the private pension and personal savings tiers need much work and enhancement. Undermining our current social security system would be a counterproductive move in American history. Instead, we believe it would be more effective to adapt and strengthen the private sector retirement system. For example, private defined benefit plans should be targeted for deregulation and creative reform. Full-funding limits should be loosened. Congress must reorient itself towards supporting employer-sponsored plans and move away from its revenue-driven fiscal policies. Policymakers should also promote more innovation and flexibility in DB plans, such as provisions for employee contributions and partial phase-out retirements. The tax advantages of private pension plans should not be weakened.

Public opinion surveys indicate that workers are expecting to depend much more on their own retirement savings and their employer's pension plans than on social security in the future (Rother and Wright, this volume). If these expectations are to be realized, and if workplace conflict is to be avoided in the twenty-first century, here is where the work needs to be done. Privatizing Social Security is not the solution to our national retirement problems. Promoting and expanding private pension plans presents safer opportunities for policymakers to enhance our retirement system.

References

Advisory Council on Social Security. *Final Report of the 1994–1996 Advisory Council on Social Security*. Vol. 1, *Findings and Recommendations*. Washington, D.C.: USGPO, 1997.
Baker, Dean. "Granny Bashing." *These Times*, December 23, 1996.
———. *Saving Social Security with Stocks: The Promises Don't Add Up*. Twentieth Century Fund/Economic Policy Institute Report. New York, 1997.
Fraser, Douglas. "Too Old to Work, Too Young to Die: A Union Program for Retired Workers." In Irving Bluestone, Rhonda J. V. Montgomery, and John D. Owens, eds., *The Aging of the American Work Force*. Detroit: Wayne State University Press, 1990.
Starr, Paul. "Social Security and the American Public Household." In Theodore R. Marmor and Jerry L. Mashaw, eds., *Social Security: Beyond the Rhetoric of Crisis*. Princeton, N.J.: Princeton University Press, 1988.

Chapter 16
Women as Widows Under a Reformed Social Security System

Karen C. Holden

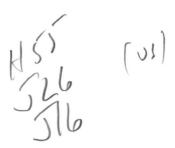

The U.S. social security system has two missions: to insure workers and their immediate families against the loss of income due to workers' disability or retirement, and to provide those benefits in a way that favors workers and families who are less likely to be otherwise insured. The current debate over the structure of social security is in large part a discussion over the attributes of individuals and families to whom redistributive benefits are paid, and the current financial importance and social value of these benefits. Women, more often than men, are the beneficiaries of the redistributive compo-nents — as recipients of spouse and survivor benefits and of the higher replacement of covered earnings for low-wage workers — so the debate is about the value to women and their families of retaining these redistributive benefits.

This chapter focuses on the economic and social rationale for and value of social security survivor benefits. We first describe the historical reasoning for the provision of survivor benefits, and for their payment without actuarial reduction in the married worker's benefits prior to death but subject to an implicit means test. Understanding the motivation for the structure of survivor benefits is the first step in debating whether they remain economically and socially relevant today. We next review recent findings about the economic consequences of widowhood during the early 1990s. This discussion is followed by discussion of the treatment of widows under the two proposals of the recent Advisory Council on Social Security that include individual accounts. Whether a widow's economic status improves under reform proposals that would provide greater individual discretion over the payment of survivor benefits will depend, in part, on whether the widow shares in the individual accounts of her deceased husband, in the form of either a joint-and-survivor annuity elected at the husband's retirement or the inheritance of undistributed accumulations at his death. A review of results from an analysis of predictors of the joint-and-survivor selection, presented in the final section, suggests the role of regulatory policies governing the bequeathing of individual accounts to surviving spouses.[1]

A Brief History of Social Security Survivor Benefits

The social security system is sometimes described as based on a now-outmoded "traditional" view of the family, though in fact the framers of the social security system were quite sophisticated. Benefit proposals did take account of the greater prevalence of one-earner couples at that time, but women were not expected to remain permanently out of the work force. The 1937–38 Advisory Council on Social Security recommended benefits for younger widows only if they were caring for their deceased spouses' minor children on the basis that "It is normal for a large majority of younger widows without dependent children to reenter employment" (Brown 1977: 31). Benefits for older widows were argued largely on income adequacy grounds, targeting a group of individuals in need of additional income "to tide themselves over the period of income stoppage for which social insurance benefits are *payable without the necessity of recourse to public assistance*" (Burns 1949: 413, emphasis added).

Upon that Advisory Council's recommendation, the 1939 Social Security Amendments provided for a supplemental benefit to aged wives and widows (if 65 and older), but it also imposed a "dual entitlement" provision. This mandated a dollar-for-dollar reduction in spouse and survivor benefits if the wife or widow received her own retired-worker benefits.[2] For this reason, it is more accurate to characterize the original social security model as one that overlaid a strict earnings-related insurance system offering women and men identical retired-worker benefits with an income-transfer system whose provisions were akin to means testing in other income-transfer programs. Targeting supplemental benefits to wives and widows was considered to be consistent with the adequacy goals of the social security system during the early years of the program, at a time when retired-worker benefits were low and most married women would be unlikely to contribute much earnings-based retirement income toward the consumption needs of the married household, or toward their own consumption needs when their husbands died. At the same time, the adequacy goals motivating these benefits also dictated reduced benefits for married women and survivors when other sources of income were available — principally their own retired-worker benefits accompanied, perhaps, by pension income connected to longer market careers.

Dramatic increases in labor market attachment by women during the second half of the 20th century, along with changes in family structure, have made the dual entitlement provision an increasingly apparent factor in determining the benefits of married women. In 1960, 57 percent of female social security beneficiaries were eligible for benefits solely as a spouse or survivor, but by 1995 this was true for only 37 percent of female beneficiaries. Conversely, in 1960, only 9 percent of all female retired-worker beneficiaries were dually entitled — that is, eligible for both a retired-worker benefit and a spouse or survivor benefit higher than their own retired-worker benefits; by 1995, 43 percent of all retired-worker beneficiaries were dually entitled (Social Security Administration 1997).[3] These changes would be expected in a population in which paid labor market activity is an increasingly important component of women's lives. At the same time, women's lengthening work careers have led to a rise in the percentage of female social security beneficiaries who experience (and are aware of) small or no marginal gains in their social security benefits with longer years of covered employment. Every proposal for reform — including those of the recent Social Security Advisory Council — embodies a view about the value of these benefits to individuals and families.

The Continuing Vulnerability of Widows

As described, during the 1930s, the relatively low incomes of elderly couples and widows motivated the provision of spouse and survivor benefits (paid initially only to women). Today, the poverty rate for families headed by a retired worker now lies below rates for all working-age families with a male present, a gain attributable to increases in the real wages of workers and to improvements in the social security benefit formula. Despite improvements in the income levels of older households over the past several decades, including those of women living alone, incomes of widowed women remain substantially below those of married households, even when household incomes are adjusted for differences in consumption needs.

Research using data from the 1970s and early 1980s attempts to separate the contribution to the relatively low income of widows of widowhood itself from the relatively low income of about-to-be widowed households (Bound et al. 1991; Burkhauser, Holden, and Feaster 1988; Hurd and Wise 1989). The picture emerging from these studies is that while a share of the lower average income of widows and intact couples, widowhood itself had a large, negative impact on the economic wellbeing of women widowed during those decades. Since then, women's labor-force participation rates have continued to rise, the life insurance and pension industries have expanded survivor policy options, and pension legislation has been passed that aimed to increase the share of a couple's resources paid to a widow after her husband's death (e.g., the 1974 Employee Retirement Income Security Act and the 1984 Retirement Equity Act). These forces might be expected to reduce the impact of widowhood on women more recently widowed.

A recent study by Holden and Zick (1997) shows that even for women widowed during the 1990s, widowhood continued to be accompanied by a large and abrupt decline in income. Figure 1 shows the pattern of average monthly income-to-needs ratios of women whose widowhood was observed over the 1990, 1991, and 1992 panels of the Survey of Income and Program Participation (SIPP). These "eventually widowed couples" are defined as women who at the first SIPP interview were 40 or older, married with husbands present, and whose husbands died at some point during the 32-month SIPP panel, after which the widows were observed for at least one interview as a widow.[4] Figure 1 also shows average monthly income-to-needs ratios for a comparison group of "intact couples" in which the wife was also 40 and older at the first interview but who remained married throughout the 32-month SIPP panel. This comparison group is presented as an estimate of the income changes that might otherwise have been observed among the eventually widowed couples but for their having been widowed. In this way it is possible to separate the contribution to the relatively low income of widows of pre-widowhood differences in income levels (which may or may not be attributed to pending widowhood itself), changes in real income upon widowhood that may be attributable to broader economic forces (e.g., to high rates of inflation), and the change that is attributable to widowhood itself. Since intact couples in the SIPP sample are on average younger than eventually widowed couples, the age distribution of the intact-couple group are "matched" to that of the eventually widowed couples. This forced comparability in age structure means that differences in income and income change between the two groups of women are net of differences in age structure.[5]

In Figure 1 the data for each eventually widowed woman are arrayed around the month of widowhood, which may occur at different SIPP months for the widows in the sample.[6] A month of "widowhood" is randomly assigned to intact-couples using an approach suggested by Zick and Smith (1991). While the continuously married couples are in fact never widowed, arraying their monthly incomes around an assigned widowhood month provides a comparison over the same extended time period.

The story told in Figure 1 is strikingly similar to the findings of the studies using earlier years' data. Prior to widowhood, eventually widowed households have lower incomes than do their continuously married counterparts. The eventual widows' average income-to-needs (using the standard U.S. Census Bureau needs calculations) was 3.41 in the two months preceding widowhood, but this ratio dropped to 2.38 immediately after the husbands' deaths. While the average pre-widowhood income-to-needs ratio of eventual widows is only 10 percent below that of continuously married couples, in the post-widowhood months their monthly income-to-needs falls to and stabilizes at roughly 70 percent of that of the comparison couples. Compared to women widowed in the 1984 SIPP, the 1990s widows are only slightly better off both before and after widowhood—women widowed in the 1984 panel had income-to-needs ratios of 3.1 in the pre-widowhood months, declining

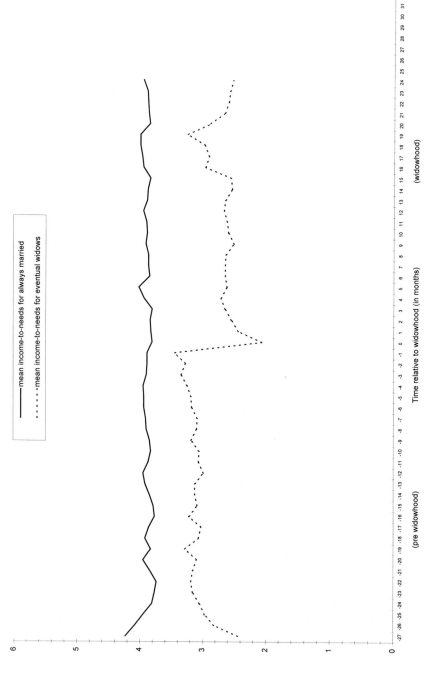

Figure 1. Income-to-needs ratios for always-married women and eventual widows. Source: Author's calculations.

to 2.0 for the two months after widowhood (Holden 1990). In sum, while widows' lower economic status as compared to married couples appears to be explained in part by pre-widowhood income differences, a decline by almost one-third in income-to-needs occurs at the time of the husband's death.[7]

Why women on average suffer a large decline in income upon their husbands' deaths is not fully understood. The analysis of the predictors of income-to-needs and of income changes by Holden and Zick (1997) finds that while these two groups of couples are remarkably alike in the pre-widowhood months on many demographic dimensions, there are marked differences in the sources of income before and after the husband's death. Husbands about to die are more likely to be drawing on social security and pension benefits and less likely to have labor income than are their married counterparts. This is not surprising, given the lower labor market involvement among the about-to-die husbands.

It is also clear from the SIPP analysis of widowhood that the receipt of a pension both is associated with higher pre-widowhood income and lessens the economic shock of the widowhood event itself. Among the women who were widowed in the SIPP panels, those who received a pension as a widow both had higher pre-widowhood income-to-needs ratios than those who did not (4.13 vs. 3.03) and had a significantly smaller decline in that ratio (11% vs. 38%). Compared to the 74 percent of the men in eventually widowed couples who were receiving pensions prior to their deaths, only 45 percent of the widows received a pension. The loss of this pension explains an important part of the decline in income among widows. It is clear that, while not all husbands are eligible for a pension before they die, the receipt of pension following the husbands' death cushions the fall in income upon widowhood. Ironically, the expansion in pension coverage, which has increased the proportion of men who receive a pension, has increased the importance of pensions as an explanation of income declines upon widowhood.

Social Security Reform Proposals

Two of the three reform plans described in Chapter 1 by the Advisory Council on Social Security have a defined-contribution layer on top of a basic defined-benefit plan.[8] The Personal Savings Account (PSA) plan would add a mandated defined-contribution individual account (financed by a 1.6 percent increase in the payroll tax rate) to a defined-benefit plan whose benefits would be somewhat less generous than the current system.[9] The Individual Account plan proposes that the major share of social security benefits be derived from a fully funded, privately held individual account that would be a second tier of a system that also provided a flat retirement benefit tied to a number of years covered. Under both proposals, the surviving spouse would be eligible for a benefit that is no less than 75 percent of the combined benefits received by the couple from the defined-benefit component of the plan. Under the PSA plan, while the worker is alive, the spouse would be eligible for a spouse's benefit equal to one-third of the other spouse's Primary Insurance Amount (before any early-retirement reduction). When both spouses in a couple claim benefits at the normal retirement age, the 75 percent survivor benefit would leave the surviving spouse in a one-earner couple with a benefit equal to that of the deceased worker's and the surviving spouse of a two-worker, equal-earner couple with a benefit equal to 150 percent of the (equal) individual benefit (i.e., .75* 200%). The 75 percent survivor benefit across all couples compares to the current system in which survivor benefits range from two-thirds to 50 percent of the couples' combined pre-widowhood benefit.[10]

Under the Individual Account alternative the non-working spouse of a one-earner couple would be eligible for a benefit equal to 50 percent of the flat benefit. Consequently, the 75 percent survivor benefit for a widow would amount to between 112.5 percent of the flat benefit for a one-earner couple (75% of 1.50 of the flat benefit) to 150 percent of the one-person single flat benefit for a two-worker equal-earner couple. While this percentage is higher than the current 100 percent of deceased-worker benefit for survivors first claiming benefits at or after the normal retirement age, it is a percentage of a much lower proposed flat benefit — $410 per month (in 1996 dollars) for a single earner. The resulting survivor benefit is between $461 and $615 and is lower than the average benefit award of $781 paid in 1995 to nondisabled widows 65 and older (Social Security Administration, 1996).[11] Under both the Individual Account and the PSA plans, widows would be assured only the survivor benefits based on the lower, basic benefits. Whether, as widows, wives would share in the projected higher social security benefits paid to workers from both tiers, would depend on their sharing as wives and widows in their husbands' individual accounts. As widows they would not be assured a share unless an explicit bequest was made or a survivor annuity chosen by their husbands prior to death. In the next section of this chapter we present evidence on the probability of husbands' making this choice and the policy implications of that evidence.

Joint-and-Survivor Benefits

The married individual who applies for social security retired-worker benefits now has no choice as to whether survivor benefits will be paid to a surviving spouse or a former spouse nor as to the amount paid. Divorced individuals automatically are entitled to a survivor benefit based on their former spouse's covered earnings. Individual accounts introduce choice into the payment of survivor benefits, unless the option to choose against a joint-and-survivor option is restricted by accompanying federal regulation. The

PSA plan would require annuitization but allow a married worker to choose a single-life benefit (a benefit that ceases upon the worker's death) or a joint-and-survivor benefit (a benefit that continued to be paid to the designated survivor). The proposed regulation of annuitized accounts in the PSA roughly mirrors federal regulation now governing private employer-provided pensions (Kushner and Domone 1995). The Individual Account alternative would not require annuitization, nor did proponents of this plan propose regulations on the type of annuity selected when the accounts are annuitized.

Critical to how widows will fare under the two individual-accounts proposals is whether workers will choose to share these pension assets across the years when only one of them may be alive. As wives' labor force participation, earnings, and pension coverage increase, it is not known how husbands may consider these changes in making their choice about annuity type.

Pension Legislation

In 1974, the Employee Retirement Income Security Act (ERISA) established minimum fiduciary, coverage, and vesting requirements governing qualified *private* pension plans. ERISA (as amended) applies only to an "employee benefit plan . . . established or maintained by any employer . . . [except that it] shall not apply to . . . a governmental plan" (ERISA Sec.4).

The "joint-and-survivor annuity requirements" of ERISA specify that when the primary form of plan payout is an annuity, the default payout form to married workers must be at least a joint-and-one-half survivor annuity which is actuarially equivalent to the single-life worker pension. That is, the spouse of the married worker is eligible for a survivor benefit equal to at least one-half of the benefit payable to the retired worker under this option. A joint-and-survivor benefit that is actuarially equivalent to a single-life pension will pay a lower benefit during the retired worker's lifetime. ERISA originally allowed the married worker to choose a single-life annuity, a lump-sum distribution, or some other option instead of the default option without notification to the spouse. The 1984 Retirement Equity Act (REA) amended ERISA to require the spouse's notarized signature when the default joint-and-survivor option is rejected.

This default joint-and-survivor annuity must be provided by defined-benefit plans and by defined contribution plans unless participants do not elect benefits in the form of an annuity and the nonforfeitable accrued benefit is payable in full to the participant's spouse. While ERISA also regulates Individual Retirement Accounts and 403(b) tax deferred annuities, the distributions from these accounts fall outside the joint-and-survivor regulations. Likewise, ERISA rules on distributions do not apply to privately purchased annuities from life insurance companies. In other words, ERISA requirements regulate the joint-and-survivor annuity selection, but workers may opt not to take the joint-and-survivor option or may roll over pension distributions into accounts that are not regulated.

Exploring the degree to which men who now receive a pension choose to insure their wives through a joint-and-survivor option provides insight into the protection that widows may receive from their husbands' individual accounts and into which widows would be vulnerable to the loss of a pension under a more privatized system. The next section examines the predictors of the decision by married men to take a joint-and-survivor pension.

Predictors of Joint-and-Survivor Annuity Selection

The data used are for married male retired workers in the New Beneficiary Survey (NBS). The NBS surveyed a sample of individuals who first received social security benefits during 1980–81. They and their spouses, if married, were interviewed approximately one year later. Here we examine male retired-worker beneficiaries who were married and reported pension receipt at the time of the 1982 survey. Respondents were asked when their pensions were first received, from which it is possible to determine whether their pensions began prior to or after the effective date of ERISA. In addition, pensioners were asked whether their pension would continue to their spouse, if they died today. It is from this question that the estimate of joint-and-survivor selection is derived.[12] Because the NBS sample is of men who were already pension recipients, the analysis does not throw any light on the consequences for widows when husbands vested in a pension die prior to pension receipt. In addition, the pension-option selection of these men was not governed by the 1984 provisions of the Retirement Equity Act, and so the effects of that act cannot be examined with these data.[13] We examine the probability that the married man chose a pension that would continue to be paid to his wife after death, as a function of explanatory variables affecting the willingness of the couple to suffer a reduction in pension income when both were alive, the "need" of the widow for the additional pension income, and the likelihood of the husband's dying earlier than his wife.

For the total sample of married men, 62 percent had elected a pension that would continue to be paid to the widow after the husband's death. This is a weighted average of the 48 percent of the men whose pension benefits began prior to 1974 who elected a joint-and-survivor pension, and the 64 percent whose benefits began in 1974 or later who did so.

The difference in these two groups of men's election suggested an effect of the 1974 legislation, but establishing exactly which kinds of men elect a joint-and-survivor pension is more complex. An earlier analysis of men's pension-option selection in the pre-ERISA years (Holden and Burkhauser 1986) hypothesized that the pension-option selection was shaped by economic factors affecting both the value and the affordability of a pension that continued to a widow. For a group of men electing a pension in the pre-1974 legislation years, the joint-and-survivor pension was more likely to be selected (a) by husbands who were economically better off (implying that the couple was better able to afford a reduction in the husband's pension while both were alive), (b) when the wife's expected widowhood period was longer (implying a longer survivor pension pay-out period for these couples), and (c) whose pension wealth was a higher proportion of his total wealth (implying that he was constrained in resources that could be bequeathed to the widow).[14] For this pre-ERISA sample, the wife's own income and pension eligibility failed to have an influence on the husband's pension-option selection, implying that the couple's decision was shaped primarily by the costs and consequences of reducing his own pension income when both spouses were alive. We replicate and extend this earlier analysis, taking advantage of the more up-to-date and detailed NBS data.

The results of the analysis of the survivor-option selection are presented in Table 1. Predictors include wealth measures (total wealth of the husband, the share of his wealth that is his pension, and the wife's own wealth), an indicator of whether the wife is eligible for her own pension (the wealth value of which is included in her wealth measure), an indicator of the husband's poor health, and indicators of the difference in age between husband and wife. We include additional measures of the timing of the pension selection (POST-ERISA=1 if the pension began in 1974 or later), of the husband's marital history (MARRIED BEFORE=1 if the husband was married before), and if there were children from the current marriage (CHILDMAR=1 if there were children from the current marriage). The last variable is included since adult children may provide support to a widowed parent, should resources in widowhood be insufficient.

A husband with greater wealth (TWEALTH) is expected to allocate more wealth to the period of his wife's widowhood. The greater is the share of husband's wealth that is his pension (PWEALTH), the more important is the selection of a joint-and-survivor pension as a means of bequeathing wealth to the widow.[15] The greater the wealth value of the wife's on pension and social security benefits (WIDWLTH), the less dependent is her well-being as a widow on her husband's pension selection. The wife's pension eligibility (WIFEELIG) indicates whether eligibility for her own pension, versus other forms of wealth, has a unique influence on the husband's pension decision. Finally, the health and age variables are included to indicate observable — to the couple — differences in the probability that the wife will survive the husband.[16]

The results using the new data are largely consistent with earlier findings (Burkhauser and Holden 1986). The share of wealth accounted for by the husband's pension increased the probability that a joint-and-survivor was selected, indicating that couples who are most likely to take the joint-and-survivor pension are those for whom cessation of pension income would

TABLE 1. Predictors of Joint-and-Survivor Selection (Probit Estimate)

Variables	Coefficients
INTERCEPT	−.698***
TWEALTH	−.001
PWEALTH	2.270***
WIDWLTH	−1.062***
WIFEELIG	−.124*
HEALTH	.116*
AGE1	−.252*
AGE2	−.084
AGE4	−.342***
POST-ERISA	.703***
CHILDMAR	.122*
MARRIED BEFORE	−.096
WHITE	.239*
N	2058

Source: Author's computation using data from the New Beneficiary Survey, 1982.
*Significant at .1 level; **significant at .05 level; ***significant at .01 level.
Variable definition
TWEALTH   The wealth value of asset, pension, and Social Security that the husband can consume over his lifetime.
PWEALTH   Share of his pension wealth comprising TWEALTH (%)
WIDWLTH   Wealth value of widow's Social Security benefits, her own retirement pension, and other assets owned by her over her expected widowed life.
WIFEELIG   Equal 1 if wife is eligible for a pension in her own right, zero otherwise.
HEALTH   Equal 1 if husband reports any one of three serious health conditions.
AGE1   If husband is 11 or more years older than wife.
AGE2   If husband is 10–4 years older than wife.
AGE3   If husband is within 3 years of wife's age.
AGE4   If wife is 4 or more years older than husband.
POST-ERISA   If pension was initiated after 1974
CHILDMAR   If couple had children from current marriage (adult or minor)
MARRIED BEFORE   If husband was married before.
WHITE   If husband was white

seriously reduce the wealth that continued into widowhood. Consistent with the earlier study, couples appear to consider their own differential risk of widowhood. The husband's own poor health (HEALTH) increases the probability of his selecting a joint-and-survivor pension. When the wife is substantially older than her husband (AGE4), and consequently, her expected widowhood shorter than average, the husband is less likely to take a survivor pension. It is also the case that much older husbands (AGE1) are less likely to choose a joint-and-survivor pension, probably due to the large benefit cut as compared to the single-life pension for such couples. The positive effect of being white may reflect the much longer expected lifetimes of white women (and the greater value to them of a survivor pension) in a world of race-neutral pension calculations. Finally, whether a husband is in a first marriage or subsequent marriage has no effect beyond the effect prior marriages may have had on his current wealth.[17]

Conclusion

A major policy question is why women remain vulnerable to sharp income changes when their husbands die. The risk of poverty among widows has diminished in part because of the greater resources that women bring into widowhood, but widowhood is still accompanied by a large fall in income. To the extent that social policy is designed not only to guarantee minimum income levels, but also to reduce the likelihood of severe income changes for all widows, this goal has not been fully achieved.

Proposals to provide a larger share of couples' combined social security benefits to survivors, financed by lowering benefits paid to the couple, would diminish the sharp decline in income upon widowhood (Burkhauser and Smeeding 1994). However, reforms that would substitute an individual account component for some share of current benefits might increase the widow's losses, depending on the share of the husband's individual account bequeathed to his widow. The PSA plan would require annuitization with a joint-and-survivor option that could be rejected by the annuitant. The Individual Account plan would not mandate annuitization or regulate the form of the annuity.

Our empirical analysis of the joint-and-survivor selection among married male pensioners offers insight into the characteristics of widows who might be most vulnerable to income declines under an individual account system. We find that smaller social security survivor benefits would increase the probability of the husband's joint-and-survivor selection. We also find that as women's pension coverage increases, the joint-and-survivor probability falls, leaving wives more vulnerable to income declines upon widowhood. The effect of ill health and age differences on the probability of electing a joint-and-survivor benefit implies a rational weighing of the relative value of that benefit. At the same time, it means that a man who dies "against the odds" — e.g., a healthy man or a husband younger than his wife who dies unexpectedly early — will leave a widow without the assured income protection now provided through a uniform survivor benefit.

The results suggest that reform proposals that include a major individual accounts component should include discussion of the details of the regulations governing the annuity options that workers may elect. It is important to note that the Individual Account plan would leave these accounts largely unregulated, and the PSA plan, which would require annuitization, would allow workers to choose against a joint-and-survivor option.

Under the current social security system, survivors (including divorced spouses) are eligible for a social security benefit at least as large as that of their deceased (ex-)spouse, although that benefit may be reduced for early acceptance, for continued earnings, or by the survivor's receipt of her own social security retired-worker benefit. Under the individual account options, a survivor pension would be paid without regard to other income and assets. Widows who now have their social security survivor benefits reduced would be better off with inherited individual accounts. However, if husbands select against the joint-and-survivor annuity when their wives have their own social security or employer-provided pensions, widows might be no better off — and perhaps worse off — under a system with far smaller guaranteed survivor benefits. Among the women widowed in the 1990, 1991, and 1992 SIPP panels, less than half as many reported pension receipt after their husbands' death as would have been expected had all pension-recipient husbands chosen a joint-and-survivor pension, and women who had no pensions after their husband died experience sharper declines in income.

Other studies of widowhood have found that social security survivor benefits are as important to the economic well-being of widows as are benefits from private pension plans (Holden, Burkhauser, and Feaster 1988). Longer work histories and greater pension coverage among women have not eliminated the economic risk of widowhood. Our findings, using the NBS data, also suggest that proposals to restructure the social security system so that a greater share of the system's protection is derived from individual accounts may pay greater attention to the consequences for widows — still an economically vulnerable group — of allowing holders of those accounts to choose an annuity that ceases upon the death of the spouse. The passage of legislation making a joint-and-survivor option the default payment in private plans was an important contributor to a substantial rise in the percentage of men taking that option after 1974. Even as these findings suggest that couples rationally weigh the relative value of postponing potential consumption to the years when the wife alone survives, they also suggest that untimely deaths will leave widows without survivor benefit protection. For the widow whose husband chose a single-life annuity, however rational that decision may have been, the death of the husband and her loss of his pension would result in the continuation of the income declines now experienced by widows.

Support for this research was provided in part by a grant from the Social Security Administration and a training grant in the Economics of Mental Health from the National Institute of Mental Health. Sean Nicholson and Stuart Kipnis provided valuable assistance with the NBS and SIPP estimates, respectively. All findings, interpretations, and conclusions of this paper represent the views of the author and not necessarily those of the funding agencies.

Notes

1. Gender neutrality in the social security system means that all issues discussed in this chapter may apply to a surviving husband. On the other hand, continuing differences in earnings of women and men mean that women are at much greater risk of poverty as widows than are men as widowers, so the public policy issue is addressed here as a widowhood issue.

2. The payment of survivor benefits initially only to women does reflect a traditional view of the family in which husbands were expected to be the primary earners. Payment was extended to husbands in 1950, but only if pre-widowhood economic dependency could be established. After 1975, when the dependency test for men and not for women was ruled discriminatory by the U.S. Supreme Court, all remaining sex-based differences in social security rules were eliminated.

3. This is an underestimate of women eligible for both a retired-worker and a spouse or survivor benefit, since the Social Security Administration defines as dually entitled only persons eligible for retired-worker benefits and a *higher* spouse or survivor benefit. If dual entitlement were defined as persons eligible for both a retired-worker benefit and a subsidiary benefit, regardless of size, virtually all ever-married women and men would be so deemed.

4. Each SIPP panel is a nationally representative sample of households whose members are interviewed at four-month intervals over approximately a 32-month period (U.S. Bureau of Census 1987).

5. Before weighting the intact-couple sample to achieve age comparability, each sample was weighted by the SIPP sample weights that adjust for the specific sampling criteria used in SIPP and panel attrition. The age weighting of the intact-couple sample means that their data do not reflect the actual average experience of this group, but only of this group with a reweighted age structure.

6. The aggregate data are arrayed over a 64-month period, even though for any single couple we have a maximum of 32 months of data. This is because some women are observed for a longer period as married women and are widowed near the end of the panel, while others are widowed early and are observed for a longer period as widows.

7. The 0 month is the month in which the husband dies. The first month of post-widowhood is the first full month spent as a widow. See Holden (1989) and Burkhauser, Holden, and Myers (1986) for a discussion of the problems associated with the accounting period during which a husband dies. Surveys (including SIPP) generally do not count the husband's income during the month of his death even though he may have been present part of the month. This is probably the reason for the lower income in month "0" and the rise in month "1" a more accurate measure of the income the widow could draw on as a new widow.

8. The details of these plans are described in Chapter 1.

9. Under this plan the computation period for the Average Indexed Monthly Earnings, which is used to compute benefit amounts, would be increased from 35 to 38 years and the move to age 67 as the earliest age of receipt for unreduced benefits would be accelerated.

10. The 50 percent "survivor benefit" arises when both spouses receive equal retired-worker benefits. In this case no additional benefits would be paid to the survivor beyond his or her own retired-worker benefits.

11. Note the anomaly that a single worker gets less than the surviving spouse does in a married couple.

12. Pensioners might have answered this question affirmatively if they had chosen

a period-certain option. Thus, the analysis is not strictly of the joint-and-survivor selection. Nevertheless, any survivor selection indicates that the pensioner is willing to forgo some share of his own pension in order to have it continue to his widow, even if only in the case of his relatively early death and for a relatively short period of widowhood.

13. ERISA did not mandate a survivor pension when pension vested workers died prior to the earliest age of retirement. REA extended survivorship protection to spouses of pre-retirement deceased workers. The NBS data are for retired men; thus survivor pension receipt is not affected by the pre-retirement death provisions. Tegen (1997), using data from the National Survey of Families and Households, concludes that the REA did increase the percentage of widows receiving joint-and-survivor pensions when husbands died prior to retirement.

14. This study used a sample of married men interviewed in the Retirement History Study and who died between the survey years 1969 and 1979. Their pension-option selection was estimated by their widows' receipt of pension income that could be attributed to their husbands' pension continuation.

15. The estimate of pension wealth is the actuarial value of the single-life option, adjusting for the actual pension option selection of these men. While we know when a survivor pension is chosen, we do not know what specific choice was made. We assume a joint-and-one-half pension (the minimum allowed by ERISA) when estimating the actuarial value of the pension of men who chose a survivor option.

16. Education-level variables were also included but statistically insignificant and made little difference to the estimates. Education was hypothesized to influence the information husbands sought when faced with the pension-option decision.

17. The effect of wife's marital history on the husband's pension-option selection also was found to have no influence. The husband's marital history variable was included in these estimates since the effect of a divorce on his assets and any obligations to a former wife are not observed while the assets the wife gained from a divorce are observable and included in the WIDWLTH measure.

References

Bound, John, Greg J. Duncan, Deborah S. Laren, and Lewis Oleinick. "Poverty Dynamics in Widowhood." *Journal of Gerontology: Social Sciences* 46 (1991): S115–24.

Brown, J. Douglas *Essays on Social Security*. Princeton, N.J.: Industrial Relations Section, Princeton University, 1977.

Burkhauser, Richard V., Karen C. Holden, and D. A. Myers. "Marital Disruption and Poverty: The Role of Survey Procedures in Artificially Creating Poverty." *Demography* 23 (1986): 621–31.

Burkhauser, Richard V., Karen C. Holden, and Daniel Feaster. "Incidence, Timing, and Events Associated with Poverty: A Dynamic View of Poverty in Retirement." *Journal of Gerontology* 43 (1988): 546–52.

Burkhauser, Richard V. and Timothy M. Smeeding. *Social Security Reform: A Budget Neutral Approach to Reducing Older Women's Disproportionate Risk of Poverty*. Policy Brief 2/1994 Syracuse, N.Y.: Center for Policy Research, Maxwell School of Citizenship and Public Affairs, 1994.

Burns, Eveline M. *The American Social Security System*. New York: Houghton Mifflin, 1949.

Holden, Karen C. "The Transition from Wife to Widow: Data Issues in Measuring First-Period Income Effects in SIPP and the RHS." In *Individuals and Family in Transition: Understanding Change Through Longitudinal Data*. Washington, D.C.: U.S. Bureau of Census, 1989.

———. "Social Security Policy and the Income Shock of Widowhood." Robert M. La Follette Institute of Public Affairs Working Paper 3. University of Wisconsin, Madison, 1990.

Holden, Karen C. and Richard V. Burkhauser. "Pensioners' Annuity Choice: Is the Well-Being of Widows Considered?" Discussion Paper 802. University of Wisconsin, Institute for Research on Poverty, 1986.

Holden, Karen C., Richard B. Burkhauser, and Daniel J. Feaster. "The Timing of Falls into Poverty After Retirement and Widowhood." *Demography* 25 (1988): 405–14.

Holden, Karen C. and Cathleen Zick. "The Economic Impact of Widowhood in the 1990s: Evidence from the Survey of Income and Program Participation." *Consumer Interests Annual* 43 (1997).

Hurd, Michael and David A. Wise. "The Wealth and Poverty of Widows: Assets Before and After the Husband's Death." In David A. Wise, ed., *The Economics of Aging*. Chicago: University of Chicago Press, 1989.

Kushner, Michael G. and Dana J. Domone, eds. *ERISA: The Law and the Code*. 1995 edition. Washington, D.C.: Bureau of National Affairs, 1995.

Social Security Administration. *Annual Statistical Supplement to the Social Security Bulletin*. Washington, D.C.: USGPO, 1996.

———. *Annual Statistical Supplement to the Social Security Bulletin*. Washington, D.C.: USGPO, 1997.

Tegen, Karen. "Influence of Survivor Pensions on the Income of Widows: Role of Legislation, Rules, and Consumer Information." M.S. Thesis: University of Wisconsin, Department of Consumer Science, 1997.

U.S. Bureau of Census. *Survey of Income and Program Participation Users' Guide*. Washington, D.C.: U.S. Department of Commerce, 1987.

Zick, Cathleen D. and Ken R. Smith. "Patterns of Economic Change Surrounding the Death of a Spouse." *Journal of Gerontology: Social Sciences* 46 (1991): S310–20.

Chapter 17
Investment and Administrative Constraints on Individual Social Security Accounts

Robert C. Pozen and John M. Kimpel

Several practical issues would become important if Congress decided to allow a modest portion of the OASDI contribution (currently 12.4 percent of annual compensation up to $68,400 for 1998) to be directed toward an individual social security account. Such an individual account would provide a variable part of a participant's social security benefit in addition to a guaranteed social security floor. For example, Congress could decide to enact legislation similar to the Kerry-Simpson bill[1] with its 2 percent contribution to "Personal Investment Plans," which would supply a supplemental social security benefit in addition to certain guaranteed social security payments. Alternatively, Congress could adopt the proposal by two members of the last Advisory Council on Social Security for a 1.6 percent Individual Account, or the proposal by five members of the Council for a 5 percent Personal Security Account to be invested by individual participants. As noted in Chapter 1, these proposals share the common strategy of converting the social security structure from one that is entirely defined benefit to one that is partially defined contribution.

One practical issue that deserves attention is the range of investment constraints that might be placed on individual social security accounts such as those discussed in this volume. Another is the administrative alternatives for implementing such an individual account system. We discuss both below.

Investment Constraints

Several approaches to investment alternatives might be adopted in an individual account system. Since defined contribution plans shift the risk and rewards of investment experience from the plan sponsor to the plan participant, investments that can be held in an individual account should seek to maximize individual choice. However, this goal may be moderated by a desire to maintain an appropriate balance between risk and return for investments that constitute part of the social security system.

One possible investment model is that of the Individual Retirement Account (IRA). IRAs currently allow an individual to choose among many different investments. These include individual stocks and bonds, bank accounts, mutual funds, and various types of physical commodities. It is, however, unclear whether Congress is prepared to allow a similar breadth of investment choice in an individual social security account. Since this account is intended to provide part of a participant's social security benefit, albeit a modest and variable portion of such a benefit, Congress may be reluctant to allow participants to take a significant degree of risk in this portfolio.

For example, Congress might prohibit participants from investing social security contributions in any individual stock, bond, or commodity. Instead, Congress might limit participant choices to diversified securities pools, where the aggregate risk is reduced by investments in multiple issuers. Such diversified pools could be in the form of common trust funds maintained by banks, separate accounts run by insurance companies, or mutual funds managed by investment advisers. The Congressional view is also likely to be influenced particularly by the level of guaranteed social security payments under the reformed plan relative to the poverty line.

Another investment model is presented by the Federal Thrift Savings Plan. That plan offers currently only three investment options, all of which are diversified pools. One pool is a Government Securities Fund, which purchases securities directly from the United States Treasury. The other two pools, a Stock Index Fund (based on the S&P500) and a United States Debt Index Fund (based on the Lehman Brothers Aggregate bond index), are run by a private firm. This firm is selected through competitive bidding by an independent body, the Federal Retirement Thrift Investment Board, appointed by the President.

While the Thrift Savings Plan provides diversification at a low expense rate, the range of investment choices is quite narrow. In fact, over 60 percent of the assets of the Thrift Savings Plan are currently invested in the Government Securities Fund. In practice, some participants might want returns with reasonable risk from a diversified pool of smaller stocks or international securities, rather than a S&P index fund. Other participants may want the opportunity to choose among investment managers, instead of being required to use the one selected by the Federal Retirement Thrift Investment Board. Among the 200 largest defined benefit plans, only 30 percent of the assets are invested in bonds.[2] Among Fidelity 401(k) and other participant-directed defined contribution plans, fixed income and money market investments constitute less than 30 percent of assets.[3]

An intermediate model between the IRA and Thrift Savings Plan models would allow participants to direct some amount, say 2 or 5 percent of their OASDI contributions, to any qualified provider offering an appropriate array of diversified pools. A "qualified provider" could be defined as an investment manager qualified under Section 3(38) of the Employee Retirement Income Security Act (ERISA), which would limit qualification to insured banks, insurance companies, and SEC registered investment advisers. There could be additional qualifications, such as bonding and reporting, designed to assure the integrity and solvency of providers.

An appropriate range of investments could be based on the model reflected in the regulations issued under Section 404(c) of ERISA. These regulations require a provider to offer at least three diversified pools as "core" options, each of which has materially different risk and return features. One of these core options must be a money market fund, a managed income account consisting of GICs and other stable value investments, or a FDIC-insured bank account. In addition, providers who seek the benefit of Section 404(c) must distribute to participants written material on each core option, as well as other options available under the plan, designed to educate participants about the range of investment choices. Among other things, such disclosure is intended to educate participants about the investment objectives of each option and the risk and return characteristics of each such alternative.[4]

Under such an intermediate model, each qualified provider would have to offer three core options, with risk and return characteristics similar to those provided under the Thrift Savings Plan. But participants could also choose among other diversified pool options that focused on subasset classes, such as international stocks or small cap growth stocks. Providers offering such alternatives would be required to meet disclosure requirements comparable to those required by ERISA.

Administrative Constraints

The administration of an individual account system should maximize individual control and minimize costs, but these objectives are difficult to achieve because of the small size of many of these accounts. For example, if only 2 percent of the OASDI contribution were invested in an individual social security account, this would amount to only $600 invested per year for the average social security participant. Moreover, social security payments are made by most employers on a weekly basis, which would mean investments of $12 per week on average. If as much as 5 percent of pay were invested in an individual social security account, as suggested by members of the Advisory Council on Social Security proposing a Personal Security Account, it would amount to a $1500 annual contribution amount or only $30 per week.

The situation becomes even worse if we move beyond averages. Two-thirds (67 percent) of all workers covered by social security earned less than $25,000.[5] As a consequence, one could expect two-thirds of those covered by individual social security accounts to contribute less than $300 per year (or less than $6 per week) if the contribution rate were 2 percent, and less than $1,250 (of less than $25 per week) if the contribution rate were 5 percent. In other words, one of social security's greatest virtues — its universality — is also one of its problems. Administering social security in its current defined benefit form, without individual accounting or investment management requirements, is expensive: 0.42 percent when expressed as a percentage of contributions, and 0.57 percent when expressed as a percentage of benefits paid (Mitchell 1998). This compares to the 0.09 percent cost of administering the considerably smaller Thrift Savings Plan (137 million vs. 2.3 million workers), even though the Thrift Savings Plan cost includes individual accounting and investment management expenses (Mitchell 1998).

The universality of social security creates another administrative burden: by covering all workers, social security must interface with all employers. Of the approximately 6.5 million employers in the United States, 4 million have fewer than 10 employees; almost 5.5 million have fewer than 250 employees. Currently more than 5.4 million employers file their wage reports with social security by paper and not electronically (NASI 1998). Contrast this to the Federal Thrift Savings Plan, where the employer is the Federal Government (this covers many different agencies, but virtually all of them submit wage data electronically).

In the private plan arena, the average employer Fidelity deals with has over 1,000 employees. Virtually all of them submit most contribution and other data electronically (to do otherwise would require us to convert paper data manually to electronic format for input to our recordkeeping system). The high cost of manual data inputting is a barrier to providing a low-cost defined contribution plan to small employers.

In addition to participant account size and employer size, the administrative cost of individual social security accounts will be driven by the number of annual transactions. The Social Security Administration's current transactions are generally limited to the annual reconciliation of wage data (the actual collection of weekly or less frequent payroll tax contributions is handled by the Internal Revenue Service), and the payment of monthly benefits to retirees. Contrast this to the typical private sector defined contribution plan, where multiple investment options, daily transaction capabilities, and 24 hour telephone service are the norm. Last year, for example, Fidelity's recordkeeping operation performed over 90 transactions per participant, or over 450 million monetary transactions for 5 million participants. These included periodic contribution allocations among investments, daily exchanges among investment options, and distributions. In addition, Fidelity's recordkeeping operation handled over 140,000 telephone calls daily. These are the costs of giving participants maximum control over the investment of their accounts. The Federal Thrift Savings Plan, by contrast, curtails monetary transactions (and thereby expenses) by limiting participant control (for example, by limiting investment options and by limiting the number of exchanges to once a month rather than daily).

What administrative system would provide the best compromise between maximizing participant control over individual social security accounts and retaining reasonable administrative costs? One possible administrative system would be for the U.S. Treasury to continue to collect social security tax payments from employers, and subsequently to send the individual account portion to the provider selected by the participant. This system could operate through an additional page in the annual income tax filing, on which a participant would compute his applicable OASDI tax, designate his preferred qualified provider, and direct the Treasury to deposit his monies in a specific investment alternative offered by that provider.

While a governmental model would have the advantage of piggybacking on existing procedures for collecting social security payments and making Internal Revenue Service filings, it would have several disadvantages. First, there would be a substantial delay between the collection of the social security payments and the transmission of funds to the individual account provider. For example, 1998 social security payments could not be transmitted to the investment provider until the social security Administration had reconciled the individual's wage data and the Internal Revenue Service had received the individual's tax return. This would probably not occur until the end of 1999 or even the beginning of 2000. Second, this system would impose a new computer burden on the Internal Revenue Service, an agency already hard pressed to cope with its current computer demands. Procedures would have to be established to rectify any mistakes in individual social security accounts, perhaps requiring participants to deal with both the Social Security Administration and the Internal Revenue Service. Third, requiring all allocations to be made by the Internal Revenue Service might subject the individual account process to a broad range of government constraints unrelated to the system itself (for instance, an elaborate set of government contractor rules).

A different administrative model would piggyback an individual account system on the existing 401(k) plans offered by many employers to their employees. Under this model, the 401(k) plan's recordkeeper would allocate the employee's 2 percent or 5 percent contribution to a sub-account under the employer's 401(k) plan, to be periodically invested under the plan in the appropriate investment pool at the appropriate provider. Employers would have the same fiduciary responsibilities with respect to those sub-accounts that they now have to the plan as a whole.

The latter model has the advantage of utilizing an existing processing system in the private sector that has proved to be relatively efficient, but it too has several serious drawbacks. First, while 401(k) plans are virtually universal at large firms, they are almost nonexistent at small firms (although the new SIMPLE plan created by Congress in 1996 is beginning to make a dent). At present, however, only about 20 percent of employees working for small businesses with fewer than 100 employees participate in any type of pension plan. A national system for administering individual accounts would therefore need another procedure to address employees of small businesses as well as the self-employed. Second, participants in a 401(k) plan at a large firm may desire to invest their social security contributions with financial institutions other than the provider involved in their 401(k) program. If a business must allocate contributions to several different providers, administrative costs would increase significantly. Third, it is unclear who would absorb the incremental cost of piggybacking individual account allocations on 401(k) systems. Even some large employers may not want to take on the task of implementing an individual social security account system. A result of these drawbacks, this model may best serve as an optional administrative arrangement for those employers willing to undertake it.

Yet a third administrative model would be to utilize the procedures developed for annual IRA contributions. Under this scenario, a participant would instruct his or her employer to withhold only 10.4 percent or 7.4 percent (rather than 12.4 percent) of his or her paycheck for OASDI payroll tax. Then, each participant would periodically (perhaps annually) deposit 2 or 5 percent of his wages in an individual account at a qualified provider selected by the participant. He would then submit to the IRS a receipt for such contribution along with his income tax form. While this IRA model would minimize bureaucratic constraints and maximize individual control, the Treasury is likely to express concerns about possible social security fraud. The Treasury would have difficulty ferreting out those individuals who falsified receipts, underpaid their social security tax, or simply forgot to make a deposit.

A variant of the IRA model could be developed to address Treasury's concerns. Under this variant, Treasury would continue to collect all social security payments, but a participant could obtain a tax credit if he chose to make contributions to a qualified provider selected by the participant. Accordingly, participants could make an individual account contribution to providers of their choice and reduce their tax payments on their income tax filings. Alternatively, participants could reduce their withholding taxes or estimated taxes to reflect their anticipated tax credit. This variant gives participants maximum control over their individual social security accounts, though it does require participants to adjust their tax payments in order to avoid advancing the government the amount of their contributions. In addition, the tax credit should be refundable for participants who are not currently paying income tax. This variant, however, shifts much of the administrative complexities imposed on the employer under the 401(k) model to the individual. While it may be a workable solution for many individuals, it may be simply too complicated for others.

Under another variant of this alternative, participants could avoid adjusting their withholding and writing a check by instead presenting a copy of their W-2 form to the qualified provider of their choice and requesting that their tax credit be sent directly by the Internal Revenue Service to such provider. By establishing such a system (which perhaps could be built on the existing electronic refund system), participants would be sure to have the funds available to make the contribution. While such an alternative eliminates the need for writing a check, it might share some of the problems described above with regard to the governmental model (such as the potential delay between the collection of the social security payments and the transmission of the contribution to the qualified provider).

Conclusion

This discussion suggests that a system of individual social security accounts can be designed with a reasonable range of investment choices. Arguments can be made for very broad or very narrow investment choices, but the most powerful case is from an array of diversified investment pools including one stable value fund. Such an array of options has worked for private pension plans under ERISA by providing a reasonable balance between risk and return.

The administrative issues posed by a system of individual social security accounts is more difficult to resolve. The 401(k) model would be attractive to some large employers, but most small employers will not want to participate in such a program. The Treasury could both collect social security taxes and allocate contributions under a governmental model, but this would be a bureaucratic and slow system with relatively little individual control. By contrast, an IRA model maximizes individual control and minimizes bureaucracy, but may be vulnerable as a tax collection system. The best middle ground, in our view, is an IRA-type model under which the Treasury would continue to collect social security taxes and participants would be allowed a tax credit upon making their own individual account contributions. But this model might shift too much of the administrative burden to participants to be universally accepted. Perhaps the best result would be a program encompassing multiple solutions. It is not hard to envision a scenario where some employees held individual social security accounts in their employer's 401(k) plans, while others held them in an IRA.

In any event, the administrative issues presented by individual social security accounts are significant. The factors most affecting administrative costs are account size, employer size, and number of transactions. Further analysis of the effect of these factors on the various individual account proposals needs to be done before any of them are implemented.

Notes

1. S. 825, 104th Congress. Similar bills have been introduced by others.

2. Overall assets for the 200 largest DB plans were divided as follows: stocks, 60 percent; bonds, 30.5 percent; and other, 9.4 percent (Barr 1998).

3. Fidelity is the nation's largest defined contribution plan recordkeeper, with over 6,000 plans covering more than five million participants. As of 12/31/97, investment allocations (excluding company stock) were as follows: equities, 75 percent; fixed income and GIC, 17 percent; and money market, 8 percent.

4. See Labor Regulations 2550.404c-1(b)(2)(B)(1)(ii). More extensive information must be disclosed on request, including a description of the annual operating expenses which reduce the rate of return on the diversified pool.

5. Office of the Actuary, SSA, as cited in NASI (1998).

References

Barr, Paul G. "Largest Funds Top $4 Trillion in Assets." *Pension and Investments* (January 26, 1998): 1.

Mitchell, Olivia S. "Administrative Costs in Public and Retirement Systems." In Martin Feldstein, ed., *Social Security Privatization*. Chicago: University of Chicago Press, 1998.

National Academy of Social Insurance (NASI). "Setting up Individual Social Security Accounts." Working Draft, Washington, D.C., 1998.

Chapter 18
Americans' Views of Social Security and Social Security Reforms

John Rother and William E. Wright

Because of the importance that most Americans place on social security, public values and attitudes are likely to play an influential role in Congressional action. This chapter describes public values and preferences regarding the current social security program along with options for reform. We do not advocate any particular reform proposal; instead, we draw from a range of public opinion surveys to highlight which parameters should be considered in the upcoming debate.

Our conclusions may be summarized in four points. First, Americans know there is a problem with social security, but they do not regard it as a crisis (Jacobs and Shapiro 1998). Second, there is a high level of continuing support for the social security system, despite the public's increasing lack of confidence in the program (Jacobs and Shapiro 1998; AARP 1985, 1995, 1996). Third, the evidence suggests that the American public may need more time and information to work through some of the policy trade-offs that will be a necessary part of any effort to keep social security strong for the next century (Heclo 1998). Fourth, as the public works through these issues, we hypothesize that this debate will have a "centering effect" — i.e., a shifting from the position of "no change is needed" at one extreme, and "scrap the social security system and start over" at the other extreme, toward the position of moderate change in the present system.

Values and Attitudes About Social Security

Several studies of public values and attitudes about social security have been commissioned by the American Association of Retired Persons (AARP). Here we report detailed findings taken from the 1996 survey; where possible, comparisons are made with the 1995 and 1985 surveys.

Americans Feel Informed About Social Security

The survey evidence suggests that "[the public's] knowledge of social security is much higher than widely assumed" (Jacobs and Shapiro 1988). Most Americans, 7 in 10 in 1996, believe they are "very well informed" or "fairly well informed" about how social security works, an increase from 6 in 10 in 1985 (AARP 1985, 1996). As would be expected, more seniors (85 percent of those age 65 or older) report being at least fairly well informed; this represents an increase from 67 percent of those age 62 or older in 1985. Seventy-three percent of those age 50–64 feel at least somewhat informed, as do 71 percent of the baby-boomer group (age 30–49), and 59 percent of Generation X (those in their twenties). All age groups report being better informed about social security in 1996 than in 1985.

Americans Are Strongly Committed to the Program

Nearly 9 in 10 (88 percent) of nonretired Americans believe that they may not need social security when they retire (Table 1). However, they definitely want to know it is there for them just in case they do. (This question was not asked in the 1985 survey.) Sixty percent of Americans believe social security is one of the very most important government programs; this figure is down slightly from 65 percent in 1985 (AARP 1985, 1996). This belief rises with age: among those age 18–29 it is 48 percent; for those age 30–49 it is 55 percent; for those age 50–64 it is 70 percent; and at age 65 or older it is 83 percent.

Eight in 10 Americans of all ages believe that the government made a commitment to people a long time ago about social security being there for them when they retire and that the government cannot break this commitment (AARP 1996). There is a broad consensus on this across age, gender, and income categories, since 8 in 10 women, men, and people of all income categories hold this belief. (There are no corresponding data from 1985.)

The fraction of people reporting they are very confident or somewhat confident in social security declined from 46 percent in 1985, to 36 percent in 1996 (Figure 1). But confidence generally increases with age (Figure 2): one-third of Gen Xers are either very or somewhat confident, compared with 40 percent of those age 50–64 and 60 percent of seniors. However, baby-boomers are the age group with least confidence in the future of the social security system: only 23 percent are either very or somewhat confident. There are no gender differences, but there are income differences: the higher a respondent's income, the lower the confidence in social security. Confidence figures range from 48 percent among those with incomes of under $15,000, to 25 percent among those with incomes of $50,000 or more (AARP 1996).

There is some controversy on how to interpret the time trend. Jacobs and

TABLE 1. Attitudes Toward Social Security (1996) (percent)

	Agree		Disagree		
	Completely	*Somewhat*	*Somewhat*	*Completely*	*DK/Ref*
Maybe I won't need social security when I retire, but I definitely want to know it's there just in case I do.	70	18	4	8	—
The government made a commitment a long time ago about social security being there for them when they retire. The government can't break that commitment.	62	17	8	11	2
Everyone who pays into social security should receive it no matter what other income they have.	59	18	11	11	1
To ensure that social security will be there for me when I retire, I would be willing to pay more now in payroll taxes.	17	27	17	37	2
To ensure that social security will be there for today's older people, I would be willing to pay more now in payroll taxes.	18	32	18	31	1

Source: AARP/DYG/ICR (1996).

Shapiro (1998) forcefully challenge the assumption that declining confidence inevitably leads to declining support for social security; instead, they argue that "that even with low confidence, the public's support has remained virtually unchanged — a flatliner, according to available trend data." Heclo (1998) suggests, " 'It won't be there for me' appears to be a way of registering a generalized mistrust about government and politics today rather than a focused judgment about the sustainability of the social security program in particular."

Half of nonretired Americans (52 percent) believe that social security

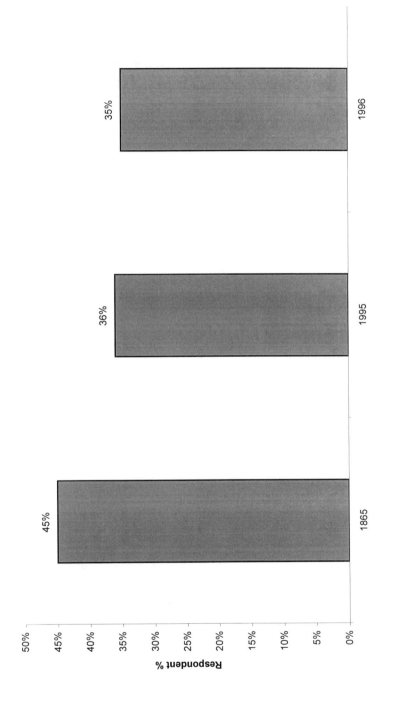

Figure 1. Respondents very/somewhat confident in the future of social security (various years). Source: AARP/DYG (1985, 1995), AARP/DYG/ICR (1996).

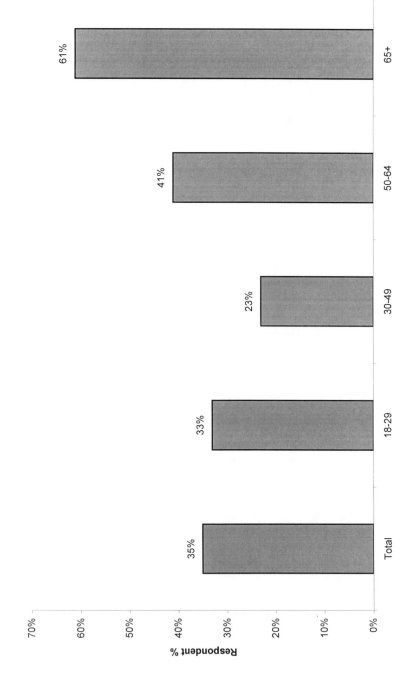

Figure 2. Respondents by age very/somewhat confident in social security (1996). Source: AARP/DYG/ICR (1996).

payments are too low (AARP 1996). In 1985, 4 in 10 nonretired Americans perceived social security payments as being "inadequate," in a differently worded question (AARP, 1985). This view was held more often by mid-life Americans (those age 50–64) (58 percent) and boomers (56 percent) than it was by Gen Xers (42 percent) (AARP 1996). In 1996, one-quarter of the nonretired believed that social security payroll taxes are "too high"; this represents almost no change over 1985 (23 percent) (AARP 1985, 1996).

Americans Support a Universal Program, but Are Also Interested in Private Retirement Options

More than three-quarters (78 percent) of Americans believe that everyone who pays into social security should receive it no matter what other income they have (AARP 1966). (There are no corresponding data from 1985.) There are no age differences in this view in the combined agreement categories (agree completely plus agree somewhat). Only at the highest income level ($50,000 or more household income) is there less overall agreement (73 percent). Thus, there is a broad consensus across age, gender, and income categories regarding the universal nature of the program.

More than two-thirds (68 percent) of the nonretired say they should stay in and support the social security system rather than get out of it. Nevertheless, this figure is down from 73 percent in 1985 (AARP 1985, 1996). There is a slight but statistically significant rise in interest in the option of "dropping out" of the social security system, from 24 percent in 1985 to 28 percent in 1996. There are also substantial gender differences (Figure 3): nonretired men (37 percent) are almost twice as likely as women (20 percent) to say they would like to drop out of social security. Male boomers (43 percent) are twice as likely as female boomers (21 percent) to say they would opt out. Higher-income respondents ($50,000+) are more likely to want to opt out (Figure 4).

Americans' Willingness to Pay More Now Has Declined

Less than half of nonretired Americans say they are willing to pay more now in the form of payroll taxes to assure that social security will be there for them when they retire (44 percent), and to assure that social security will be there for today's older people (49 percent; Table 1). (There are no corresponding 1985 data.) Nearly half (49 percent) of those age 50–64 are willing to pay more for their own retirement and 57 percent are willing to pay more for today's older people. Willingness to pay more for their own retirement was at the same level (49 percent) among Xers, 53 percent of who are willing to pay more now for today's older people. Boomers are the least willing to pay higher payroll taxes, either for themselves (39 percent) or for today's older people (45 percent). Willingness to pay is also related to income. Willingness to pay more for themselves is greatest among those with in-

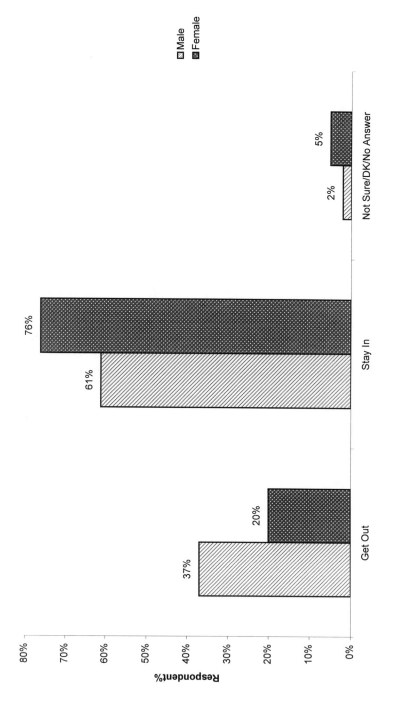

Figure 3. Response to 1996 question by sex: "If you could get out of the Social Security system, would you?" Source: AARP/DYG/ICR (1996).

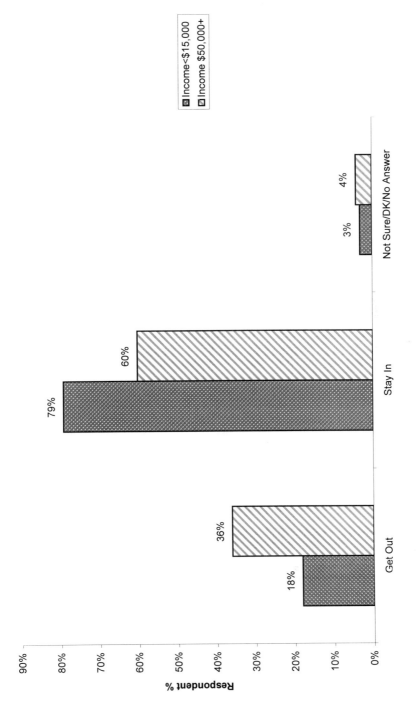

Figure 4. Response to 1996 question by income: "If you could get out of the Social Security system, would you?" Source: AARP / DYG/ICR (1996).

comes less than $15,000 (62 percent), and least among those with incomes over $50,000 (43 percent). Willingness to pay more for today's older people is likewise greater among the lowest income group (88 percent) and least (42 percent) among the highest income group.

Public Opinion on Social Security Reform Proposals

There have also been several surveys regarding a range of social security reform options, which we summarize next.

Are Cuts in Social Security Needed?

Americans have traditionally consistently opposed cutting in social security benefits as a way of balancing the system. According to Jacobs and Shapiro (1998), "Support [for maintaining or expanding the social security program] remains enormous and opposition to cutting back massive." A 1996 poll found that 59 percent of respondents do not think it will be necessary to cut back on future social security payments to keep the system financially sound. One-third thought cuts would be necessary, and 8 percent were not sure (Time/CNN 1966).

Cut Social Security Benefits to Balance the Budget?

A majority of Americans believe that the federal budget *can* be balanced without cutting social security or Medicare. A 1995 survey found that more than three-quarters of respondents (77 percent) believed that the federal budget could be balanced without cutting social security. More than a fifth (21 percent) thought it must be cut and 3 percent did not know (AARP 1995).

When asked a direct question, "Should the federal government cut back spending on social security?" to reduce the federal budget deficit, 85 percent of respondents answered in the negative. Only 14 percent replied in the affirmative and 2 percent did not know (AARP 1995). In the same poll, the choice was posed between balancing the federal budget or preventing social security from being significantly cut. Here 69 percent of the respondents chose protecting social security from being significantly cut versus balancing the budget (27 percent). Twenty-seven percent opted for the reverse and 3 percent did not know or did not answer the question (AARP 1995).

Changing the Cost-of-Living Adjustment

A majority of Americans oppose most proposals to change the social security cost of living adjustment (COLA). In 1996, nearly two-thirds (62 percent) opposed "reduc[ing] automatic increases in [social security] benefits." Thirty-four percent favored this proposal and 4 percent did not know.

TABLE 2. Attitudes Toward Social Security Cost-of-Living (COLA) Reductions (1995) (percent)

	Oppose	Favor	Don't Know
Lower increases in social security benefits (COLAs) to about 2% for each of the next two years	62	34	4
Eliminate the increase entirely for just one year	70	27	3
Cut in half the cost of living adjustments paid to social security recipients for two years	76	19	5
Provide increases over the next two years just for people with lower incomes	41	54	4

Source: Readers Digest/Institute for Social Inquiry/Roper (1995).

Mid-life Americans (age 50–64) and seniors (age 65+) were more likely than Boomers and Generation Xers to oppose this proposal (EBRI 1996).

A poll in 1995 asked about several proposals for changing the COLA in the context of helping cut the federal deficit and balancing the budget (Table 2). Half the respondents (54 percent) favored only "providing increases over the next two years just for people with low incomes," 41 percent opposed the proposal, and 4 percent did not know (Readers Digest 1995). Large majorities opposed halving the cost of living adjustments paid to social security recipients for two years (76 percent); delaying the increase entirely for just one year (70 percent); and limiting benefit COLAs to 2 percent for each of the next two years (Readers Digest 1995).

Should the Retirement Age Be Raised?

Raising the retirement age appears to be among the least popular social security reform proposals, and the higher the proposed new retirement age is, the greater the opposition. A 1997 poll found that nearly two-thirds (64 percent) opposed "gradually increasing the retirement age for social security from 65 to 69 without affecting people now receiving benefits," 31 percent favored this proposal, and 5 percent did not know (Newsweek 1997). Another 1996 poll found that a proposal raising the retirement age to 70 was opposed by 68 percent and favored by 31 percent, whereas 9 percent did not know. Younger respondents were most likely to oppose this proposal and those without any college education were more likely to strongly oppose this reform proposal (Table 3).

Should the Payroll Tax Be Increased?

Increasing the payroll tax is an unpopular social security reform proposal. When asked a general question about raising this tax, over two-thirds (68 percent) opposed the idea in 1996, while 28 percent favored it (EBRI 1996). Boomers and Gen Xers were more likely to strongly oppose an increase in the payroll tax. A 1997 poll found that a majority (54 percent) of respondents opposed "increasing the social security payroll tax by one and a half to two percent," while 41 percent favored this proposal and 5 percent did not know (Newsweek 1997).

Should Social Security Benefits Be "Means-tested" or Fully Taxed?

Subjecting all of social security benefits to taxes is an unpopular reform proposal. However, taxing all social security benefits for retirees with household incomes over $50,000 found favor with 61 percent of the respondents in 1996. This proposal was more likely to be favored by seniors, those with at least some college education, and those with annual incomes *less than* $50,000 (EBRI 1996).

A 1996 proposal prefaced a question regarding taxes with the statement, "As you may know, most people receiving social security payments today get more money in payments than they put into the system in taxes." Respondents were then asked if they thought social security recipients should have to pay federal income taxes on the difference between what they paid in taxes and the amount they received in benefits. This proposal is decidedly unpopular: 71 percent of the respondents are opposed to this proposal and 21 percent are favorable, with only 8 percent volunteering that they were not sure (Time/CNN 1996).

By contrast, "means-testing" (see Neumark and Powers, this volume) social security benefits is one of the more popular reforms, as long as the income level at which it takes effect is safely above the respondent's own annual income. In 1966, 61 percent favor, either strongly or somewhat, "cut[ting] future social security benefits for retirees with income over $50,000," while 35 percent oppose this proposal. Respondents in the 35–54 age group are more likely to favor cutting benefits for retirees with high incomes (Table 3).

The public is roughly evenly divided over the general issue of "scaling social security benefits so that the more outside income retirees have, the less they receive in social security": 46 percent favor this proposal whereas 47 percent are opposed, with 7 percent having no opinion on this issue (Newsweek 1997). When specific income amounts are stipulated, the higher the income, the greater the favorability ratings.

Should Social Security Funds Be Invested in the Stock Market?

Regarding the question of whether social security funds should be held in equities, public opinion changes, depending on how the questions are phrased. Jacobs and Shapiro (1998) argue that "[f]airly probing the public's views on privatization requires asking balanced questions that pose the potential rewards and risks of equity." Relatively more "abstract" questions about "letting individuals decide how some of their own social security contributions are invested" meet with favorable responses. In 1997, 71 percent favored this proposal, whereas 22 percent opposed it, and 7 percent did not know (Newsweek 1997). Similarly, nearly two-thirds (64 percent) of the respondents in a 1996 survey favored "invest[ing] some of the social security Trust Fund into private sector stock markets." This was opposed by only 29 percent of the respondents (EBRI 1996). Respondents under the age of 55, those with a college education, those with household incomes of $25,000 or more, and men were more likely to indicate they favored investing some of the Trust Fund in the stock market.

Interestingly, a small change in question wording can alter findings somewhat. In one 1997 survey, the proposal was phrased as "investing some social security revenues in the stock market, instead of putting them all into government bonds." Faced with this question, half of the respondents are in favor, 40 percent opposed, and 10 percent have no opinion (Newsweek 1997). Another 1997 survey posed the question differently: "[T]hinking about social security, do you favor or oppose investing a portion of the social security tax funds in the stock market?" Here again, half are in favor, 36 percent are opposed, and 13 percent are not sure (Time/CNN 1997).

When risk is explicitly mentioned, opposition to investing social security funds in the stock market increases sharply. A 1997 poll posed the question as follows: "Some people have suggested investing some of the social security Trust Funds in the stock market, which might make more money for the Funds, but would involve greater risk" (CBS/NYT 1997). Nearly 7 in 10 respondents (69 percent) thought this was a bad idea; a quarter thought it a good idea; 6 percent did not know or did not answer the question. Similarly, a different 1997 poll mentioned that subsequent social security "benefits could either be higher or lower than expected, depending on the stock market's performance" (NBC/WSJ 1997). Respondents were asked to judge whether "the risk of losing money in the stock market outweighs the potential of high returns from investing in the stock market," or whether "the potential of higher returns from investing in the stock market outweighs the risk of losing money in the stock market." Fifty-seven percent believe that risk outweighed potential returns, 37 percent take the position that potential returns outweigh the risks, and six percent are not sure (NBC/WSJ 1997).

Should Social Security Benefits Be Cut for All Future Recipients?

Cutting benefits for all future retirees appears to be the least popular proposed reform. More than three-quarters (76 percent) oppose this reform, and a majority (56 percent) of those surveyed in 1996 opposed it strongly.

TABLE 3. Attitudes Toward Social Security Reforms (percent)

	Strongly Favor	Somewhat Favor	Somewhat Oppose	Strongly Oppose
Popular social security reforms				
Cut future benefits for retirees with income over $50,000	30	31	16	19
Fully tax all social security benefits of retirees with income over $50,000	30	31	17	18
Invest some of the social security trust fund into private sector stock market	25	39	13	16
Social security reforms opposed by a majority				
Reduce automatic increases in benefits	12	22	28	34
Raise retirement age to 70	10	21	23	45
Increase the existing payroll tax on workers	6	22	25	43
Cut future benefits payments for all future recipients	4	16	20	56

Source: EBRI (1996).

Not surprisingly, seniors were relatively more willing to entertain this proposed reform (Table 3).

Conclusion

Americans' views about the social security program appear relatively stable and supportive, and somewhat slow to change. Attitudes towards specific reform proposals, however, are not consistent. The public is generally opposed to cuts in social security benefits, is not convinced they are needed, and is not willing to endure much "pain" to achieve long-term solvency. The only clearly popular reforms involve reducing social security benefits or fully taxing all social security benefits of retirees with annual incomes over $50,000. Investing some of the social security trust fund in the stock market is popular "in the abstract," but decidedly less so when risk is introduced.

In overview, public opinion has not yet coalesced around reforms needed to bring about system solvency. Important differences along income and gender lines remain significant. It is perhaps more striking that age differences are not a more salient important predictor of attitudes towards social security. Jacobs and Shapiro (1998) confirm this when they state: "Although seniors are more sensitive to threats to social security, younger Americans are consistently just as supportive (if not more so) of the overall program."

Americans will apparently require more time and information to reconcile their views on these policy trade-offs. The danger, as Jacobs and Shapiro (1998) point out, is that "instead of public opinion research driving policy decisions, policy decisions will drive public opinion research toward identifying the best language and policy arguments for presenting the preferred policy." This is an even greater danger of this happening, Jacobs and Shapiro contend, if the media continue "by-pass[ing] substance in favor [of] disproportionate coverage of conflict and crisis [instead of substantive coverage of the social security debate]."

Should substantive issues regarding social security reform be covered, it might be expected that this debate will have a "centering effect" of a shift towards the moderate "middle" from the positions on both extremes, no change and radical change. This accords with experience from the 1994 health care reform debate: as people were exposed to the pro and con arguments, they retreated to a moderate middle position, rather than one of radical change.

References

AARP/Yankelovich, Skelly, and White. *A Fifty-Year Report Card on the Social Security System: The Attitudes of the American Public.* Washington, D.C., August 1985.

AARP/DYG. *Social Security and Medicare Anniversary Research: A Study of Public Values and Attitudes.* Washington, D.C., June 1995.

AARP/DYG/ICR. *Social Security and Medicare Anniversary Research: A Study of Public Values and Attitudes — 1996 Update with Comparisons to 1995.* Washington, D.C., October 1996.

AARP/Wirthlin Group. *A National Survey Measuring Sentiment Towards the Balanced Budget Amendment.* Washington, D.C., January 1995.

CBS News/New York Times Poll. *National Adult Survey, Age 18 and Older.* 1997.

Employee Benefit Research Institute (EBRI). *Retirement Confidence Survey.* Washington, D.C., 1996.

Heclo, Hugh. "A Political Science Perspective on Social Security Reform." Paper presented at the Tenth Annual Conference of the National Academy of Social Insurance, Washington, D.C., 1998.

Jacobs, Lawrence R. and Robert Y. Shapiro. "Myths and Misunderstandings About Public Opinion Toward Social Security: Knowledge, Support, and Reformism." Paper presented at the Tenth Annual Conference of National Academy of Social Insurance. Washington, D.C., 1998.

NBC News/Wall Street Journal Poll. *National Adult Survey, Age 18 and Older.* New York, 1997.

Newsweek/Princeton Survey Research Associates. *National Adult Survey, Age 18 and Older.* Princeton, 1997.

Readers Digest/Institute for Social Inquiry/Roper Center. *National Adult Survey, Age 18 and Older.* Hartford: University of Connecticut, March 1995.

Time/CNN/Yankelovich. *National Adult Survey, Age 18 and Older.* New York, 1996.

Time/CNN/Yankelovich. *National Adult Survey, Age 18 and Older.* New York, 1997.

Contributors

u/lt →

David S. Blitzstein is the Director of the United Food and Commercial
Workers International Union (UFCW) Office of Negotiated Benefits, ad-
vising UFCW local unions in collective bargaining on pension and health
insurance issues and strategic planning for the UFCW. In addition, he
acts as an advisor to the Union's 150 jointly trusted health and welfare and
pension plans nationwide and is a trustee of the $2.2 billion UFCW Indus-
try Pension Fund and the UFCW National Health and Welfare Fund. He
is also a member of the working committee of the National Coordinating
Committee for Multiemployer Plans, a member of the Employee Benefits
Research Institute (EBRI), and a Board Member of the Pension Research
Council of the Wharton School — University of Pennsylvania. He is a graduate of the University of Pennsylvania and holds a M.S. in labor studies
from the University of Massachusetts in Amherst.

Christopher Bone is Chief Actuary with Actuarial Sciences Associates. His
work has focused on consulting involving the modeling, analysis, and
design of postretirement employee benefits (pensions, health and life
insurance). He has also worked on proposed changes in the legislative
and financial reporting areas. Active in both trade associations and professional organizations, he currently chairs the Society of Actuaries Task
Force on Retirement Income models and is a member of its Social Insurance Committee. He is a fellow of the Society of Actuaries, an Enrolled Actuary under ERISA, and a member of the American Academy of
Actuaries.

John Geanakoplos is the James Tobin Professor of Economics and Director
of the Cowles Foundation for Research in Economics at Yale University.
His research interests include general equilibrium models of international finance and trade, game theory, and financial markets. He received
the Ph.D. in economics from Harvard University.

Gordon P. Goodfellow is a senior associate at the Research and Information
Center at Watson Wyatt Worldwide, where he has specialized in the anal-

ysis of social security policy and private defined contribution plans. Previously, he worked with the Office of the Assistant Secretary for Planning and Evaluation as a senior policy analyst and project manager of the Panel Study of Income Dynamics.

Stephen C. Goss is a Supervisory Actuary in the Office of the Actuary at the Social Security Administration. He is an Associate in the Society of Actuaries and a member of the National Academy of Social Insurance. He received the M.S. degree in mathematics from the University of Virginia.

Janice M. Gregory is Vice President at The ERISA Industry Committee, an association of 130 major companies, all of which maintain comprehensive pension, health, and welfare benefit plans for their employees, and which together provide health coverage to approximately 25 million individuals. She previously worked with the Chairman of the Subcommittee on Social Security, and served as legislative aide, press assistant and chief speech writer for Rep. J. J. Pickle (Texas). She is a Founding Member and Member of Board of Directors of the National Academy of Social Insurance. She received the B.A. with Special Honors from the University of Texas.

Karen C. Holden is an Associate Professor of Consumer Science and Public Affairs at the University of Wisconsin-Madison. Her research interests include the relationship between disability, life expectations, and insurance purchase. She is also Associate Director of the Robert M. LaFollette Institute of Public Affairs, a member of the National Academy of Social Insurance, a Fellow of the Gerontological Society of America and the Employee Benefit Research Institute. She received the Ph.D. in economics from the University of Pennsylvania.

Martin R. Holmer is President of the Policy Simulation Group. His research interests focus on the design, implementation, and use of micro-sample and cell-based policy simulation models for risk assessment and risk management in the pension, health insurance, portfolio management, and housing finance areas. Previously, he was Director of Income Security Policy Research at the U.S. Department of Health and Human Services. He received the Ph.D. in economics from MIT.

Robert M. Hutchens is a Professor of Labor Economics at Cornell's School of Industrial and Labor Relations. His current research encompasses government transfer programs, long-term implicit contracts, and the market for older workers. He received the Ph.D. in economics from the University of Wisconsin, specializing in labor economics, public finance, and econometrics.

Stephen G. Kellison is Vice President and Chief Actuary at the Variable Annuity Life Insurance Company and a Public Trustee of the Social Security and Medicare Trust Funds. He is a fellow of the Society of Actuaries and a member of the American Academy of Actuaries. He is also a member of the National Academy of Social Insurance. Previously, he was a Professor in the Department of Risk Management and Insurance at Georgia State University. He received the M.S. from University of Nebraska-Lincoln.

John M. Kimpel is Senior Vice President and Deputy General Counsel for Fidelity Investments, where he is responsible for all legal issues relating to the management of retirement plan assets. Prior to joining Fidelity, he was a partner at Gaston Snow & Ely Bartlett in Boston, where he was in charge of the law firms' ERISA group. He is former Chairman of the Investment Company Institute Pension Committee, a member of the Profit Sharing / 401(k) Council of America Legal & Legislative Committee, and a member of the University of Chicago Law School Visiting Committee. He received the B.A. from Denison University and a J.D. from the University of Chicago.

Joyce Manchester is an economist at the Social Security Board, and previously worked at the Congressional Budget Office. Her research covers analysis of macroeconomic aspects of social security reform in the United States, consumption taxes, baby boomers in retirement, the North American Free Trade Agreement, and the savings and loan crisis. She recently served as Visiting Fellow at The World Bank, working on various aspects of social security reform around the world, and she previously taught at Dartmouth College. She received the B.A. from Wesleyan University and the Ph.D. in economics from Harvard University.

Olivia S. Mitchell is the International Foundation of Employee Benefit Plans Professor of Insurance and Risk Management, and Executive Director of the Pension Research Council, of the Wharton School at the University of Pennsylvania. Her research interests include the economics of retirement and benefits, social security and pensions, and public as well as private insurance. She is also a Research Associate at the National Bureau of Economic Research and serves on the Steering Committee for the University of Michigan's HRS/AHEAD projects, funded by the National Institute on Aging. Her previous academic positions included a faculty appointment at Cornell University and visiting scholar at Harvard University. She received the B.S. in economics from Harvard University, and the Ph.D. in economics from the University of Wisconsin.

Marilyn Moon is a Senior Fellow in the Health Policy Center of the Urban Institute and a Public Trustee of the Social Security and Medicare Trust Funds. Her research interests include Medicare, poverty, health, income distribution, and long-term care issues. She is also a founding member, and serves on the Board of Directors, of the National Academy of Social Insurance. She received the Ph.D. in economics from the University of Wisconsin.

Robert J. Myers is a special consultant to the Social Security Division of William M. Mercer. He was previously chief actuary for Social Security Administration during 1947–1970 and deputy commissioner in 1981–1982. He is a fellow of the Society of Actuaries and a member of the

American Academy of Actuaries. He received the B.A. from Lehigh University in engineering physics and the M.S. in actuarial mathematics from the University of Iowa.

David Neumark is Professor of Economics at Michigan State University. His research fields include labor economics and applied econometrics. He is a Research Associate at the National Bureau of Economic Research. He received the Ph.D. from Harvard University.

George G. Pennacchi is Associate Professor of Finance and a co-director of the Office for Banking Research at the University of Illinois at Urbana-Champaign. His research is in the areas of banking, the valuation of derivative securities, fixed-income securities pricing, and international finance. He has consulted with private and public organizations including the International Monetary Fund, the World Bank, the Federal Reserve Board, the Federal Reserve Banks of Chicago and Cleveland, the Central Bank of Finland, and the U.S. Office of Management and Budget. He received the B.A. in applied mathematics from Brown University and the Ph.D. in economics from the Massachusetts Institute of Technology.

Elizabeth Powers is Assistant Professor of Economics and a faculty member of the Institute of Government and Public Affairs at the University of Illinois at Urbana-Champaign. Her research interests are in the areas of poverty, consumption and saving, and income redistribution policies. Previously she worked at the Federal Reserve Bank of Cleveland and the Council of Economic Advisers. She holds the B.A. in economics from Vassar College and the Ph.D. in economics from the University of Pennsylvania.

Robert C. Pozen is the CEO of Fidelity Investments; he is also Senior Vice President and General Counsel of FMR Corp. He is a member of the Commerce Department's Advisory Committee on Trade in Services, and the Treasury Department's Advisory Committee on the Future of Financial Services. He is also a member of the Executive Committee of the Investment Company Institute and the International Advisory Committee of the New York Stock Exchange. Previously, he taught at Harvard University, Georgetown University and New York University. Mr. Pozen received the B.A. from Harvard University and the law degree and Ph.D. from Yale University, where he was an editor of the Yale Law Journal.

Joseph F. Quinn is Professor of Economics at Boston College. His research focuses on the economics of aging, with emphasis on the economic status of the elderly, the determinants of individual retirement decisions, and patterns of labor force withdrawal among older Americans. He is a founding member of the National Academy of Social Insurance, and serves on the Board of Governors of the Foundation for International Studies on Social Security, the (Massachusetts) Governor's Council on Economic Growth and Technology, the Executive Board of the Gordon Public Policy Center at Brandeis University, and the Editorial Board of the Review of

Income and Wealth. He recently co-chaired (with Olivia Mitchell of the Wharton School) the Technical Panel on Trends and Issues in Retirement Saving for the 1995–96 Social Security Advisory Council. He received his undergraduate education at Amherst College and the Ph.D. in economics from the Massachusetts Institute of Technology.

John Rother is the Director of Legislation and Public Policy for the American Association of Retired Persons (AARP), where he is responsible for the federal and state legislative advocacy activities of the Association, and for the policy research and public education programs that support that effort. Previously, Mr. Rother worked on Capitol Hill for Senator Jacob Javits (R-NY), and as Staff Director and Chief Counsel for the Special Committee on Aging under its Chairman, Senator John Heinz (R-PA). He is an Honors Graduate of Oberlin College and the University of Pennsylvania Law School, where he was editor of the Law Review.

Sylvester J. Schieber is the Director of Watson Wyatt Worldwide's Research and Information Center in Washington. During his professional career he has specialized in the analysis of public and private retirement policy and health policy issues. He has been responsible for the development of a number of special ongoing survey programs at Watson Wyatt focusing on these issues. Previously, he worked as Research Director of the Employee Benefits Research Institute and also held positions at the Social Security Administration. He serves on Watson Wyatt's Board of Directors and was a member of the 1994–95 Social Security Advisory Council. He received the Ph.D. in economics from the University of Notre Dame.

Kent A. Smetters is an Assistant Professor of Insurance and Risk Management at the Wharton School. Previously he worked at the Congressional Budget Office. His recent research has focused on tax reform, national saving, and Social Security reform. He received the Ph.D. from Harvard University.

William E. Wright is a Senior Research Advisor of the American Association of Retired Persons. He is responsible for conducting, analyzing, and reporting all of AARP's member and public opinion polling on entitlement programs (Social Security, Medicare, Medicaid). Previously, he taught at the University of British Columbia in Vancouver, Canada, and at the University of Georgia. He received the B.A. in mathematics from Millsaps College and the Ph.D. in political science from Vanderbilt University.

Howard Young is an Adjunct Professor in the Department of Mathematics at the University of Michigan, teaching actuarial courses. In addition, he is Adjunct Associate Research Scientist at the University's Institute of Labor and Industrial Relations. He is a member of the Pension Research Council at the Wharton School, and is a Founding Member of the National Academy of Social Insurance. Previously he was Special Consultant to the President at the United Auto Workers Union (UAW) and held other senior positions as well, working on assignments in areas of direct interest to four UAW Presidents. He received the M.S. in economics from the University of Michigan.

Stephen P. Zeldes is the Benjamin Rosen Professor of Economics and Finance at Columbia University's Graduate School of Business. His research examines applied macroeconomics issues including the determinants of household saving and portfolio choice, the effects of government budget deficits, the relationship between consumer spending and the stock market, and social security reform. He is also a Research Associate with the National Bureau of Economic Research and a Visiting Academic Economist at the Federal Reserve Bank of New York. He previously served on the Technical Panel on Trends and Issues in Retirement Saving that reported to the 1994–96 Advisory Council on Social Security, and is now a member of the National Academy of Social Insurance Panel on Social Security Privatization. He received the Ph.D. in economics from the Massachusetts Institute of Technology.

Index

Aaron, Henry J., 188, 199, 200, 243, 266
Abel, Andrew B., 142, 148 218
Access Research, Inc., 155, 182
Actuarial approach, 11, 67, 333–27
Actuarial imbalance in social security, 19–36, 60–76
Actuarial Standards Board, 16
Adequacy of income in old age, 39–45, 201, 243–67. *See also* Means test; Poverty; Wealth
Administrative costs, 3, 50, 73, 155–59, 182, 321–23, 372–79. *See also* Social security
Adverse selection, 214, 222
Advisory Council on Social Security. *See* Social Security Advisory Council
AFL-CIO, 350
Aging, 3–15, 23–24, 54–55, 61, 202–5, 243, 325–26. *See also* Demography; Poverty; Retirement; Wealth
Alm, James, 301, 311
Altig, David, 211, 219, 261, 266
American Academy of Actuaries, 347
American Association of Retired Persons (AARP), 12, 380–93
Ameriks, John, 137, 148
Andrews, Emily S., 300, 305, 311
Annuity, 14, 218, 335, 350, 367–68; and inflation, 14, 353; and social security reform, 14, 73–74, 153, 156, 177, 214, 353, 363. *See also* Individual Account plan; Personal Security Account plan; Social security
Argentina, 301, 305–6, 308
Arrau, Patricio, 261, 266
Asset: allocation, 154–57; income, 39–42; test, 248. *See also* Bonds; Equities; Means test; Portfolio; Return; Risk; Saving; Wealth

Assumptions for social security projections, 29–36, 61–62, 153–59, 184–200, 353–55. *See also* Social security
Attitudes toward social security, 380–93. *See also* American Association of Retired Persons; Discount rates; Means test; Saving
Auerbach, Alan J., 243, 266, 297, 311
Australia, 218, 247–48
Austria, 272–73, 300
Average-cost method for social security, 20–36

Baby boomers, ix, 5–15, 23–24, 45–47, 71, 180, 202–5, 15–16, 385 *See also* Aging; Demography
Bailey, Clive, 299, 311
Bajtelsmit, Vickie L., 162, 182
Baker, Dean, 352, 354–55
Bakija, Jon M. 46, 59, 143, 150, 290, 292, 300, 312
Balanced funds, 154–55. *See also* Investment; Portfolio; Stable value
Balduzzi, Pierluigi, 139, 147, 150
Ball, Robert, 13
Bankruptcy, 4, 223–25, 316, *See also* Funding
Barr, Paul G., 379
Barreto, Flávio Ataliba, 215, 220, 240, 242
Barro, Robert J., 188–89, 198, 200, 218–19
Bequests, 218
Benefits, 3, 16–36. *See also* Social security
Benefit to tax ratio in social security, 8–10. *See also* Money's worth
Berkowitz, Edward D., 44, 55, 57
Binder, Michael, 188, 200
Bipartisan Commission on Entitlement Reform, 246, 266

Black, Fischer, 222, 224, 232, 240
Blitzstein, David S., 11, 349–55
Bodie, Zvi, 240, 241
Bohn, Henning, 126, 148, 209, 218–19
Bonds, 13–14, 154–19, 164–65, 172–73, 373.
    See also Government bonds; Investment;
    Mutual funds; Pension; Stable value funds
Bone, Christopher, 11, 333–47
Book reserves, 224–25
Borden, Karl, 206, 219
Borowski, Allan, 261, 267
Boskin, Michael J., 56, 58, 143, 148
Bosworth, Barry P., 55–56, 58, 68, 75, 188,
    199, 200, 204–5, 219
Boudreau, John W., 281, 291
Bound, John, 358, 369
Boyle, Phelim, 227, 241
Brazil, 306–7
Breyer, Friedrich, 211, 219
Brown, J. Douglas, 357, 369
Brown, Stephen, 121, 148
Bryce, David V., 55, 58
Budget impact of social security, 5, 49–50,
    165
Burdett, Kenneth, 289, 291
Bureau of Economic Analysis, 191, 200
Burkhauser, Richard V., 56, 59, 358, 364–65,
    367–68, 370
Burns, Eveline, 357, 370
Burtless, Gary, 55, 58, 188, 199, 200, 246, 266

Caldwell, Steven, 143–44, 148
Campbell, G. R., 304, 311
Canada, 225, 300
Canan, Michael J., 319, 331
Capital income taxation, 211
Capital markets, ix, 4, 9, 11, 69–75, 154–83,
    209–10. *See also* Bonds; Equities; Portfolio;
    Return; Risk; Stocks
Carter, Marshall N., 15, 154, 158
Casey, Bernard, 273, 291
Chamorro, Claudio, 304, 311
Chen, Andrew H., 240, 241
Chile, 10, 214–15, 218, 232–33, 236–39, 261,
    304–6
Christenson, Laurtis R., 188, 200
Chu, Hoaquan, 307, 312
Citro, Constance, 347
Civil Service Retirement System, 32
Clark, Robert L., 327, 331
Clinton, Bill, 206
Closed group method for social security, 31–
    36. *See also* Social security

Cohen, Wilbur J., 261, 266
Cohort: perspectives on social security, 79–
    156, 380–93; returns under social security,
    46, 79–151, 154–83. *See also* Privatization;
    Social security
Committee for Economic Development
    (CED), 15, 153, 183, 345, 347
Committee on Economic Security, 55, 58
Committee on Ways and Means, 249, 262,
    266
Company responses to social security reform,
    10–11, *See also* Employees; Employers
Compliance, 295–312
Concord Coalition, 244, 261
Confidence, 12, 16, 50–51, 380–93. *See also*
    AARP; Polls
Congressional Budget Office, 189, 191, 200,
    219
Consumption-saving behavior, 48–49
Contingent claims, 10, 221–42. *See also* Guar-
    anteed retirement benefits
Contributions. *See* Social security; Taxes
Cooperstein, Richard L., 227, 240, 241
Corruption. *See* Evasion
Corsetti, Giancarlo, 298, 311
Cost of living adjustments in benefits, 6, 37,
    341. *See also* Inflation; Social security
Costs of managing retirement system, 3, 158–
    59, 372–79. *See also* Administrative costs;
    Social security
Council of Economic Advisors, 48, 54, 56, 58
Coverage of social security. *See* Evasion
Cowell, Frank A., 298, 301, 311
Cox, John, 222, 224, 241
Crown, William M., 261, 267
Cummings, Dianne, 188, 200
Current Population Survey (CPS), 272, 290

da Motta, L. F. J., 240, 241
Danziger, Sheldon, 49, 58
Das-Gupta, Arindam, 308, 311
Davis, E. Philip, 240, 241
Deadweight loss, 297. *See also* Efficiency
Debt, 5–7, 189, 203–5, 209–10, 224. *See also*
    Bonds; Investment; Macroeconomy; Re-
    turn; Risk; Social security; Transition costs
Deficit, 203–5, 210, 216
Defined benefit plan, 11–12, 185, 191, 212–
    16, 221, 223–32, 296, 308, 334–47, 352–
    53; and asset/liability management, 223–
    39; and risk, 214–15, 223–32. *See also*
    Defined contribution; Social security; So-
    cial Security Advisory Council

Defined contribution plan, 10–12, 154–56, 185, 191, 212–16, 221, 232–39, 308, 334–47, 352–53; and administrative costs, 158, 372–79; and guarantees, 10, 232–39; investment in, 72–75, 154–59; payouts from, 10; and risk, 72–75, 154–59, 214–15, 232–39, 352–53. *See also* Defined benefit; 401(k); Privatization; Social security; Social Security Advisory Council

Demography, ix, 3, 23, 46–47, 184–85, 201–3. *See also* Aging

Depression. *See* Great Depression

Developing countries, 304–7, 310. *See also* Latin America

Devine, Theresa, 302, 311

Diamond, Peter A., 126, 146, 148, 210, 216, 218–19, 236, 241

Dickson, Joel, 155–59, 181–82

Disability, 4, 14, 16, 18, 34–35, 44, 63, 189, 328, 352. *See also* Social security

Discount rates. *See* Return; Risk

Distribution and social security. *See* Means test; Poverty; Redistribution; Wealth

Diversification of retirement assets, 72–75, 96–151; and social security,10–11, 72–75. *See also* Equities; Investment; Mutual funds; Social security; Privatization

Divorce, 6, 309. *See also* Marital status; Social security; Widowhood

Domone, Dana, 363, 370

Dougherty, Christopher, 188, 200

Duffie, Darrell, 240, 241

Duggan, James E., 101, 143, 149

Dynamic assumptions, 20, 183–200. *See also* Social security projections

Early retirement. *See* Retirement; Social security

Earned Income Tax Credit (EITC), 216

Earnings, 4–6, 63; and social security, 154–83, test, 244. *See also* Assumptions; Jobs

Economic growth, 43–45, 47–50, 71, 183–200

Economic security, 37–59. *See also* Evaluation criteria; Saving; Social security

Efficiency, 201, 210, 296. *See also* Administrative costs

Elderly, 3–15, 23. *See also* Aging; Demography

Employee Benefit Research Institute (EBRI), 50–51, 199, 314, 322, 325, 331–32, 391

Employee Retirement Income Security Act (ERISA), 12, 32, 336, 358, 363, 374

Employees, 4, 10, 268–92, 324–25; and control over retirement assets, 153. *See also* Employers; Workers

Employers, 268–92; and pensions, 39–40, 52–53; and social security reforms, 3, 10–11, 52–53, 313–32, 333–46. *See also* Administrative costs; Communication; Social security

Engen, Eric M., 56, 58

Equity under social security system, 43–47, 201, 208–18, 353–54, 372–79

Equities as investment, 8–10, 13–14, 50, 69–75, 79–151, 154–83, 201–19, 327, 343–44, 373. *See also* Mutual funds; Social security; Stable value funds

ERISA. *See* Employee Retirement Income Security Act

ERISA Industry Committee, 316, 330, 331–32

Estrella, Arturo, 227–28, 231

European social security systems, 10, 297, 300

Evaluation criteria for reform, 37–59

Evasion and social security, 10–11, 46, 295–312. *See also* Social security

Exhaustion of social security trust fund, 16–36. *See also* Social security

Expectations of social security, 16, 154–60

Expense of managing account. *See* Administrative cost

Experience rating, 268–92

Fallon, Peter, 307, 311

Feaster, Daniel, 358, 367–68, 370

Federal budget, 3, 189, 205–6. *See also* Social security

Federal employee thrift savings plan. *See* Thrift Savings Plan

Feinstein, Jonathan, 301, 311

Feldstein, Martin S., 49, 58, 132, 143, 149,152, 154, 171, 183, 189, 200, 202–5, 211–13, 218–19, 243, 245, 247, 261, 266, 289, 291, 297, 303, 311

Ferris, Kenneth R., 240, 241

Fertility, 6, 23, 63–66. *See also* Aging; Demography

Fidelity, 12, 373, 375, 379

Fields, Gary S., 308, 312

Financial Accounting Standards Board, 347

Financial adequacy of social security, 17–36, 152–83. *See also* Social security; Wealth

Financial markets. *See* Capital markets

Findlay, M. Chapman, 240, 241

Firm. *See* employer

Fischer, Stanley, 182
Fixed-income investments, 154–60. *See also*
    Investments
Food stamps, 152
Forbes, Stephen, 79, 149
Forecasts. *See* Projections
France, 223
Fraser, Douglas, 350, 355
Friedland, Robert B., 51, 55, 59
Friedman, Benjamin, 218–19
Friedman, Milton, 261, 266
401(k) plan, 49, 153–83, 316, 327, 373–78.
    See also defined contribution plan; Mutual
    funds
Funding of social security, 4, 16–36, 201–18.
    See also Privatization; Social security

Gale, Douglas, 209, 219
Gale, William G., 56, 58
Gallup poll, 50–51
Gang, Ira N., 302, 308, 311
Geanakoplos, John, 8–10, 55, 58, 79–151,
    157, 171, 181–82, 211, 220
Gender. *See* Marital status; Social security;
    Women
Generations, 4–7, 13, 209, 210–11, 380–93.
    See also Aging; Demography; Social security
Germany, 223, 295, 304
GICs. *See* Stable value funds
Gillingham, Robert, 101, 143, 149
Global capital markets, 4, 13, 69–75. *See also*
    Equities; Bonds; Capital markets
Goetzmann, William, 121, 148
Gokhale, Jagadeesh, 211, 219, 261, 266
Goodfellow, Gordon P., 9, 14, 55, 58, 152–83
Goss, Stephen C., 6–7, 16–36, 62, 80–49,
    178, 182, 198, 200, 218–19
Goswami, Omkar, 302, 311
Government Accounting Standards Board,
    335, 346
Government bonds, 164, 181, 373
Government budget, 165
Grad, Susan, 39–42, 55, 58
Graham, Avy D., 314, 331–32
Gramlich, Edward M., 13, 56, 58, 219
Great Depression, 3, 43, 84, 88, 142–43,
    201–2
Greenlees, John S., 101, 149
Gregory, Janice M., 11, 313–32
Gruber, Jonathan, 101, 146, 149, 310, 312
Growth and social security, 183–200, 201–5
Guaranteed Insurance Contract (GIC), 155.
    See also Stable value funds

Guaranteed retirement benefits, 8–10, 72–
    73, 221–42, 352–53. *See also* Social security
Guarantees for social security, 221–42
Gustman, Alan, 246, 255, 261, 266

Hammond, P. Brett, 207, 219
Hanushek, Eric, 347
Harrison, Michael, 222, 242
Hausman, Jerry A., 56, 58
Haveman, Robert, 49, 58
Health insurance, 68, 303. *See also* Benefits;
    Medicaid; Medicare
Heclo, Hugh, 380–82, 393
Heston, Alan, 188, 200
Hirtle, Beverly, 227–28, 241
Holden, Karen C., 11–12, 350–70
Holmer, Martin R., 9, 56, 58, 184–200
Holzmann, Robert, 298, 312
Hoopengardner, Tom, 307, 311
Hoshino, Shinya, 261, 267
Hotchkiss, Julie, 289, 292
Housing, 39–41. *See also* Saving; Wealth
Howe, Neil, 189, 200
Hsieh, Su-Jane, 240, 241
Hubbard, R. Glenn, 262, 266
Hull, John, 240, 241
Hurd, Michael D., 56, 58, 143, 149, 358, 370
Hutchens, Robert M., 268–92

Ibbotson, R., 121, 129, 149, 182
Implicit contract, 269, 290
Incentives and social security, 243–67, 268–
    92
Income and social security reform, 12. *See
    also* earnings; Poverty; Redistribution;
    Wealth
Income redistribution, 41–45, 152–83,
    201–2
Index fund, 9–10, 72–73, 207–8, 217. *See also*
    Administrative costs; Equities; Mutual
    funds; Return; Risk; Social security
India, 308
Individual Account (IA) plan, 7–10, 13–14.
    See also Social Security Advisory Council
Individual accounts in social security, 8–12,
    72–75, 152–83, 221–42, 343–45, 350–70,
    372–79. *See also* Social security
Individual equity as evaluation criterion, 43–
    45, 201–2. *See also* Evaluation criteria
Individual Retirement Account (IRA), 47–
    48, 69, 79, 181, 286, 316, 345, 354–55, 363,
    373–78
Inflation, 4–6, 17, 63, 159, 164, 314, 353,

388–89, *See also* Annuities; Assumptions; Social security
Informal labor markets, 297–98
Insolvency, 4–15, 221–42. *See also* Bankruptcy; Social security; Solvency
Insurance, 30–31, 221–22; social, 4–5, 41–45, 201–2, 221–42. *See also* Disability; Guarantee; Social security; Unemployment
Integrated pension plans, 318–20
Internal rate of return in social security, 8–10, 79–151, 152–83. *See also* Social security money's worth
Interest rate, 22, 63, 79–151. *See also* assumptions; Money's worth; Rate of return
Intermediate assumptions for social security projections, 20–36, 152–83. *See also* Social security
Investment in social security, 69–75, 79–151, 152–83, 201–19, 343, 372–79. *See also* Bonds; Equities; Mutual funds; Portfolio; Return; Risk; Social security
Ippolito, Richard A., 56, 58
Italy, 240

Jackson, Richard, 189, 200
Jacobs, Lawrence R., 380, 393
James, Estelle, 308, 312
Japan, 223, 300
Jobs, 4, 268–92. *See also* Tenure; Unemployment; Workers
Johnson, Herbert, 240, 241
Johnson, Richard D., 162, 182
Jones, Thomas, 206, 219
Jorgenson, Dale W., 188, 200

Kahn, Arthur L., 249, 262, 266
Kellison, Stephen G., 6, 60–75
Kennickell, Arthur, 137, 149
Kimpel, John M., 322, 332, 372–79
Kocherlakota, Narayana, 205–6, 212, 219
Kollmann, Geoffrey, 218–20
Kotlikoff, Laurence J., 145, 149, 211–12, 220, 243, 245, 261, 266, 297, 311
KPMG, 317, 332
Kreps, David, 222, 241
Kushner, Michael, 363, 370

Labor supply, 47–48, 211, 213, 243–67, 269–92, 297–98, 357–58, 363. *See also* Retirement; Workers
Langetieg, T. C., 240, 241
Latin America, 10, 222, 240
Leimer, Dean R., 56, 59, 80, 101–13, 142, 149

Leon, Carol Boyd, 290, 291
Level cost approach, 19–20
Lewis, Christopher, 225, 227, 240, 241
Liability of social security system. *See* Social security
Libanova, Ella, 307, 311
Lillard, Lee A., 143, 150
Liquidity constraints, 79–151
Longevity, 13, 63–64, 237, 353, 366. *See also* Assumptions; Demography; Mortality
Long range projections for social security, 19–36, 62–66, 79–151
Longstaff, Francis A., 224, 240, 241
Lumsdaine, Robin, 146, 150

Macroeconomy, 9, 48–49, 79–151, 184–200, 211–18
Maintain Benefits (MB) plan, 7–10, 13–14. *See also* Social Security Advisory Council
Maintain Tax Rate (MTR) benchmark for social security, 167–83
Manchester, Joyce, 10, 146, 150, 202, 220, 295–312
Mankiw, N. Gregory, 142, 148
Marcus, Alan, 225–26, 240, 241
Margrabe, William, 240, 241
Marital status, 6, 157–58, 309, 358–70. *See also* Divorce; Widowhood; Women
Market volatility, 69–75, 152–83, 184–200
Marr, M. Wayne, 218, 220
Martingale pricing, 222–42
McCurdy, Thomas E., 161, 183
McGarry, Kathleen, 262–63, 267
McGill, Dan M., 335–48
Means test for social security, 8, 10, 37, 243–67, 342, *See also* Social security
Medicaid, 262
Medicare, 5, 13, 22, 29, 68, 165, 388
Mehra, Rajnish, 121, 150
Merton, Robert C., 222, 224–25, 240, 241
Meyer, Jack A., 262, 267
Mexico, 310
Michelitsch, Roland, 305, 312
Minorities, 5. *See also* Poor; Retirement; Social security; Wealth
Miron, Jeffrey, 144, 150, 203, 206, 220
Mitchell, Olivia S., 3–15, 50, 52, 55, 58, 79–151, 157, 159, 171, 175, 181–82, 210–11, 215, 218, 220, 240, 242, 244–45, 261, 266, 308–9, 312, 375, 379
Moffitt, Robert A., 56, 58, 143, 150, 246, 266
Money market funds, 155–57

Money's worth, 3, 8–10, 79–151, 152–83. *See also* Social security; Returns
Monte Carlo simulations. *See* Projections; Social security
Moon, Marilyn, 6, 60–75
Moore, Stephen, 141, 150
Moral hazard, 216, 222
Morningstar, 159
Mortality, 11–12, 125–26, 144, 237, 300, 350–70
Moynihan, Daniel P., 131
Munnell, Alicia H., 49, 58
Mutual funds, 13–14, 158. *See also* Administrative cost; Social security
Myers, Daniel A., 56, 59, 368–69
Myers, Robert J., 3–15, 56, 59, 101, 117, 143–50, 152, 183, 314, 342
Myopia, 44, 299

Naschold, Frieder, 273, 291
National Academy for Social Insurance, 323, 331–32, 375, 379
National Commission for Social Security Reform, 350
National saving, 73–74, 184–200, 202–18. *See also* Saving
Netherlands, the, 224
Net present value in social security, 8–10, 79–151, 52–83. *See also* Social security money's worth
Neumark, David, 10, 55, 58, 243–67, 390, 393
New Beneficiary Survey, 364
Newsweek, 390, 393–94
Nofsinger, John, 218, 200
Normal retirement. *See* Retirement
Nugent, Mistene M., 162, 182

O'Connell, Stephen A., 145, 150
OECD, 300, 312
Old age. *See* Aging; Demography
Old Age, Survivors, and Disability Insurance (OASDI) system, 3, 11–12, 16, 27–29, 37–38, 61, 162, 189, 202–5, 218, 277, 372. *See also* Social security
Older worker. *See* Aging; Demography; Employees; Employers; Retirement
Olsen, Kelly, 59, 341, 348
Open group projections, 31–36, 184–200. *See also* Social security
Opinion, 12, 313, 380–93. *See also* AARP; Polls
Option pricing, 10, 221–42
Organized labor, 11, 349–55

Panis, Constantijn W. A., 143, 150
Pay. *See* Earnings
Pay-as-you-go system, 19, 35, 83–87, 201–18, 243, 247, 350. *See also* Privatization; Social security
Payout method. *See* Annuity; Lump sum; Pension loans
Payroll taxes, 3–6, 10–11, 79–151, 152, 201–5, 296–312. *See also* Social security
Pennacchi, George G., 9–10, 75, 218, 220, 221–42, 261, 267
Penn Aging Research Center (PARC), x
Pension Benefit Guaranty Corporation (PBGC), 221, 228, 316; and Pension Insurance Management System, 228
Pension: funding, 328–30; Joint and survivor, 363–68; plan, 222–42, 313–32; response to social security reform, 313–31, 333–46. *See also* Defined benefit; Defined contribution; 401(k)
Pension Research Council, ix
Personal finance. *See* Saving; Wealth
Personal Retirement Accounts (PRA), 152
Personal Security Account (PSA) plan, 5, 7–10, 13–14, 34–46, 372. *See also* Return; Risk; Social Security Advisory Council
Pesando, James E., 240, 242
Pesaran, M. Hashem, 188, 200
Pillars in social security system, 14. *See also* Social security
Plotnick, Robert, 49, 58
Political risk, 179, 207–8, 216–18, 373–74
Polls, 12, 50–51, 380–93. *See also* AARP; Opinion
Portfolio, 5, 154–47, 152–83, 206–7; restrictions, 372–74. *See also* Asset; Investment; Return; Risk; Social security
Poterba, James M., 56, 59, 161, 175, 183
Poverty, 3–5, 41–45, 152–83, 243–67, 350–70. *See* Adequacy; Income; Poor; Redistribution; Wealth; Women
Powers, Elizabeth T., 10, 55, 59, 243–67, 390, 393
Pozen, Robert C., 12, 322, 332, 372–79
Prefunding, 79–151. *See also* Privatization of social security; Transition costs
Prescott, Edward, 121, 150
Present-law benchmark for social security, 154–83, 167–83
Present-value approach for costing social security, 20–36
Privatization of social security, ix, 79–151, 153–83, 184–200, 201–18, 349–55; and re-

distribution, 72–75, 153–83, 221–42; and returns, 72–75, 79–151, 153–83; and risk, 72–75, 79–151, 153–83, 184–200, 221–42. *See also* Social security
Production function, 187–91, 198, 270–71
Productivity, 198
Projections for social security, 19–36, 79–151, 152–83, 184–200, 222, 351–52. *See also* Assumptions; Social security
Public opinion polls, 12. *See also* Opinion
Public sector pensions, 11, 313, 335
Puffert, Daniel, 143, 148
Putnam, Robert D., 59
Put option, 225–32

Quadagno, Jill, 56, 69
Queissar, Monika, 240, 242, 303, 312
Quinn, Joseph F., 7, 15, 37–59, 74, 315, 332

Rate of return, 79–151, 153–83. *See also* Inflation; Money's worth; Risk; Volatility
Rashid, Mansoora, 300, 305, 311
Rationality, 210
Readers Digest, 389, 393
Rebick, Marcus, 273, 291
Recession, 4. *See also* Unemployment
Recordkeeping. *See* Administrative costs; Investment
Redburn, F. Stevens, 227, 241
Redistribution and social security, 53, 79–151, 152–83, 203–5, 216–28, 245–67, 350–70. *See also* Poverty; Social security
Regulation of pensions, 222
Reid, Gary A., 301, 309, 312
Reinganum, Jennifer F., 301, 312
Reno, Virginia, 51, 59
Replacement rate, 44–45, 327–28
Retirees. *See* Aging; Demography; Retirement
Retirement, 13–14, 47–48, 64, 268–92, 324–26, 343, 389; and standard of living, 4, 152–83. *See also* Aging; Demography; Means test; Poverty; Social security
Retirement Equity Act of 1984 (REA), 363–64
Retirement History Survey (RHS), 369
Return, 46, 69–75, 79–151, 152–83, 184–200, 201–18, 221–42, 353–54, 373. *See also* Money's worth; Portfolio restrictions; Risk; Social security
Riboud, Michelle, 307, 312
Risk, 4–5, 8–10, 45, 69–75, 79–151, 152–83, 184–200, 209–19, 221–42, 352–54, 373;

references, 222. *See also* Investment; Portfolio restrictions; Return; Social security
Romano, Roberta, 218, 200
Rones, Philip L., 290, 291
Roosevelt, Franklin Delano, 202–3, 351
Ross, Stephen, 121, 148, 222, 241
Rother, John, 12, 74, 380–93
Rust, John, 273, 290, 291

Sachs, Jeffrey, 243, 245, 266
Sala-i-Martin, Xavier, 188–89, 198, 200
Samwick, Andrew, 132, 149,152, 154, 171, 183, 189, 200, 202–5, 211–13, 219, 297, 303, 311
Sanyal, Amal, 302, 311
Saving, 9–10, 48–49, 73–75, 184–200, 201–5, 243–67, 315–17; attitude toward, 44–45, 79–151; and risk, 69–75, 79–151, 184–200; and social security, 10, 41–45, 68–69, 71, 79–151, 184–200, 202–18, 243–67, 298–99, 323–24
Schieber, Sylvester J., 9, 14, 55, 58, 152–83, 327, 332
Schleifer, Andrei, 302, 312
Schmidt-Hebbel, Klaus, 261, 266, 298, 312
Schoebel, Bruce, 101, 143, 150
Scholes, Myron, 222, 232, 240
Scholz, John Karl, 56, 58
Schultz, James H., 247, 261, 267
Schwartz, Eduardo S., 224, 240, 241
Select Committee on Aging, 331–32
Sex and pensions. *See* Women
Shapiro, Robert Y., 380–81, 393
Shipman, William G., 15, 154, 158
Shoven, John B., 143, 149, 161, 165, 183
Siegel, Jeremy J., 145, 150, 183
Simulations. *See* Projections; Social security
Skill obsolescence, 44
Skinner, Jonathan, 262, 266
Slemrod, Joel, 300, 312
Smallhout, James H., 235, 240, 242
Smetters, Kent A., 15, 126, 150, 209, 220
Social insurance, 16, 30–31, 35, 44–45, 79–151, 201–2, 243–67, 269–92, 303–4, 353–55; and survivors, 350–70. *See also* Redistribution; Disability; Social security; Unemployment; Women
Social investment criteria, 373–78
Social Security: actuary, 101–41, 378; administrative costs, 3, 50, 73, 155–59, 321–23, 358, 370, 372–79; annuitization, 175–77, 363; assets, 68–69, 79–151, 152–83, 201–19; assumptions, 31–36, 60–75, 79–151,

Social Security (*cont.*)
  154–60, 184–200, 351–52; behavioral responses and, 7, 79–151, 184–200, 243–67,
  269–92; benefits, 6, 17–36, 38–41, 79–151,
  152–83, 184–200, 202–5, 297–99, 320–22,
  352–53, 383–85, 391–93; burden, 7, 203–
  5; compliance, 295–312; contingency reserve, 17, 60–75, 221–42; contributions, 6,
  79–151, 202–5; cost rate, 16–36, 60–75,
  79–151, 184–200; crisis, 4, 60–65, 79–151;
  criteria for evaluating reform, 5, 7, 79–
  151; debt, 5–7, 79–151, 201–20; disability
  benefits, 14, 328; and distribution of benefits, 79–151, 152–83, 246–67, 350–70; evasion, 46, 295–312; flat benefit under, 162–
  83; funding status, 3–15, 60–75, 79–151,
  184–200, 202–5, 221–42; future of, 3–15,
  65–67, 79–151, 154–83, 184–200; goals of
  the system, 7, 38–43, 268; and Individual
  Account (IA) plan, 7–8, 13–14, 38, 50,
  153, 158–83, 352–53, 362, 367; individual
  accounts, 8–10, 13–14, 79–151, 153–83,
  184–200, 321–23, 350–70; and inflation, 6,
  17, 353, 388–89; insolvency, ix, 3–15, 16–
  36, 60–75, 79–151, 184–200, 201–5, 212;
  integration, 318–20; investment, 46–47,
  69–74, 79–151, 154–83, 184–200, 201–20,
  343–44; liabilities, 79–151, 205, 212; and
  Maintain Benefits (MB) plan, 7–8, 13–14,
  38, 50, 153, 158–83, 207–9, 349; and marital status, 6, 350–70; means testing of benefits, 8, 10, 246–57, 342, 385, 390; money's
  worth, 3, 8–10, 46–47, 79–151, 154–83,
  184–200; participation, 46, 295–312; pay-
  as-you-go system, 19, 35, 68–69, 79–151,
  201–2; payroll tax, 10–14, 47–48, 79–151,
  162, 201–5, 208–9, 212–16, 318–20, 385;
  and Personal Security Account (PSA)
  plan, 7–8, 13–14, 38, 50, 52, 153, 158–83,
  221, 352–53, 361–62, 367, 374; privatization, 8–10, 79–151, 154–83, 184–200,
  201–20, 221–42, 344–45, 350–55; portfolio, 5, 9–10, 69–75, 79–151, 154–57,
  201–19; projections, 19–36, 61–66, 79–
  151, 152–83, 184–200, 201–19, 282–85,
  351–52; reform, 3–15, 7–8, 67–75, 79–
  151, 153–83, 184–200, 201–19, 246–57,
  246, 380–93; retirement, 13–14, 64, 168,
  268–92, 325–26, 343, 389; reserve, 18–36,
  79–151, 202, 210; return, 3, 46, 69–75, 79–
  151, 154–83, 184–200, 201–20, 221–42,
  353–54; revenue, 16–36, 209–10; risk, 8–
  10, 79–151, 154–83, 184–200, 201–19,
  221–42; 75-year perspective, 8, 16–36, 53,
  62–66, 79–151, 152–83, 201–19; and saving, 68–69, 79–151, 184–200, 201–5, 243–
  67; surplus, 49, 201–5; survivors' benefits,
  14, 350–70; system, 3–15, 79–151, 184–
  200, 201–19; taxes, 6, 10–22, 17–36, 79–
  151, 162–83, 184–200, 243, 295–312, 338–
  41, 389–90; ten-year perspective, 62–66;
  termination, 31–36, 79–151; transfers, 5,
  79–151, 152–83, 184–200, 201–19, 221–
  42; transition, 7–10, 31–36, 51–52, 79–
  151, 170–71; unfunded liabilities, 5–7,
  16–36, 60–76, 79–151, 201–5; valuation
  period, 16–36, 60–76, 152–83, 184–200,
  201–5. *See also* Individual Account plan;
  Maintain Benefits plan; Money's worth;
  Personal Security Account plan; Projections; Return; Risk; Solvency; Taxes; Technical Panel
Social Security Act, 16, 18–19, 201–2
Social Security Administration, 17, 55, 59,
  101, 153, 198–99, 262, 266
Social Security Advisory Council, 4–15, 18,
  25–26, 37–38, 50, 55, 59, 79–151, 75, 152–
  83, 192, 200, 205–8, 285–86, 295, 328, 332,
  335, 349–55, 361–62, 372
Social Security Trustees, 16–17, 19–36, 49,
  61–65, 74–75, 128, 144, 148, 188, 198,
  200–202, 314, 331
Social Security Trust Fund, 3, 8–10, 13–14,
  16–36, 79–151, 184–85, 201–18, 244; and
  investment in equities, 69–72, 68–72, 79–
  151, 205–19, 221–42
Socially responsible investments, 206
Society of Actuaries, x
Solvency of social security system, 16–36, 60–
  76, 79–151, 184–200, 201–18, 221–42. *See
  also* Social security
Special Committee on Aging, 331–32
Stable value funds, 155, 374
Stakeholders in social security, 4–5, 152–83,
  206, 350. *See also* Employees; Employers;
  Families; Social security
Starr, Paul, 350, 355
Starr-McCluer, Martha, 137, 149
Steinmeier, Thomas L., 246, 255, 261, 266
Steurle, C. Eugene, 46, 59, 143, 150, 290, 292
Stochastic modeling, 9, 29–31, 152–83, 184–
  200
Stock market, 45, 69–75, 79–151. *See also*
  Great Depression; Return; Risk; Social se-
  curity
Stocks in retirement plans, 45, 72–74, 79–

151, 152–59, 201–19, 221–42. *See also* Equity; 401(k) plan; Mutual fund; Pension investment

Straub, Martin, 211, 219

Stulz, Rene M., 240, 242

Summers, Lawrence H., 142, 148, 188, 200

Summers, Robert, 188, 200

Sunden, Annika K., 137, 149

Supplemental Security Income (SSI), 10, 53, 152, 244–67

Survey of Income and Program Participation (SIPP), 248–60, 359–61

Survivor benefits, 14, 350–70. *See also* Social security; Widowhood

Tanner, Michael, 128, 146, 151

Taxes, 7, 190, 211; and social security, 6, 10–11, 79–151, 152–59, 174–75, 184–200, 201–5, 243, 295–312, 378–79, 389–90. *See also* Social security

Technical Panel: on Assumptions and Methods, 25, 102, 192, 199, 200; on Trends in Income and Retirement Saving (TIRS), 7, 53, 37–38, 43, 53, 56, 59, 205–9, 220, 246. *See also* Social security

Tegen, Karen, 369–70

Thompson, Lawrence, 55, 59, 144, 150

Thrift Savings Plan (TSP), 207–8, 215–16, 373–76

Tiers in social security system, 14, 38, 243–44. *See also* Social security

Tobin, James, 145, 151

Topel, Robert H., 280, 289–90, 292

Towers Perrin, 325, 327, 332

Transition costs, 8–10, 14, 79–151, 170–71, 184–200. *See also* privatization of social security

Treasury Bills, 160, 164

Treynor, Jack L., 240, 242

Trimble, John, 218, 220

Trust Fund, 3, 13–14, 16–36, 138–39, 201–19, 221–42. *See also* Social security

Turkey, 307

Turner, John A., 75, 235, 240, 242, 299, 312

Uncertainty, 79–151, 152–83, 184–200, 221–42. *See also* Insurance; Projections; Return; Risk

Unemployment, 4, 6, 63, 303; and social security benefits for older workers, 10, 268–92. *See also* Disability; Social security

Unfunded liability in social security, 14, 16–36, 69–76, 79–151. *See also* Social security; Transition costs

Union approach to social security reform, 11, 349–55

United Auto Workers, 349

United Mine Workers, 349

United Kingdom, 225, 240, 300–301

United States, 225

U.S. Bureau of the Census, 192, 200, 368, 370

U.S. Congress, 35, 68, 372; House of Representatives, 36, 55, 58; Senate, 55

U.S. Department of the Treasury, 32–33, 36

U.S. President, 35

U.S. Social Security Advisory Council. *See* Social Security Advisory Council

Upp, Melinda, 55, 59

Uruguay, 232

Valdés-Prieto, Salvador, 236, 241

Valuation of social security benefits, 16–36, 60–76, 79–151, 152–83, 184–200

Vazques-Caro, Jaime, 301, 312

Vasicek, Oldrich A., 236, 242

Venti, Steven F., 56, 59, 161, 183

Vishny, Robert W., 302, 312

Vittas, Dmitri, 305, 312

Volatility, 11, 79–151, 152–83, 184–200, 221–42. *See also* capital markets; Investment; Return; Risk

Wagner, Gert, 235, 242

Walliser, Jan, 211–12, 218, 220

Warshawsky, Mark J., 175, 183, 207, 218, 220

Watanabe, Noriyasu, 75, 235, 240, 242

Watson Wyatt, 181, 313, 318, 332; and asset model, 163

Wealth, 12, 243–44; and opinions about social security reform, 12. *See also* Poverty

Weaver, Carolyn, 14, 36

Weil, David, 143, 150, 203, 206, 220

Welfare program, 152

West Germany, 273

Wharton School, x

White, Lawrence, 147, 151, 208, 220

Widowhood, 11–12, 350–70. *See also* Marital status; Social security

Wilde, Louis L., 301, 312

Winter-Ebner, Rudolf, 272, 292

Wise, David A., 56, 58–59, 161, 183, 358, 370

Women: and confidence in social security, 380–93; and wellbeing in retirement, 5, 11–12, 302–3, 309, 350–70

Woods, John, 55, 59

Workers, 4, 366–69; and social security benefits, 10. *See also* Education; Employees; Employers; Organized labor

Work incentives. *See* Labor supply

World Bank, 218, 298, 311, 306–8, 312

Wright, Randall, 289, 292

Wright, William E., 12, 74, 380–93

Young, Howard, 3–15

Zarita, Salvador, 235, 242

Zedlewski, Sheila R., 262, 267

Zeldes, Stephen P., 8–10, 55, 58, 79–151,
157, 171, 181–82, 206, 211, 220, 244–45,
261–62, 266

Zick, Cathleen, 358–59, 370

Pension Research Council

The Pension Research Council of the Wharton School of the University of Pennsylvania is an organization committed to generating debate on key policy issues affecting pensions and other employee benefits. The Council sponsors interdisciplinary research on the entire range of private and social retirement security and related benefit plans in the United States and around the world, and seeks to broaden public understanding of these complex arrangements through basic research into their social, economic, legal, actuarial, and financial foundations. Members of the Advisory Board, appointed by the Dean of the Wharton School, are leaders in the employee benefits field, and share a strong desire to strengthen private and public sector approaches to economic security.

Executive Director

Olivia S. Mitchell, *International Foundation of Employee Benefit Plans Professor*, Department of Insurance and Risk Management, The Wharton School, University of Pennsylvania, Philadelphia.

Institutional Members

Marc M. Twinney, Jr., F.S.A., *Consultant*, Bloomfield Hills, Mich.

Michael Useem, *Professor of Management and Sociology*, The Wharton School, Philadelphia, Pa.

Jack L. VanDerHei, *Associate Professor of Risk and Insurance*, Temple University, Philadelphia, Pa.

Paul H. Wenz, F.S.A., *Second Vice President and Actuary*, The Principal Financial Group, Des Moines, Iowa.

Stephen P. Zeldes, *Benjamin Rosen Professor of Economics and Finance*, Columbia University, New York, N.Y.

Other Related Pension Research Council Publications

Demography and Retirement: The Twenty-First Century. Anna M. Rappaport and Sylvester J. Schieber, eds. 1993.

An Economic Appraisal of Pension Tax Policy in the United States. Richard A. Ippolito. 1990.

The Economics of Pension Insurance. Richard A. Ippolito. 1989.

Fundamentals of Private Pensions. Dan M. McGill, Kyle N. Brown, John J. Haley, and Sylvester J. Schieber. Seventh edition. 1996.

The Future of Pensions in the United States. Ray Schmitt, ed. 1993.

Inflation and Pensions. Susan M. Wachter. 1987.

Living with Defined Contribution Pensions. Olivia S. Mitchell and Sylvester J. Schieber, eds. 1998.

Pension Mathematics with Numerical Illustrations. Howard E. Winklevoss. Second edition. 1993.

Pensions and the Economy: Sources, Uses, and Limitations of Data. Zvi Bodie and Alicia H. Munnell, eds. 1992.

Pensions, Economics, and Public Policy. Richard A. Ippolito. 1986.

Positioning Pensions for the Twenty-First Century. Michael S. Gordon, Olivia S. Mitchell, and Marc M. Twinney, eds. 1997.

Providing Health Care Benefits in Retirement. Judith F. Mazo, Anna M. Rappaport, and Sylvester J. Schieber, eds. 1994.

Retirement Systems in Japan. Robert L. Clark. 1990.

Search for a National Retirement Income Policy. Jack L. VanDerhei, ed. 1987.

Securing Employer-Based Pensions: An International Perspective. Zvi Bodie, Olivia S. Mitchell, and John A. Turner, eds. 1996.

Social Investing. Dan M. McGill, ed. 1984.

Social Security. Robert J. Myers. Fourth edition. 1993

Available from the University of Pennsylvania Press, telephone: 800-445-9880, fax: 410-516-6998.

More information about the Pension Research Council is available at our web site: http://prc.wharton.upenn.edu/prc/prc.html